Transnational Aging

This book focuses on the diverse interrelationships between aging and transnationality. It argues that the lives of older people are increasingly entangled in transnational contexts on the social, as well as the cultural, the economic, and the political, level. Within these contexts, older people both actively contribute to and are affected by border-crossing processes. In addition, while some may voluntarily opt for adding a transnational dimension to their lives, others may have less choice in the matter. Transnational aging, therefore, provides a critical lens on how older people shape, organize, and cope with life in contexts that are no longer bound to the frame of a single nation-state. Accordingly, the book emphasizes the agency of older people as well as the personal and structural constraints of their situations. The chapters in this book reveal these aspects by approaching transnational aging from different methodological angles, such as ethnographic research, comparative studies, quantitative data, and policy and discourse analysis. Geographically, the chapters cover a wide range of countries in Africa, Asia, Europe, and North and South America, such as Namibia, Thailand, Russia, Germany, the US, and Ecuador.

Vincent Horn is a PhD candidate and resesarch associate in the Institute of Education at the University of Mainz (Germany).

Cornelia Schweppe is a professor of Social Pedagogy in the Institute of Education and the director of the Research Center for Transnational Social Support (TRANSSOS) at the University of Mainz (Germany).

Routledge Research in Transnationalism

5 Communities across Borders
New Immigrants and Transnational
Cultures
*Edited by Paul Kennedy
and Victor Roudometof*

6 Transnational Spaces
*Edited by Peter Jackson, Phil
Crang and Claire Dwyer*

7 The Media of Diaspora
Edited by Karim H. Karim

8 Transnational Politics
Turks and Kurds in Germany
Eva Østergaard-Nielsen

**9 Culture and Economy in the
Indian Diaspora**
*Edited by Bhikhu Parekh,
Gurharpal Singh and Steven
Vertovec*

**10 International Migration and the
Globalization of Domestic
Politics**
Edited by Rey Koslowski

11 Gender in Transnationalism
Home, Longing and Belonging
among Moroccan Migrant Women
Ruba Salih

12 State/Nation/Transnation
Perspectives on Transnationalism
in the Asia-Pacific
*Edited by Brenda S. A. Yeoh and
Katie Willis*

13 Transnational Activism in Asia
Problems of Power and
Democracy
*Edited by Nicola Piper and
Anders Uhlin*

14 Diaspora, Identity and Religion
New Directions in Theory and
Research
*Edited by Waltraud Kokot,
Khachig Tölölyan and Carolin
Alfonso*

**15 Cross-Border Governance in the
European Union**
*Edited by Olivier Thomas
Kramsch and Barbara Hooper*

**16 Transnational Connections and
the Arab Gulf**
Edited by Madawi Al-Rasheed

17 Central Asia and the Caucasus
Transnationalism and Diaspora
*Edited by Touraj Atabaki and
Sanjyot Mehendale*

18 **International Migration and Security**
Opportunities and Challenges
Edited by Elspeth Guild and Joanne van Selm

19 **Transnational European Union**
Towards a Common Political Space
Edited by Wolfram Kaiser with Peter Starie

20 **Geopolitics of European Union Enlargement**
The Fortress Empire
Edited by Warwick Armstrong and James Anderson

21 **Rethinking Transnationalism**
The Meso-link of Organisations
Edited by Ludger Pries

22 **Theorising Transnational Migration**
The Status Paradox of Migration
Boris Nieswand

23 **Migration, Nation States, and International Cooperation**
Edited by Randall Hansen, Jobst Koehler and Jeannette Money

24 **Beyond Methodological Nationalism**
Research Methodologies for Cross-Border Studies
Edited by Anna Amelina, Devrimsel D. Nergiz, Thomas Faist and Nina Glick Schiller

25 **Transnationalism and Urbanism**
Edited by Stefan Krätke, Kathrin Wildner, and Stephan Lanz

26 **Transnational Marriage**
New Perspectives from Europe and Beyond
Edited by Katharine Charsley

27 **Transnational Politics and the State**
The External Voting Rights of Diasporas
Jean-Michel Lafleur

28 **Transbordering Latin Americas**
Liminal Places, Cultures, and Powers (T)Here
Edited by Clara Irazábal

29 **Transnational Families, Migration and the Circulation of Care**
Understanding Mobility and Absence in Family Life
Edited by Loretta Baldassar and Laura Merla

30 **Transnational Agency and Migration**
Actors, Movements, and Social Support
Edited by Stefan Köngeter and Wendy Smith

31 **Languages and Identities in a Transitional Japan**
From Internationalization to Globalization
Edited by Ikuko Nakane, Emi Otsuji and William S. Armour

32 **Transnational Aging**
Current Insights and Future Challenges
Edited by Vincent Horn and Cornelia Schweppe

Transnational Aging
Current Insights and Future Challenges

Edited by Vincent Horn and Cornelia Schweppe

NEW YORK AND LONDON

First published 2016
by Routledge
711 Third Avenue, New York, NY 10017

and by Routledge
2 Park Square, Milton Park, Abingdon, Oxon OX14 4RN

*Routledge is an imprint of the Taylor & Francis Group,
an informa business*

© 2016 Taylor & Francis

The right of the editors to be identified as the authors of the editorial
material, and of the authors for their individual chapters, has been
asserted in accordance with sections 77 and 78 of the Copyright,
Designs and Patents Act 1988.

All rights reserved. No part of this book may be reprinted or reproduced or
utilised in any form or by any electronic, mechanical, or other means, now
known or hereafter invented, including photocopying and recording, or in any
information storage or retrieval system, without permission in writing from
the publishers.

Trademark notice: Product or corporate names may be trademarks or
registered trademarks, and are used only for identification and explanation
without intent to infringe.

Library of Congress Cataloging-in-Publication Data
Transnational aging : current insights and future challenges / edited by Vincent
   Horn, Cornelia Schweppe. — 1st Edition.
     pages cm. — (Routledge research in transnationalism ; 32)
   Includes bibliographical references and index.
  1. Older people.   2. Transnationalism.   I. Horn, Vincent,
editor.   II. Schweppe, Cornelia, 1955– editor.
  HQ1061.T745 2016
   305.26—dc23
   2015019523

ISBN: 978-1-138-79070-4 (hbk)
ISBN: 978-1-315-75639-4 (ebk)

Typeset in Sabon
by Apex CoVantage, LLC

Contents

List of Figures	x
List of Tables	xi

Introduction: Transnational Aging: Current Insights
and Future Challenges   1
VINCENT HORN AND CORNELIA SCHWEPPE

PART A
Aging and the Family in Transnational Contexts:
Cross-Border Activities and Intergenerational Relationships

1 Migration Regimes and Family-Related Transnational Activities
of Older Peruvians in Spain and the United States   19
VINCENT HORN

2 Intergenerational Solidarity in Migrant Families From the
Former Soviet Union: Comparing Migrants Whose Parents
Live in Germany to Migrants with Parents Abroad   45
ELENA SOMMER AND CLAUDIA VOGEL

3 Remaking the *Yanga Kawsay*: Andean Elders, Children,
and Domestic Abuse in the Transmigration Logics
of Highland Ecuador   64
JASON PRIBILSKY

4 Transnational Babushka: Grandmothers and Family
Making Between Russian Karelia and Finland   85
TATIANA TIAYNEN-QADIR

viii *Contents*

PART B
Migration in Later Life: Transnational Strategies and Managing Risk in Old Age

5 Transnational Aging as Reflected in Germany's
Pension Insurance 107
RALF HIMMELREICHER AND WOLFGANG KECK

6 Maintaining Dual Residences to Manage Risks in Later Life:
A Comparison of Two Groups of Older Migrants 125
ANITA BÖCKER AND CANAN BALKIR

7 Pendular Migration of the Older First Generations
in Europe: Misconceptions and Nuances 141
TINEKE FOKKEMA, ERALBA CELA, AND YVONNE WITTER

PART C
Facets of Old-Age Care in a Transnational World: Traveling Institutions, Boundary Objects, and Regimes of Inequality

8 "Moving (for) Elder Care Abroad": The Fragile Promises of
Old-Age Care Facilities for Elderly Germans in Thailand 163
VINCENT HORN, CORNELIA SCHWEPPE, DÉSIRÉE BENDER,
AND TINA HOLLSTEIN

9 Traveling Institutions as Transnational Aging: The Old-Age
Home in Idea and Practice in India 178
SARAH LAMB

10 Negotiating the Potato: The Challenge of Dealing with
Multiple Diversities in Elder Care 200
KARIN VAN HOLTEN AND EVA SOOM AMMANN

11 More Than Demand and Demographic Aging:
Transnational Aging, Care, and Care Migration 217
SUSAN MCDANIEL AND SEONGGEE UM

PART D
Social Protection and Transnational Aging: The Circulation of Ideas and the Role of Nongovernmental Actors

Contents   ix

12 Older Persons' Rights: How Ideas Travel in
International Development   231
CARMEN GRIMM

13 From Alms to Rights: Boundaries of a Transnational
Nongovernmental Organization Implementing an
Unconditional Old-Age Pension   248
KATRIN FRÖHLICH

Contributors   267

Figures

2.1	Exchange of instrumental help between respondents and their parents	55
2.2	Exchange of different types of instrumental help between respondents and their parents	56
2.3	Exchange of practical help with housework between respondents and their parents	57
2.4	Exchange of financial support between respondents and their parents	59
4.1	Babushka reading a book for her grandchild	92
4.2	Young babushka and her granddaughter	94
5.1	In- and out-migrations, net migration, and total volume of migration of foreigners in Germany (1954–2012)	112
5.2	In- and out-migrations, net migration, and total volume of migration of Germans in Germany (1954–2012)	113

Tables

1.1	Older Peruvians in Spain and the US	20
1.2	Arrival periods of older Peruvians in Spain and the US	21
1.3	Time of arrival and migration status	26
1.4	Socio-economic profiles of Peruvians aged 50 years and older in Spain and the US	29
1.5	Family visits of Peruvians aged 50 years and older in Spain and the US	32
1.6	Peruvians aged 50 years and older in Spain and the US sending remittances	35
1.7	Peruvians aged 50 years and older in Spain and the US using the Internet for communication purposes	37
2.1	Percentage of respondents with at least one parent still alive and geographic distance to parents by age groups	52
2.2	Main characteristics of respondents with parents abroad compared to respondents with parents in Germany	54
5.1	Framework of migration based on the data of the German Federal Pension Insurance	115
5.2	Migration in the stock statistics of the German Federal Pension Insurance 2013, pensioners with full old age pensions (people older than 60)	117
5.3	Migration in the pension inflow statistics of the German Federal Pension Insurance 2013, pensioners aged between 60 and 65 years with new full old-age pensions	119
5.4	Number and total percent of insured persons of the German Federal Pension Insurance 2012 by place of residence and citizenship	120
A.5.1	Top five countries by numbers of pensions paid in foreign countries in the stock statistics of the German Federal Pension Insurance 2013, pensioners with full old-age pensions	124
8.1	Elderly care and the portability of social benefits	168
13.1	Social protection strategies	250
13.2	Model of a needs-based and rights-based approach of the TNGO	261

Introduction
Transnational Aging
Current Insights and
Future Challenges

Vincent Horn and Cornelia Schweppe

Over the past few decades, aging and transnationality have become buzz-words in academic, political, and popular debates. However, only recently have both terms been connected to each other. Long-standing and persistent ideas about aging in place and the far greater interest of transnational researchers in prime-aged individuals are two explanations for this reluctance. Nevertheless, as Kobayashi and Preston (2007) emphasize, transnational practices are not bound to a specific phase in the life course. This point is reflected by a growing body of research on children and older people from a transnational vantage point (Faulstich et al. 2001; Menjívar 2002; Montes de Oca, Molina and Avalos 2009; Parreñas 2005; Poeze and Mazzucato 2014; Zhou 2012). Since the late 1990s, different strands of research have emerged and revealed the manifold ways in which older people are entangled in an increasingly transnational and globalized world. However, the strands of research remain selective and internationally scattered and have not been brought under a common framework yet. The aim of this book is to present transnational aging as both a research perspective and an agenda for further research, related but not limited to several, partly overlapping broader strands of research identified in this field.

The first strand of research emerged in the broader field of retirement migration, which focuses on the migration of older Asian, European, and North American citizens to countries with better climates and often lower living costs. These studies reveal how older people develop transnational lifestyles and identities; engage in transnational social, cultural and political activities; and maintain close relationships with friends and family members back home (Ackers and Dwyer 2002; Banks 2009; Casado-Díaz, Kaiser and Warnes 2004; Croucher 2012; Gustafson 2008; Huber and O'Reilly 2004; Kaiser 2011; Ono 2008; Toyota 2006). In order to grasp the geographic orientation and the social frames of reference, researchers in this field developed a wealth of typologies, differentiating for example between long-stay international tourists, second-home owners, "snowbirds," and permanent residents (King, Warnes and William 2000; Williams et al. 2000) or between full residents, returning residents, seasonal visitors, peripatetic visitors, and

2 *Vincent Horn and Cornelia Schweppe*

tourists (O'Reilly 2000; see also Warnes et al. [2004] for a typology of older migrants in Europe in general).

Closely related to the first, a second strand of research focuses on aging migrants in wealthier countries. Researchers in this strand examine practices, strategies, and mobility patterns that are employed to manage long-distance relationships or optimize resources in the host and home societies (Baykara-Krumme 2013; Chong and Li 2012; Bolzman, Fibbi and Vial 2006; Dietzel-Papakyriakou 2005; Krumme 2004; Strumpen 2012). In this regard, pendular migration has been identified as a widespread strategy of aging migrants to combine resources in different countries, such as enjoying proximity with family members in the country of origin, on one hand, and access to social benefits and health care services in the host society, on the other hand. Pendular migration is also used as a strategy to reconcile one's desire to maintain close ties to the country of origin with the reluctance of family members to permanently return (De Haas and Fokkema 2010).

A third strand of research emerged in the broader field of transnational family research, with a specific focus on older people as both providers and receivers of care and support in transnational settings. These studies emphasize the role of older nonmigrant women as "flying grandmothers" (Goldbourne and Chamberlain 2001) who travel back and forth to spend periods of physical co-presence with family members abroad (Deneva 2012; Lie 2010). Other researchers focus on older people who join their emigrated kin abroad (Lamb 2002; Treas 2008; Zhou 2012), examining, for example, which patterns of intergenerational reciprocity emerge in the context of migration and globalization (Izuhara 2010). These studies show that older people engage in frequent and extended visits to their country of origin, maintain residences and keep bank accounts in both countries, and acquire dual citizenship (Lamb 2002).

However, studies also reveal how unfulfilled expectations of reciprocity and prolonged periods of caregiving have an impact on the older people's well-being. Treas and Mazumdar (2004) found evidence of older people working extensive hours in their children's households while suffering from social isolation and economic dependence at the same time. Still other researchers consider older people in their role as "mother and father surrogates" who aim to fill the gap left by the emigrated mother and/or father (Bernhard, Landolt and Goldring 2006; Levitt 2001; Pantea 2012; Parreñas 2001; Romero 1997). Finally, some studies look at transnational aged care provided and organized by emigrated kin (Baldassar 2007; Baldassar and Baldock 2000; Baldock 2000; Díaz Gorfinkiel and Escrivá 2012; Zechner 2008). These studies demonstrate that intergenerational relationships and care commitments are not dissolved in transnational settings, with families being able to circulate resources (money, hands-on care, emotional support, etc.) across borders and large geographic distances. Nevertheless, providing transnational care for older family members should not be assumed to be a general pattern among migrants (Mazzucato 2008; Vullnetari and King 2008).

A fourth strand of research comprises a variety of studies related to health and care migration, in particular looking at the care deficits of older people in richer countries that in many respects are not prepared for the changing needs and demands in old age care. On one hand, this refers to the migration and recruitment of mainly female migrants from poorer countries to care for older people in wealthier countries in both private and institutionalized settings (e.g., Agrela 2012; Huang, Yeoh and Toyota 2012; Hooren 2012). Although not mobile themselves, the care needs of these older people are addressed by migrants who often maintain close ties to their families and communities in their country of origin. This phenomenon, known as "global care chains" (Hochschild 2000), has led to a growing industry of transnational recruitment agencies that place foreign care workers into the households of wealthier countries (Di Santo and Ceruzzi 2010; Krawietz 2014). Additionally, public employment agencies and old-age care providers in wealthier countries increasingly aim to recruit migrant care workers and nurses to address local labor shortages (Cangiano and Walsh 2014).

On the other hand, this strand of research refers to older people who seek health care outside their country of residence (Bilicen and Tezcan-Güntekin 2014; Lee, Kearns and Friesen 2010; Sun 2014). These studies investigate the regulatory framework of transnational health care, as well as motivations, patterns and outcomes of transnational health care strategies, often characterized by multiple medicine consumption, diverse medical treatments, and paradigms. More recently, growing academic interest has been given to the migration of older Western Europeans to old-age care facilities in Asia and Eastern Europe (Bender et al. 2014, Horn et al. in this volume), and North Americans to Latin American countries, especially Mexico (Ibarra 2011). Although there are still very few insights into the scope and social implications of this development, the rapid emergence of old-age care providers in these countries indicates a new trend of care demand following care supply. That is, so to speak, a trend towards reversed global care chains. Similarly underresearched is a further feature of this trend: transnational marriages for old-age care (Lu 2012).

Implicitly or explicitly, a fifth strand of research has emerged which identifies and examines the challenges and changes of social services and social policy brought along by transnational aging (Krawietz and Schröer 2010; Lunt 2009). For example, examining the division of labor between outpatient care services and private transnational agencies within care households illustrates how the provision of social interventions and offers is increasingly embedded in a transnational welfare mix. At the same time, it also indicates the complex restructuring that could develop through transnational cooperation in local forms of care provision in the future. The entanglement of local service structures with transnationally organized 24-hours care

4   *Vincent Horn and Cornelia Schweppe*

services shows, for example, features of a "two-class-service-provision" (Krawietz and Schröer 2010).[1]

Altogether, the different strands of research provide a wide array of perspectives and approaches to transnational aging that reflect the multifaceted nature of this phenomenon. Despite this diversity, to a greater or lesser extent all studies refer to the interplay of micro-, meso- and macro-level factors regarding the construction of aging in transnational settings or spaces. We argue, accordingly, that transnational aging is constructed within these different, often interlinked dimensions. On the micro-level, transnational aging is constructed within older people's life histories, biographical projects and identities, and everyday life experiences. On the meso-level, it is constructed within social security systems, social institutions and services available for older people, including public, nonprofit and market-based providers, and on the macro-level within the process of welfare state development, global and supranational politics, and ideologies of aging (Horn, Schweppe and Um 2013). In this sense, a holistic approach to transnational aging requires the analysis of multiple levels and their interrelationships.

Additionally, the different strands of research show that we need to include not only the traditional units of analysis such as aging and retirement migrants in transnational aging research but also those without or with less familiar migration histories. On one hand, this refers to older non-migrants who often make important contributions to the well-being of their emigrated kin. To establish this group as an analytical category, Nedelcu (2009) coined the term *generation zero*, which is currently taken up by other researchers (e.g., King et al. 2014). On the other hand, it refers to older individuals who are not entangled in transnational family settings but whose lives are still affected by transnational processes, such as older people who receive care in a transnational welfare mix or those who move abroad to receive health or long-term care. Moreover, older people's lives may be affected by transnational organizations or traveling ideas and institutions. Lamb (2009), for example, has shown how the culturally transformed adoption of the Western institution of old-age homes in India considerably changed the aging experiences of older Indian residents.

On the macro-level, studies emphasize that the nation-state has by no means lost its importance with regard to transnational aging (Westwood and Phizacklea 2000). Indeed, despite increasingly blurred boundaries, the nation-state still has a deep impact on people's life courses, through relevant jurisdictions, sociocultural conditions, and/or economic and political systems. For example, the question of whether pensions and health insurances can be received in another country than the country of residence may "shape decisions of older immigrants who are considering whether to retire to their country of origin, whether to follow their child/ren overseas or whether to stay" (Lunt 2009: 247). Similarly, mobility and citizenship rights shape the transnational activities and relationships of older people by configuring the spatial and temporal dimension of their involvement (Kilkey and Merla 2014).

Because of the enduring importance of boundaries set by nation-states, transnational aging is often embedded in different and oftentimes incongruent (national) contexts and frames of reference. These incongruences need to be worked on in order to moderate and compensate for incompatibilities (Mau 2007). Accordingly, transnational aging requires effort to relate and combine the different frames of reference with each other. These efforts can place high coping demands on the actors who need to reconnect what seemingly falls apart and who have to make things suitable that do not belong well together (Mau 2007). It is precisely through this that their coping efforts can also be risky, crisis-afflicted or over demanding. As Mau puts it,

> [o]ne can rightly raise the question, whether a new level of the scope, fluidity and heterogeneity of social relations is achieved by transnationalization, which overreaches the risks of disintegration and individual overload. Per definitionem, cross-border relations are more demanding and precarious . . . As with any form of individualization and the magnification of opportunities, the new possibilities to expand the horizon of action transnationally are a matter of "risky freedom" (Beck and Beck-Gernsheim 1994). (Mau 2007: 61, translation by the authors)

At the same time, it becomes evident that, because of these entanglements, transnational aging cannot be considered just as a geographic expansion of aging or the continuation of previous concepts beyond national borders. These entanglements influence aging and can change its related institutions and policies. In this regard, Bender and colleagues (2014) refer to the relevance of the concept of translation. Processes of translation ask how knowledge, practices, ideas, and organizations, among others, spread, that is, how they circulate between different social worlds and frames of reference and how they are transformed. In this process ideas, organizations, practices, and so on are not simply received or rejected, accepted or discarded but, rather, they form new, previously nonexistent connections through processes of "displacement, drift, invention, mediation, creation" (Latour 1993, cited from Czarniawska and Joerges 1996: 24). In translation processes, something is linked to something else that exists and simultaneously something new is created. Translation processes signify imitation and creation, variation and uniformity, change and status quo. With regard to transnational aging, the question arises of how much these processes widen possibilities of action and are related to new or further burdens and restrictions.

On this matter, debates on agency and structure prove to be fruitful. The concepts of agency and structure are quite contested, and little consensus exist about how to adequately define them. A useful approach is provided by Marshall and Clarke (2010), who propose to distinguish between at least four constructs in order to grasp the complexities of aging. The

6   Vincent Horn and Cornelia Schweppe

first construct is the human capacity to make a choice, to be intentional. Second, resources refer to the individual's additionally acquired capacities (e.g., literacy) and other possessions (e.g., economic or social capital). The third construct referred to is behavior in the Weberian sense (when the actor's behavior is meaningfully orientated to that of others). Finally, the fourth construct refers to the social and physical structuring of activities and therefore to the "de facto structure of opportunities or life chances that is open within the range of action of the actor" (Marshall and Clarke 2010: 302). This construct "constitutes the field that constrains but also facilitates the choices made by all people, all of whom possess agency but who vary widely in the person, social, and economic resources they can employ as they try to construct their biographies over the life-course" (ibid.).

In such an understanding, agency does not focus on the individual characteristics of the actor's capacity to act. Rather, the focus is on social processes and structures through which people are strengthened in their agency. When this point is taken up, transnational aging can be considered within the frame of social processes, and the question of agency can be situated in the social and political contexts (Homfeldt, Schröer and Schweppe 2006). The analysis then focuses not only on coping with individual challenges but also, and especially, on the structural, organizational, and legal framing of possibilities and restrictions of action.

This perspective also opens the view to social inequalities. Hence, it can be assumed that the uneven distribution of resources accumulated by older people over time is likely to turn into unequal possibilities of action within transnational settings (Ackers and Dwyer 2002; Dahinden 2010). Thus, older people may deliberately opt for types or experiences of transnational aging according to their resources, by choice or because of constraint (e.g., because of the lack of access to local social services or denied family reunification). The study of social inequalities is an important dimension in transnational aging research; however, within an increasing transnational world with actors related to different national contexts, these social inequalities can no longer be theorized solely within the borders of the nation-state (Weiss 2005). Transnational aging can be considered a multiclass phenomenon experienced by individuals with highly diverse socioeconomic, ethnic, and religious backgrounds.

Within the diversity of transnational aging, it is also important to take into account that transnational lifeworlds are not limited to mobile people and that mobility is not a necessary requirement. Many studies show the importance of information and communication technologies (ICTs) for establishing and being involved in transnational relationships (Baldassar 2008; Wilding 2006); however, immobile people without access to or the ability to use, ICTs can be involved in transnational lifeworlds. In this respect, transnational references to life can emerge or be sustained through symbolic or mental connections that are border crossing, such as memory, nostalgia or imagination (Huber 2013). These connections concern, inter alia, actors who have strong affiliations with religious and/or political groups. Therefore, transnational aging research does not limit its focus to mobile older people. An analytical lens that includes both the "ways of being" and "ways of belonging" of older people in transnational processes, as suggested by Levitt and Glick-Schiller (2004), proves to be helpful. According to these authors, "ways of being" refer to the actual social relations and practices in which individuals engage, in contrast to "ways of belonging" which refer to a transnational connection through memory, nostalgia, or imagination. It is through the latter that we might be able to grasp the significance of different forms of mental border crossing in older people's lives, and not only immigrants.

With such a broad understanding of the transnational and diverse units of analysis, we certainly go beyond the well-known definition of transnationalism as the "process by which immigrants build social fields that link together their country of origin and their country of settlement" (Glick Schiller, Basch and Szanton 1992). With transnational aging we refer instead to "the process of organizing, shaping, and coping with life in old age in contexts which are no longer limited to the frame of a single nation state" (Horn, Schweppe and Um 2013: 7). This is not to say that we assume transnational processes to be a ubiquitous phenomenon in older people's lives. They may simply be absent or may not have a significant influence on aging experiences. They may also be selective, ebbing and flowing depending on a range of conditions and circumstances (Vertovec 2009).

We argue, however, that the relevance and scope of transnational processes in the lives of older people will increase in the near future. We base this assumption on two broader developments: first, the growing number of older people benefiting from increasing economic, technological and health-related possibilities and, second, the growing number of older people with limited financial resources and access to affordable health and long-term care in their countries of residence. For the former group we expect the development of resource-based transnational lifestyles in old age, whereas the transnational entanglement of the latter group represents a reaction to limited resources in their ancestral environments. Both developments are enhanced by the gradual transnational opening of social security systems to allow for the portability of (certain) social benefits to other countries. Additionally, ICT skills and traveling experiences among older people can be expected to increase with every younger cohort.

OVERVIEW OF CHAPTERS

The contributors of this book were asked to provide insights into current findings and debates on aging. The different chapters, therefore, reflect the diversity of perspectives and methods currently used to explore the

8   *Vincent Horn and Cornelia Schweppe*

phenomenon of transnational aging; the book brings them together in a single publication.

The book is structured in four parts. Part A examines the relation between aging and the family in transnational contexts from different perspectives, showing the many dimensions and ambivalences that transnational contexts have regarding the roles, functions, and experiences of the elderly within the family and its exchanges.

Vincent Horn examines the influence of migration regimes on family-related transnational activities of older Peruvian migrants in Spain and the United States. This comparative analysis is based on data taken from the first Worldwide Survey on the Peruvian Community Abroad (WSPCA) from 2012. Horn shows that migration regimes shape the socioeconomic profile of migrant populations, mediate the migrants' incorporation into the labor market and welfare regime, and determine the migrants' family structures. These factors shape the type, as well as the scope and frequency, of engaging in family visits, sending remittances, and using the Internet for communication purposes by the older Peruvians.

Elena Sommer and Claudia Vogel examine the effects of geographic distance on the functional solidarity of migrant families, as illustrated by adult migrants from the former Soviet Union in Germany and their parents. The authors use a quantitative data analysis of the Survey on Ageing of Soviet Union Migrants (2011) to show that the exchange of instrumental help decreases with increasing distance. The analysis also reveals that the older generation is the giver of financial support if both parents and children live in Germany, while parents living abroad are more often the receivers of monetary assistance.

Jason Pribilsky addresses the issue of abuse and neglect of Andean elders in a rural indigenous community in the Ecuadorian highlands, a region that is highly influenced by international emigration. Pribilsky analyzes the ways "transnational logics" have upended the lives of elderly in this area as well the forces that shape the context of abuse. He highlights the tensions and ambiguities surrounding the meanings of social obligations, generational differences between rural youth and their elderly caregivers, and the economic necessities of family separation.

Tatiana Tiaynen-Qadir examines the role and experiences of grandmothers in their family making between Russian Karelia and Finland. She suggests that these roles and experiences are substantially informed by the practices and understandings of the "babushka," a Russian grandmother figure. In re-creating family solidarity and women's networks, the figure of the "transnational babushka" is at the core of transnational social support that provides a feeling of comfort and existential security as women age.

The topic of "migration in later life" is at the center of Part B. Even though this topic has been under academic scrutiny for quite a while, due to often severe methodological obstacles, there is hardly any reliable statistical

Introduction 9

data on the scope of this phenomenon. Ralf Himmelreicher and Wolfgang Keck face the challenge of estimating the number of older people who migrate from Germany by using data from the statutory German Pension Insurance. They find strong evidence that migration in old age connected to Germany has increased in the last 20 years and will probably continue to increase in future.

Anita Böcker and Canan Balkir turn to the topic of dual residences in old age. The authors examine whether and how increasing care needs or an awareness of future needs influences the migratory decisions of older migrants, by comparing Dutch retirement migrants and Turkish retirement returnees. They especially explore if and how different social and mobility rights granted to different groups of older migrants impact their mobility preferences.

Tineke Fokkema, Eralba Cela, and Yvonne Witter focus on pendular migration in old age and challenge some of the current assumptions attached to it. In contrast to beliefs that pendular migration is a temporary event followed by a permanent stay or a definite return, a second-best option, a time of relaxation, and a private matter, the authors demonstrate that the available empirical evidence paints a more complex and nuanced picture.

Elder care has been given much attention within transnational aging research. While so far this has mainly focussed on the family and on the recruitment of migrant household workers, increasing evidence shows the importance of transnational challenges and changes of organizations for elder care as well as the importance of framing transnational elderly care within a macro perspective. Part C, called "Facets of Old-Age Care in a Transnational World," examines these challenges.

Vincent Horn, Cornelia Schweppe, Désirée Bender, and Tina Hollstein turn to the relatively new phenomenon of old-age care and retirement facilities for elderly Germans abroad, which are mainly established in Asia and Eastern Europe. They show the close relationship between the emergence of these facilities and the so-called old-age-care crisis in Germany and identify the ambivalence of these facilities, designed as promising structures for care and support.

Old-age homes in India are at the center of the chapter by Sarah Lamb. She uses the concept of "traveling institutions" to show that institutions and the ideas embedded in them play a vital role in constituting the experience of aging in the current transnational era. She explores how residents, kin, and proprietors are creating unique Indian cultural versions of the modern, increasingly globally ubiquitous institution of the old-age home.

Karin van Holten and Eva Soom Ammann examine elderly care settings in Switzerland, which—like in other northwestern countries—are increasing diverse, both with regard to the caregivers and to those receiving care. By focusing on food and feeding and by introducing the potato as a symbol for difference and belonging in debates on "good" care, they discuss

10 *Vincent Horn and Cornelia Schweppe*

the negotiation of diversity and power asymmetry in institutional and home-based elder-care settings.

Susan McDaniel and Seonggee Um apply a macro perspective to elderly care and challenge the prevalent script that ageing populations in more developed countries, combined with more women in the labor force and more families living distantly from older relatives, lead to increased demand for care and, therefore, increased demand for international elder-care workers. The authors contest this script and explore the complexity of alternative patterns, arguing that growing inequalities, both globally and within many countries, create regimes of inequality that position and reposition transnational care work in new, emerging, and heretofore largely unexplored ways.

Social protection becomes of growing importance in the debate on transnational aging. Part D, therefore, turns to this debate and discusses it, especially in the field of international development cooperation where old age is increasingly on the agenda.

Carmen Grimm explores the traveling of ideas in the area of international development cooperation concerned with old age. Through the empirical example of a nongovernmental organization, she follows age-related ideas over time and across locations, circulating between Latin America and the Caribbean, Germany, and international organizations. She demonstrates how ideas about older persons trespass national and thematic borders and assume shapes in different contexts.

Katrin Fröhlich analyzes an unconditional pension project that is implemented by a nongovernmental organization (NGO) in Tanzania. She shows how this NGO positions itself amongst other local and global actors, and how it justifies this uncommon and internationally not (yet) fully accepted measure of social protection to its donors. She also explores how the NGO, in addressing its own limitations, is expanding its role from service provision to a human rights–based approach giving the responsibility for social protection to the state and to the older people themselves.

ACKNOWLEDGMENTS

The book could not have been published without the participation and support of many people. We would like to thank the authors for their extraordinary work and fruitful collaboration as well as Routledge for accepting and publishing this volume. Our gratitude goes particularly to Max Novick from Routledge, who stood by us with great calm and fortitude. Special thanks to Manuela Popovici, for her comments and distinguished proofreading skills, and to Simon Rosenkranz, Pascal Ludwig, and Anne Winterhager, for editing and formatting the manuscript. Finally, a special thank you goes to our friends and families who accompanied us during this process and provided us with support—locally, translocally, and transnationally.

NOTES

1 Local providers facilitate the qualified and therefore recognized and legally secured medical and nursing activities. In contrast, the migrant care workers in precarious and insecure employment situations take over all those activities that are not or are only insufficiently covered or provided by the welfare state. Those are the activities that the families have to deal with themselves (e.g., all time-consuming and household-related care activities).

REFERENCES

Ackers, Louise/Dwyer, Peter (2002): *Senior Citizenship? Retirement, Migration and Welfare in the European Union.* Bristol: Policy Press.

Agrela, Belén (2012): Towards a Model of Externalisation and Denationalisation of Care? The Role of Female Migrant Workers for Dependent Older People in Spain. In: *European Journal of Social Policy* 15, 1, pp. 45–61.

Baldassar, Loretta (2007): Transnational Families and Aged Care: The Mobility of Care and the Migrancy of Ageing. In: *Journal of Ethnic and Migration Studies* 33, 2, pp. 275–97.

Baldassar, Loretta (2008): Missing Kin and Longing to Be Together: Emotions and the Construction of Co-presence in Transnational Relationships. In: *Journal of Ethnic and Migration Studies* 33, 2, pp. 275–297.

Baldassar, Loretta/Baldock, Cora (2000): Linking Migration and Family Studies: Transnational Migrants and the Care of Ageing Parents. In: Agozino, Biko (ed.): *Theoretical and Methodological Issues in Migration Research. Interdisciplinary and International Perspectives.* Aldershot: Ashgate, pp. 61–89.

Baldock, Cora (2000): Migrants and Their Parents: Caregiving from a Distance. In: *Journal of Family Issues* 21, 2, pp. 205–224.

Banks, Stephen P. (2009): Intergenerational Ties Across Borders: Grandparenting Narratives by Expatriate Retirees Living in Mexico. In: *Journal of Aging Studies* 23, 3, pp. 178–187.

Baykara-Krumme, Helen (2013): Returning, Staying, or Both? Mobility Patterns Among Elderly Turkish Migrants After Retirement. In: *Transnational Social Review—A Social Work Journal* 3, 1, pp. 11–29.

Bender, Désirée/Hollstein, Tina/Horn, Vincent/Huber, Lena/Schweppe, Cornelia (2014): Old Age Care Facilities and Care-Seeking Elderly on the Move. In: *Transnational Social Review: A Social Work Journal* 4, 2–3, 290–293.

Bernhard, Judith P./Landolt, Patricia/Goldring, Luin (2005): Transnational, Multi-local Motherhood: Experiences of Separation and Reunification among Latin American Families in Canada. *CERIS Working Paper 40.*

Bilecen, Başak/Hürrem, Tezcan-Güntekin (2014): *Transnational Healthcare Practices of Retired Circular Migrants.* Bielefeld: Working Papers—Center on Migration, Citizenship and Development: 127.

Bolzman, Claudio/Fibbi, Rosita/Vial, Marie (2006): What to Do After Retirement? Elderly Migrants and the Question of Return. In: *Journal of Ethnic and Migration Studies* 32, 8, pp. 1359–75.

Cangiano, Alessio/Walsh, Kieran (2014): Recruitment Processes and Immigration Regulations: The Disjointed Pathways to Employing Migrant Carers in Ageing Societies. In: *Work Employment Society* 28, 3, pp. 372–89.

Chong, Wendy W./Li Mark D. (2012): Transnationalism, Social Wellbeing and Older Chinese Migrants. In: *Graduate Journal of Asia-Pacific Studies* 8, 1, pp. 29–44.

12 Vincent Horn and Cornelia Schweppe

Casado-Díaz, María/Kaiser, Claudia/Warnes, Anthony M. (2004): Northern European Retired Residents in Nine Southern European Areas: Characteristics, Motivations and Adjustment. In: *Ageing & Society* 24, 3, pp. 353–81.

Croucher, Sheila (2012): Privileged Mobility in an Age of Globality. In: *Societies* 2, 1, pp. 1–13.

Czarniawska, Barbara/Joerges, Bernward (1996): Travels of Ideas. In: Czarniawska, Barbara/Sevón, Guje (eds.): *Translating Organizational Change*. Berlin/New York: Walter de Gruyter, pp. 13–48.

Dahinden, Janine (2010): Wer entwickelt einen transnationalen Habitus? Ungleiche Transnationalisierungsprozesse als Ausdruck ungleicher Ressourcenausstattung. In: Reutlinger, Christian/Baghdadi, Nadia/Kniffki, Johannes (eds.): *Die soziale Welt quer denken: Transnationalisierung und ihre Folgen für die Soziale Arbeit*. Berlin: Frank & Timme, pp. 83–108.

De Haas, Hein/Fokkema, Tineke (2010): Intra-Household Conflicts in Migration Decisionmaking: Return and Pendulum Migration in Morocco. In: *Population and Development Review* 36, 3, pp. 541–61.

Deneva, Neda (2012): Transnational Aging Carers: On Transformation of Kinship and Citizenship in the Context of Migration Among Bulgarian Muslims in Spain. In: *Social Politics* 19, 1, pp. 105–28.

Di Santo, Patrizia/Ceruzzi, Francesca (2010): *Migrant Care Workers in Italy. A Case Study*. Report presented for the project 'Health system and long-term care for older people in Europe—modelling the interfaces and links between prevention, rehabilitation, quality of services and informal care'. INTERLINKS. Rome/Vienna, February 2010.

Díaz Gorfinkiel, Magdalena/Escrivá, Angeles (2012): Care of Older People in Migration Contexts: Local and Transnational Arrangements Between Peru and Spain. In: *Social Politics* 19, 1, pp. 129–41.

Dietzel-Papakyriakou, Maria (2005): Potenziale älterer Migranten und Migrantinnen. In: *Zeitschrift für Gerontologie und Geriatrie* 38, 6, pp. 396–406.

Faulstich, Marjorie/Thorne, Barrie/Chee, Anna/Wan Shun, Eva L. (2001): Transnational Childhoods: The Participation of Children in Processes of Family Migration. In: *Social Problems* 48, 4, pp. 572–91.

Glick-Schiller, Nina/Basch, Linda/Szanton-Blanc, Cristina (1992): *Towards a Transnational Perspective on Migration*. New York: New York Academy of Sciences.

Goulbourne, Harry/Chamberlain, Mary (eds.) (2001): *Caribbean Families in the Trans-Atlantic World*. London: Macmillan.

Gustafson, Per (2008): Transnationalism in Retirement Migration: The Case of North European Retirees in Spain. In: *Ethnic and Racial Studies* 31, 3, pp. 451–75.

Hochschild, Arlie (2000): Global Care Chains and Emotional Surplus Value. In: Hutton, Will/Giddens, Anthony (eds.): *On the Edge: Living with Global Capitalism*. London: Sage Publishers, pp. 130–46.

Homfeldt, Hans G./Schröer, Wolfgang Schröer/Schweppe, Cornelia (eds.) (2006): *Transnationalität, soziale Unterstützung, agency*. Nordhausen: Traugott Bautz.

Hooren, Franca J. van (2012): Varieties of Migrant Care Work: Comparing Patterns of Migrant Labour in Social Care. In: *Journal of European Social Policy* 22, 2, pp. 133–47.

Horn, Vincent/Schweppe, Cornelia/Um, Seong-gee (2013): Transnational Aging—A Young Field of Research. In: *Transnational Social Review—A Social Work Journal* 3, 1, pp. 7–10.

Huang, Shirlena/Yeoh, Brenda S. A./Toyota, Mika (2012): Caring for the Elderly: The Embodied Labour of Migrant Care Workers in Singapore. In: *Global Networks* 12, 2, pp. 195–215.

Huber, Andreas/O'Reilly, Karen (2004): The Construction of *Heimat* Under Conditions of Individualized Modernity: Swiss and British Elderly Migrants in Spain. In: *Ageing & Society* 24, pp. 327–51.

Huber, Lena (2013): Analyserahmen und Arbeitsdewfinitionen für eine sozialpädagogische Konzeption von Transmigration—ein Entwurf. In: Herz, Andreas/Olivier, Claudia (eds.): *Transmigration und Soziale Arbeit. Ein öffnender Blick auf Alltagswelten.* Baltmannsweiler: Schneider Verlag Hohengehren, pp. 45–69.

Ibarra, Roberto A. (2011): The Initiative to Extend Medicare into Mexico: A Case Study in Changing U.S. Health Care Policy. In: *Health, Culture and Society* 1, 1, pp. 91–109.

Izuhara, Misa (ed.) (2010): *Ageing and Intergenerational Relations. Family reciprocity from a global perspective.* Bristol: The Policy Press.

Kaiser, Claudia (2011): *Transnationale Altersmigration in Europa. Sozialgeographische und gerontologische Perspektiven.* Wiesbaden: Verlag für Sozialwissenschaften.

Kilkey, Majella/Merla, Laura (2014): Situating Transnational Families' Care-Giving Arrangements: The Role of Institutional Contexts. In: *Global Networks* 14, 2, pp. 210–29.

King, Russell/Warnes, Anthony M./Williams, Allan M. (2000): *Sunset Lives: British Retirement Migration to the Mediterranean.* Oxford/New York: Berg.

King, Russell/Cela, Eralba/Fokkema, Tineke/Vullnetari, Julie (2014): The Migration and Well-Being of the Zero Generation: Transgenerational Care, Grandparenting, and Loneliness Amongst Albanian Older People. In: *Population, Space and Place* 20, pp. 728–38.

Kobayashi, Audrey/Preston, Valerie (2007): Transnationalism Through the Life Course: Hong Kong Immigrants in Canada. In: *Asia Pacific Viewpoint* 48, 2, pp. 151–67.

Krawietz, Johanna (2014): *Pflege grenzüberschreitend organisieren. Eine Studie zur transnationalen Vermittlung von Care-Arbeit.* Frankfurt am Main: Mabuse.

Krawietz, Johanna/Schröer, Wolfgang (2010): Transnationale Sorge im lokalen Dienstleistungsmix—Neue Forschungsperspektiven Sozialer Arbeit. In: Reutlinger, Christian/Baghdadi, Nadia/Kniffki, Johannes (eds.): *Die soziale Welt quer denken: Transnationalisierung und ihre Folgen für die Soziale Arbeit.* Berlin: Frank & Timme, pp. 207–20.

Krumme, Helen (2004): Fortwährende Remigration: Das transnationale Pendeln türkischer Arbeitsmigrantinnen und Arbeitsmigranten im Ruhestand. In: *Zeitschrift für Soziologie* 33, 2, pp. 138–53.

Lamb, Sarah (2002): Intimacy in a Transnational Era: The Remaking of Aging Among Indian Americans. In: *Diaspora* 11, 3, pp. 299–330.

Lamb, Sarah (2009): *Aging and the Indian Diaspora. Cosmopolitan Families in India and Abroad.* Bloomington: Indiana University Press.

Lu, Melody C.-W. (2012): Transnational Marriages as a Strategy of Care Exchange: Teteran Soldiers and their Mainland Chinese Spouses in Taiwan. In: *Global Networks* 12, 2, pp. 233–51.

Lunt, Neil (2009): Older People Within Transnational Families: The Social Policy Implications. In: *International Journal of Social Welfare* 18, pp. 243–51.

Lee, Jane Y./Kearns, Robin A./Friesen, Wardlow (2010): Seeking Affective Health Care: Korean Immigrants' Use of Homeland Medical Services. In: *Health & Place* 16, pp. 108–15.

Levitt, Peggy (2001): *The Transnational Villagers.* Berkeley/Los Angeles: University of California Press.

14 Vincent Horn and Cornelia Schweppe

Levitt, Peggy/Glick-Schiller, Nina (2004): Conceptualizing Simultaneity: A Transnational Social Field Perspective on Society. In: *International Migration Review* 38, 3, pp. 1002–39.

Lie, Mabel L. S. (2010): Across the Oceans: Childcare and Grandparenting in UK Chinese and Bangladeshi Households. In: *Journal of Ethnic and Migration Studies* 36, 9, pp. 1425–43.

Marshall,Victor W./Clarke, Philippa J. (2010): Agency and Social Structure in Aging and Life Course Research. In: Dannefer, Dale/Phillipson, Chris (eds.): *International Handbook of Social Gerontology*. London: Sage, pp. 294–305.

Mau, Steffen (2007): *Transnationale Vergesellschaftung. Die Entgrenzung sozialer Lebenswelten*. Frankfurt am Main/New York: Campus.

Mazzucato, Valentina (2008): Transnational Reciprocity: Ghanaian Migrants and the Care of Their Parents Back Home. In: Alber, Erdmute/van der Geest, Sjaak / Whyte, Susan R. (eds.): *Generations in Africa: Connections and Conflicts*. Münster: LIT Verlag, pp. 111–33.

Menjívar, Cecilia (2002): Living in Two Worlds? Guatemalan-Origin Children in the United States and Emerging Transnationalism. In: *Journal of Ethnic and Migration Studies* 28, 3, pp. 531–52.

Montes de Oca, Veronica/Molina, Ahtziri/Avalos, Rosauro (2009): *Migración, redes transnacionales y envejecimiento*. México: UNAM, Instituto de Investigaciones Sociales; Gobierno del estado de Guanajuato.

Nedelcu, Mihaela (2009): La Generation Zero : Du Sedentaire a L'acteur Circulant. Effets de Mobilite sur la Generation des Parents des Migrants Roumains Hautement Qualifies a Toronto A L'ere du Numerique. In: Cortes, Geneviève /Faret, Laurent (eds.): *Les circulations transnationales. Lire les turbulences migratoires contemporaines*. Paris: Armand Colin, pp. 197–98.

Ono, Mayumi (2008): Long-Stay Tourism and International Retirement Migration: Japanese Retirees in Malaysia. In: Yamashita, Shinji/Minami, Makito/Haines, David W./Eades, Jerry S. (eds.): *Transnational Migration in East Asia. Japan in a Comparative Focus*. Senri Ethnological Reports 77. Osaka: National Museum of Ethnology, pp. 151–62.

O'Reilly, Karen (2000): *The British on the Costa del Sol: Transnational Identities and Local Communities*. London: Routledge.

Pantea, Maria-Carmen (2012): Grandmothers as Main Caregivers in the Context of Parental Migration. In: *European Journal of Social Work* 15, 11, pp. 63–80.

Parreñas, Rhacel S. (2001): *Servants of Globalization: Women, Migration and Domestic Work*. Stanford, CA: Stanford University Press.

Parreñas, Rhacel S. (2005): *Children of Global Migration. Transnational Families and Gendered Woes*. Stanford, CA: Stanford University Press.

Poeze, Miranda/Mazzucato, Valentina (2014): Ghanaian Children in Transnational Families: Understanding the Experiences of Left-Behind Children Through Local Parenting Norms. In: Baldassar, Loretta/Merla, Laura (eds.): *Transnational Families, Migration and the Circulation of Care. Understanding Mobility and Absence in Family Life*. New York: Routledge, pp. 140–69.

Romero, Mary (1997): Who Takes Care of the Maid's Children? Exploring the Costs of Domestic Service. In: Nelson, Hilde L. (ed.): *Feminism and Families*. Routledge: New York, pp. 151–69.

Strumpen, Sarina (2012): Altern in fortwährender Migration bei älteren Türkeistämmigen. In: Baykara-Krumme, Helen/Motel-Klingebiel, Andreas/Schimany, Peter (eds.): *Viele Welten des Alterns? Ältere Migranten im alternden Deutschland*. Wiesbaden: Verlag für Sozialwissenschaften, pp. 411–33.

Sun, Ken C.-Y. (2014): Transnational Healthcare Seeking: How Ageing Taiwanese Return Migrants View Homeland Public Benefits. In: *Global Networks* 14, 4, pp. 533–50.

Toyota, Mika (2006): Ageing and Transnational Householding: Japanese Retirees in Southeast Asia. In: *International Developmental Planning Review* 28, 4, pp. 515–31.

Treas, Judith (2008): Transnational Older Adults and Their Families. In: *Family Relations* 57, pp. 468–78.

Treas, Judith/Mazumdar, Shampa (2004): Caregiving and Kin Keeping: Contributions of Older People to America's Immigrant Families. In: *Journal of Comparative Family Studies* 35, pp. 105–22.

Vertovec, Steven (2009): *Transnationalism*. London: Routledge.

Vullnetari, Julie/King, Russel (2008): 'Does Your Granny Eat Grass?' On Mass Emigration, Care Drain and the Fate of Older People in Rural Albania. In: *Global Networks* 8, 2, pp. 139–71.

Warnes, Antony, M./Friedrich, Klaus/Kellaher, Leonie/Torres, Sandra (2004): The Diversity and Welfare of Older Migrants in Europe. In: *Ageing & Society* 24, 3, pp. 307–26.

Weiss, Anja (2005): The Transnationalization of Social Inequality: Conceptualizing Social Positions on a World Scale. In: *Current Sociology*, 53, 4, pp. 707–28.

Westwood, Sallie/Phizacklea, Annie (2000): Trans-Nationalism and the Politics of Belonging. London: Routledge.

Wilding, Raelene (2006): 'Virtual' Intimacies? Families Communicating Across Transnational Contexts. In: *Global Networks* 6, 2, pp. 125–42.

Williams, Allan M./King, Russel/Warnes, Anthony M./Patterson, Guy (2000): Tourism and International Retirement Migration: New Forms of an Old Relationship in Southern Europe. In: *Tourism Geographies* 1, pp. 28–49.

Zechner, Minna (2008): Care for Older Persons in Transnational Settings. In: *Journal of Aging Studies* 22, 32–44.

Zhou, Yanqiu R. (2012): Space, Time, and Self: Rethinking Aging in the Contexts of Immigration and Transnationalism. In: *Journal of Aging Studies* 26, pp. 232–42.

Part A

Aging and the Family in Transnational Contexts

Cross-Border Activities and
Intergenerational Relationships

1 Migration Regimes and Family-Related Transnational Activities of Older Peruvians in Spain and the United States

Vincent Horn

A growing academic interest can be observed concerning the impact of institutions on family related transnational activities, especially within the field of transnational family care (e.g., Kilkey and Merla 2013; Merla and Baldassar 2011). Researchers in this field tend to draw on case studies to disentangle the complex interrelationships between laws and regulations, on one hand, and the families' capacities to circulate care on the other. This chapter chooses a different approach by drawing on statistical data in order to generate assumptions about how migration regimes shape the opportunities of older Peruvians in Spain and the US to engage in family related transnational activities. It does so by analyzing the scope and/or frequency of three different transnational activities, namely, family visits, the sending of remittances, and the use the internet for communication purposes. All three have been covered by the first Worldwide Survey on the Peruvian Community Abroad (WSCPA) from 2012.

More specifically, this chapter addresses the following questions: First, how are older Peruvians residing in Spain and the US incorporated into the corresponding migration regimes in terms of income, employment, and legal status? Second, to what extent do older Peruvians engage in family related transnational activities, and how far do the patterns of engagement differ between the two groups? Third, what assumptions can be made about the interrelationship between the migration regimes and the older Peruvians' involvement in family-orientated border-crossing activities? To contextualize these discussions, the chapter starts with a brief overview of Peruvian migration to Spain and the US, emphasizing the different histories and entry channels for older Peruvians. In the second section, the chapter introduces Kilkey and Merla's (2013) framework for situating transnational family-care arrangements in institutional contexts. This conceptual framework is then used to compare the incorporation of older Peruvians into the migration regimes of Spain and the US, respectively. Against the backdrop of this comparison, the third section presents the findings and assumptions of the interrelationships between the older Peruvians' family related transnational activities and the two migration regimes.

20   *Vincent Horn*

OLDER PERUVIANS IN SPAIN AND THE US

Spain and the US have been the two major destination countries of Peruvian emigrants in the recent past. Thus, of the approximately 2.4 million Peruvian who left their country between 1990 and 2009, 32.6 percent are estimated to reside in the US and 16.6 percent in Spain (IOM et al. 2010). As shown in Table 1.1, between 2001 and 2010 the number of Peruvians registered in Spain increased from 34,000 to 140,000 and in the US from 145,000 to 600,000. Alternative estimates assume that the number of Peruvians in the US has already exceeded the 1 million threshold (Takenaka, Paerregaard and Berg 2010), based on the assessment that a large number of Peruvians live as irregular migrants and avoid registration in order to remain undetected. The official statistics in the US thus refer to those with legal status, including both foreign and domestic born migrants. In contrast, in Spain migrants usually register regardless of their legal status in order to gain access to health care and education. However, unlike in the US, naturalized migrants tend to fall out of the official statistics (Escrivá 2013). Estimates that also include naturalized Peruvians therefore calculate that 240,000 Peruvians are residing in Spain (Carpio and García 2011).[1] Evidently, because of the recent economic crisis, the recruitment of labor in Peru by the Spanish government, as well as the demand for work permits and family visas by Peruvian migrants, has diminished dramatically. Thus, the number of long-term visas issued to Peruvians has decreased from almost 30,000 in 2008 to little more than 3,000 in 2012 (Horn 2013).

During the same period, the number of older Peruvians in the two countries increased significantly. In the US today every one out of four Peruvians has already reached the age of 50. In contrast, in Spain, the Peruvian proportion has remained stable at around 13 percent, but in absolute terms the number of older Peruvians had more than tripled. The different relative proportion of older Peruvians in the two countries can be explained primarily by the longer tradition of Peruvian migration to the US and the recent flow

Table 1.1   Older Peruvians in Spain and the US

	Peruvians 50 years and older	
	Registered in 2000/1	Registered in 2010
USA	47,000	145,000
(total)	(233,926)	(609,000)
% of total	20	23.8
Spain	4,495	18,253
(total)	(34,690)	(141,309)
% of total	12.9	12.9

Sources: INE (2014); Census Bureau (2014).

Migration Regimes and Transnational Activities   21

Table 1.2   Arrival periods of older Peruvians in Spain and the US

	Peruvians aged 50 years and older who arrived		
	22 or more years ago	10–21 years ago	9 or less years ago
US	25.7%	47.5%	26.4%
Spain	3.8%	32.5%	63.6%

Source: WSCPA (2012).

of younger Peruvian adults into Spain. As a consequence of this, the age structure of Peruvians in Spain is still very young, whereas the age structure of the Peruvians in the US has become quite similar to the one of the overall population. However, with Peruvian migration to Spain having slowed considerably during the last years, the pool of younger and middle-aged adults is not constantly replenished anymore. It can therefore be expected that the demographic structure of Peruvians in Spain is going to change in the future, as well.

The longer tradition of Peruvian migration to the US is also reflected in Table 1.2, which compares different arrival periods of older Peruvians in the two countries. According to the data, the share of older Peruvians who arrived 22 or more years ago is much larger in the US (25.7 percent) than in Spain (3.8 percent). In contrast, almost two-thirds of older Peruvians in Spain arrived in the last nine years, compared to one-quarter in the US. This indicates that a larger group of older Peruvians in the US aged in the country, whereas older Peruvians in Spain were more likely to have arrived already at an advanced age (Escrivá and Skinner 2006). On one hand, this can be attributed to the comparatively easy access for older Peruvians to the Spanish labor market, which has been facilitated by a bilateral labor recruitment program between Spain and Peru. In fact, one out of four older Peruvians who arrived in Spain during the last nine years signed a labor contract before migrating (WSCPA 2012). On the other hand, the relatively lax regulations for family reunification in effect in Spain until 2009 facilitated reuniting with elderly parents (Escrivá 2013). In contrast, older Peruvians who arrived in the US recently entered almost entirely through family reunification.[2] Indeed, only 4.6 percent gained entry to the US because of a labor contract (WSCPA 2012). However, a common practice among Peruvian migrants in both countries was to overstay short-term visas and hope to regularize their status at a later date (Altamirano 1990).

INSTITUTIONAL CONTEXTS AND TRANSNATIONAL FAMILY ACTIVITIES

Research on the impact of institutions such as migration laws on transnational family activities and dynamics is still quite rare (Baldassar 2008a;

22 Vincent Horn

Mazzucato and Schans 2011). Among the few contributions in this field are Bernhard and colleagues' (2006) study of Latin American mothers in Canada and Fresnoza-Flot's (2009) study of female Filipino domestic workers in France. Both studies focus on the phenomenon of transnational motherhood by analyzing the impact of migration policies (Bernhard, Landolt and Goldring 2006) and different migration statuses (Fresnoza-Flot 2009) on women's experiences, practices, and strategies to mother from afar and their difficulties before and after reuniting with their children. In turn, studies from transnational family care research highlight the impact of institutions on the multidirectional and multigenerational circulation of care. These studies tend to follow a comparative approach, for example, by contrasting the transnational family care capabilities of Italian and El Salvadoran migrants in Australia (Merla and Baldassar 2011) or of Polish migrants in the United Kingdom and El Salvadoran migrants in Belgium (Kilkey and Merla 2013). Ariza's (2014) case study looks at the relationship of care circulation and migration regimes by comparing Mexican migrants in the US with Dominican migrants in Spain. Ariza concludes that the restrictive migration policies toward Mexicans in the US tend to hinder care circulation, whereas the Spanish migration regime facilitates it. Finally, some studies are concerned with older family members and with how they navigate immigration laws and other institutions in order to balance their transnational family commitments (Lamb 2002, 2009; Treas 2008).

However, applying an institutional perspective to the activities of transnational families is a complex exercise because of the range of policies, laws, and regulations, as well as social norms, that shape their "spatial and temporal configuration" (Kilkey and Merla 2013: 3). Therefore, the analytical approach of Kilkey and Merla (2013) is of particular value, because it systematically situates transnational family care arrangements within the institutional contexts of the sending and receiving countries. It provides an analytical toolkit for cross-ethnic and cross-national research and is applicable to different kinds of family-related transnational activities, not just to care. Thus, this approach can be used to compare family-related transnational activities of different immigrant populations that are subject to the institutional context of the same receiving country. Similarly, it can be used to examine whether certain institutional contexts are more favorable for these activities than other contexts by comparing migrants from the same country of origin who reside in different host societies. Evidently, it should not be assumed that a favorable institutional context necessarily intensifies family-related transnational activities or that a rather hostile institutional context necessarily diminishes them. In fact, transnational families are creatively circumventing institutional barriers in order to maintain what Bryceson and Vuorela (2002) called "familyhood" (Boehm 2012; Kilkey and Merla 2013). Thus, an institutional approach does not neglect the agency of families but, rather, interprets the institutional context as a structure of opportunity with which transnational families are dealing.

Migration Regimes and Transnational Activities 23

According to Kilkey and Merla's (2013) comprehensive approach, this structure of opportunity is shaped by four core regimes, namely, the migration regime, the welfare regime, the gendered care regime and the working time regime. In addition, transport and communication policies are included because of their influence on the availability and affordability of international passenger transport and the accessibility of the communication infrastructure.[3] The four core regimes are related to different key parameters; in the case of the migration regime, these are the "exit/entry/residency rights for migrants and their family members," policies and regulations which govern "the insertion of migrants and their family members into the labour market" and the welfare regime, and the migration cultures in the sending and receiving societies (Kilkey and Merla 2013: 7). The different regimes are interrelated in manifold ways and a focus just on migration regimes inevitably comes short in grasping the complexity of the framework. However, as Merla (2014: 121) puts it, migration regimes are of "primary importance . . . for the lives of transnational families in general and for the circulation of care in particular" and can therefore be seen as the most powerful set of rules, practices, and social norms that influence the activities of transnational families.

DATA AND METHODS

Most of the data presented in this chapter are taken from the first Worldwide Survey on the Peruvian Community Abroad (WSPCA), conducted in 2012 as a joint project of the Peruvian Ministry of External Affairs, the Statistical Office, and the International Organization for Migration in Peru. Almost 13,000 Peruvian migrants in 49 countries who attended a Peruvian consulate during the time of data collection were interviewed. Approximately one-quarter of all respondents had already reached the age of 50; of those, 393 resided in Spain and 1,492 in the US. A focus on individuals of this specific age group seems to be of particular interest because of their multiple roles as parents, grandparents, and often as children of older generations. In addition to the WSCPA, official data sources (census data and national surveys in Spain and the US) are used to provide complementary information about older Peruvians in both countries. Descriptive statistical analysis (frequencies, cross-tables) is utilized in order to detect common or contradictory patterns and to generate assumptions about possible relationships between the different migration regimes and the scope and/or frequency of the older Peruvians' involvement in family-related transnational activities.

Given that family relationships are at the core of these activities, the survey data used for the comparisons in this chapter are subject to several limitations. For instance, the survey does not include information about the migrants' relationship to family members and about where these family members are located. Moreover, it only includes activities that are directed

24 Vincent Horn

toward the country of origin and thus omits the multidirectionality of family-related transnational activities (Zontini and Reynolds 2007). Therefore, the survey does not contain any information about visits from the older Peruvians' significant others in Peru or elsewhere or about reverse remittances. Additionally, the survey tells us little about the concrete presence of state policies in the older Peruvians' lives and about how these policies actually have an impact on their engagement in family-related activities across borders. It does, however, allow for certain assumptions about relationships between migration regimes and family-related transnational activities on an aggregated level, which is useful both for future research and for contrasting findings from qualitative research.

MIGRATION REGIMES IN SPAIN AND THE US

This section applies the conceptual framework proposed by Kilkey and Merla (2013) to the case of older Peruvians in Spain and the US. The first part focuses on the migration cultures in Peru, Spain, and the US and the older Peruvians' entry and residence rights. The second part examines the older Peruvians' insertion into the labor market and welfare regime.

Migration Cultures and Entry and Residence Rights

According to Kilkey and Merla (2013: 7), migration cultures encompass the "norms around appropriate (family) migration strategies in sending societies" and the "overarching approach to migrants" in the receiving countries. As far as Peru is concerned, migration can be described as a widely accepted strategy for survival and social mobility (de Bruine et al. 2013) based on the economic breakdown and political uncertainties in the 1980s and 1990s (Takenaka, Paerregaard and Berg 2010). However, despite a longer period of economic growth and political stability in Peru and the economic crisis in various destination countries, the trend of massive migration outflows continues almost unabated.[4] Regarding the specific impact of migration on the family level, the spatial fragmentation of families for longer or shorter periods is not particularly new for Peruvians. Because of massive rural-to-urban migration during the last 50 years, many Peruvians left—and still leave— their children or elderly parents in the hands of relatives, care workers, or friends. Indeed, in the Andes, child fostering "has been practiced as far back as living memory extends" (Leinaweaver 2010: 72). While this common practice may diminish the social and moral pressure on migrants, it does not alleviate the emotional costs of physical separation, nor does it reduce the support expectations of those "left behind" or the felt obligations of those who left.

The migration cultures in Spain and the US are defined as the countries' "overarching approach to migrants" (Kilkey and Merla 2013: 7), commonly categorized as multicultural or assimilationist/integrationist. The underlying assumption is that multicultural migration regimes tend to have a greater sensibility to the migrants' needs and therefore are more likely to promote measures that facilitate family-related activities across borders (Kilkey and Merla 2013; Merla and Baldassar 2011). For instance, multicultural migration regimes may tolerate dual or multiple citizenship, support bilingual education, fund migrant associations and activities, ensure religious freedom, and promote equal rights.[5] Certainly, neither Spain nor the US can be classified as multicultural migration regimes in the sense that multiculturalism has been adopted as a public policy (MPI 2014). However, both countries officially recognize the cultural diversity of their societies and promote multiculturalism in certain policy areas such as education. Accordingly, the Multiculturalism Policy Index (MPI) ranks Spain and the US in the group of countries with modest multiculturalism policies. Nonetheless, the two countries differ with regard to the mechanisms employed to achieve the migrants' integration and the role the state plays in this process. In the US, robust antidiscrimination policies and citizenship are the key mechanisms for easing the migrants integration (Bloemraad and de Graauw 2012), and "it is not seen as the role of the state to work for social justice or to support the maintenance of ethnic cultures" (Castles and Miller 2009: 248). In contrast, in Spain the state and its administrative bodies seek to play an active role in promoting equal opportunities, managing cultural diversity, and improving the migrants' civic, cultural, economic, and social participation, as well as their access to public benefits and services (Plan Estratégico de Ciudadanía e Integración 2011–2014; Solé et al. 2011).[6]

This contrast can be exemplified by focusing on the more concrete parameter of exit/entry and residence rights (Kilkey and Merla 2013), which illuminates the preferential treatment of migrants from Peru and other Ibero-American countries in Spain[7] with regard to both entry and residency rights (Ariza 2014; Escrivá 2003).[8] The most striking aspect of this preferential treatment is the right to apply for citizenship after only two years of legal residency; otherwise, a period of ten years is required.[9] This quick way to citizenship is used extensively, with 95 percent of the 12,008 Peruvians who were naturalized in 2012 filing their applications after two years of legal residency (MTE 2013). Moreover, Peruvians benefit from a bilateral agreement on citizenship (1959, Art. 7) that includes the automatic recognition of nonnaturalized migrants' work permits, which are usually subject to a quota system based on the evaluation of the national employment situation.

In contrast, in the US, Peruvians do not receive any preferential treatment. Indeed, the US immigration law aims to avoid unequal treatment based on nationality by establishing annual per-country caps. Of the current 675,000 permanent residence permits available per year, only 7 percent can be issued to migrants with the same nationality (Ewing 2012). According to these annual ceilings, migrants are admitted and selected by

26 Vincent Horn

a preference system that differentiates between employment-based and family-sponsored migrants. However, with more than two-thirds of permanent residence permits allocated for the latter, the preference system heavily favors family-related migration. As a consequence of both annual ceilings and per-country caps, the waiting lists for migrants are long, especially for those from the major sending countries such as Mexico, China, or the Philippines. A total of 51,023 Peruvians are currently on the waiting list as well (US Department of State 2013; for wait times, see also Bergeron 2013). Additionally, the pathway to citizenship for Peruvians and other migrants in the US is longer: with the exception of spouses of US citizens who can apply for citizenship after three years of permanent legal residency, all other migrants are required to wait for at least five years.

According to official data sources, the 44 percent of foreign-born Peruvians in the US are US citizens, (Pew Research Center 2012)[10] compared to 33 percent in Spain (Carpio and García 2011). Interestingly, the data provided by the WSPCA (2012) deviate considerably, indicating that only 23 percent of Peruvians acquired citizenship in both countries so far (see Table 1.3). While this seems to be a methodological question,[11] it should be emphasized that older Peruvians in both countries are more likely to possess citizenship than other migrants. As Table 1.3 shows, one out of three older Peruvians residing in Spain or the US obtained the host country's nationality; however, it is the time spent in the receiving country, rather than age, that augments the likelihood to naturalize (Portes and Rumbaut 2006). This correlation is apparently confirmed when different arrival periods are compared. What stands

Table 1.3 Time of arrival and migration status

	Migration status Peruvians 50 + * (total)	Peruvians aged 50 years and older arriving. . .		
		22 or more years ago*	10–21 years ago*	9 or less years ago*
US		25.7%	47.5%	26.4%
Citizenship	33.4% (23.3%)	63.4%	28.6%	13.6%
Permanent residents	39% (39.8%)	32.5%	35.2%	52.6%
Irregular	17% (20%)	1.6%	25.7%	17%
Spain		3.8%	32.5%	63.6%
Citizenship	34.7% (23.4%)	78.6%	62.4%	17.8%
Permanent residents	42.3% (47.3%)	14.3%	32.5%	49.1%
Irregular	2.2% (1.8%)	**	—	3.1%

*Missing percentages: working visas, student visas, tourist visas and others.
**Only one respondent.

Source: WSCPA (2012).

out is that older Peruvians who spent more than ten years in Spain show a two times higher citizenship rate than their counterparts in the US.

As argued by Naujoks (2012), the propensity to apply for citizenship is likely to be influenced by the availability of dual citizenship. With regard to this, no obstacles are raised by the Peruvian government, which grants its citizens the right to dual citizenship. Because of the bilateral agreement, Peruvian migrants can also claim this right in Spain, which otherwise does not allow dual citizenship (Faist and Gerdes 2008). The US allows dual citizenship but has not signed a bilateral agreement with Peru. In fact, the US migration law does not refer to dual citizenship specifically, although the US Department of State (2014) emphasizes that the "[g]overnment recognizes that dual nationality exists but does not encourage it as a matter of policy because of the problems it may cause." These concerns are related to questions of allegiance and do not consider that migrants may naturalize not because of loyalty but because it facilitates family related transnational activities (Baldassar 2011; see also the chapter by Böcker and Balkir in this volume). Nevertheless, the US does not require migrants to give up their previous citizenship once they naturalize, which can be seen as a de facto recognition of dual citizenship.

Given that legal permanent residency is the precondition for acquiring citizenship (Bosniak 2006), regularization programs are of major relevance. Policy makers in Spain and the US show little consensus about the use of regularization programs as a measure to control irregular migration. Thus, whereas Spain ran six regularization programs since 1985 (Levinson 2005) and established a settlement program in 2006 to provide "permanent channels for social integration of migrants in illegal status" (Sabater and Domingo 2012: 194), the US so far only ran two onetime regularization programs under the Immigration Reform and Control Act of 1986.[12] This might partly explain why the share of irregular migrants among those who arrived in the US 22 or more years ago is very small compared to those who arrived more recently. However, the overall share of older Peruvians without regular status, 17 percent, is noticeable and at the same time is significantly higher than in Spain. The question remains whether older Peruvians in Spain who still have other types of visas (20 percent) will get their visas prolonged, become permanent residents, or lose their regular status.

Evidently, citizenship goes along with various benefits in the migration regime. One benefit is that citizenship holders can stay outside the host country for longer periods without running the risk of losing their status or needing to apply for a reentry visa. Another benefit is that citizens from Spain and the US can travel to many countries without being required to have a visa, which facilitates family member visits spread over different countries. Probably the most attractive benefit of citizenship, however, is related to family reunification. Both Spanish and US migration laws favor the reunification of citizenship holders compared to permanent legal residents, although in different ways. While naturalized migrants in the Spanish migration regime have fewer requirements to meet (Escrivá 2013), in the US

28   Vincent Horn

they are exempted from the quota ceilings that otherwise limit family-related immigration. Moreover, in the US only naturalized migrants can apply for reunification with adult children and parents. The exemption from quota ceilings can be of great value, since massive backlogs and long waiting lists can otherwise extend by many years the time until an approved family reunification applicant finally gets their US visa.[13] In contrast, estimates for Spain suggest that migrants need an average time of two years after arrival to reunite with their spouses and/or children (González Ferrer 2008).

To sum up, the parameter on entry and residence rights indicates that older Peruvians in Spain have better opportunities to gain mobility rights through a regular status and can reunite with family members more easily because of a quicker pathway to citizenship, fast proceedings, and the lack of family-visa quota for nonnaturalized migrants. The vast majority of the older Peruvians in the US also have mobility rights, but one out of five is not allowed to travel because of irregular status and runs a constant risk to be detected and eventually deported.

The Older Peruvians' Insertion into the Labor Market and Welfare Regime

Let's now take a closer look at the last parameter of migration regimes as defined by Kilkey and Merla (2013), namely, the insertion of the migrant and his or her family into the labor market and the welfare regime. A concept helpful in analyzing the insertion into the labor market is the segmented labor market, according to which migration regimes tend to channel immigrant workers into certain low-pay and often dangerous occupations with little chances for social mobility (DeFreitas 1988; Gordon, Edwards and Reich 1982). This seems to be the case particularly in Spain where, according to the WSPCA (2012), half the older Peruvian women have jobs as care and domestic workers, and one-third of the older Peruvian men work in the agricultural and manufacturing industries. Many older Peruvians arrived not many years ago and were quickly faced with high and persistent countrywide unemployment rates of 25 percent and more. However, compared to other migrant populations in Spain, Peruvians were more likely to step out of their labor-market niches and to experience social mobility, especially Peruvian women (Parella 2003). This can partly be explained by the educational profile of Peruvians, who have the largest share of individuals with university degree after immigrants from Argentina and Venezuela (Pajares 2010).

In contrast to Spain, the migration regime in the US channels migrants into an hourglass labor market characterized by an "upper tier of professional and technical occupations, requiring advanced educational credentials, and a lower tier of manual occupations, requiring physical strength and few skills in sectors such as agriculture, construction, the food industry, and personal services" (Portes and Rumbaut 2006: 351). For Peruvians, insertion tends to take place in the upper tier of the US labor market. In fact, the median household income of Peruvians is one of the highest among the numerous Latin American migrant populations in the US and is only surpassed by Asians, Colombians, and households of non-Hispanic whites (Bergad 2010). However, one-quarter of the older Peruvian men and women in the US are working as care and domestic workers (WSPCA 2012), which points to a certain polarization in the labor market.

The country-specific differences concerning the insertion into the labor market are also expressed in Table 1.4, which summarizes the socioeconomic profiles of older Peruvians in the two countries. Thus, while older Peruvians in Spain cluster in the lower income groups, the majority of their counterparts in the US receive middle and higher incomes compared to 35.4 percent of lower-income receivers. Consequently, the average monthly income of older Peruvians in the US is considerably higher, with US$2,790 compared to US$1,244 in Spain. Table 1.4 also shows that the income disparities between older Peruvians in Spain and the US are apparently related to the different educational profiles. However, more factors should be considered, such as economic growth and restructuring, as well as the demand for labor and the creation or loss of employment. The overall employment

Table 1.4 Socioeconomic profiles of Peruvians aged 50 years and older in Spain and the US

	Employment rate	**Educational level**		**Income in US$**	
USA	44.5% (50–64 years)	Primary	4.0%	<500	30.8%
	44% (65+ years)	Secondary	29.2%	501–1,500	31.6%
		Higher, no university	25.7%	1,501–3,000	39.7%
		University	34.2%	3,001–5,000	15.9%
		Post-graduate	6.6%	>5,001	9.0%
Spain	36.5% (50–64 years)	Primary	9.3%	<500	60.6%
	32.3% (65+ years)	Secondary	41.5%	501–1,500	68.3%
		Higher, no university	23.0%	1,501–3,000	22.7%
		University	25.1%	3,001–5,000	10.2%
		Post-graduate	1.1%	>5,001	10.2%

Source: WSCPA (2012).

30   *Vincent Horn*

rate of older Peruvians is significantly higher in the US than in Spain, according to the WSPCA (2012). Interestingly, in both countries reaching retirement age does not seem to affect very much the desire or necessity to receive money from employment. In fact, in both countries it is very common that Peruvians aged 70 years and older are still working (28.5 percent in the US; 38.7 percent in Spain).

The previous position in the labor market and the time span of contributions made to public pension systems and/or private funds are crucial for one's economic situation in old age. Given the rather short periods of time older Peruvians spent in Spain and their rather low income, their prospects seem gloomier than their counterparts in the US. Those who arrived without enough time to accumulate the minimum time of contributions to the Spanish pension system (15 years) or worked in the shadow economy face quite dim economic prospects. Nevertheless, apart from relying on other sources of income such as work or family members, older Peruvians in Spain have access to a means-tested noncontributory pension if they have ten years of legal residency in the country (Escrivá 2013). Moreover, those who contributed to the Peruvian pension system before may benefit from the bilateral agreement on social security between Spain and Peru, although formalities are often complex and slow (Díaz-Gorfinkiel and Escrivá 2012). Apart from this, migrants in Spain benefit from free public health care and complete coverage regardless of their legal status. However, as part of a larger austerity program enacted in 2012, the Spanish government seeks to restrict the access to health care for irregular migrants.

In contrast, no bilateral agreement on social security issues has been signed between the US and Peru. To qualify for benefits, older Peruvians have to satisfy the requirements of each system separately. Thus, in the US an old age pension can only be claimed after a minimum contribution period of ten years as well as access to the federal health insurance program for individuals aged 65 and older (Medicare). Moreover, applicants have to be either naturalized or legal permanent residents in order to be eligible. A differentiation line, however, is drawn between citizens and noncitizens in case of needs-based federal programs such as Supplemental Security Income, Food Stamps, or Medicaid. According to the 1996 Personal Responsibility and Work Opportunity and Reconciliation Act (PRWORA), only citizens (or regular migrants who arrived before 1996) have unconditional access. Permanent legal residents have to wait for at least five years before they can apply, whereas irregular migrants are generally banned from these benefits (Fix and Passel 2002; Kullgren 2003; Richardson and Wasem 2002). As a consequence, irregular migrants with little resources depend very much upon the (varying) efforts of the states to provide a safety net for vulnerable groups. Those with better financial means have to purchase generally expensive individual policies (Portes, Light and Fernández-Kelly 2009). In view of this situation, it is not surprising that 70 percent of older Peruvians with an irregular migration status lack access to health care services or health insurance, compared to 16.3 percent of those with citizenship and 36.7 percent of permanent legal residents (WSPCA 2012). However, because of the 2010 Patient Protection and Affordable Care Act (PPACA), the gap between naturalized older Peruvians and those with permanent legal residency is likely to shrink.[14] Moreover, under the PPACA lawfully admitted older migrants who arrived recently (green card holders) can also purchase health insurance without a five-year waiting period.

To conclude, older Peruvians in the US are comparatively better incorporated into the labor market as measured by their employment rate, monthly income, and occupational status. They are also more likely than their counterparts in Spain to have longer employment records because of their earlier arrival and therefore have had more time to accumulate economic capital, make investments, and pay into pension funds. In turn, older Peruvians in Spain can benefit from bilateral agreements on citizenship and social security and a high degree of health care coverage.

MIGRATION REGIMES AND FAMILY-RELATED TRANSNATIONAL ACTIVITIES

Against the backdrop of the previous analysis of the Spanish and US migration regimes, this section aims to interpret different family-related transnational activities and opportunities of older Peruvians in both countries. It does so by looking at the frequency of family visits, remitting behavior, and the use of Internet for communication purposes in relationship to the migration status and history and the socioeconomic status as the central factors mediated by migration regimes.

Family Visits

The freedom to cross national borders is presumably the "main stratifying factor" within transnational family settings, as Bonizzoni and Boccagni (2014: 87–88) emphasize with reference to Baumans's (1998) well-known argument about mobility in an increasingly globalized world. Mobility, among other things, enables migrants to share key events, exchange personal care, and express unaltered feeling of belonging to the family and identification with the community left behind (Baldassar, Baldock and Wilding 2007; Mason 2004). This is not to say that visits are free of conflicts and disappointments. Longer periods of physical absence seem to increase the potential for alienation and the need for more complicated adaption processes. Additionally, migrants may feel morally obliged to visit regularly than actually being enthusiastic about it (Baldassar 2011). However,

32   Vincent Horn

frequent visits can be seen as a positive indicator for the older Peruvians' relationship with family members in Peru and for their opportunity to maintain more intimate relationships.

As Table 1.5 shows, frequent family visits of older Peruvians are not very rare, at least among those residing in the US. In fact, one out of three report visits to family members in Peru at least once a year, and 15.4 percent still travel at least every two years. In contrast, in Spain the percentage of older Peruvians who travel at least once a year is significantly lower (15.7 percent); one out of four report travel at least every two years. At the same time, one out of three older Peruvians and 40.8 percent of all Peruvians in the US never visit their family members in Peru, compared to one-quarter of the Peruvians in Spain. Interestingly, while the travel frequency of older Peruvians in the 65-and-older group increases in the US, in Spain it drops significantly.

In the US, family visits are closely linked to the migration status. Peruvians with US citizenship are traveling more often, at least once a year (43.3 percent), followed by those with permanent legal residency (32.7 percent) and working visas (26.4 percent). Interestingly, 5 percent of older Peruvians without a regular migration status report that they travel at least once a year. However, 90.8 percent of those lacking a regular migration status never visit their family members in Peru, compared to only 6.4 percent among those with US citizenship, 14.7 percent of those with permanent legal residency, and 29.4 percent of those with a working visa. In Spain, the different types of regular migration statuses seem to have less impact on the traveling patterns, although those with a working visa are more likely to travel at least once a year (22.9 percent) compared to their counterparts with Spanish citizenship (14.6 percent) and permanent legal residency (14.3 percent). Similar to the US, in Spain older Peruvians without a regular migration status report no travel at all, compared to 15.4 percent among those with Spanish citizenship, 22.4 percent of those with permanent legal residency, and 31.1 percent of those with a working visa.

Table 1.5   Family visits of Peruvians aged 50 years and older in Spain and the US

Peruvians traveling . . .	US			Spain		
	50+	65+	Total	50+	65+	Total
at least once a year	28.2%	34%	24.3%	15.7%	9.5%	20%
every two years	15.4%	16.4%	13.6%	25.5%	23.8%	26.3%
eventually	25.5%	27.2%	21.3%	35.5%	39.7%	29%
never	30.9%	22.5%	40.8%	23.5%	27%	24.8%

Source: WSCPA (2012).

While the geographical immobility of older Peruvians without regular migration status could be expected, the question occurs why older Peruvians in the US visit their family members on a yearly basis twice as much as their counterparts in Spain, especially at advanced ages. At least four assumptions can be generated. The first is that migrants who arrived more recently in the receiving country—like most of the older Peruvians in Spain—are less likely to travel than those who arrived a longer time ago (Schunck 2011). The explanation for this behavior would be that recently arrived migrants first have to go through a period of economic consolidation before they can invest in visiting family members in their country of origin. However, while such a trend can be observed in Spain, older Peruvians who arrived during the last five years are the most active travelers in the US. The second assumption is that the better the migrant's economic situation, the more likely they are to visit the country of origin frequently, especially after retirement age. Such a relationship cannot be confirmed for both countries. Thus, whereas older Peruvians with higher incomes in the US are more likely than those with lower incomes to travel at least once a year, apparently no significant differences exist between income groups in Spain.[15]

A third assumption relates to the effects of restrictive family reunification policies (Bernhard et al. 2006). Thus, it is assumed that slow processing and long waiting lists in the US affect travel activities, since close family members such as children and spouses often have to remain in Peru for many years. The higher travel activity of recently arrived migrants could be interpreted as supporting this assumption. A comparatively quick processing and the lack of numerical ceilings in Spain could diminish travel activities since families can reunite after a relatively short time.[16] A fourth and final assumption relates to the duration and costs of traveling, which could be expected to affect the likelihood of travel activity and vice versa. Indeed, older Peruvians with a short travel distance (six hours for those residing in Miami) are most likely to visit family members in Peru on a yearly basis (47.5 percent). However, older Peruvians residing in New York (34.2 percent) are more likely to travel at least once a year than are those residing in Los Angeles (25 percent) despite similar travel costs and a longer travel distance (11 vs. 9 hours, respectively). Compared with their counterparts in Spain, the travel distances for older Peruvians in the US are generally smaller and airline tickets are cheaper. To this is added the lower average monthly income of older Peruvians in Spain who—roughly calculated—spend one monthly income for an airline ticket, whereas their counterparts in the US pay one-third or even less.

Remitting Behavior

Migrant remittances are probably the transnational activity that received the most attention from both academic disciplines and international organizations. Despite the bulk of studies in this field, statistical findings about

34 Vincent Horn

determinants and patterns of remittances tend to be inconsistent if not contradictory regarding the concrete influence of factors such as age, gender, migration status, educational attainment, expectations, relative resources, return intentions, and the like (for an excellent review, see Carling 2008). For instance, Soltero (2009) shows that undocumented Mexican migrants in the US are more likely to remit than their naturalized counterparts, while Konica and Filer (2005) show the opposite pattern for Albanian migrants residing in Italy and Greece. Increasing age is often seen as positively related with remitting (Merkle and Zimmermann 1992), although a decline is predicted with advancing age (Durand et al. 1996). Moreover, it is predicted that the time spent in the receiving country diminishes the likelihood to remit (ibid.). However, as Carling (2008: 596) concludes, "the overlapping influences on remittance-sending behaviour are so numerous and complex that our ambitions for quantified explanations should be modest." The following findings should therefore not be understood as cause-and-effect relationships but rather as rough approximations of a multicausal phenomenon.

The first finding regarding the remitting behavior of older Peruvians in Spain and the US is that the majority of both groups sends money to family members in Peru (see Table 1.6). The propensity to remit is significantly higher among older Peruvians in Spain but also drops sharper when reaching retirement age. This trend confirms that migrants' remittances decline with advancing age, although in both cases more than 40 percent of those aged 65 and older still send money to family members in Peru. Regarding the relationship of remittances and time spent in the receiving country, the data show no common pattern. Thus, in Spain the propensity of older Peruvians to remit is highest among recent arrivers and declines the longer ago the arrival. Since most Peruvians arrived rather recently, the migration history helps to explain the high share of remittance senders among older Peruvians in Spain. In contrast, in the US those who arrived 22 or more years ago are more likely to send remittances than recent arrivers (58.6 percent compared to 51.1 percent of those who arrived during the last five years) and remit only slightly below average. This indicates that the majority of older Peruvians in the US still feel committed to sending money to family members in Peru even after many years.

This finding can be seen as related to the fact that older Peruvians in the US with an irregular migration status show a much higher propensity to remit than those with a regular migration status (legal permanent residents and those who obtained US citizenship).[17] Because of the very limited possibilities to adjust their status in order to qualify for family reunification or obtain mobility rights, these older Peruvians often experience very long periods of physical separation from close family members. Their higher propensity to send remittances can therefore be interpreted as a strategy to alleviate the emotional costs of their enduring absence by regular money transfers and the sending of gifts (Fresnoza-Flot 2009). Similarly, numerical ceilings and long waiting lists in the US family reunification system lead to prolonged periods of physical separation and, accordingly, a higher propensity to remit even among those who obtained legal permanent residency. What points in this direction is that older Peruvians in the US who live in the same household with family members are significantly less likely to remit than those who do not (57.1 percent compared to 77.3 percent). The same pattern can be observed in Spain, where 61.2 percent of those who live with family members remit compared to 88.6 percent of those who do not live with family members in Spain. In other words, "migrants tend to remit . . . much less once their immediate family members have joined them" (Goldring 2004, cited in Soltero 2009: 322).

While the more recent arrival of older Peruvians in Spain seems to explain partly their higher propensity to remit, a further factor deserves attention: the socioeconomic profile measured by income and educational attainment. The related assumption would be that the lower the social class, the more likely migrants are to remit. According to Solé and colleagues (2007), the explanation for this is that the migration of people from lower social strata more often represents a family survival strategy, whereas migrants from higher social strata tend to migrate in order to improve their individual career opportunities. However, regarding the (individual) monthly income, no linear trend but rather an inverted U-curve can be observed since both low- and high-income groups are less likely to send remittances than middle-income groups.

Not surprisingly, since income and education are closely related, the same pattern exists if the remitting behavior is crossed with educational attainment. Older Peruvians in both countries who obtained secondary or non-university higher education are more likely to remit than are their counterparts with primary or university education. Since older Peruvians with secondary education have a relative higher status in Spain than in the US, the educational attainment–income nexus adds another piece to the

Table 1.6 Peruvians aged 50 years and older in Spain and the US sending remittances

	US	Spain
Send remittances	60.8%	71.2%
(65+)	(44.8%)	(41.9%)
Regular status	54.5%	n/a
Irregular status	78.8%	n/a
University degree	55.6%	64.2%
Secondary education	65.4%	73.9%
Primary education	50.8%	46.9%

Source: WSCPA (2012).

36 Vincent Horn

understanding of the higher propensity to remit among older Peruvians in Spain. A further assumption might be that older Peruvians in Spain prefer to remit instead of spending the money for family visits. However, those who travel at least every two years also remit more frequently (81.4 percent) compared to those who travel eventually or not at all (62.3 percent).

Ability to Use Communication Technologies

Apart from geographical mobility and the capacity to transfer money to family members in Peru, the access to and the ability to make use of communication technologies are crucial for maintaining family relationships across borders (Baldassar 2008b; Madianou and Miller 2012; Wilding 2006). Although the question of whether and under what conditions communication technologies can replace physical co-presence is still largely unexplored, such technologies remain the main avenue to exchange information or to provide emotional and practical support transnationally.[18] In this context the notion of a digital divide can be borrowed to describe the fact that older and disabled people have less access to Internet and are less familiar with chatting, e-mailing, and videoconferencing than are younger generations. However, the digital divide is also influenced by several factors including the families' (or individual's) economic and cultural capital (Merla 2013). This point is taken into account by controlling for the use of internet in relation with income and educational attainment.

The WSCPA (2012) asked respondents if they use the internet for communication purposes. It did not specifically ask for communication with family members abroad; nevertheless, the responses can be used to interpret the older Peruvians' ability to do so if they wished and needed to. As shown in Table 1.7, this ability is more widespread among older Peruvians in the US than in Spain. As a confirmation of the digital divide, the percentage of older Peruvians who use the internet for communication purposes decreases with advancing age. Interestingly, in the US the gaps between the different age groups are smaller than in Spain. Assuming that the infrastructures in both countries provide similar access possibilities, this difference may be explained by an acculturation process. Because they usually arrive at younger ages, older Peruvians in the US could be assumed to be acquainted with the Internet earlier than their counterparts in Spain. However, no evidence can be found that a longer period in the receiving country relates to a higher percentage of Internet users among older Peruvians. The migration status, in contrast, seems to play a role since those without a regular migration status communicate via the Internet more often than do those with citizenship or legal permanent residency. Thus, 62.3 percent of older Peruvians without a regular migration status in the US and 62.5 percent in Spain use the Internet for communication purposes compared to 55.2 (US) and 44 percent (Spain) of those with citizenship or legal permanent residency.

Table 1.7 Peruvians aged 50 years and older in Spain and the US using the Internet for communication purposes

Age groups	Uses Internet for communication	
	US	Spain
50+	56.3%	45.6%
Total	65.2%	67.1%
30–39	71.8%	75.9%
40–49	65.6%	60.7%
50–59	61.7%	49.4%
60+	49.5%	37.4%

Source: WSCPA (2012).

Similarly, significant differences exist between different income groups and educational levels. Thus, the higher the income and the better the educational attainment, the more likely older Peruvians are to communicate via the internet. Only 12 percent of older Peruvians with primary education and 49.6 percent with secondary or higher (no university) education in the US report that they use the Internet for communication purposes compared to 68.8 percent of those with a university degree. Similarly, although not as pronounced, 20.7 of older Peruvians in Spain with primary and 44.2 percent with secondary or higher (no university) education use the Internet for communication purposes compared to 57.1 percent with a university degree. The larger proportion of older Peruvians with a university degree in the US is thus a partial explanation for the more widespread use of the Internet compared to their counterparts in Spain. Evidently, not using the internet for communication purposes should not be interpreted as a lack of communication with relatives in Peru. It can be expected that the preferred medium for communication of older Peruvians is still the ordinary telephone. Cheap calls are in this sense still the "social glue" (Vertovec 2004) in older Peruvians' transnational families.

CONCLUSION

Overall, the analysis of the WSCPA shows that older Peruvians engage quite actively in family related transnational activities. In fact, the majority of older Peruvians in both Spain and the US are involved in at least one of the three activities examined in this chapter. Interestingly, there are significant differences between the two groups regarding the scope and frequency of their involvement in different activities. Thus, older Peruvians in the US are much more likely than their counterparts in Spain to travel frequently to Peru, especially at an advancing age, and to use the Internet

38 *Vincent Horn*

for communication purposes. The latter, in turn, engage more actively in the sending of remittances, although a steep drop can be observed after retirement age. These findings have been partly explained by the different migration histories of older Peruvians in both countries. Thus, while usually arriving at younger ages, older Peruvians in the US are more likely to accumulate the resources necessary to travel. Older Peruvians in the US engage in family related transnational activities even decades after their arrival, which has been related to restrictive family reunification laws and regularization policies leading to prolonged periods of physical separation from close family members. Their counterparts in Spain arrived at comparatively advanced ages and dispose of comparatively low economic resources. However, an ongoing regularization program, a quick way to citizenship, and a rather favorable family reunification law facilitate their reunification with close family members after only a few years of legal residency. In fact, the percentage of older Peruvians without a regular migration status is much smaller in Spain than in the US, where one out of five is in an irregular situation. The migration status, however, is a decisive factor regarding the type of transnational activity of older Peruvians. Thus, while not having the option to visit family members abroad, those without a regular migration status tend to engage more actively in the sending of remittances and online communication. This finding has been explained based on a compensation assumption, according to which migrants seek to compensate for their physical absence through different forms of virtual co-presence (Fresnoza-Flot 2009).

The findings were also explained by the different socioeconomic profiles of older Peruvians in the two countries. According to this, older Peruvians in the US dispose of both higher incomes and are much more likely to have a university degree than their counterparts in Spain. The migration regime plays an important role here as well, since the admission of migrants in both countries is regulated by visa systems that select migrants based on their skills or family relationships. In case of the US this means that being young and highly skilled or a family member of a US citizen enhances the possibility to enter the country legally. In Spain, low- and middle-skilled older economic migrants were also admitted to satisfy the enormous demand for labor in the construction and manufacturing industries, as well as the increasing demand for care and domestic workers. In this sense, migration regimes shape the socioeconomic profile of migrant populations, mediate the migrants' incorporation into the labor market and welfare regime, and probably most important, determine the migrants' family structure. All of these factors overlap in different ways and cannot be seen as isolated from each other. Furthermore, since neither migration regimes nor the migrants' position within them is a static monolith, the set of factors that are important changes over time. These two aspects pose methodological challenges to this field. Therefore, longitudinal cross-national comparative research with both qualitative and quantitative data seems to be needed for a better understanding of how and to what extent institutional contexts modify family-related activities, dynamics, and strategies; reset caring priorities; and have an impact on intergenerational relationships.

NOTES

1 It should also be noted that Peruvian migration to Spain has been decreasing since it reached its peak in 2010. The recent official number is therefore significantly lower, with 111,268 Peruvians officially registered (-21.26 %). At the same time, naturalizations increased by 44.83 percent from 8,291 in 2010 to 12,008 in 2012 (MTE 2013). It can be assumed that at least some of the migrants who have disappeared from the official statistics are still residing in the country.

2 As a matter of fact, 88.2 percent of Peruvians who obtained legal permanent residence in the US in 2011 did so because of family-related migration (US Department of Homeland Security 2012). This is, of course, not to say that older Peruvians who arrived through this channel did not take up economic activities.

3 Because of the inherent association of "regime" with the national and in order to avoid "methodological nationalism" (Wimmer and Glick Schiller 2002), Kilkey and Merla (2013) extend their framework by a further dimension called spaces. Spaces here refer to the different levels and arenas of governance in which the institutional contexts are constituted including the "global, regional, sub-national and national" (ibid.: 9).

4 Only a modest drop of 4.9 percent in the number of Peruvian emigrants could be observed between 2009 and 2010 (IOM 2012).

5 The categorization of migration regimes is notoriously difficult also because of the different usages of terms such as *multiculturalism* or *integration* in various European and North American countries (Clyne and Jupp 2011). In fact, depending on its underlying notion and purpose, integration may "simply describe a preferred situation very like multiculturalism or alternatives very close to assimilation" (Clyne and Jupp 2011: 41). This lack of common definitions complicates the operationalization of the different concepts in order to make them measurable. Despite these difficulties, the Multiculturalism Policy Index (MPI) evaluates and measures multiculturalism policies in some of the world's main migration regimes. In brief, the MPI consists of eight indicators including the migration regimes' affirmation of multiculturalism, the adoption of multiculturalism in school curriculum, allowance of dual citizenship, and the funding of ethnic group organizations and activities (Tolley 2011).1

6 These different approaches to migration already indicate that a similar outcome in the MPI can be the result of very different policies and mechanisms, which in turn may affect family related activities across borders differently.

7 With this preferential treatment Spain seeks to recognize the special historical and cultural linkages with these countries, such as the Philippines or Equatorial Guinea.

8 The first parameter that refers to the migrants' permission to leave his or her country of origin can be neglected here since Peruvians are not banned from traveling abroad.

9 In the case of being married with a Spanish citizen, the period is even shorter (one year).

40 *Vincent Horn*

10 When considering the domestic born Peruvians who obtain citizenship by birth, the rate is 62 percent (average citizenship rate of Hispanics is 74 percent; Pew Research Center 2012).
11 For example, respondents may hide their real migration status. Irregular or undocumented status was not an answer category; instead, "expired visa" was used as a category. Additionally, those with citizenship may have fewer issues to deal with at the consulate.
12 For now, as part of a recent reform proposal of the US immigration policy, the so called *Border Security, Economic Opportunity, and Immigration Modernization Act,* the government seeks to open a door for irregular immigrants to legalize their status after a period of eight years (The White House 2011). Until then, irregular immigrants are at a high risk to be deported under the immigration enforcement measures implemented after 9/11. According to recent figures from the US Department of Homeland Security, 369,000 irregular immigrants were deported in 2013 alone (*The Economist*, February 8, 2014).
13 According to Hill (2010), it can take between one and 18 years until the family member finally enters the US, especially if the applicant is from one of the mayor sending countries (Mexico, China, India, and the Philippines).
14 The PPACA makes many kinds of legal migration statuses eligible for a health insurance except from irregular migrants; see also http://www.healthcare.gov/immigration-status-and-the-marketplace/, accessed April 21, 2014.
15 Older Peruvians who travel at least once a year according to their income group: Spain: $501–1,500, 19.8%; $1,501–3,000, 19.2 %; very few respondents in higher higher-income groups. US: $501–1,500, 21.9%; $1,501–3,000, 25.9%; $3,001–5,000, 30.5 %; >$5,000, 46.6 %.
16 Unfortunately, the WSCPA does not contain data about the structure of the migrants' families and the relationship of the family members located in different countries. It therefore remains for future research to reveal a possible relationship between family reunification laws and the migrants' travel frequencies.
17 Since the number of older Peruvians in Spain without regular migration status is very small a comparison does not allow for qualified assumptions.
18 Communication technologies allow not only for caring but also controlling across borders and may therefore be perceived ambivalently by different actors (cf. Madianou and Miller 2012).

REFERENCES

Altamirano, Téofilo (1990): *Los que se fueron. peruanos en los Estados Unidos de Norteamérica.* Lima: Fondo Editorial de la Pontificia Universidad Católica del Perú.

Ariza, Marina (2014): Care Circulation, Absence and Affect in Transnational Families. In: Baldassar, Loretta/Merla, Laura (eds.): *Transnational Families, Migration and the Circulation of Care. Understanding Mobility and Absence in Family Life.* New York: Routledge, pp. 94–114.

Baldassar, Loretta (2008a): Debating Culture Across Distance: Transnational Families and the Obligation to Care. In: Grillo, Ralph (ed.): *The Family in Question: Immigrant and Ethnic Minorities in Multicultural Europe.* Amsterdam: Amsterdam University Press, pp. 269–291.

Baldassar, Loretta (2008b): 'Missing Kin and Longing to be Together: Emotions and the Construction of Co-presence in Transnational Relationships. In: *Journal of Intercultural Studies* 29, 3, pp. 247–266.

Migration Regimes and Transnational Activities 41

Baldassar, Loretta (2011): Obligation to People and Place: The National Cultures of Caregiving. In Baldassar, Loretta/Gabaccia, Donna R. (eds.): *Intimacy and Italian Migration. Gender and Domestic Lives in a Mobile World.* New York: Fordham University Press, pp. 171–188.

Baldassar, Loretta/Baldock, Cora/Wilding, Raelene (2007): *Families Caring Across Borders. Migration, Ageing and Transnational Caregiving.* New York: Palgrave Macmillan.

Bauman, Zigmund (1998): *Globalization: The Human Consequences.* Cambridge: Polity.

Bergad, L. W. (2010): *Peruvians in the United States 1980–2008.* Center for Latin American, Carribean and Latino Studies. Latino Data Project—Report 35 — October 2010.

Bergeron, Claire (2013): *Going to the Back of the Line. A Primer on Lines, Visa Categories, and Wait Times.* Issue Brief 1, 2013. Washington, DC: Migration Policy Institute.

Bernhard, Judith/Landolt, Patricia/Goldring, Luin (2006): *Transnational, Multi-local Motherhood: Experiences of Separation and Reunification among Latin American Families in Canada.* CERIS, Policy Matters, No. 24, January 2006.

Bloemraad, Irene/de Graauw, Els (2012): Diversity and Laissez-Faire Integration in the United States. In: Spoonley, Paul/Tolley, Erin (eds.): *Diverse Nations, Diverse Responses. Approaches to Social Cohesion in Immigrant Societies.* Montreal/Kingston: Queen's Policy Studies Series, McGill-Queen's University Press, pp. 33–57

Boehm, Deborah A. (2012): *Intimate Migrations. Gender, Family, and Illegality Among Transnational Mexicans.* New York: New York University Press.

Bonizzoni, Paola/Boccagni, Paolo (2014): Care (and) Circulation Revisited: A Conceptual Map of Diversity in Transnational Parenting. In: Baldassar, Loretta/Merla, Laura (eds.): *Transnational Families, Migration and the Circulation of Care. Understanding Mobility and Absence in Family Life.* New York: Routledge, pp. 78–93.

Bosniak, Linda (2006): *The Citizen and the Alien. Dilemmas of Contemporary Citizenship.* Princeton: Princeton University Press.

Bryceson, Deborah/Vuorela, Ulla (eds.) (2002): *The Transnational Family. New European Frontiers and Global Networks.* Oxford/New York: Berg Publishers.

Carling, Jørgen (2008): The Determinants of Migrant Remittances. In: *Oxford Review of Economic Policy* 24, 3, pp. 581–598.

Carpio, Concepción/García Serrano, Carlos (2011): *Inmigración y Mercado de trabajo.* Madrid: Observatorio Permanente de la Inmigración.

Castles, Stephen/Miller, Mark J. (2009): *The Age of Migration.* New York: Palgrave Macmillan.

Census Bureau (2014): *American Community Survey.* Integrated Public Use Microdata Series. Minnesota: Minnesota Population Center.

Clyne, Michael/Jupp, James (eds.) (2011): *Multiculturalism and Integration. A Harmonious Relationship.* Canberra: Australian National University E Press.

De Bruine, Eva/Hordijk, Michaela/Tamagno, Carla/Sánchez Arimborgo, Yanina (2013): Living Between Multiple Sites: Transnational Family Relations from the Perspective of Elderly Non-Migrants in Junín, Peru. In: *Journal of Ethnic and Migration Studies* 39, 3, pp. 483–500.

DeFreitas, Gregory (1988): Hispanic Immigrants and Labor Market Segmentation. In: *Industrial Relations* 27, 2, pp. 195–214.

Díaz Gorfinkiel, Magdalena/Escrivá, Angeles (2012): Care of Older People in Migration Contexts: Local and Transnational Arrangements Between Peru and Spain. In: *Social Politics* 19, 1, pp. 129–141.

42 Vincent Horn

Durand, Jorge/Kandel, William/Parrado, Emilio A./Massey, Douglas S. (1996): International Migration and Development in Mexican Communities. In: *Demography* 33, 2, pp. 249–264.

The Economist (2014): *The Great Expulsion*. 8th of February 2014, http://www.economist.com, accessed March 2014.

Escrivá, Angeles (2003): Inmigrantes Peruanas en España. *Conquistando el Espacio Laboral Extradomestico*. Papers 60, pp. 327–342.

Escrivá, Angeles (2013): Asset Accumulation and Transfer for Old Age. A Study on Peruvian and Moroccan Migration to Spain. In: *European Journal of Ageing* 10, pp. 279–287.

Escrivá, Angeles/Skinner, Emilie (2006): Moving to Spain at an Advanced Age. In: *Generation Review* 16, 2, pp. 8–15.

Ewing, Walter A. (2012): *Opportunity and Exclusion. A Brief History of U.S. Immigration Policy*. Immigration Policy Center. http://www.immigrationpolicy.org, accessed April 15, 2014.

Faist, Thomas/Gerdes, Jürgen (2008): *Dual Citizenship in an Age of Mobility*. Washington, DC: Migration Policy Institute.

Fix, Michael/Passel, Jeffrey (2002): *The Scope and Impact of Welfare Reform's Immigrant Provisions*. Washington, DC: The Urban Institute.

Fresnoza-Flot, Asunción (2009): Migration Status and Transnational Mothering: The Case of Filipino Migrants in France. In: *Global Networks* 9, 2, pp. 252–270.

Goldring, Luin (2004): Family and Collective Remittances to Mexico: A Multi-Dimensional Typology. In: *Development and Change* 35, 4, pp. 799–840.

González Ferrer, Amparo (2008): La Reagrupación Familiar en España. Algunas cifras para el debate. In: *Anuario de Inmigración en España*, pp. 121–137.

Gordon, David M./Edwards, Richard/Reich, Michael (1982): *Segmented Work, Divided Workers*. Cambridge: Cambridge University Press.

Hill, Laura (2010): *The Immigration and Citizenship Process. Just the Facts*. Public Policy Institute of California. http://www.ppic.org, accessed April 2014.

Horn, Vincent (2013): *Geographical Mobility of Older Peruvians Non-Migrants as Care Opportunities. Impacts of the Recent Crisis*. Paper presented at the IMIS-COE 10th Annual Conference "Crisis and Migration—Perceptions, Challenges and Consequences". Malmö, Sweden, August 2013.

INE (Instituto Nacional de Estadística; Spain) (2013): Población extranjera por país de nacimiento, edad y sexo. In: *Revisión del Padrón municipal 2012*, Madrid.

IOM (International Organization for Migration) in cooperation with INEI (Instituto Nacional de Estadística e Informática) and DIGEMIN (Dirección General de Migraciones y Naturalización) (2010): *Perú: Estadísticas de la Emigración Internacional de Peruanos e Inmigración de Extranjeros, 1990–2009*. Lima: Crea Imagen S.A.C.

IOM (International Organization for Migration) (2012): *Peru Migration Profile Confirms that Peruvians Continue to Migrate Despite Economic Crisis*. October 19, 2012: http://www.iom.int/cms/en/sites/iom/home/news-and-views/press-briefing-notes/pbn-2012/pbn-listing/peru-migration-profile-confirms.html, accessed February 2014.

Kilkey, Majella/Merla, Laura (2014): Situating Transnational Families' Care-Giving Arrangements: The Role of Institutional Contexts. In: *Global Networks*, 14, 2, pp. 210–229.

Konica, Navila/Filer, Randall K. (2005): *Albanian Emigration. Causes and Consequences*. Prague: Working Paper, CERGE-EI.

Kullgren, Jeffrey T. (2003): Restrictions on Undocumented Immigrants' Access to Health Services: The Public Health Implications of Welfare Reform. In: *American Journal of Public Health* 93, 10, pp. 1630–1633.

Lamb, Sarah (2002): Intimacy in a Transnational Era: The Remaking of Aging among Indian Americans. In: *Diaspora* 11, 3, pp. 299–330.

Migration Regimes and Transnational Activities   43

Lamb, Sarah (2009): *Aging and the Indian Diaspora. Cosmopolitan Families in India and Abroad.* Bloomington: Indiana University Press.

Leinaweaver, Jessaca (2010): Outsourcing Care: How Peruvian Migrants Meet Transnational Family Obligations. In: *Latin American Perspectives* 174, 37, pp. 67–87.

Levinson, Amenda (2005): *The Regularisation of Unauthorized Migrants. Literature Survey and Country Case Studies.* Oxford: Centre on Migration, Policy and Society, University of Oxford. http://www.compas.ox.ac.uk/fileadmin/files/Publications/Reports/Regularisation%20Report.pdf, accessed June 2014.

Madianou, Mirca/Miller, Daniel (2012): *Migration and New Media. Transnational Families and Polymedia.* Oxon/New York: Routledge.

Mason, Jennifer (2004): Managing Kinship Over Long Distances: The Significance of 'The Visit'. In: *Social Policy and Society* 3, 4, pp: 421–429.

Mazzucato, Valentina/Schans, Djamila (2011): Transnational Families and the Well-Being of Children. Conceptual and Methodological Challenges. In: *Journal of Marriage and Family* 73, pp. 704–712.

Merkle, Lucie/Zimmermann, Klaus F. (1992): Savings, Remittances, and Return Migration. In: *Economic Letters* 38, pp. 77–81.

Merla, Laura (2013): Salvadoran Transnational Families, Distance and Eldercare. Understanding Transnational Care Practices in Australia and Belgium. In: Geisten, Thomas/Studer, Tobias/Yildiz, Erol (eds.): *Migration, Familie und soziale Lage.* Wiesbaden: VS Verlag für Sozialwissenschaft, pp. 295–312.

Merla, Laura (2014): A Macro Perspective on Transnational Families and Care Circulation. Situating Capacity, Obligation and Family Commitments. In: Baldassar, L./Merla, L. (eds.): *Transnational Families, Migration and the Circulation of Care. Understanding Mobility and Absence in Family Life.* New York: Routledge, pp. 115–129.

Merla, Laura/Baldassar, Loretta (2011): Transnational Caregiving between Australia, Italy and El Salvador. The Impact of Institutions on the Capability to Care at Distance. In: Addis, Elisabetta/de Villota, Paloma/Degavre, Florence/Eriksen, John (eds.): *Gender and Well-Being. The Role of Institutions.* Farnham: Ashgate Publishing Limited, pp. 147–161.

MPI (Multiculturalism Policy Index) (2014): *Multiculturalism Policies in Contemporary Democries.* Kingston: Queen's University. http://www.queensu.ca/mcp/index.html, accessed April 2014.

MTE (Ministerio de Empleo y Seguriad Social) (2013): *Concesiones de nacionalidad espanola por residencia 2012.* Madrid: Observatorio permanente de la Inmigración. http://extranjeros.empleo.gob.es/es/Estadisticas/operaciones/concesiones/, accessed April 2014.

Naujoks, Daniel (2012): *Does Dual Citizenship Increase Naturalization? Evidence from Indian Immigrants in the U.S.* Hamburg: HWWI Research Paper 125.

Pajares, Miguel (2010): *Inmigración y Mercado de trabajo.* Informe 2010. Documentos del Observatorio Permanente de la Inmigración 25.

Parella, Sonia (2003): *Mujer, inmigrante y trabajadora. la triple discriminación.* Barcelona: Anthropos.

Pew Research Center (2012): *Hispanics of Peruvian Origin in the United States.* Washington, DC: Pew Hispanic Center.

Plan Estratégico Ciudadanía e Integración 2011–2014 (2014): Madrid: Dirección General de Integración de los Inmigrantes. http://www.fundacionlengua.com/extra/descargas/des_38/INMIGRACION/II-Plan-Estrategico-Ciudadania-e-Integracion.pdf, accessed March 2014.

Portes, Alejandro/Rumbaut, Ruben G. (2006): *Immigrant America.* Berkeley: University of California Press.

Portes, Alejandro/Light, Donald/Fernández-Kelly, Patricia (2009): The U.S. Health System and Immigration: An Institutional interpretation. In: *Sociological Forum* 24, 3, pp. 487–514.

44 *Vincent Horn*

Richardson, Joe/Wasem, Ruth E. (2002): *Noncitizen Eligibility for Major Federal Public Assistance Programs. Policies and Legislation.* Washington, DC: Congressional Research Service.

Sabater, Andreu/Domingo, Andreu (2012): A New Immigration Regularization Policy: The Settlement Program in Spain. In: *International Migration Review* 46, 1, pp. 191–220.

Schunck, Richard (2011): Immigrant Integration, Transnational Activities and the Life Course. In: Winges, Michael/Windzio, Michael/de Valk, Helga/Aybek, Can (eds.): *A Life-Course Perspective on Migration and Integration.* Dordrecht, Heidelberg, London and New York: Springer Science+Business Media, pp. 259–282.

Solé, Carlota/Parella, Sonia/Cavalcanti, Leonardo (2007): *Los Vínculos Económicos y Familiares Transnacionales. Los Inmigrantes Ecuatorianos y Peruanos en España.* Bilbao: Fundación BBVA.

Solé, Carlota/Sordé, Teresa/Serradell,; Olga/Alcalde, Rosalina/Flecha, Ainhoa/ Petroff, Alisa G./Cavalcanti, Leonardo/Parella, Sònia/Pavez, Iskra/Santamaría, Enrique/Garzó, Luis (2011): Cohesión Social e Inmigración. Aportaciones Científicas y Discursos Políticos. In: *Revista Internacional de Sociología* 69, 1, pp. 10–30.

Soltero, José (2009): Determinants of Remittances to Mexico from Mexican-Born Immigrants in Chicago. In: *Journal of Poverty* 13, 3, pp. 319–330.

Takenaka, Ayumi/Paerregaard, Karsten/Berg, Ulla (2010): Peruvian Migration in a Global Context. In: *Latin American Perspectives* 37, 3, pp. 3–11.

Tolley, Erin (2011): *Multiculturalism Policy Index: Immigrant Minority Policies.* Kingston, Canada: School of Policy Studies, Queen's University. http://www.queensu.ca/sps/, accessed March 2014.

Treas, Judith (2008): Transnational Older Adults and their Families. In: *Family Relations* 57, pp. 468–478.

US Department of Homeland Security (2012): *Yearbook of Immigration Statistics 2011.* Washington, DC: Department of Homeland Security, Office of Immigration Statistics.

US Department of State (2013): *Annual Report of Immigrant Visa Applicants in the Family-sponsored and Employment-based preferences Registered at the National Visa Center as of November 1, 2013.* http://travel.state.gov/content/dam/visas/ Statistics/Immigrant-Statistics/WaitingListItem.pdf, accessed February 2014.

US Department of State (2014): *U.S. Citizenship Laws and Policies. Dual Nationality.* http://travel.state.gov/content/travel/english/legal-considerations/us-citizen ship-laws-policies/citizenship-and-dual-nationality/dual-nationality.html, accessed March 2014.

Vertovec, Steven (2004): Cheap Calls: The Social Glue of Migrant Transnationalism. In: *Global Networks* 4, 2, pp. 219–224.

The White House (2011): *Building a 21st Century Immigration System.* Washington, DC: White House.

Wilding, Raelene (2006): 'Virtual' Intimacies? Families' Communication Across Transnational Contexts. In: *Global Networks* 6, pp. 125–142.

Wimmer, Andreas/Glick Schiller, Nina (2002): Methodological Nationalism and Beyond: Nation-State Building, Migration and the Social Sciences. In: *Global Networks* 2, 2, pp. 301–334.

WSCPA (2012): *Encuesta Mundial a la Comunidad Peruana en el Exterior.* Lima: Instituto Nacional de Estadística e Informática, Ministerio de Relaciones Exteriores, International Organization for Migration.

Zontini, Elisabetta/Reynolds, Tracey (2007): Ethnicity, Families and Social Capital: Caring Relationships Across Italian and Caribbean Families. In: *International Review of Sociology* 17, 2, pp. 257–277.

2 Intergenerational Solidarity in Migrant Families From the Former Soviet Union
Comparing Migrants Whose Parents Live in Germany to Migrants With Parents Abroad

Elena Sommer and Claudia Vogel

Because of demographic and socioeconomic developments in ageing societies, families face new challenges regarding care for the growing elderly population and the exchange of support between generations. Hence, there has been a growing research interest in analyzing the role of the family and state in the provision of different types of support to the elderly population (Kohli 2004, Künemund and Rein 1999; Künemund and Vogel 2006). In developed welfare states such as Germany, one could expect a "crowding-out" effect, whereby the welfare state substitutes private support, and the need for intergenerational exchange between family members decreases because the required services and financial resources are provided by the state. Several sociological studies, however, support the "crowding in" hypothesis, arguing that the state instead complements or even facilitates familial support (Igel et al. 2009; Künemund and Vogel 2006). It is argued that family members who are relieved from responsibilities to a certain degree are stimulated to engage in the provision of support. As Künemund and Rein (1999), as well as Igel and colleagues (2009), show in their comparative studies, in European countries with a high degree of welfare social service provision, family members complement the help provided by the state ("crowding in"). Thus, the support of elderly family members can be interpreted as being the mixed responsibility of the family and the state (Daatland and Lowenstein 2005).

For a long time, intergenerational support was associated with geographic proximity (Rossi and Rossi 1990). The rationale behind this association was the assumption that increasing geographic distance between children and parents reduced the possibility of support exchange between family members. According to Rossi and Rossi (1990), increasing geographic distance between parents and children has a negative effect on the exchange of intergenerational support of all types. However, filial responsibilities and parental expectations do not fade away with increasing geographic distance (Baldassar, Baldock and Wilding2007). Whereas it seems self-evident that

46 Elena Sommer and Claudia Vogel

the exchange of instrumental help can be hindered by distance, as family members can only help each other on a regular basis if they live close to each other, exchange of emotional support and financial assistance do not depend on geographic proximity in the same way. Developments in communication technologies mean that emotional interactions can be sustained over distance (Baldassar 2008). With regard to financial assistance, a broad body of literature on remittances (Mazzucato 2010; Zimmer et al. 2008) and on familial exchange (Kohli and Künemund 2003) shows that intergenerational monetary support depends primarily on the needs of the recipients and the resources of the givers, as well as on welfare conditions in the places of residence of the giver and the receiver. Financial transfers across national borders from migrants to their relatives left behind in the country of origin are an established practice, especially if migrants live in a more economically advanced country than their former country of residence.

Although migration often leads to geographic separation of first generation migrants and their parents, there are also cases when adult migrants and their parents migrate together and live in the same country of destination. In such cases, one could expect that the opportunity structure for engaging in intergenerational support can be similar to that of the nonmigrant population, especially if migrants are entitled to social welfare services to the same degree as natives. Several empirical studies (Baykara-Krumme 2007) have indeed demonstrated that patterns of intergenerational exchange in such migrant families are similar to those found among the non-migrant population. Studies analyzing intergenerational exchange in migrant families usually compare migrant families with native families. Instead, we suggest that further differentiation between transnational families,[1] that is, families whose members live in different countries, and migrant families with family members of different generations living in the same country can be useful for analyzing patterns of intergenerational exchange. Among other factors, the geographic distance between adult children and their parents as well as differences in the degree of social welfare provision in transnational settings can have an impact on patterns of intergenerational exchange. Therefore, we hypothesize that patterns of intergenerational exchange between adult children and their parents in migrant families will differ when parents live abroad versus when both parents and adult children live in the same country.

This chapter aims to analyze patterns of intergenerational support between adult children (40 years and older) and their parents in migrant families, focusing on the aspect of "functional solidarity" or on the exchange of instrumental and financial help (Bengtson and Roberts 1991) and taking into account the effect of the geographic distance between parents and children. These patterns are analyzed by using the case of migrants from the former Soviet Union (FSU migrants), one of the largest migrant groups in Germany. Most FSU migrants came to Germany as so-called ethnic Germans. One distinctive characteristic of this migrant group in contrast to labor migrants is that they tended to migrate to Germany with their extended family, which often consisted of several generations (Dietz 2006). However, in the case of mixed marriages between FSU migrants of German origin and FSU migrants of non-German origin, the non-German spouses were not allowed to migrate with their parents, which led to the emergence of transnational families. We compare such transnational families that have parents living abroad with FSU migrant families in which both adult migrants and their parents live in Germany.

FUNCTIONAL SOLIDARITY IN MIGRANT FAMILIES

Functional Solidarity

Intergenerational support includes the transfer of financial resources as well as the exchange of instrumental help and emotional support among family members. In general, the intergenerational exchange of support between parents and adult children can be interpreted as the interplay of the need and ability of each generation to provide certain kinds of help (Eggebeen 1992). In addition, reciprocity of transfers and a sense of filial obligation acquired through the process of socialization also have an impact on intergenerational support (Lowenstein and Daatland 2006). The concept of "intergenerational solidarity" developed by Bengtson and his colleagues (Bengtson and Roberts 1991), defined as social cohesion between generations, differentiates between six main dimensions of familial solidarity: (1) structural, for example, geographic proximity between family members; (2) associational, or frequency of contacts and social activities between family members; (3) affectual, or emotional closeness; (4) consensual, or level of agreement in opinions and values; (5) normative, or "strength of obligations felt towards other family members" (Silverstein and Bengtson 1997: 432); and (6) functional solidarity, or mutual instrumental and financial assistance. Associational and affectual solidarity refer to emotional support, while functional solidarity refers to instrumental help (e.g., practical help with housework, care of elderly and sick, looking after grandchildren) and monetary transfers. Although several studies (Baldassar 2008; Baldassar Baldock and Wilding 2007) underline that emotional support is a very important aspect of intergenerational relationships in migrant families, we decided to focus our analysis on functional solidarity. First, in line with findings from recent empirical studies on transnational families (Baldassar 2008), we assume that emotional support does not primarily depend on geographic proximity. Second, there is no clear conceptual link between emotional support within families and welfare provision by the state. Functional solidarity, on the other hand, can be affected by geographic distance (in the case of instrumental help), as well as by different welfare regulations in transnational settings (especially in the case of financial transfers).

Predictors in the provision and receipt of monetary assistance and instrumental help in families are, for example, sociodemographic characteristics, health and functional status, aspects of family and social networks, cultural norms, and welfare conditions (Albertini, Kohli and Vogel 2007). Migration and increasing distance between family members can affect how these factors influence intergenerational relationships. The migration experience in itself could result in a complicated interplay between the structural frameworks for familial support in the host country and the context of origin (Baykara-Krumme 2008). Within this frame of reference, two contrasting hypotheses describe the possible scenario for postmigration changes: "family cohesion" versus "family alienation" (Baykara-Krumme 2008; Vogel 2012). According to the "family cohesion" hypothesis, migration could intensify family relationships in the new environment. Mutual assistance among family members compensates for the loss of social networks in the country of origin and the lack of social contacts in the host country. The "family alienation" hypothesis, on the contrary, assumes that relationships between the family members are weakened after migration. Integration in a new society can be a burden for the whole family, especially when family members are faced with difficulties in providing each other with the necessary help. Depending on the age at the time of relocation, different members of the same family might face different challenges in the country of destination. Adult migrants of the "sandwich generation" are often doubly burdened with the tasks of providing for both older parents and their own children. In addition, after migration some family members may develop a different understanding of solidarity and norms of responsibility that does not correspond to the expectations of other family members, particularly those from the older generation (Baykara-Krumme 2008; Vogel 2012).

Using Zechner's (2008) terminology, needs and abilities in transnational settings can be labeled as "resources" (i.e., time, money, information, social networks) that migrants have or need in order to be able to provide transnational support to their parents, and as "circumstances" of daily living of the elder generation (i.e., housing conditions, health status, care services available). In addition, Baldassar, Baldock, and Wilding (2007) include in their model of transnational care such elements as obligation and negotiation. Obligations are related to cultural expectations assigned to someone's social role as a particular family member (e.g., daughter, mother, father, or grandmother) and negotiation can be understood as a commitment in a specific relationship acquired over a longer period. Apart from these factors, visa regulations (e.g., free mobility for European Union [EU] citizens versus restricted mobility for non-EU citizens) and welfare conditions (e.g., pension system, social security), as well as various social policies related to care-providing activities both in the country of destination and in the country of origin, can influence the outcomes of intergenerational exchange in migrant families (Zechner 2008). The issue of care-related social policies has rarely been analyzed in studies on transnational familial support exchange (Zechner 2008). In Germany, for example, there are no special policies promoting transnational caregiving or encouraging migrants to bring older family members to Germany. However, migrants can apply for tax deductions if they support their relatives outside Germany financially. In summary, migrants' capacity to participate in transnational intergenerational exchange of functional solidarity depends, on one hand, on individual factors (resources, perceived norms of responsibility, etc.) and, on the other hand, on macro factors such as the structural framework, institutional regulations, and the welfare provision both in the residence country of the migrant and in the country where his or her parents live.

Migrants From the Former Soviet Union in Germany

Emigration from the former Soviet Union was highly restricted during the Soviet era. This changed dramatically with the collapse of the Soviet Union in 1991. Since the 1990s, about 2.3 million so-called Aussiedler (ethnic Germans), 220,000 Jews, and about 100,000 other migrants (e.g., labor or marriage migrants) arrived in Germany from the successor countries of the Soviet Union. Although not all FSU migrants are ethnic Germans, our analysis focuses on this group, as FSU ethnic Germans account for 92 percent of all respondents in our Survey on Ageing of Soviet Union Migrants (ASUM) 2011 sample.

Compared to other migrant groups in Germany, FSU ethnic Germans received a relatively privileged migration status: they could immigrate with their extended family, were granted German citizenship directly on their arrival in Germany, and were eligible for various welfare benefits and public integration help (e.g., free language courses), as well as material assistance (Harris 1997). Elderly ethnic Germans (but not their non-German spouses) are entitled to public pensions, which have been quite generous because the calculation includes entitlements from their employment history in the country of origin (Baumann and Mika 2012). One could therefore expect that they are less dependent on financial support from younger family members compared to other elderly migrant groups in Germany.

Although various integration aids were offered to FSU migrants, many migrants still faced some integration difficulties and had limited economic and social resources at their disposal (Geiling et al. 2011). Most of them came during the mass migration following the collapse of the Soviet Union and German local municipalities faced a challenging task providing large numbers of newly arrived migrants with social welfare and accommodation support, as well as with adequate labor market integration assistance (Harris 1997). After their arrival in Germany, many ethnic Germans decided to settle in rural areas, which was uncommon among other migrant groups (Wenzel 2004), as urban areas tend to offer more possibilities in terms of labor market integration. The proportion of FSU ethnic Germans to the population living in Germany is about 3 percent. However, in some rural

50 *Elena Sommer and Claudia Vogel*

regions in Lower Saxony their proportion has reached up to 20 percent of the total population (Geiling et al. 2011: 82) and even higher proportions in some specific neighborhoods. Despite their German ethnic background, contacts with the host population are rare among the first generation of migrants, and leisure time is spent mainly with the family (Fuchs, Schwietring and Weiß 1999).

Hardly anything is known about the ageing processes of migrants from the former Soviet Union. Of the few studies that investigate intergenerational support in migrant families, Baykara-Krumme's (2008) quantitative analysis of the data from the DEAS (German Ageing Survey) and the GSOEP (German Socio-Economic Panel) has a particular focus on migrants from the former Soviet Union. These migrants are characterized by high family orientation, where non-relatives play only a marginal role in the potential support network. Another distinctive characteristic is frequent contacts and the high rate of cohabitation with parents: "Parents . . . constitute an important cognitive and emotional support potential and support source, as immigrants from the former Soviet Union, for instance, comparatively often receive financial support from parents" (Baykara-Krumme 2008: 296). In this respect, FSU migrant families are similar to nonmigrant families in Germany who are characterized by a downward flow of instrumental help and financial support from the older to the younger generation (Albertini, Kohli and Vogel 2007; Vogel 2010). But do the patterns of functional solidarity remain the same if FSU adult migrants and their parents live in different countries?

Hypotheses

We expect to find different patterns of functional solidarity in FSU migrant families in which both migrants and their parents live in Germany as compared to FSU migrant families in which parents live abroad. With regard to instrumental help, a decrease of exchange between adult migrants and their parents is expected if parents live abroad, mainly due to the reduced possibilities of engaging in exchange of instrumental help because of increasing geographic distance. Although financial assistance does not depend primarily on geographic proximity, we expect to find different patterns of financial transfers between adult FSU migrant children with parents living in Germany as compared to those migrants whose parents live in the country of origin. Because of the previously mentioned pension entitlement of FSU ethnic Germans in Germany, in families with both migrants and parents living in Germany we expect to find a similar pattern of financial support as that found among the nonmigrant population, namely, downward financial flows from parents to children. In families in which the parents stayed in the FSU countries, we assume an opposite pattern (children in Germany supporting their parents living abroad), mainly because of the lower pensions and the lower level of welfare social support for elderly people in the countries of the former Soviet Union.

ASUM 2011

It is possible to analyze the life situation of elderly people and the patterns of intergenerational exchange in families of the native population by using representative surveys such as the DEAS or the Survey of Health, Ageing and Retirement in Europe (SHARE). However, there are shortcomings of analytical potentials with regard to the migrant population because of their underrepresentation in those surveys. Besides the low number of migrants in random samples, SHARE Germany and DEAS interviews are only conducted in the German language, which can be a burden for elderly migrants with language barriers. Apart from that, as German citizens, FSU ethnic Germans often cannot be identified as migrants in administrative data because most statistics still use citizenship as the only criterion for migration status.

In order to achieve a representative sample of FSU migrants, we conducted a postal survey called ASUM—the Survey on Ageing of Soviet Union Migrants in 2011.[2] This survey, however, is only representative for the region of Oldenburger Muensterland in the federal state of Lower Saxony, in northern Germany. We conducted the survey there because this rural region has a particularly high percentage of ethnic Germans, up to 20 percent of total population in some areas (Geiling et al. 2011). The municipal registration offices were asked to randomly choose the addresses of persons who were born in one of the republics of the former Soviet Union before 1971 (aged 40 and older). A two-language (German and Russian) questionnaire was designed and sent to the chosen individuals. The ASUM asks for information on health, socioeconomic status, living arrangements, life satisfaction, and intergenerational relationships in families of FSU migrants. Further questions are related to migration background and to attitudes and norms of responsibility. The questionnaire consists mainly of standardized questions and two open questions at the end. Questions related to functional solidarity are the main part of the questionnaire. For reasons of comparability (e.g., FSU migrants with natives or with FSU migrants in Israel), the parts of the ASUM questionnaire on instrumental help and financial support are based on the relevant parts of the SHARE questionnaire.

In total, 2,176 questionnaires were sent to the selected persons by applying the Tailored Design Method[3] (Dillman 2000). We received 684 completed questionnaires (response rate of 32[4] percent). The percentage of females in the net sample (58.6 percent) was slightly higher than in the gross sample (53.5 percent). The age distribution in the gross and net samples was similar. However, the proportion of 60- to 69-years-olds among the respondents (net sample) was somewhat higher than in the gross sample (17 percent vs. 11 percent, respectively). The interpretation of the results of the study should be framed within the context of a specific rural area, in this case, the region of Oldenburger Münsterland. Despite this limitation, we can still draw some conclusions about intergenerational relationships in

52 *Elena Sommer and Claudia Vogel*

the families of ethnic Germans in general, as living in rural areas is common for this migrant group (Wenzel 2004).

INTERGENERATIONAL RELATIONSHIPS IN FSU MIGRANT FAMILIES

Living Arrangements and Spatial Distance Between Adult Migrants and their Parents

FSU ethnic Germans constituted the majority of the ASUM sample: out of 684 respondents, 92.4 percent stated that they belonged to the category "FSU ethnic Germans or their family member," 6 percent belonged to a different FSU migrant group, and 1.6 percent of respondents did not answer this question. Most respondents had German citizenship (94 percent), and about a quarter (24 percent) had dual citizenship (German and citizenship of country of origin). The mean age of respondents was 55 years. On average, respondents had been living in Germany for 17 years. More than half (56.5 percent) resided in family-owned properties. About one-fifth (20.3 percent) were retired, but the majority (58.8 percent) were still employed. Eighty-three percent of the respondents were married. On average, respondents had 2.9 children. The majority (81 percent) of respondents reported that their children lived at a distance of less than five kilometers from them. The mean size of the household was 3.2 persons. Nine and a half percent of respondents lived in a three-generation household. Multigenerational households were common if the respondent lived in a family-owned house and rare if the family lived in rented accommodation.

About half of all respondents (51 percent, or 349 persons) in the survey had at least one parent still alive (Table 2.1). The proportion of respondents with parents still alive obviously decreases with age. The number of respondents with their mother still alive (298) was considerably higher than the number of respondents with their father still alive (178). About one-fifth of

Table 2.1 Percentage of respondents with at least one parent still alive and geographic distance to parents by age groups

	No parents still alive (N = 335)	At least one parent still alive (N = 349)	Parent lives		
Age group			same household /house	separately in Germany	in different country
40–54	24.2%	75. 8%	15.8%	59.7%	24.5%
55 or above	79.0%	21.0%	15.4%	73.8%	10.8%
Total	49.3%	50.7%	15.7%	62.4%	21.9%

Source: ASUM (2011).

Intergenerational Solidarity in Migrant Families   53

respondents with parents still alive (22 percent, or 75 respondents) had at least one parent living outside Germany (Table 2.1). In comparison, the percentage of respondents with at least one child living abroad was relatively low (7.5 percent).

Geographic distance does not necessarily reduce contacts between family members living in different countries. Modern technologies enable relatively cheap communication across national borders and contribute to the maintenance of close ties (Zechner 2008). However, older generations might not be able to use the new communication technologies (Künemund and Tanschus 2013). In addition, in the case of FSU migrants, relatives left behind usually do not possess EU citizenship. Therefore, visa regulations as well as relatively high travel costs can be barriers to family visits. The family's participation in transnational intergenerational exchange can also be limited by national administrative regulations. One of the ASUM respondents wrote the following response to the open question related to worries and hopes for the future (translated from Russian [Elena Sommer]):

> My elderly parents live in Russia. I am worried about the fact that I am helpless to take care of them. I would really be very happy to take care and support them if they lived close to me. Sometimes I am really scared when I think about the future. I wish with all my heart that the government implement a law that allows migrants to take their elderly parents from abroad to live with them, so that they can spend their last days surrounded by family members and grandchildren. It is the dream of my life that my children can grow up close to their grandparents.

Although 22 percent of respondents report having parents living abroad, transnational families are less common among ethnic Germans compared to other migrant groups. In fact, geographic proximity between family members and a high rate of cohabitation are distinctive features of FSU ethnic Germans (Baykara-Krumme 2008). About 16 percent of ASUM respondents live in the same household or building as their parents (Table 2.1), and another 30 percent live at a distance of less than five kilometers away from their parents. It is more common for one parent to live in the same household as the respondent if the other parent is deceased or lives abroad. In some cases, cohabitation can be viewed as a coping strategy of pooling limited resources, because migrant families are often economically disadvantaged compared to the native population (Lowenstein and Katz 2005). Such multigenerational living arrangements can facilitate an intensive exchange of instrumental help between generations but are related to psychological distress and poorer personal well-being, too (Lowenstein and Katz 2005). Respondents cohabiting with their parents report having experienced conflict situations with their parents more often (at 46.3 percent) than did migrants living separately from their parents (28.5 percent if parents live separately in Germany and 29.3 percent if parents live abroad).

54   *Elena Sommer and Claudia Vogel*

Respondents with parents living abroad differ in several ways from respondents with both parents living in Germany. Table 2.2 shows the main characteristics of these two groups. While parents of 80.8 percent of FSU ethnic Germans from the sample live in Germany, the majority of respondents (61.1 percent) with a different migration status than FSU ethnic Germans (e.g., labor or marriage migration) have parents living outside Germany. Respondents with parents outside Germany have been living in Germany on average for a shorter time themselves, and 22.7 percent of them do not have German citizenship. Among respondents with parents living in Germany, only 1.5 percent did not possess German citizenship. Only 9.4 percent of respondents with parents living abroad also have at least one child living abroad. In cases of labor migration, there are limited legal possibilities for adult children or parents of labor migrants to join labor migrants in the host country. Therefore, the proportion of transnational families is higher in this migrant group than among ethnic Germans. Respondents with parents

Table 2.2   Main characteristics of respondents with parents abroad compared to respondents with parents in Germany

Characteristics		Parent lives in . . .		
		Germany (N = 274)	abroad (N = 75)	total (N = 349)
Visits to country of origin	At least once a year	1.8%	13.3%	4.3%
	Every 2–3 years	8.4%	40.0%	15.2%
	Every 4–5 years	10.2%	20.0%	12.3%
	Less than every 5 years	37.6%	17.4%	33.2%
	Never	42.0%	9.3%	35.0%
Citizenship	German	70.1%	57.3%	67.3%
	German and country of origin	28.4%	20.0%	26.6%
	Country of origin	1.5%	22.7%	6.1%
Living situation	Property owner	67.0%	58.7%	65.2%
	Tenant	33.0%	41.3%	34.8%
Mean duration of stay in Germany (years)		17.4	14.0	16.7
Mean age (years)		49.8	46.8	49.0
At least one child abroad		4.2%	9.4%	5.3%
Felt lonely		44.1%	58.7%	47.3%

Source: ASUM (2011).

outside Germany visited their country of origin more frequently than did respondents with parents in Germany. In addition, FSU migrants with parents living abroad felt lonely more often than did respondents with parents in Germany (58.7 percent vs. 44.1 percent, respectively).

Exchange of Instrumental Help

The ASUM questions on the exchange of instrumental help are divided into three types of support: (1) personal care (e.g., assistance with dressing, washing or eating), (2) practical household help (e.g., cooking, renovating, cleaning the house, shopping), and (3) help with paperwork (e.g., help with administrative issues). Respondents were asked about instrumental help received and given during the last 12 months prior to the time point of participating in the survey. There are some limitations on such operationalization of instrumental help. First, it does not include the information on grandchild care, which is an important kind of instrumental help elder generations are often engaged in (Albertini; Kohli and Vogel 2007; Igel and Szydlik 2011). Unfortunately, our data have only limited information on the grandchild care provided by respondents who have grandchildren and no information on whether respondents receive childcare assistance from their parents. The second problem is related to the temporal character of instrumental help. The data only reflect a snapshot of a period of 12 months. As Kofman (2012: 159) indicates, "[t]o investigate the different forms, orientations, and directions of care, one would need as a first step to adopt an approach that follows longitudinally and spatially the migrant so as to capture care giving and receiving." Furthermore, the data only illustrate the perspective of the respondent that might involve some aspects of "social

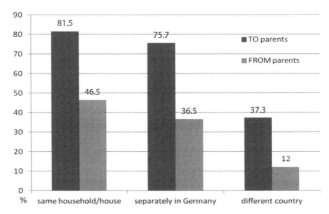

Figure 2.1 Exchange of instrumental help between respondents and their parents
Source: ASUM (2011).

desirability" (ibid.). In an ideal case, information provided by parents is needed to analyze the reliability of such statements. Figure 2.1 shows that, regardless of geographic distance, respondents more often give instrumental help to their parents rather than receive it: 68.2 percent of all respondents with parents reported that they gave instrumental help to their parents at least once in the last 12 months, while only 32.7 percent stated that they received this type of support from their parents.

In all three types of instrumental help analyzed, respondents reported more help given to their parents than received from their parents, regardless of where their parents lived (Figure 2.2). However, with growing spatial distance, the proportion of giving as well as receiving of instrumental help is decreasing. The degree of exchanging instrumental help between respondents and their parents in both directions is lowest in transnational families. Practical household help is the most common type of instrumental help both respondents and their parents are involved in, and personal care is the least common type of support received by respondents from their parents. This is to be expected, as the need for personal care among the younger generation may not be as high. Need for personal care usually occurs in late life stages, and elderly parents are more often in need of this type of help than the respondents. Compared with other types of support that can be provided sporadically when one has an opportunity (e.g., during visiting parents in the country of origin), the provision of personal care requires more intensity, regularity, and geographic proximity (Brandt, Haberkern and Szydlik

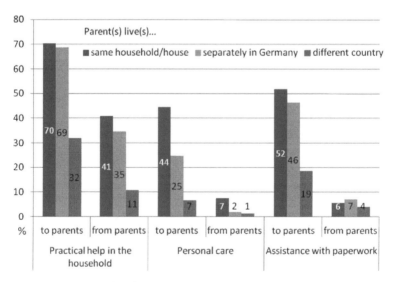

Figure 2.2 Exchange of different types of instrumental help between respondents and their parents
Source: ASUM (2011).

Intergenerational Solidarity in Migrant Families 57

2009). In cases in which this type of help is given or received from parents, respondents and their parents often live in the same household or building.

With regard to assistance with paperwork, the younger generation is again usually the giver of this type of support to the older generation. Provision of this type of help is especially important in migrant families, as older generations might not be familiar with administrative procedures in the host country or might experience language-related difficulties. Although an exchange of this type of support is less dependent on geographic proximity, Figure 2.2 shows that with growing distance, giving this help to parents decreases. Assistance with paperwork also includes such support as accompanying persons to different administrative appointments. The possibility of accompaniment can, however, be limited by spatial distance between family members. Apart from this, parents staying in the country of origin might need this kind of help to a lesser extent as they can use their native language and are familiar with the administrative procedures.

The effect of geographic distance manifests itself not only in the possibility of exchanging instrumental help but also in the frequency by which help is exchanged. As shown in Figure 2.3, exchange of practical help between adult children and parents is most intensive if respondents and parents live in the same household or building: 44.4 percent offered this support daily to their parents and 27.8 percent received it from their parents on a daily basis. While 30.4 percent of respondents living separately from their parents in Germany still provided their parents with practical help at least once a month, only 6.7 percent of respondents with parents living outside Germany

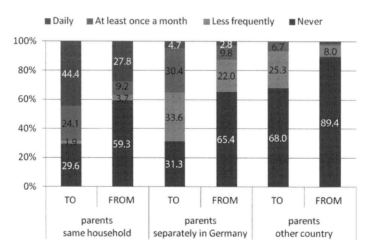

Figure 2.3 Exchange of practical help with housework between respondents and their parents
Source: ASUM (2011).

58 *Elena Sommer and Claudia Vogel*

gave this type of help to their parent on a monthly basis. The frequency of exchange of all three kinds of instrumental help between respondents and their parents in both directions was highest among families living in the same building and lowest in transnational families. These findings are in line with the dominant assumption of the negative effect of geographic distance on the exchange of instrumental help.

Financial Transfers

A different pattern can be observed with regard to financial transfers. About 43 percent of ASUM respondents with children gave support of 250 euro or more to their children in the previous 12 months, while only 11 percent received monetary help from their children. In comparison, the percentage of respondents that gave financial support to parents was relatively low. Only 12 percent of all respondents with parents still alive stated that they gave financial support to their parents, and about 20 percent received monetary help from parents. This pattern is in line with the general pattern of intergenerational financial support in Western Europe, which is characterized by the downward flow from parents to children, because in the last decades there has hardly been any need for adult children to financially support their parents (Kohli 2004; Vogel 2010). Elderly FSU ethnic Germans (but not their non-German spouses) receive a public pension as German citizens, calculated from their employment history in both Germany and their country of origin. Because full-time employment for both men and women was guaranteed by and demanded from the government in the Soviet era, public pensions of FSU ethnic Germans who are eligible tend to be comparatively high. Therefore, when both parents and children live in Germany, one could expect the same pattern of financial transfer in FSU migrant families as among native population, namely a downward financial flow from older to younger generations. Indeed, if a respondent's parents lived in Germany, the respondent is more often the receiver of financial transfers than the giver (Figure 2.4). However, a reverse pattern is observed in transnational families. In total, 26.7 percent of FSU migrants with parents outside Germany support their parents financially, and only 5.3 percent receive monetary assistance from parents living abroad.

In addition, statistical analysis of correlations shows that, with all other factors constant, having parents abroad has the highest effect on providing financial support to parents. We assume that it is not the geographic distance in a physical sense that plays a significant role for financial assistance but, rather, the location of migrants' parents and the context that defines their living situation. In less economically developed countries of the former Soviet Union with a less generous welfare regime, relatively low pensions, and lack of care-related policies for the elderly, parents might be more in need of financial assistance than parents who live in Germany. Unfortunately, our data do not contain information about the needs of the

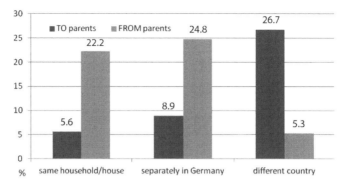

Figure 2.4 Exchange of financial support between respondents and their parents
Source: ASUM (2011).

respondents' parents and their living conditions. Elderly people in rural areas in particular often live in relatively poor conditions with inadequate infrastructure, for example, no supply of running water, heating with wood (Zechner 2008). Thus, one possible explanation for the different patterns of financial transfers between migrants and parents in Germany compared to those with parents outside Germany is the differing needs of parents partly due to the differences in the welfare systems that guarantee different levels of provision for old age.

Another possible interpretation for financial support of parents living abroad could be the respondents' wish to fulfill filial obligations. Attitudes and expectations regarding norms on family support can have an impact on intergenerational familial support. A study conducted by Daatland and colleagues (2011), in which seven European countries are compared with regard to attitudes to family obligation, shows that in Western European countries with well-developed welfare social services (Norway, Germany), parental obligations (opinion that parents should support their adult children) are stronger than filial obligations (opinion that children should support their parents). In Eastern European countries with less developed welfare services (Russia, Georgia), support of parental and filial norms are balanced to almost the same level, with stronger degree of family norms support in general as compared to West-European countries.

As in the SHARE, ASUM respondents were asked, "Should the state or the family be responsible for the financial support of elderly people?" While the majority of all respondents think that both family and state should take care of elderly people, those who actually give financial support to their parents regardless of whether their parents live in Germany or abroad tend more often to think that the family should be mainly responsible for the financial support of elderly family members. In the former Soviet Union the family was expected to take care of elderly people: ". . . it was assumed that

60   *Elena Sommer and Claudia Vogel*

the needs of older persons are met by the families, usually by the women in the families. The idea was enforced by not providing services helping families to care for their elderly members or by making the use of such services stigmatizing and unpleasant" (Zechner 2008: 41). Findings of several qualitative studies that examine the attitudes of ethnic Germans toward care of elderly family members in Germany (Schnepp 2002) show that care is primarily perceived as a family responsibility and accommodation of elderly family members in a nursing home is not acceptable among FSU ethnic Germans. Such cultural expectations of filial obligations, on one hand, and the limited possibilities to provide regular practical help or care due to long distances, on the other hand, might result in a "compromising compensation" in the form of monetary support.

CONCLUSION

The aim of this chapter was to explore the patterns of intergenerational solidarity between adult children and parents in families of migrants from the former Soviet Union in Germany. The analysis based on ASUM (2011) has shown relatively close distances between children and parents when both children and parents live in Germany. High percentage of cohabitations with parents and close geographic proximity between parents and children enabled a favorable opportunity structure for the exchange of instrumental help. Supporting the "family cohesion" hypothesis, family is an important resource for different types of help. Although migrating to Germany with the whole family consisting of several generations is a distinctive characteristic of FSU ethnic Germans, about one in five (22 percent) of respondents with at least one parent alive has a parent living outside Germany. With regard to financial transfers, respondents with parents living abroad report different patterns of monetary assistance than those with parents living in Germany. Whereas parents who live in Germany behave similarly to the host population and are more often the givers of financial support to the younger generation, parents who live abroad are in most cases the receivers of financial support. There are two possible interpretations for this pattern. On one hand, one can look at this financial transfer to parents living abroad as a mechanism to compensate for the inability to provide instrumental help that is only possible on a regular basis when family members live close to each other in order to fulfill filial obligations. On the other hand, one can interpret these findings as a result of different welfare systems with different levels of provision for old age (Vogel and Sommer 2013). The welfare provision via public pensions for elderly FSU migrants enables them to live comparatively independent of financial support provided by their children, and even to support financially their children and grandchildren in Germany. This is not the case for migrants' parents living abroad. What is most plausible, however, is that the tendency among FSU migrant children to provide

Intergenerational Solidarity in Migrant Families   61

financial support to parents living abroad falls within the transnational arrangement that families adapt to maintain intergenerational relationships.

NOTES

1 By "transnational family" we refer to the framework of "transnationalism" introduced by Glick-Schiller and colleagues (1992), which states that migrants maintain social ties to their former home country while acquiring new social contacts in the receiving country. These ties can be especially intense if migrants have family members left behind in the country of origin. Transnational families are characterized by multidirectional flows of support across the borders between family members living in different nation states (Baldassar, Baldock and Wilding 2007; Faist 2000). For simplification purposes, the term *transnational family* is used in this chapter to refer to transnational child–parent relationships, regardless of the degree to which the migrant is involved in transnational social activities.
2 This survey is a part of the collaboration project "Intergenerational Relationships of Elderly Migrants from the Former Soviet Union—an Israeli-German Comparison" between the Gerontology Institute at the University of Vechta (Germany) and the Israel Gerontological Data Center at the Hebrew University of Jerusalem (Israel), which was financed by Niedersaechsisches Vorab: Niedersaechsisch-israelische Projekte des Ministeriums fuer Wissenschaft und Kultur (MWK).
3 After sending the questionnaire for the first time in September 2011, we sent reminder postcards two weeks later, and two weeks after that we sent the questionnaire for the second time to persons who had not replied.
4 Thirty-six letters could not be delivered and were excluded from the gross sample.

REFERENCES

Albertini, Marco/Kohli, Martin/Vogel, Claudia (2007): Intergenerational Transfers of Time and Money in European Families: Common Patterns—Different Regimes? In: *Journal of European Social Policy* 17, pp. 319–334.

Baldassar, Loretta (2008): Missing Kin and Longing to Be Together: Emotions and the Construction of Co-presence in Transnational Relationships. In: *Journal of Intercultural Studies* 29, 3, pp. 247–266.

Baldassar, Loretta/Baldock, Cora/Wilding, Raelene (2007): *Families Caring Across Borders: Migration, Ageing and Transnational Caregiving.* New York: Palgrave Macmillan.

Baumann, Jochen/Mika, Tatjana (2012): Steigende Ungleichheit unter Aussiedlern und Spaetaussiedlern im Alter. In: Baykara-Krummer, Helen/Motel-Klingebiel, Andreas/Schimany, Peter (eds.): *Viele Welten des Alterns. Ältere Migranten im alternden Deutschland.* Wiesbaden: VS Verlag für Sozialwissenschaften, pp. 127–157.

Baykara-Krumme, Helen (2007): *Gar nicht so anders: Eine vergleichende Analyse der Generationenbeziehungen bei Migranten und Einheimischen in der zweiten Lebenshälfte.* WZB Discussion Paper, SP IV 2007–604. Berlin: Wissenschaftszentrum Berlin.

62 Elena Sommer and Claudia Vogel

Baykara-Krumme, Helen (2008): *Immigrant Families in Germany: Intergenerational Solidarity in Later Life*. Berlin: Weißensee Verlag.

Bengtson, Vern L./Roberts, Robert (1991): Intergenerational Solidarity in Ageing Families: An Example of Formal Theory Construction. In: *Journal of Marriage and Family* 53, pp. 856–870.

Brandt, Martina/Haberkern, Klaus/Szydlik, Marc (2009): Intergenerational Help and Care in Europe. In: *European Sociological Review* 25, 5, pp. 585–601.

Daatland, Sven O./Herlofson, Katarina/Lima, Ivar A. (2011): Balancing Generations: On the Strength and Character of Family Norms in the West and East of Europe. In: *Ageing and Society* 31, pp. 1159–1179.

Daatland, Sven O./Lowenstein, Ariela (2005): Intergenerational Solidarity and the Family-Welfare State Balance. In: *European Journal of Ageing* 2, pp. 174–182.

Dietz, Barbara (2006): Aussiedler in Germany: From Smooth Adaptation to Tough Integration. In: Lucassen, Leo/Feldman, David/Oltmer, Jochen (eds.): *Paths of Integration: Migrants in Western Europe (1880–2004)*. Amsterdam: IMISCOE Research, Amsterdam University Press, pp. 116–138.

Dillman, Don A. (2000): *Mail and Internet Surveys: The Tailored Design Method*. New York: J. Wiley.

Faist, Thomas (2000): Transnationalism in International Migration: Implications for the Study of Citizenship and Culture. In: *Ethnic and Social Studies* 23, 2, pp. 189–222.

Eggebeen, David J. (1992): Family Structure and Intergenerational Exchanges. In: *Research on Ageing* 14, pp. 427–447.

Fuchs, Marek/Schwietring, Thomas/Weiß, Johannes (1999): Leben im Herkunftsland. In: Silbereisen, Rainer K./Lantermann, Ernst-Dieter/Schmidt-Rodermund, Eva (eds.): *Aussiedler in Deutschland: Akkulturation von Persönlichkeit und Verhalten*. Opladen: Leske+Budrich, pp. 69–90.

Geiling, Heiko/Gardemin, Daniel/Meise, Stephan/König, Andrea (2011): *Migration—Teilhabe—Milieus. Spätaussiedler und türkischstämmige Deutsche im sozialen Raum*. Wiesbaden: VS Verlag für Sozialwissenschaften.

Glick-Schiller, Nina/Basch, Linda/Blanc-Szanton, Cristma (1992): Transnationalism: A New Analytical Framework for Understanding Migration. In: *Annals of the New York Academy of Science* 645, 1, pp. 1–24.

Harris, Paul A. (1997): *The Politics of Repatriation and Return: Soviet Jewish and Ethnic German Immigration to the New Germany*. Alabama: Auburn University.

Igel, Corinne/Szydlik, Marc (2011): Grandchild Care and Welfare State Arrangements in Europe. In: *Journal of European Social Policy* 21, 3, pp. 210–224.

Igel, Corinne/Brandt, Martin/Haberkern, Klaus/Szydlik, Marcu (2009): Specialization Between Family and State—Intergenerational Time Transfers in Western Europe. In: *Journal of Comparative Family Studies* 40, 2, pp. 203–226.

Kofman, Eleonore (2012): Rethinking Care Through Reproduction: Articulating Circuits of Migration. In: *Social Politics* 19, 1, pp. 142–162.

Kohli, Martin (2004): Intergenerational Transfers and Inheritance: A Comparative View. In: Silverstein, Merril (ed.): *Intergenerational Relations Across Time and Place*. New York: Springer, pp. 266–289.

Kohli, Martin/Künemund, Harald (2003): Intergenerational Transfers in the Family: What Motivates Giving? In: Bengtson, Vern L./Lowenstein, Ariela (eds.): *Global Aging and Challenges to Families*. New York: Aldine de Gruyter, pp. 123–142.

Künemund, Harald/Rein, Martin (1999): There Is More to Receiving Than Needing: Theoretical Arguments and Empirical Explorations of Crowding in and Crowding out. In: *Ageing and Society* 19, pp. 93–121.

Künemund, Harald/Tanschus, Nele M. (2013): Gero-Technology: Old Age in the Electronic Jungle". In: Komp, Katrin/Aarsten, Marja (eds.): *Old Age in Europe: A Textbook of Gerontology*. New York: Springer, pp. 97–112.

Künemund, Haral/Vogel, Claudia (2006): Öffentliche und private Transfers und Unterstützungsleistungen im Alter—"crowding out" oder "crowding in"? In: *Zeitschrift für Familienforschung* 18, pp. 269–289.

Lowenstein, Ariela/Daatland, Sven O. (2006): Filial Norms and Filial Support in a Comparative Cross-national Context (the OASIS Study). In: *Ageing and Society* 26, pp. 203–233.

Lowenstein, Ariela/Katz, Ruth (2005): Living Arrangements, Family Solidarity and Life Satisfaction of Two Generations of Immigrants in Israel. In: *Ageing and Society* 25, pp. 749–767.

Mazzucato, Valentina (2010): Reverse Remittances in the Migration–development Nexus: Two-way Flows Between Ghana and the Netherlands. In: *Population, Space and Place* 17, 5, pp. 454–468.

Rossi, Alice S./Rossi, Peter H. (1990): *Of Human Bonding: Parent-Child Relations Across the Life Course*. New York: Aldine de Gruyter.

Schnepp, Wilfried (2002): *Familiale Sorge in der Gruppe der russlanddeutschen Spätaussiedler*. Bern: Hans Huber Verlag.

Silverstein, Merril/Bengtson, Vern L. (1997): Intergenerational Solidarity and the Structure of Adult Child-Parent Relationships in American Families. In: *American Journal of Sociology* 103, 2, pp. 429–460.

Vogel, Claudia (2010): Generationenbilanzen familialer Unterstützungsleistungen im europäischen Vergleich. In: Ette, Andreas/Ruckdeschel, Kerstin/Unger, Rainer (eds.): *Potentiale intergenerationaler Beziehungen*. Wiesbaden: VS Verlag für Sozialwissenschaften, pp. 301–319.

Vogel, Claudia (2012): Generationenbeziehungen der (Spät-)Aussiedler—Forschungsstand und exemplarische Befunde zu Einstellungen in Bezug auf familiale Unterstützungsleistungen. In: Baykara-Krummer, Helen/Motel-Klingebiel, Andreas/Schimany, Peter (eds.): *Viele Welten des Alterns. Ältere Migranten im alternden Deutschland. Wiesbaden*. Wiesbaden: VS Verlag für Sozialwissenschaften, pp. 289–314.

Vogel, Claudia/Sommer, Elena (2013): Financial Transfers Between Adult Children and Parents in Migrant Families from the Former Soviet Union. In: *Journal of Comparative Family Studies*, Special Issue on Family and Migration, XLIV, pp. 783–796.

Wenzel, Hans-Joachim (2004): Aussiedler: Wachstumsimpulse für den ländlichen Raum. In: *Geographische Rundschau* 9, 4, pp. 34–38.

Zechner, Minna (2008): Care of Older Persons in Transnational Settings. In: *Journal of Ageing Studies* 22, pp. 32–44.

Zimmer, Zachary/Korinek, Kim/Knodel, John/Chayovan, Napaporn (2008): Migrant Interactions with Elderly Parents in Rural Cambodia and Thailand. In: *Journal of Marriage and Family* 70, pp. 585–598.

3 Remaking the *Yanga Kawsay*
Andean Elders, Children, and Domestic Abuse in the Transmigration Logics of Highland Ecuador

Jason Pribilsky

To date, my ethnographic work on migration from highland Ecuador to the United States and Spain has mostly been in the service of addressing questions of how, what many transnational migration scholars call "economies of care," are produced and managed in the thick networks that form between sending and receiving communities (Pribilsky 2001; 2007).[1] Specifically addressing issues of fatherhood, masculinity, and the refashioning of marriages, I have tried to understand the complex relationships between transnational migration strategies, on one hand, and new family forms and practices on the other, probing these developments through ethnographic fieldwork in both rural indigenous communities of Ecuador's south-central highlands and New York City. My multisited research began in 1999 and extended to 2004, at which point I initiated an unrelated project in Peru.

However, while my research changed, I increasingly became a magnet for multiple solicitations by immigration attorneys in their defense of Ecuadorian clients fighting deportation by the Department of Homeland Security. Their clients, almost invariably minors, had migrated illegally to reunite with parents already in the US and had been detained during their passage north. While distinct in many of their details, taken together the cases reveal a patterned set of issues. All of them entail situations where children—ranging in age between of 11 and 17—came to live in the households of elderly grandparents (and sometimes aunts and uncles) when their own parents migrated abroad. Instead of care and support, these children found themselves both neglected and actively abused, both physically and mentally, by their new caretakers. The documented abuse takes many forms, including beatings, persistent threats of violence and intimidation, starvation, and general neglect with respect to meeting basic needs and school attendance; photographic evidence of burns, lacerations, and poorly healed bone fractures that occasionally accompany case files lend a visceral sense of the violence meted about by elderly kin. For the attorneys assigned to these cases, justification for asylum hinges on the argument that deportation will necessarily land youth back in dangerous, and potentially life-threatening, situations with little to no protection from the state or local authorities.

Remaking the Yanga Kawsay   65

Since 2003, I have provided background research and expert testimony on nine such cases and have consulted more informally on at least ten others.

A typical case that I have worked on would be that of Serifin.[2] When his parents migrated together to the US in 2009, he was just 11 years old and was left in the care of his maternal grandparents, along with his three-year-old sister, Jenifer. Together, they occupied a small and dilapidated three-room adobe-walled home with a large courtyard. His grandparents were in their late 60s, but their worn bodies suggested they were deeper into old age. According to Serifin, they "worked all the time" often to a point of exhaustion, tending to a few plots of land and pasturing animals. Cash income, while small, came from occasionally selling eggs, pigs, or sheep, yet mostly they lived by subsistence. Serifin always considered his grandfather to be an angry person, yet he attributed his grandfather's demeanor to heavy drinking. However, within months of living in his house, his grandfather turned particularly violent and told Serifin that he was not wanted in the house. If his grandfather were at the house he would swat Serifin's legs and arms with a thorny branch and aim rocks his way to make him flee. His grandmother, who also suffered abuse, worked in small ways to temper the tinderbox conditions by telling the grandfather that she required Serifin's help to watch his sister, Jenifer. When the grandfather was away, she would sneak him into the house for food. However, despite such gestures, she, too, was prone to abusive behavior, most of which she reserved for Jenifer. The girl would be tasked with impossible chores for a child her age and would be beaten when she fell short of expectations. Serifin tried his best to protect her but was often barred access. The children's only respite came when they could take refuge at an uncle's house nearby, where they could sleep for a day or two at a time, cramped in a room of four. The household, though, had little extra food to share, and the children would pass days without eating before they would be forced to return to their grandparents to beg. The last straw came when Serifin's grandfather tried to pin him down and burn him with hot coals. By then 14, and appreciably stronger than the old man, Serifin fended him off and escaped. Soon after, his parents, who had achieved some stability cobbling together a series of jobs in a Boston suburb, raised the funds, in cash and credit, to hire a migrant smuggler (*pasador*) to bring the children to the US. The trip passed relatively quickly, with only three weeks of difficult travel by boat, truck, and train before crossing the border by foot into Arizona. Then, the pair was apprehended in a delivery truck crammed with other migrants as they entered New York State. They were taken to Boston and temporarily reunited with their parents as they awaited their asylum hearing.

To be sure, well-crafted affidavits (from which I draw parts of Serifin's story) paint a potentially exaggerated picture of abuse, prepared for the purposes of approximating the US's strict criteria for asylum.[3] Yet, demographic studies conducted in Ecuador do point to profound changes in the composition of family and economies of care stemming from migration,

66   Jason Pribilsky

many with addressing the risk to children's well-being. Since the late 1990s, Ecuador has witnessed a steady rise in the number of children left behind by migrating parents. At the height of the out-migration boom, between 1991 and 2000, the figure climbed from an estimated 17,000 to more than 150,000 (INEC/SIISE 2000). In Cañar Province in the south-central region of the country, the site of my research, the situation has been particularly arresting, prompting the aid organization Plan International to dub the county (*cantón*) seat of Cañar, a "ciudad sin padres" (city without parents; Mediatools TV 2011). Overall demographic changes in the *cantón* of Cañar have been dramatic as a result of out-migration with a reduction in population by almost half in the past ten years; half of those residents (approximately 28,000) are minors (INEC/SIISE 2000). A comprehensive report issued by Ecuador's Observatorio de los Derechos de Niñez y Adolescencia (ODNA) in 2008 presents a particularly stark picture: children occupy 61 percent of households in Cañar province where one or both parents has migrated, a figure double the national average (ODNA 2008; see also Torres 2009). An adult older than 58 heads 48 percent of households affected by migration. In 24 percent of these cases, the household head is older than 65 (ODNA 2008). Qualitative data in the ONDA report detail conditions of chronic malnutrition, physical and mental abuse, and missed schooling for children living with elderly grandparents in their parents' absence (Camacho and Hernández 2008).

UNDERSTANDING ABUSE WITHIN TRANSNATIONAL LOGICS

This chapter seeks to make cultural sense of issues of abuse and neglect at the hands of Andean elders that sit uncomfortably in the context of Ecuadorian transnational migration. While children's experiences are the catalyst for this work, the central focus is the situation of the elderly and their experience of aging at the start of the twenty-first century. As I argue, paying close attention to the ways the life course of elderly Andeans has been affected by transnational migration provides a broad view to better understand larger family dynamics that have an impact on migrant households. Few researchers studying family dynamics in transnational migration globally have paid sustained attention to the deleterious effects of migration on children's lives (see Parreñas [2005] for a notable exception). And a similar picture emerges for studies of the elderly in transnational migration contexts, in their roles both as dependents in need of care and as caregivers. Most research tends to focus on various ways migrants attempt to unite with elderly parents in receiving countries with strong welfare states (Baldassar, Baldock and Wilding2007; Lie 2010; Powell and Cook 2009; Zhou 2012), addressing the lives of well-resourced migrants from cultural backgrounds with strong traditions of filial piety (Lamb 2002; Lan 2002). Ironically, while trenchant critiques of the political economic injustices of care economies are by now

Remaking the Yanga Kawsay   67

quite commonplace (Ehrenreich and Hochschild 2003; Yeates 2004) the ways, for instance, sending communities act as subsidized dependent care for migrant laborers in the global North—less critical attention is paid to the underside of actual care provided back home or issues of abandonment of elderly in sending communities (Vullnetari and King 2008 for a promising exception). In this chapter I aim to address this gap.

In doing so, I invariably must navigate through a number of thorny issues concerning Ecuador's migration politics, the ethics of the cross-cultural study of abuse, and the interpretations of family life within transnational migration studies. First, writing about domestic abuse at the hands of Andean elders in Ecuador's sending villages falls dangerously close to the kinds of racism and entrenched class positioning that pervade critiques of migration (Klaufus 2012; Miles 2004; Pribilsky 2007). In Ecuador, local journalists, public health officials, and policy makers have roundly derided rural sending communities, especially in indigenous regions of highland Ecuador, for what they see as the pathologies of migration. *Hogares disorganizadas*, or disrupted households, are faulted for a number of childhood and adolescent ailments said to be reflexes of migration, including gender confusion, poor school performance, and even suicide.[4] Scholars, including myself, have written against these portrayals by addressing the frequently paradoxical ways migration solidifies households, rural agricultural economies, and ethnic identification (Jokisch 1997; Miles 2004; Torres 2009). Yet the collective net result of this approach may be an overly optimistic image of migration.

In addition to the challenges for migration scholarship, making comprehensive the beliefs and behaviors surrounding child abuse and neglect at the hands of elders is difficult to square with anthropology's deep relativist underpinnings. Anthropologists researching child abuse often find themselves confronting an ethically difficult set of opposing choices (Korbin 1981; Scheper-Hughes 1987). On one hand, psychological or individual-based explanations of abuse behaviors can easily slip into "blaming the victim" and obfuscate significant sociocultural contexts of stress and vulnerability. Conversely, more culturally informed studies run the risk of excusing forms of abuse as acceptable "traditional" practices and fail to identify new fissures in social life. Deciding how to maneuver between these options can leave researchers avoiding the topic altogether. My approach draws on anthropologist Donna Goldstein's call for a "tough ethics of care" (1998: 391), a perspective that first privileges the social and cultural dimensions that shape abusive contexts and then asks how people derive meaning from this system rather than trying to solely theorize individual agents of abuse.

In highland Ecuador, this ethic, I argue, emerges out of a specific context shaped by the profound ways migration has altered village life in the rural Andes. I characterize this context as a set of "transnational logics" as a means of capturing the various ways migration deeply alters senses of time, space, family, money, and traditional forms of exchange for elderly family

68 Jason Pribilsky

members left behind, as well as profoundly informing their conduct and action. At the root of the "logics" of transnational migration are the logics of global capitalism and the political economy of labor, where controlled borders have ripple effects that sister together undocumented migrants in Manhattan cleaning bathrooms, doing factory work, and chopping vegetables in restaurants, with everyday decision making within rural Andean households. For elderly in charge of youth, these logics of transnationalism often confront them as *illogical* or at best confusing.[5] Some parents see money while others do not; some remittances trickle in some months, while others not; migrant parents promise to return and don't, while some migrant return surprisingly early—unable or unwilling to adopt the migrant's life. Similarly, as children's lives develop entirely in migration's shadow, the cultural gulf between youth and elders widens considerably. Differences over food preferences, cultural tastes, future outlooks, the loss of the Quichua language, and divergent values of what is considered meaningful work (*llankay*) split generations in a local context already tension filled by the absence of parents.

In what follows, I train my focus on elders themselves living in transnational migration sending communities of south-central Ecuadorian Andes, a population who has received little ethnographic attention in the region.[6] My arguments unfold in three parts. After a brief contextual overview of migration history and dynamics in highland Ecuador, I sketch an ethnographic picture of ageing in Andean communities, with stress placed on the issues of life course and age-related expectations. I address the experience of ageing in Cañar through the experience of the concept of *sami* and forms of exchange and obligation (*ayni*) forces that shape social relationships as well as physical and mental well-being. In the third part, addressing the impact of transnational migration on rural Cañari households, I focus on ways role expectations have been upended for the elderly through the example of one particular family's experience.

Given the crosscutting challenges of epistemology and the politics of representation inherent in this analysis, I echo anthropologist Nelson Graburn's sentiment regarding studying domestic abuse among the Inuit (1987: 211), namely, that this is "a paper I did not want to write because I would be happier if the data did not exist." Yet the data for this work do exist and are available from a number of sources. In addition to asylum cases noted earlier (which include reading court reports, affidavits, and my interview notes), I primarily draw from nearly ten years of ethnographic and collaborative research among indigenous Cañari communities in Ecuador's south-central Andes since 2005 on themes of health, family dynamics, and household economics. While my fieldwork has not engaged old age directly, the changing life circumstances of elderly Cañaris nonetheless figure prominently in my work as a population profoundly affected by migration. Additional data come from a handful of invaluable large-scale studies addressing migration and childhood (Camacho et al. 2009; ONDA 2008) and the

Remaking the Yanga Kawsay 69

status and needs of Ecuador's *tercera edad*, or elderly population (Freire et al. 2010; Waters and Gallegos 2012).

ECUADORIAN TRANSMIGRATION AND THE REORDERING OF HOUSEHOLDS

Distinct from the 1980s and 1990s, it is difficult to speak of international migration from Ecuador in terms of specific sending and receiving areas. Whereas the phenomenon of migration was once largely restricted to the country's south-central Andean highlands, Ecuador as a whole has become, if fitfully, a diasporic nation, with fully 10 percent of its citizenry living abroad and with large migrant populations in the urban United States, Spain and other countries of Western Europe. Between 1993 and 2006 alone, approximately 900,000 people left Ecuador without returning, a figure that represents almost 8 percent of the total population of the country and 20 percent of its economically active population according to the country's 2001 census (Herrera 2008; see also Jokisch and Pribilsky 2002).[7] There is also no single demographic profile of migrants. While young men constituted the original rank and file of migrants, a wholesale "feminization" of migration has occurred over the past decade with the large-scale migration of women, largely to Spain (Boccagni 2013; Herrera 2013).

The view presented here, then, is partial one, focused on the south-central province of Cañar, Ecuador's first major migrant-sending region (Jokisch 1997; Jokisch and Pribilsky 2002). Despite the influx of remittances and a landscape dotted with new homes paid for by migrants abroad, Cañar remains one of Ecuador's poorest regions (INEC 2012). Rural indigenous households, many of them originally constituted on hacienda lands, can be characterized as "semiproletariatized," whereby family units, nucleated around a parental unit and some extended family, secure their livelihood from a combination of subsistence farming (mainly of corn, potatoes, beans, and barley), and piecemeal day labor (*jornada*). Aside from a fortunate small group of men who find work as local truck transport drivers, and a handful of women who own small stores selling basic groceries, alcohol, and medicines, few villagers secure steady work outside their home communities (Torres 2009).

As in many rural villages throughout the Ecuadorian sierra, intensive international migration from Cañar has suspended rural households between the market and subsistence economy. Beginning in the mid-1980s, as the pace of migration accelerated substantially, a pattern of transnationalization of familial arrangements began to predominate (Kyle 2000; Miles 2004; Pribilsky 2007). Typically, men initially left their households, in a preferred pattern of first getting married and not infrequently having a child. If successful abroad, many migrant men would seek to establish an independent household for their family through the purchase of land

70   *Jason Pribilsky*

or the construction of a home in their home community, with the eventual plan of returning to Ecuador. Such a base allowed men to establish households apart from their natal kin and to consolidate remittances within their newly formed nuclear household (Pribilsky 2007: 147–54). However, in the wake of financial crisis, dollarization of the Ecuadorian economy in 2000, and increased securitization and militarization of border enforcement post-9/11, many households found this model increasingly untenable, prompting women to begin leaving Ecuador as well.[8] In many cases, women joined already established husbands with employment connections and, in the case of Western European destinations, found opportunities in the feminized sectors of child care and domestic labor (Bertoli, Moraga, and Ortega 2011; Herrera 2013).

By 2008, many of the transnational migrant households I had been tracking for almost a decade were beginning to experience diminishing returns on their migration investment. Emotional toll aside, rising smuggling costs, high interest rates on informal loans to pay for smuggling, and global economic crises all served to upend the once sure-fire model driven by male migration. "No vale como antes" (It doesn't pay like it used to) was a common refrain from within these households. Husbands and wives both migrating to redouble their chances of success abroad, either at the same time or staggered, invariably meant that children would need to be left in charge of relatives, mostly grandparents. Often seen as a temporary solution (as migrants often either believe they will stay for a short time or will earn enough money to have their child united with them), many arrangements become indefinite affairs. Of the core fifteen households constituted in this way that I have followed, the average age of children living without their parents is 13, a modest step from adulthood. For their part, children, like parents and grandparents, eventually come to find a normalcy in the separation. Young children old enough to recognize their parents' departure are often lied to—told that their parents are only leaving the village for a few days to purchase a car or to visit a doctor. As children age and learn the truth, their own lives become intimately transnational despite the fact that they themselves may never migrate. Aided by cellphones and video-calling applications such as Skype and FaceTime, children interact with their parents only distally—cultivated by the sending and receiving of gifts and remittances (Leifsen and Tymczuk 2012; Pribilsky 2007; Rae-Espinoza 2011). In the everyday, kids interact with a different world separated not only by distances but by generations as well.

AGING IN THE TRANSNATIONAL ANDES: THE UNRAVELING OF OBLIGATION

Elderly populations form a slight demographic in Ecuador (approximately 6 percent of the country is older than 65 years of age), and only scant research has been directed their way (de Vos 1998). Likewise, within the highland regions of Ecuador, Peru, and Bolivia, home to sizable Quechua and Aymara-speaking populations, few studies on ageing in Andean communities exist[9]. It is, then, with only slight exaggeration, true to say that a good starting place is the sixteenth-century writer and illustrator Guaman Poma de Ayala and his nearly 1,200-page protest letter-cum-ethnography addressed to King Phillip III of Spain. Amid details of life under the Inca and Spanish conquests, Guaman Poma describes the working lives, rights, and responsibilities of different age grades. In one particular drawing of four age grades, Poma details how age-related identities were closely matched with types of work and people's capacities. Of the eldest group, he wrote,

> Being so ancient, they were not expected to do much more than eat and sleep . . . They were greatly respected and honored. Value was attached to their influence over the young, their advice and capacity to hand down the knowledge of religion with their little remaining understanding. They were clothed free of charge and allowed to have their own garden plots.[10]

While certainly much has changed in the organization of old age in the Andes since this time, evoking Poma's description captures two enduring feature of the modern condition: (1) a slow unraveling of the obligations, ties, and commitments elderly members have to society and (2) a general level of elevated honor and respect despite their lack of societal contributions. In Cañar, as throughout the Andes, subsistence farming is backbreaking work. As people age, they are slowly relieved of this labor. Older people still tend to work—managing a few sheep or continuing to pasture a cow, yet their tasks are not critical to generating food supplies; the important tasks of sowing or harvesting are never expected of old people.

As they age, elders' status becomes one largely related to symbolic honor. They are donned with the honorific titles *tayta* (father)/*mama* (mother), although the labels' meaning extends beyond simple kinship descriptors. When pressed, Cañari will describe these terms as reserved only for *ñaupa yayacuna* (very respected elders). If elders' minds and faculties sustain during aging, distinctive community members also may be elevated to the status of "wise one" (*amauta*), revered for their possession of special knowledge. In Cañar, *amautakuna* typically command a mastery of ancestral medicinal plants and their uses or possess extensive knowledge and (interpretation of) past historical conditions.[11] Throughout the region, particularly distinguished senior men recount history through singing the *jahuay*, or harvest song form performed at key religious holidays (Corpus Christi in particular). In times of the hacienda, the lilting, infectious rhythm of the *jahuay*, carried across the manorial field, served to revitalize worn-out hacienda workers exhausted by days of harvest.

72 Jason Pribilsky

Despite such reverence for the elderly in Cañar, I have often been taken aback by the frequent reference I have heard to aged Cañari as *abandonados*, or "abandoned ones." As one Cañari friend described matter-of-factly during a discussion about his 85-plus-year-old father, "Old people [*ancianos*] are abandoned by society, their family, and their former lives. Their last days are about separation, moving away, and leaving this world." Indeed, elderly Cañari often seem placed at a distance from the goings on around them. Within households, old people will routinely occupy their own houses (or more realistically, huts, or *chozas*) separate from their adult children, in both single and married capacities. They will also spend much of their time alone, including taking meals. In my field experiences, aside from very special occasions (baptisms, weddings, house raisings), elderly are not typically and automatically included in events.

Becoming *abandonados*, however, is not generally perceived in negative terms but is rather seen as a natural, if often difficult, transition from the world. For many elderly, almost invariably men, this state of being "abandoned" is frequently accompanied by heavy consumption of cheap contraband sugarcane liquor (*puro*). It is a common scene in a household compound to find an elderly man alone, hopelessly sodden without a clear demarcation between sober and inebriated states, while others are off at school or work. For those willing to stop and talk, conversations often unfold into fascinating monologues where personal and community histories are remembered, recounted, and interpreted. For the speaker, the act can be tremendously emotional, and perhaps cathartic, and frequently pulls him into deep grief (*dolientes*) accompanied by spontaneously breaking down and sobbing. Typical socially acceptable drinking, by contrast to this scene, is predominately an act heavily marked by sociality and conviviality and rarely takes a companionless form (Pribilsky 2007: 226–230; Sánchez-Parga 1997). However, not all solitary drinking commands respect. In contrast, a *viejo chumado* (literally an "old drunk") derisively labels an elderly person whose constant intoxication speaks to a wasted and lazy life—someone who has presumably never earned their alcohol. Elderly Cañari whose physical bodies are considered debilitated (*tullyaska*) and no longer allow them to carry out productive work may find solace in drinking without shame or moral rebuke. Such actions, while alarming to outsiders, can also often go uncontested by all around. To be sure, many of my interlocutors considered this type of imbibing to be a necessary condition for unraveling the bonds of obligation to family and other close community members.

When I would worriedly inquire with my Cañari informants about their persistently drunken elderly relatives, I would often be told, assuredly, that old persons drink to remember in a process that allows them to give up pieces of their lives, to review their pasts, and take stock in relationships.[12] This giving up was also repeatedly framed to me as a necessary social practice to prepare for death. Two key terms frame this thinking. Many people, young and old, spoke of giving up (*liquidando*) as a natural process

Remaking the Yanga Kawsay   73

of the unraveling of the bonds of obligation, which they generally glossed using the exchange term *ayni*. While denoting specific kinds of exchange elsewhere in the Andes (see, e.g., Mayer 2002), *ayni* in Cañari thought and speech contains a nested set of multivalent meanings including "connection," "obligation," and "reciprocity." Holding together these bonds and ensuring the flow and circulation of "things" in exchange—goods, labor, even thoughts—is provided for by the force of *sami* or, as phrased in Spanish, *energía*. In Cañari Quichua, *sami* (and the closely related term *camay*, or "disposition") are frequently translated as "luck" or "fortune" as characteristics of one's being (Cordero 1992; see also Urbano 1993). To possess *sami* is to live a right and healthy life (*sumak kawsay*), free of forces or predispositions that can cause sickness.[13] Yet, *sami* is not a vague *mana*-like force that can be tapped into at will. *Energías*, I have often been reminded, must be generated and fostered by good actions, as well as by good thoughts. (Strong emotions such as jealousy and anger can bring a pollution of *sami* and causing one ill health, perhaps because they focus energies inward). To possess *sami*, paradoxically, is to keep it in flow (Allen 2002).

The cultivation of *sami* and *energías* in old age is a positive, welcomed force, yet at the same time can be painful and problematic. To ensure the healthy flow of *sami*, bonds of *ayni* must be attended to as one ages. As people age, the accumulation of debts—usually in the form of reciprocal labor in farming, irrigation canal cleaning, and house building—become increasingly hard to pay back and older people tend to accumulate more than they can provide. The burden of relationships, I have been repeatedly told, must "liquefy themselves" (*se liquida*) or else death may bring unwanted misfortunes (*llaquicuna*) for one's soul (*alma*) (Allen 2002). Like the few possessions that occupy one's life, thick bonds of obligation should go away at death. The verb *liquidar*, frequently used by people in Cañar to describe the burdens at the end of life, hints at the myriad ways the stresses of old age entangle powerful meanings of impending death, the settling of debts, and the squaring off of personal commitments formed through reciprocal relationships over time. *Liquidar* simultaneously means to cancel a debt and to wind up a transaction (such as a business deal), as well as to eliminate or even kill. Therefore, to prepare for one's degeneration and death is an inherently social process.

One of the new transnational logics of migration is the reconfiguration of life courses in Cañar. As many older persons settle into a life that entails loosening the thick bonds of reciprocity, of accepting a life with an unproductive body (often framed as "decay," *decaimiento*; Waters and Gallegos 2012), they have been thrust into a new course as the caregivers of their children's children. Traditional transformations of role expectations where adult children are to take care of aged parents have been augmented as grandparents have been enlisted to subsidize the child-care needs of migrants abroad. While this situation does not inherently breed conflict and tension, in the final section of this chapter I explore some of unintended consequences that

74 Jason Pribilsky

accompany this new logic, including the rise of child abuse and neglect as rural households are further upended by the necessities of transnational migration.

THE WORK OF TWO GENERATIONS: ELDERS AS CAREGIVERS[14]

In Cañar, older people in their own words, with a mix of resolve and self-deprecation, frequently label their age set as the *yanga kawsay* or, in the mixed Quichuaized Spanish of the region, the *yanga vida*. Colloredo-Mannsfeld (1999) has described the ubiquity of the term's use in Ecuador's northern Andes as a sign of class distinction and self-deprecation whereby indigenous peoples note how agricultural lives often prove "fruitless" as evidenced by the few material rewards acquired after years of toil. Among older Cañari I have known, *yanga kawsay* means something slightly different, often used to express a life at the end of its rope, where one is of little utility to family and community. For older Cañari, who find themselves in charge of grandchildren when their own children migrate, the experience of *yanga kawsay* can be particularly difficult, unsettling, and anathema to their standard life course. One elderly woman in Cañar described the confusion she felt when she found herself parenting three of her daughter's children when her daughter and son-in-law migrated to Spain:

> When they first left, it was easy and I had help from other relatives, but overtime it's only me and my husband to watch over these kids. What kind of life is this? What use are we? This is not the course our lives were to take!

What constitutes an ideal life course in Cañar and the Ecuadorian Andes, as expressed in this quote, cannot be detached from the historic ways new households have been formed (Weismantel 1989) and expectations elderly bring to their new experiences. Invariably in the Ecuadorian Andes, few adults are accorded adult status, for instance, until they form their own autonomous households. Elderly status, in contrast, is marked by the unraveling of obligations within an unproductive household. What, however, constitutes a household within a transnational migration frame and what is the natural evolution of such a household? As already mentioned, during earlier historical moments of migration when newly married men were the primary sojourners, the creation of new households followed a more or less clear trajectory. Once abroad and generating sufficient revenue to remit, a couple's first goal would be to build a house in an effort of establishing autonomy from their natal kin. Beyond the benefit of accelerating the pace of how households have traditionally been formed, the model served an important secondary function of consolidating remittances within new nuclear households anchored by women. While migrants abroad are likely to help aging

Remaking the Yanga Kawsay 75

parents, this is not compulsory within the local rules of kinship. In my experience, migrant children abroad are unlikely to send regular remittances to parents in Cañar yet willingly provide financial help in cases of dire need, such as paying for medical treatments, or through the purchase of expensive ticket items such as refrigerators, televisions, and electric showers that can lessen the hardships of rural life. In the words of one male return migrant, "[C]hildren must respect their parents in old age, but that respect does not often include money. When I was abroad [in Spain], I would occasionally send my parents money, but they did not expect it. They only asked in times of dire need and then only rarely."

The assumption of the duties of caring for children, however, both the obligation migrant children have to their parents, and the obligation grandparents have to their grandchildren become unclear. An overarching tension exists as couples abroad juggle their limited options for getting ahead with obligations to family in sending communities. Without a mechanism to easily form a new household back in their home communities, young migrant couples weigh a host of options. Some work to save money for an eventual return to Ecuador; others seek to accelerate the process by investing in their home communities as much as possible in land, animals, and, in some cases, small-business operations that they hope to assume once they return. And, others, and perhaps all migrants at some point, contemplate permanent lives abroad. In this case, they may direct much of their energies and financial resources to bringing their children still in Ecuador to their destination. For migrants abroad, the situation is one of limbo as they try to figure out how best to maximize their migration decisions. Alba, a mother of three, living in Queens, New York, described her thinking this way:

> I am here working, but my mind is always back in Ecuador. Will I go back? I miss my children so badly. Or can I get them here with me somehow? Then we may never go home and my parents will die before I can say good-bye.

Whatever approach is taken—and often it can be a combination of all of them—the effect on elderly is usually one of tension. A typical situation can be illuminated by highlighting the experiences of an elderly couple I know well, both in their late seventies. Alejandro and Maria Elena have three children, two sons living abroad in Spain (José Miguel) and Queens, New York (Alberto, age 35), respectively. Their third child, a daughter (Vincente, age 25) lives with an aunt in the city of Cuenca, two hours away by bus. While José Miguel migrated alone to Spain, Alberto left with his wife Carmen, leaving their three children (ages 7, 9, and 11) in the care of Alejandro and Maria Elena. The arrangement, as with Maria Elena, was a mutual one, and when I asked how the decision to foster the children came about, I was met with a blank stare. It was an obvious choice and an obligation.

76 Jason Pribilsky

Yet, like many households stretched by migration, the consequences of the move were unforeseen. More of an immediate burden than three additional mouths to feed was the loss of labor felt when the adult children migrated. Alejandro and Maria Elena own almost six acres of land, an unusually large landholding in a region historically defined by small plots (Kyle 2000). On their plots, they grow most of their own food but also trade or sell portions of their potato harvests to obtain other goods. While potatoes are a lucrative commodity and have a high exchange value, the labor and farm inputs (pesticides and fertilizers) make planting almost prohibitive without significant (unpaid) labor. Over time, pinched by cost, Alejandro and Maria Elena switched to monocropping corn, a much less labor-intensive crop, but also one with a lower exchange value. Taking care of children on top of new farming burdens can easily leave elderly parents resentful, especially if remittances from abroad are not forthcoming. No longer are they *abandonados*, yet what their new status entails is unclear.

Part of this lack of clarity resides with the ways new transnational logics have disrupted, both temporally and spatially, practices of exchange and inheritance long in place in the Andes. In the southern Ecuadorian Andes, bilateral kinship and parallel descent are flexible except with respect to inheritance of land and other forms of wealth which spouses receive and retain separately from their respective sides of family (Belote and Belote 1977; Brownrigg 1971; Muñoz Bernand 1996). While adult children have few strict obligations to parents, traditionally the necessity of acquiring land through inheritance from parents strengthened bonds between generations. Moreover, passing inheritance to children provided one of the key ways affective *ayni* bonds could be liquidated late in life. Dividing inheritances (which typically happens prior to death) is often fraught with tensions and anxieties, especially when resources are few and children are many.[15] In Cañar, transnational migration has exacerbated this process by temporally stretching the process. Without the physical help of adult children, elderly parents remain in need of land much longer to care for themselves and often not in a place to bequeath land on the schedules of aging as they once did. Conversely, the value of land in the eyes of adult children functioning within the logics of transnationalism is often fraught with ambiguity. For adult children abroad, inheritance of land either may come too late in the course of their life planning or may altogether be of no value as they stronger consider settling permanently abroad. In either case, a fundamental form of reciprocal obligation—parents to adult children, and vice versa—has been upset by migration. In Alejandro and Maria Elena's household, tensions often focused less on the value of inheritance and more on the issue of remittances. While the elderly couple did not expect to receive direct compensation for taking care of children, because migration put pressures on their own household's finances, resentments began to emerge. In many cases, these resentments take as their focal point the children left behind.

Remaking the Yanga Kawsay   77

Before detailing some of the relational aspects between elderly Cañaris and their grandchildren, it is important to note how these relationships are clarified within local kinship systems. A critical starting point is perhaps obvious, yet crucial: bonds of consanguineal kinship ties that might otherwise bind youth and their grandparents do not predict affective relationships within transnational households. Assuming the charge of caring for grandchildren does not presume a certain quality of relationship. Moreover, Christine Ho's (1993) important concept of the "internationalization of kinship" to describe ways regular forms of care and nourishment replicate themselves despite time and space constraints, as well as who is doing the actual caring, does not adequately capture the situation at hand. In the Andes, practices of "child circulation" and adoption, whereby children are placed within childless households and largely accepted as if they were blood relations are well documented (Leinaweaver 2008; Weismantel 1995). By contrast, taking in children in elderly households entails a different relationship form. Language again is key to deciphering the core texture of these relationships. Many elderly Cañari I have interviewed describe their grandchildren not as grandchildren (*nietos*), or as *their* children, but more often as *hijos de crianza* (children by raising or foster children) and describe themselves as *encargados* (those in charge). The use of such terms, however, arguably does not signal a lack of affection toward children, and indeed, in my observations, levels of affection run a continuum from unconditional love to neglect. Rather, these categories say more about the ambiguities of the new transnational logic of care and the mismatched obligations and expectations of elders and youth. In migrant households, the main role for older people—to serve as a source of knowledge (as in the case of the honorable position of *amauta*)—has been replaced by one of caregiving.

At a very immediate level, stark age differences leave rural youth and their elderly caregivers with little in common. The experiences of Serifín and Jenifer that opened this chapter are similar to many in Cañar, where a generational gulf has been only widened through the transnationalization of rural highland households. Elderly Cañari often complain that children do not speak Quichua (or at least are reluctant to do so), know little about and take only scant interest in farming, and are generally uninterested in their community's past (King and Haboud 2011). An obvious, though potent, source of conflict can also be seen in changing food preferences. Cañar, like many areas deeply affected by migration and buoyed by remittances, is experiencing a new wave of "diet delocalization," a process by which traditional food sources, typically corn, potatoes, and grains grown for subsistence, have been replaced by purchased commodities with lesser nutritional value (Karnes 2008; Leatherman 1994). While a process fueled by migration, but not ultimately caused by it, elders disdainfully label new foods as *comida chatarra* (junk food) and complain that indigenous foodways have gone the way of *los blancos* (white-identified Ecuadorians).

78 Jason Pribilsky

Tensions over food cut deeper than the surface issues of fickle children with too many food choices. Many households involved in migration, whether they are headed by elders with grandchildren or by single women whose husbands have migrated, undergo a shift in their agricultural regimes (Jokisch 1997). As mentioned earlier, production of a wide variety of crops (including potatoes, wheat, barley, and quinoa), all of which can require costly inputs of fertilizers and pesticides and significant labor needs for weeding and harvesting, is often jettisoned for lower-risk, less-cost-intensive corn (*maíz*). Corn has a modest trade value, it cannot be a staple crop, and households are often compelled, by both convenience and taste, to purchase processes carbohydrates, mostly packaged noodles (*fideos*) and polished rice. While this process has only minimally to do with children's taste, the discourse within elder-headed households often truncates the problem in a way that mystifies the larger structural forces at work. Parents abroad, I was often told, spoil children through their encouragement of "white food" and, as a consequence, devalue traditional *grano* (grain) diets. As a tangible sign of change, children easily become the symbol for what is wrong with changing Cañari foodways.

Food offers just one tangible focal point to direct tensions concerning new transnational logics. More generally, grandparents tacitly "in charge" of youth are often excluded from the transnational flows of knowledge that bind sending and receiving communities. Most elderly lack proficiency in the preferred communication technologies (cell phones that seem to require constant recharging and purchased minutes, Skype that requires navigating around an Internet café) and are dependent on youth to communicate with their own children. Cañari youth with little in the way of disposable income often find a way to own a cell phone and the ability to communicate regularly with their parents. In some cases, a child's phone and a bank of numbers may be the only way to get a hold of a migrant relative abroad. This situation causes confusion as to the proper channels of communication and the role of grandparents as primary caregivers. Alejandro shared with me his frustration with feeling excluded from the discussions between his grandchildren and his own son. He felt "tricked" when the children would appear with new clothes or other gifts obviously sent from abroad. "I wasn't jealous," he explained, "but I did not know my role. I grew angry—I am the parent now or what?" While Alejandro's anger never spilled over into violence directed at the children (to the best of my knowledge), his telling of the situation revealed a palpable frustration and a lack of control.

This issue can grow most pronounced with respect to remittances. If the new care relationships confuse, the fractious politics of migration add fuel to the fire. In many cases, elderly caregivers are one degree removed from the negotiations and decision-making that goes on between rural households and migrants abroad. In the 15 interviews I conducted with elderly caregivers, I found only one household that actually knew about the earnings of their migrant children. In all other cases, elderly caregivers had no idea of amount of remittances that were being sent back to care for children. In most cases, remittances were funneled to the migrant's sibling or cousin, even to neighbors—usually someone of their own generation.

CONCLUSION

This chapter, which began with the puzzle of child abuse afflicted by elderly caregivers, in the end says very little about actual acts of domestic violence. Indeed, my experience in Cañar is similar to how anthropologist Penelope Harvey describes sexual violence in the Peruvian highlands: "highly visible yet strangely inaccessible" (1994: 67). Visitors to the Andes, ethnographers included, often make passing reference to the public hitting of children and all forms of neglect, from young children wielding machetes to kids being left for long periods without supervision. But what is known of the logics behind abuse or why it takes the forms it does remains murky. Grandparents falter in the difficult task of raising grandchildren for a host of reasons both individual and structural. Instead of detailing cases of abuse from court reports, of which little can be said of the agency of perpetrators, I have instead focused on the contexts of abuse in what I have called transnational logics of family life. As a researcher, I have cast my lot with the latter by focusing on what Deborah Boehm and her colleagues (2011) characterize as the "everyday ruptures" of living transnationally. These ruptures, often felt as new demands placed on elderly, are quotidian and trivial in the moment: disputes over food preferences, feeling left out of the loop of knowledge, a child's refusal to speak Quichua. Yet, they do not arise in a vacuum. Instead, they occur within what might be profitably termed "incongruent life courses"—an acknowledgment of the ways transnational migration has both altered the demographic profile of rural communities in Ecuador's migrant sending regions as well as the life trajectories of its generations. In Cañar, the specifics of culture matter including powerful ideas about well-being (*sumac kawsay*), the importance of the circulation of *sami*, and the intimate link between social obligation and one's emotional and physical health. Migration pulls Cañari youth outward even if they do not physically migrate, while the elderly in their recruitment at the end of their life course forces them to assume new duties as caregivers, pulling them into the flows of village life at a time where obligations should be liquidating.

Last, singularly focusing on cultural factors should not mean we miss the larger forces at play that structure migrant livelihoods and constrict agency. A final way to understand child abuse in these contexts is to see it not as aberration, but as a harsh by-product of the political economy of transnational migration. In her ethnographic work on everyday violence in Brazilian favelas, Goldstein (1998) suggests that individual cases of abuse should be labeled *social abuse* since they are structurally produced. Extreme conditions of inequality, poverty, and the state exercise of violence perpetrate

80   Jason Pribilsky

abuses on the poor and vulnerable that, in turn, shape a domestic culture of violence. While migrant sending communities are not favelas, especially with respect to presences of everyday violence, many of the households are sites of grinding poverty where conditions of life make family separation a necessary part of getting by. It may well be profitable to consider abuse as socially produced yet individually executed, shaped by the logics of transnationalism. Suspending notions of North American bourgeois childhood and abhorrence of abuse, the abuse exacted by grandparent may be seen as a kind of harsh discipline emerging at a time when elders feel relatively powerless.

NOTES

1   On uses of the economies of care, see Leinaweaver (2010), Parreñas (2005), and Yeates (2005).

2   The name Serifin, and all additional names in this chapter, are pseudonyms. I have also changed minor details in this brief case to further obscure the identities of those discussed.

3   See Good (2007) for a useful overview of issues and ethics concerning anthropological expertise in courtrooms, especially with respect to asylum cases.

4   For a discussion of this critique, see Pribilsky (2001).

5   My use of the term *logics* draws from Fischer (2001: 13) on the cultural logics of globalization in Mayan Guatemala: "Cultural logics [give] old forms new and meaning and . . . new forms old meaning."

6   In Peru, this needed kind of research is well underway, yet the findings only partially speak to the Ecuadorian context. See, for example, Leinaweaver (2008, 2010) and de Bruine et al. (2013).

7   Because of space constraints, I have not included a discussion of the process of migration, both largely undocumented migration to the US and short term visa holders to Spain. See Pribilsky (2007: 160–73) for details of migrant smuggling practices to the US and the important work of Ramírez and Álvarez (2009) on "transit migration."

8   See Gerlach (2003) for a history of recent economic gyrations in Ecuador.

9   There are few exceptions to this claim, yet none comprehensively focus on old age: Barnett (1986), Holmberg (1961), Loughran (1988), Mitchell (1994), and Shenk and Mahon (2009). Leinaweaver's (2008, 2010) work on child circulation in the Peruvian Andes, and transnationally (with Spain) represents the most comprehensive work on aging in the Andes to date.

10   This translation comes from Dilke's (1978).

11   The title of *amauta* in the Ecuadorian Andes is, in practice, rarely bestowed on old people and its contemporary use arguably speaks more to revitalization efforts within the indigenous movement concerning "rescuing" autochthonous knowledge than an enduring tradition.

12   The link between intoxication and the evocation of memory, as opposed to Euro-American motivations of drinking to forget, has a long history in the Andes (Bray 2008).

13   This is a general utilization of this term, overlapping yet distinct from its more recent politicized connotations within Ecuador's indigenous political sphere (Radcliffe 2012).

Remaking the Yanga Kawsay   81

14 This subheading is taken from Sando (1986), whose work addresses similar effects of rural–urban migration on elderly in rural Taiwan.
15 The film *The Spirit Possession of Alejandro Mamani* poignantly captures this tension in a farming community in Bolivia (Smith 1974).

REFERENCES

Allen, Catherine (2002) [1988]: *The Hold Life Has. Coca and Cultural Identity in an Andean Community.* Washington, DC: Smithsonian Institution Press.
Baldassar, Loretta/Wilding, Raelene/Baldock, Cora (2007): *Families Caring Across Borders. Migration, Ageing and Transnational Caregiving.* Basingstoke: Palgrave Macmillan.
Barnett, Elyse Ann (1986): *Perceptions of Menopause: Importance of Role Satisfaction in a Peruvian Town.* Doctoral Dissertation, Department of Anthropology. Stanford University, Stanford.
Belote, Jim/Belote, Linda (1977): The Limits of Obligation in Saraguro Kinship. In: Bolton, Ralph/ Mayer, Enrique (eds.): *Andean Kinship and Marriage.* Washington, DC: American Anthropological Association, pp. 106–116.
Bertoli, Simone/Moraga, Jesús Fernández-Huertas/Ortega, Francesca (2011): Immigration Policies and the Ecuadorian Exodus. In: *The World Bank Economic Review* 25, 1, pp. 57–76.
Boccagni, Paolo (2013): Migration and the Family Transformations It 'Leaves Behind': A Critical View from Ecuador. In: *The Latin Americanist* 57, 4, pp. 3–24.
Boehm, Deborah A./Hess, Julia Meredith/Coe, Cati/Rae-Espinoza, Heather/Reynolds, Rachel R. (2011): Introduction. Children, Youth, and the Everyday Ruptures of Migration. In: Coe, Catie/Reynolds, Rachel R./Boehm, Deborah A./Hess, Julia Meredith/Rae-Espinoza, Heather (eds.): *Everyday Ruptures. Children, Youth and Migration in Global Perspective.* Nashville: Vanderbilt University Press, pp. 1–22.
Bray, Tamara (2008): The Role of Chicha in Inca State Expansion. In: Jennings, Justin/Bowser, Brenda J. (eds.): *Drink, Power, and Society in the Andes.* Gainesville: University of Florida Press, pp. 108–132.
Brownrigg, Leslie (1971) *Cañari Kinship Variations.* Paper presented at the 70th Annual Meeting of the American Anthropological Association, New York City.
Camacho Zambrano, Gloria/Basante, Kattya Hernández (2008): Niñez y migración en el Ecuador : diagnóstico de situación. Quito: UNICEF/CEPLAES/INFFA.
Camacho Zambrano, Gloria/Basante, Kattya Hernández (eds.) (2009): *Miradas transnacionales: visions de la migración ecuatoriana desde España y Ecuador.* Quito: Centro de Planificación y Estudios Sociales (CEPLAES)/SENAMI.
Colloredo-Mansfeld, Rudi (1999): *The Native Leisure Class. Consumption and Cultural Creativity in the Andes.* Chicago: The University of Chicago Press.
Cordero, Luis (1992) [1895]: *Diccionario Quichua-Castellano y Castello-Quichua.* Quito: Corporación Editora Nacional.
de Bruine, Eva/Hordijk, Michaela/Tamagno, Carla/Arimborgo, Yanina Sánchez (2013): Living Between Multiple Sites. Transnational Family Relations from the Perspective of Elderly Non-Migrants in Junín, Peru. In: *Journal of Ethnic and Migration Studies* 39, 3, pp. 483–500.
De Vos, Susan (1998) Regional Differences in Living Arrangements among the Elderly in Ecuador. In: *Journal of Cross Cultural Gerontology* 13, pp. 1–20.
Dilke, Christopher Wentworth (1978): *Letter to a King. A Peruvian Chief's Account of Life Under the Incas and Spanish Rule.* Boston: E. P. Dutton.

82   Jason Pribilsky

Ehrenreich, Barbara/Hochschild, Arlie Russell (2003): Introduction. In: Ehrenreich, Barbara/Hochschild, Arlie Russell (eds.): Global *Women. Nannies, Maids, and Sex Workers in a New Economy.* New York: Metropolitan Books, pp. 1–14.

Fischer, Edward F. (2001): *Cultural Logics and Global Economies. Maya Identity in Thought and Practice.* Austin: University of Texas Press.

Freire, W. B./Rojas, E./Pazmiño, L./Fornasini, M./Tito, S./Buendía, P./Waters, W. F./ Salinas, J./Álvarez, P. (2010): *Encuesta de Salud, Bienestar y Envejecimiento 2009.* Aliméntate Ecuador/USFQ. Quito Ecuador.

Gerlach, Allen (2003): Indians, Oil, and Politics: A Recent History of Ecuador (Latin American Silhouettes). Wilmington: Scholarly Resources Inc.

Good, Anthony. (2007): *Anthropology and Expertise in the Asylum Courts.* London/New York: Routledge.

Goldstein, Donna M. (1998): Nothing Bad Intended. Child Discipline, Punishment, and Survival in a Shantytown in Rio de Janeiro, Brazil. In: Scheper-Hughes, Nancy/Sargent, Carolyn (eds.): *Small Wars. The Cultural Politics of Childhood.* Berkeley: University of California Press, pp. 389–415.

Graburn, Nelson H. H. (1987): Severe Child Abuse Among the Canadian Inuit. In: Scheper-Hughes, Nancy (ed.): *Child Survival.* Dordrecht: D. Reidl, pp. 211–225.

Harvey, Penelope (1994): Domestic Violence in the Peruvian Andes. In: Harvey, Penelope and Gow, Peter (eds.): *Sex and Violence. Issues in Representation and Experience.* London/New York: Routledge, pp. 66–89.

Herrera Mosquera, Gioconda (2008): *Migration and Trends in the Field of Social Policy in Ecuador, 1990–2005.* Policy Paper. Rome: CESPI.

Hererra Mosquera, Gioconda (2013): *"Lejos de tus pupilas": familias transnacionales, cuidados y desigualdad social en Ecuador.* Quito: FLACSO-Ecuador/ONU Mujeres.

Ho, Christine (1993): The Internationalization of Kinship and the Feminization of Caribbean Migration: The Case of Afro-Trinidadian Immigrants in Los Angeles. In: *Human Organization* 52, 1, pp. 32–40.

Holmberg, Allan R. (1961): Age in the Andes. In: Watson Kleemeier, Robert (ed.): *Aging and Leisure.* New York: Oxford University Press, pp. 86–90.

INEC (Instituto Nacional de Estadísticas y Censos) (2012): *Consejo provincial del Cañar. Azogues, Cañar, Ecuador: Instituto Nacional de Estadísticas y Censos.* http://www.hcpcanargov.ec/hcpc_ccanar.asp, accessed September 2013.

INEC (Instituto Nacional de Estadísticas y Censos)/Sistema Integrado de Indicadores Sociales del Ecuador (SIISE)/Programa Nuestro Niños, Instituto Nacional del Niño y Familia/Centro de Estudios de Población y Desarrollo (EMEDINHO): (2000): *Encuesta de Medición De Indicadores De La Niñez y Los Hogares.* Quito: Instituto Nacional de Estadística y Censo.

Jokisch, Brad D. (1997): Migration and Agricultural Change: The Case of Smallholder Agriculture in Highland Ecuador. In: *Human Ecology* 3, 4, pp. 523–550.

Jokisch, Brad D./Pribilsky, Jason (2002): The Panic to Leave: Economic Crisis and the "New Emigration" from Ecuador. In: *International Migration* 40, 4, pp. 75–102.

Karnes, Daniel A. (2008): *To Grow or to Buy: Food Staples and Cultural Identity in the Southern Ecuadorian Andes.* MA Thesis. Department of Anthropology, Oregon State University, Corvallis, Oregon.

King, Kendall A./Haboud, Marleen (2011): International Migration and Quichua Language Shift in the Ecuadorian Andes. In: McCarty, Teresa (ed.): *Ethnography and Language Policy.* London/New York: Routledge, pp. 139–159.

Klaufus, Christien (2012): *Urban Residence. Housing and Social Transformations in Globalizing Ecuador.* Oxford /New York: Berghahn Books.

Korbin, Jill (ed.) (1981): *Child Abuse and Neglect. Cross-Cultural Perspectives.* Berkeley: University of California Press.

Kyle, David (2000): *Transnational Peasants. Migrations, Networks, and Ethnicity in Andean Ecuador.* Baltimore: Johns Hopkins University Press.

Lamb, Sarah (2002): Intimacy in a Transnational Era: The Remaking of Aging Among Indian Americans. In: *Diaspora* 11, 3, pp. 299–330.

Lan, Pei-Chia (2002): Subcontracting Filial Piety: Elder Care in Ethnic Chinese Immigrant Families in California. In: *Journal of Family* 23, pp. 812–835.

Leatherman, Thomas L. (1994): Health Implications of Changing Agrarian Economies in the Southern Andes. In: *Human Organization* 53, 4, pp. 371–380.

Leifsen, Esben/Tymczuk, Alexander (2012): Care at a Distance: Ukrainian and Ecuadorian Transnational Parenthood from Spain. In: *Journal of Ethnic and Migration Studies* 38, 2, pp. 219–236.

Leinaweaver, Jessaca B. (2008): *The Circulation of Children. Kinship, Adoption, and Morality in Andean Peru.* Durham/London: Duke University Press.

Leinaweaver, Jessaca B. (2010): Outsourcing Care How Peruvian Migrants Meet Transnational Family Obligations. In: *Latin American Perspectives* 37, 5, pp. 67–87.

Lie, Mabel L. S. (2010): Across the Oceans: Childcare and Grandparenting in UK Chinese and Bangladeshi Households. In: *Journal of Ethnic and Migration Studies* 36, 9, pp. 425–443.

Loughran, Diane (1988): The Challenge of Aging in the Peruvian Andes. In: *Ageing International* 15, 1, pp. 9–12.

Mayer, Enrique (2002): *The Articulated Peasant: Household Economies in the Andes.* Boulder, CO: Westview Press.

MediatoolsTV (2011): *15 de Mayo: Dia Internacional de la Familia,* 14 May, http://mediatoolstv.blogspot.com/2011/05/15-de-mayo-dia-internacional-de-la.html, accessed October 2013.

Miles, Ann (2004): *From Cuenca to Queens. An Anthropological Story of Transnational Migration.* Austin: University of Texas Press.

Mitchell, Winifred L. (1994): Women's Hierarchies of Age and Suffering in an Andean Community. In: *Journal of Cross-Cultural Gerontology* 9, pp. 179–191.

Muñoz Bernard, Carmen (1996) Estategias Matrimoniales, Apellidos y nombres de pila: libros parroquiales y civiles en el sur del Ecuador. In: Yápez, S. Moreno (ed.): *Antropología del Ecuador: memorias de Primero Simposio Europeo sobre Antropología del Ecuador.* Quito: Abya Yala, pp. 223–224.

Observatorio de los Derechos de Niñez y Adolescencia (ODNA) (2008): *Niñez y migración en el cantón Cañar.* Quito: ONDA.

Parreñas, Rhacel Salazar (2005): *Children of Global Migration: Transnational Families and Gendered Woes.* Stanford: Stanford University Press.

Powell, Jason L./Cook, Ian G. (2009): Global Ageing in Comparative Perspective: A Critical Discussion. In: *International Journal of Sociology and Social Policy* 29, 7/8, pp. 388–400.

Pribilsky, Jason (2001): *Nervios* and 'Modern' Childhood: Migration and Shifting Contexts of Child Life in the Ecuadorian Andes. In: *Childhood* 8, 2, pp. 251–273.

Pribilsky, Jason (2007): *La Chulla Vida: Gender, Migration, and the Family in Andean Ecuador and New York City.* Syracuse: Syracuse University Press.

Radcliffe, Sarah A. (2012): Development for a Postneoliberal Era? Sumak Kawsay, Living Well and the Limits to Decolonisation in Ecuador: In: *Geoforum* 43, 2, pp. 240–249.

Rae-Espinoza, Heather (2011): The Children of Émigrés in Ecuador. Narratives of Cultural Reproduction and Emotion in Transnational Social Fields. In: Coe, Catie/Reynolds, Rachel R./Boehm, Deborah A./Hess, Julia Meredith/Rae-Espinoza,

84 Jason Pribilsky

Heather (eds.): *Everyday Ruptures: Children, Youth and Migration in Global Perspective.* Nashville: Vanderbilt University Press, pp. 115–138.

Ramírez Gallegos, Jacques/Álvarez Velasco, Soledad (2009): Cruzando Fronteras: una aproximación etnográfica a la migración clandestina ecuatoriana en tránsito hacia Estados Unidos. In: *Confluenze Rivista di Studi Iberoamericani* 1, 1, pp. 89–113.

Sánchez Parga, José (1997): Antropo-lógicas andinas. Colección Biblioteca "Abya-Yala" Nr. 47. Quito: Abya-Yala.

Sando, Ruth Ann (1986): Doing the Work of Two Generations: The Impact of Out-Migration on the Elderly in Rural Taiwan. In: *Journal of Cross-Cultural Gerontology* 1, pp. 163–175.

Scheper-Hughes, Nancy (ed.). (1987): *Child survival. Anthropological perspectives on the treatment and maltreatment of children.* Dordrecht, The Netherlands: D. Reidel.

Shenk, Dena/Mahon, Joan (2009): Standing Up for Others: The AMIGOS Volunteer Model for Working with Elders in Peru. In: Jay Sokolovsy (ed.): *The Cultural Context of Aging: World Wide Perspectives* (3rd ed.). Santa Barbara: ABC-CLIO.

Smith, Hubert (dir.) (1974): The Spirit Possession of Alejandro Mamani. (film recording, 27 mins.). Watertown, MA: Documentary Educational Resources.

Torres Proaño, Alicia (2009): *Quilloac: memoria, etnicidad y migración entre los Kañaris,* Ecuador. MA Thesis. Anthropology Program, FLACSO. Quito, Ecuador.

URBANO, Henrique (1993): Sami y ecaco: Introducción a la noción de "fortuna" en lose Andes. In: Duviols, Pierre (ed.): *Religions des Andes et langues indigènes: Équateur, Pérou, Bolivie, avant et après la conquête espagnole.* Quebec: Université de Laval, pp. 237–244.

Vullnetari, Julie/King, Russell (2008): 'Does your Granny Eat Grass?' On Mass Migration, Care Drain and the Fate of Older People in Rural Albania." In: *Global Networks* 8, 2, pp. 139–171.

Waters, William F./Gallegos, Carlos Andrés (2012): *Salud y bienestar del adulto mayor indígena.* Quito–Ecuador: Universidad de San Francisco—Quito.

Weismantel, Mary J. (1989): Making Breakfast and Raising Babies. The Zumbagua Household as Constituted Process. In: Wilk, Richard (ed.): *The Household Economy. Reconsidering the Domestic Mode of Production.* Westview Press: Boulder, CO, pp. 55–72.

Weismantel, Mary J. (1995): Making Kin: Kinship Theory and Zumbagua Adoptions. In: *American Ethnologist* 22, 4, pp. 685–704.

Yeates, Nicola (2004): Global Care Chains. In: *International Feminist Journal of Politics* 6, 3, pp. 369–391.

Yeates, Nicola (2005): Global care chains: a critical introduction, *Global Migration Perspectives 44,* Global Commission on International Migration, Geneva.

Zhou, Yanqiu Rachel (2012): Space, Time, and Self: Rethinking Aging in the Contexts of Migration. In: *Journal of Aging Studies* 26, pp. 232–242.

4 Transnational Babushka

Grandmothers and Family Making Between Russian Karelia and Finland

Tatiana Tiaynen-Qadir

The central concept of this chapter[1] is the *babushka*, which is a Russian word for "grandmother" that is also informally applied to any elderly woman. Historically, the babushka construct has grown into an anchor of Russian belonging, not least due to the key role of grandmothers in family care. In prerevolutionary agrarian Russia, a grandmother could have great authority, supervising female household members as a *matushka*, the wife or mother of the eldest man of the peasant household (Matossian 1992: 23). Babushkas helped women deliver babies as *povitukhi* or *babki* (midwives; Dmitrieva 1999), while as *znakharki* (healers) they were revered and in demand in peasant communities in rural Russia (Glickman 1991: 151). The Soviet babushka was often at the heart of everyday family routine (Tiaynen 2013), praised as a symbol of "stoic endurance" in Russian discourse during Perestroika (Ries 1997: 88). The babushka has been carrying numerous celebratory and powerful qualities. Love, care, wisdom, the babushka's *borscht* (red-beet soup) or *shchi* (cabbage soup), homemade pies, "all-seeing" and "all-knowing" babushkas in the urban yard, or "church babushkas" are some such representations and discourses.

Babushka has recently started receiving academic attention as an object of study (Krasnova 2000; Novikova 2005; Ries 1997; Semjonova 1996), particularly in a transnational context (Fogiel-Bijaoui 2013). There are also some sociological studies that discuss Ukrainian transnational grandmothers in which the same term *babushka* is applied (Solari 2010; Tolstokorova 2012). However, there is a lack of ethnographic research on the subject, especially drawing on grandmothers' narratives and taking place in a multisited context.

I am interested in what happened to the babushka—as both the practice and the imagination—amid the changes that occurred after the dissolution of the Soviet Union. In contrast to people's highly restricted mobility in the USSR, Russia has become part of the "world on the move" (Appadurai 1996), with numerous Russian-speaking diasporas in Israel, the US, the UK, Canada, Germany, Greece, and the Nordic countries. This chapter focuses on the babushka from a transnational anthropological perspective that addresses a "condition in which, despite great distances and notwithstanding

86 Tatiana Tiaynen-Qadir

the presence of international borders, certain kind of relationships" (Vertovec 2009: 3) globally evolve, implying linkages and ongoing exchange among such nonstate actors as business, nongovernmental organizations (NGOs), families, and individuals.

The chapter is based on an initial exploratory long-term ethnographic journey into the lives of grandmothers in a particular context between Russian Karelia[2] and Finland, with its specific trans(cultural), historical, and geopolitical trajectories. My multisited ethnography (Marcus 1998) encompassed long-term immersion in two sites, including participant observation and ethnographic interviews with 20 grandmothers in Petrozavodsk, the capital of the Republic of Karelia, and 12 women in Tampere, the third-largest city in Finland, in the period of 2006 through 2009. My truly "on the move" cross-border ethnography in minibuses that take passengers across borders was invaluable in capturing the dynamism and scale of transnational grandmothering and family making, enabling me to grasp the "spatial depth" (Falzon 2009: 9) of the phenomenon.

I suggest the term *transnational babushka*, which, on one hand, emphasizes the Soviet (Russian) legacy in the continued significant role of grandmothers in child care and family making, and, on the other hand, captures important changes in grandmothering that emerged as the result of intensified transnational mobility. According to Vertovec's (2004) theorizing, transnationalism has different effects on people depending on whether they (a) mainly stay in a receiving country, (b) travel regularly between specific states, and (c) have never moved but whose locality is considerably influenced by the activities of others abroad.

In contrast to the above mentioned studies on transnational babushkas (Fogiel-Bijaoui 2013; Solari 2010) that primarily focus on grandmothers in a receiving context, I argue that transnational grandmothers live on both sides of the border and between. Thus, I distinguish between (1) migrant grandmothers, who moved permanently from Russia and Finland; (2) transnationally mobile grandmothers, who commute regularly between the two states, combining living "here" and "there"; and (3) grandmothers staying put, who live in Russian Karelia but have children, grandchildren, or other relatives in Finland. In total 17 (or 20, depending on the definition, as explained later) of my co-interlocutors can be referred to as transnational grandmothers,[3] who are members of so-called *transnational families* defined in scholarship as families that "live some or most of the times separated from each other, yet hold and create something that can be seen as a feeling of collective welfare and unity, namely 'familyhood', even across national borders" (Bryceson and Vuorela 2002: 3). In addition, as part of my participant observation I also met and talked to grandmothers from other parts of Russia.

In some transnational studies, aging women are portrayed as "burdens" to their migrant children (Izuhara and Shibata 2002: 162) or as frail parents "abandoned" by their adult children who migrated elsewhere (Vullnetari

Transnational Babushka 87

and King 2008). In contrast, I focus on the agency of grandmothers, who often are at the heart of mobilizing "transnational social support" (Bender et al. 2012), including their families and aging women's networks. Undoubtedly, grandmothers' important roles are also evident in other contexts, for instance, in a Serbian setting with aging women having the important affectual power in families and local communities (Simic 1983), among African Caribbean-born grandmothers in a British context, struggling "in order to carve out a niche for themselves within their families locally and internationally" (Plaza 2000: 100), or Bulgarian Muslim traveling grandmothers in Spain (Deneva 2009).

Babushka is a particular cultural manifestation and expression of an aging woman and a grandmother in the context of Russia and the former Soviet republics with their peculiar histories. While the traditional imagination about the babushka remains the dominant point of reference for many women, grandmothering practices have diversified in the postsocialist and transnational context. To address continuities and changes in the transnational grandmothers' lives, I distinguish between two major tendencies in the ways women see themselves and act as babushkas: *(neo)traditional babushka* and *(neo)liberal babushka*. The purpose of this chapter is to illustrate that women's transnational aging is a diverse and subjective process that is closely intertwined with specific (trans)cultural and geopolitical configurations.

GEOGRAPHICAL PROXIMITY AND CROSS-BORDER REGULATIONS

In recent literature related to transnational caregiving, particularly in relation to the experiences of old age and transnational mothering, it has been argued that physical distances may become an obstacle for maintaining day-to-day family relations and providing "hands-on" care (Baldassar, Baldock and Wilding 2007; Parreñas 2010). Parted family members can often experience this separation as painful and stressful, especially if the sending context is characterized by the prominence of extended family relationships with the pertinent mutual care across generations, for instance, between Italy with the "homeland kin" and Australia as the receiving country (Baldassar 2007). Nesteruk and Marks (2009: 84–85), analyzing the transnational family ties of Eastern European migrants (including Russians) in the United States, describe decreased connection and interaction with grandparents as the "biggest immigration-related loss" given "the central role of grandparents in raising grandchildren."

Compared to the complicated circumstances of maintaining family relations and grandmothering between Eastern Europe and the United States or Italy and Australia, transnational grandmothering between Russian Karelia and Finland appears to be easier to sustain in practical terms, logistically

88 Tatiana Tiaynen-Qadir

and financially. Although there is no direct railway connection between Petrozavodsk and Helsinki (or any other Finnish city), and while traveling by air is far too expensive, there are always easily available and affordable minibuses and private cars that take passengers between these states. In fact, for somebody who lives in Russian Karelia to go to Finland to visit family members, meet friends, or just do shopping may be something more "natural" than going to Moscow (not to mention other, more remote parts of Russia). This geographic proximity, along with well-established procedures for getting Finnish visas in Petrozavodsk and the predominantly legal character of migration from Russia to Finland, can be seen as significant factors facilitating transnational grandmothering. This is in contrast, for instance, to the Albanian case, where, although the distances are not huge, neither migrants nor their relatives can visit because of the illegal ways some migrants moved to Greece; moreover, traveling is pricy and not easily affordable for both migrants and their aging parents in Albania (Vullnetari and King 2008).

Russian grandmothers with an Ingrian ethnic background are a particular case in my research. Ingrian migrants had a special place in Finnish migration policy; they were seen as "returnees" based on their Ingrian Finnish belonging (Huttunen 2002).[4] The repatriation program initiated by Finnish president Mauno Koivisto in the 1990s resulted in more than 30,000 Ingrians moving to Finland from the former Soviet space.[5] Now they are part of approximately 71,000 Russian speakers in contemporary Finland (1.3 percent of the total population) (Tilastokeskus 2013).

Among the 12 *migrant grandmothers* I interviewed, 7 had an Ingrian background, and 2 Ingrian were staying-put grandmothers, whom I met in Petrozavodsk. There are differences in the ways grandmothers with ethnic Ingrian, Slavic, or Karelian backgrounds may see themselves in terms of their ethnic and national belonging (Tiaynen 2013). However, irrespective of their ethnic backgrounds, their roles and understandings of grandmothering largely revolve around the values of Soviet and Russian family culture. In fact, Ingrian grandmothers often organized and facilitated the moves of their extended families to Finland. Babushka care was often behind their attempts to provide a more secure future for their grandchildren.

There are, of course, grandmothers of non-Ingrian backgrounds who have also migrated to Finland, for instance, as a result of marriage or family reunification. Some actually moved for the purpose of providing child care, when the move was organized by their relatives. For instance, Julia's (born in 1930) move was organized by her daughter to help with her child. Now that the child is grown up, she and her daughter's family live in different flats but in the same house and on the same floor to see each other as often as they want.

The institutional barrier that migrant grandmothers face in their transnational grandmothering and family practices consists of the travel restrictions that define the eligibility for social security benefits in Finland. For instance, women who have not yet reached their retirement age (65–67) and who attend language courses or work practices are allowed 21 days of traveling abroad in a year. This institutional barrier in transnational mobility is one of the explanations why migrant grandmothers do not travel as frequently as they would want.

However, the early retirement age of 50 in Russian Karelia and 55 in Russia[6] is something that greatly facilitates transnational commuting of *transnationally mobile grandmothers*, the other category of grandmothers among transnational babushkas. The Finnish visa agreement with the Russian Federation allows Russian citizens to apply for a visa stay of maximum 90 days within half a year. If grandmothers have children residing in Finland, the visa is given free of charge, usually for a period of two years, although with the same rule of 90 days per half a year. Among my interlocutors, two grandmothers could be seen as transnationally mobile grandmothers, although my cross-border ethnography illustrated that many babushkas frequently travel between these two sites in their continued grandmothering and family efforts. It is necessary to emphasize the Soviet legacy in this practice: grandmothering "on the move" is not a new phenomenon as such for Soviet women who had experiences of maintaining translocal families.[7] More important, transnational grandmothering between Finland and Russia may vary a lot. If it is manageable between Russian Karelia and Finland (also between Finland and St. Petersburg or Moscow, as my participant observation proved) because of the relative geographical proximity and well-developed traveling infrastructure, visiting becomes an obstacle for those who reside in or migrate from other parts of Russia.

The other category of transnational babushkas is *grandmothers* (three among my interlocutors) *staying put*, who are often either "too old" to travel or "too young." They host their children's families during the latter's stays in Petrozavodsk, spend summer holidays with their grandchildren, and participate in sustaining family-togetherness through other means, as discussed below. Once I was traveling with an elderly grandmother in a minibus who frequently visited her daughter and grandchildren in Finland. She told me that it was "the last time" she would be visiting Finland: "I am getting too old for this." This illustrates that the suggested categories of transnational grandmothers are not fixed as grandmothering practices may vary across a woman's life cycle. Grandmothering staying put may in fact be a stage that follows transnationally mobile grandmothering. Likewise, migrant grandmothers may be those who had experiences of transnational mobile grandmothering prior to their move to Finland (this is the case of Julia, mentioned earlier).

When adopting a more flexible notion of the transnational babushka, including also aging women who maintain transnational family ties with other relatives living in Finland (not necessarily with their children and grandchildren, but, for instance, sisters, nieces, nephews, etc.), then three more of my interlocutors can be referred as transnational babushkas staying

90   *Tatiana Tiaynen-Qadir*

put. For instance, Olga has a niece living in Finland, and because she is like a "second mother" to her niece, she is also acting as a babushka to niece's children. Talking on the phone or via Skype across the borders involves Olga herself, her two nieces, each with two children and a husband, one in Tampere and one in Petrozavodsk, as well as the grandmother, Olga's sister, and the nieces' mother. When the two children from Finland come to stay in Petrozavodsk during their summer vacation, their interaction with Olga is as active as with their grandmother.

(NEO)TRADITIONAL BABUSHKA

The active involvement of migrant, transnationally mobile and staying put grandmothers in transnational family space is closely linked to the (neo) traditional tendency in contemporary grandmothering. This tendency is strongly informed by Soviet family culture and today's Russian neofamilialism. By using the term *(neo)traditional*, I want to emphasize two significant aspects of the phenomenon. First, it reflects the traditional understanding of the babushka, which draws on prerevolutionary Russian and Soviet imaginations and practices of the babushka. Second, it depicts the enhanced glorification of the traditional family values (including babushka) in contemporary Russia. Similar tendencies were strong in many new national states formed out of the former Soviet republics, where nationalism was often expressed through an imagined return to tradition (often as opposed to Soviet), particularly to the traditional family ideal (Graney 2004). In the context of the babushka, Soviet practices did not erase active grandmothering practices, quite the opposite. Therefore, Soviet practices can be seen as part of the traditional understanding of the babushka.

Drawing on the prerevolutionary legacy, Soviet power "made" grandmothers into omnipotent figures of Soviet families in the period between 1917 and 1970, which was marked by the continued lack of available places in public child-care institutions,[8] highly restrictive legislation for working mothers, and significant shortages in the pension system. In view of Soviet representations and practices that discouraged men from active child upbringing and care, coupled with the actual shortage of men in the postwar period, women were expected to be the children's primary caregivers. An obligatory "right" to work (Lapidus 1978) was glorified alongside a motherhood that was defined as a "noble and rewarded service to the state" (Ashwin 2000: 11). Some researchers have suggested that the dominant Soviet gender system can be formulated as the "working mother contract" (Temkina and Rotkirch 1997). Babushkas, both grandmothers and other midlife female family members, or even neighboring or "relativized" babushkas[9] often eased the "double burden" of Soviet women.

Transnational grandmothering practices carry this Soviet legacy among all three types of grandmothers of my study. It becomes clear that two pillars of the Soviet working mother contract—work and motherhood—emerge as the decisive criteria and values against which grandmothers evaluate the success of their own lives, the lives of their daughters, daughters-in-law, and granddaughters. Many grandmothers pointed out that they were willing to help with child care in order to enable their daughters or daughters-in-law to work or study. For instance, a migrant grandmother, Elina (born in 1952), started taking care of her three-month-old granddaughter so that Elina's daughter would be able to attend Finnish language courses and start working. While working and having special work practices, many migrant grandmothers set up special routines to pick up their grandchildren from kindergarten or school, explaining these arrangements by the fact that the parents need to work or study. Weekend and Sunday babushkas, as working grandmothers sometimes call themselves, consider it their duty to spend quality time with their grandchildren over weekends. Transnational grandmothers Vesta (born in 1943) and Elena (born in 1950) travel back and forth to help their daughters with child care to enable them to study and work in Finland. Grandmothers staying put spend two to three months during the summer holidays with their grandchildren (from Finland) at a village or take them to the seaside. Galina (born in 1936), a grandmother staying put, said that her grandson (whom she "raised by herself") moved to Finland and now regularly calls her. During summer holiday, her great-grandson spends lots of time with her. Transnational babushkas on both sides of the border mobilize traditional babushkas' skills such as homemade cooking (pies, soups, pancakes), berry picking, pickling, or cultivating vegetables in their continued efforts to ensure the well-being of their extended family members, and especially their grandchildren.

Rooted in the Soviet ideological culture they lived in, grandmothers as often try to convey such values of Soviet modernity as culturedness (*kul'turnost'*) (Kelly 1998). They teach their grandchildren to read (see Figure 4.1) or take them to a museum exhibition. In addition, in view of the postsocialist resurgence of Russian Orthodoxy (Rousselet and Agadjanian 2010), babushkas have often become those who transfer religious values to their grandchildren. In fact, religion and magic have never been fully erased in the Soviet period: many babushkas continued to be committed to religious practices, often secretly and especially in rural areas (Keinänen 2002). This suppressed religious self became reactivated in postsocialist Russia. While the cultural upbringing can be seen as something traditionally Soviet, the religious upbringing emerges as neotraditional, as a return to religion, which was seen as "superstition" and "backwardness" in the project of the Soviet modernity.

I suggest that "active" grandmothering[10] can, on one hand, be seen as a *postponed* motherhood. Contemporary grandmothers are former Soviet women who often lacked opportunities for engaged hands-on mothering because of their paid work and who shared practical child-care duties with their mothers, mothers-in-law, or other female elderly family members,

Figure 4.1 Babushka reading a book for her grandchild. Painting by Irina Chernyuk.

complemented by the public child-care facilities from the 1970s. At that time, the idea that modern upbringing should be provided by "experts" in the public child-care system became prominent, and many young mothers felt compelled to place their children in nurseries. Contemporary grandmothers who used to be working mothers may be active in their grandmothering in order to fully experience engaged hands-on care of their grandchildren, the emotional need that could not be fully fulfilled once they were young mothers themselves. Elena often mentioned during our meetings that she now regrets that she placed her daughter in a nursery when she was only 11 months old:

> "Work, work, work! Is work more important than a child? Now I understand it. This is why I said to my children: My grandchildren will not go to a kindergarten until they are three years old. I am at your disposal to take care of them. (Elena, born in 1950)"

On the other hand, their grandmothering can be also interpreted as *prolonged* motherhood. Grandmothering can also appear as a subtle combination of an aging woman's need, desire, and culturally informed obligation to continue the care as mother of her adult child through involvement with grandchildren. In this role, they continue to be caring mothers toward their adult daughters. For instance, maternal grandmothers are especially active transnationally mobile grandmothers, and through this they support their daughters to become successful working mothers. It is also a prolonged motherhood in a sense that it means a prolongation of youth. Some grandmothers in their 50s or early 60s enjoy it when somebody mistakes them for the mother of a child (see Figure 4.2). While the terms *prolonged* and *postponed motherhood* help to attain deeper understandings of different aspects of grandmothering, they are, of course, not mutually exclusive categories but, rather, are overlapping and complementary. This is also evident in Fogiel-Bijaoui's (2013) finding, who points out that her respondents, Russian babushkas in Israel, frequently mentioned that because of their hard work they have not been "good mothers" and that as grandmothers they want to do as much as they can.

In this context, the Finnish gender context provides more continuity than it is apparent at a first glance. With all the differences in ideological and political framing, two pillars of Soviet female subjectivity—work and motherhood—have been both deliberate choices and necessities in the everyday lives of Finnish women (Lähteenmäki 1999). The housewife idea, which used to be popular among middle-class Finnish women in the first half of the twentieth century, was never realized in Finland simply because Finland was considered too much of "a poor country" to keep its mothers at home (Lähteenmäki 1999). Thus, the receiving context of Finland, with similar ideas of women's work and maternity duties, makes it easier for the "working mother" contract to be reproduced in transnational grandmothering.

94 *Tatiana Tiaynen-Qadir*

Figure 4.2 Young babushka and her granddaughter.
Source: Painting by Irina Chernyuk.

By suggesting that grandmothering can be interpreted as postponed or prolonged motherhood, I do not claim in any way that grandmothers substitute for mothers. Babushkas provide generational family continuity, as well as love, care, and the maturity that often can be only accumulated and cultivated with age. Contemporary babushkas contribute to the emotional and physical well-being of their grandchildren, complementing parents' care and public child care. Importantly, babushkas often foster a sense of familyhood and mutual care across generations, which nourishes the feeling of existential security among their children and grandchildren. More important, being a caring babushka is what makes women's lives meaningful and complete. For instance, Vesta (born in 1943) talked of her grandchildren and children as "the essence" of her life: "I feel the grain of my life in them."

Drawing on other empirical research, it is also possible to conclude that a (neo)traditional understanding of the babushka has informed ageing strategies of women in other transnational contexts, for instance among Russians transnational babushkas in Israel (Fogiel-Bijaoui 2013), Ukrainian grandmothers in Italy supporting their extended families back in Ukraine (Solari 2010), as well as staying put Ukrainian grandmothers providing care for their grandchildren in the absence of the mothers working in Italy (Tolsto-korova 2012).

(NEO)LIBERAL BABUSHKA

Alongside this (neo)traditional babushka, there is another tendency in grandmothering that can be seen as (neo)liberal. By using the term (neo)liberal, I aim to highlight two aspects of being a contemporary transnational babushka in this context. First, it addresses the particular features of the liberal self: active, hardworking, goal-oriented, planning for change, and succeeding in shaping its own destiny, that is, the "enterprising" self (Hazleden 2011). This tendency is also influenced by Soviet values of women's public involvement, particularly work. This liberal aspect depicts individualization trends (Zdravomyslova, Rotkirch and Temkina 2009) in grandmothering. Second, the term *(neo)liberal* reflects the changes in subjectivities within the "epochal rise" of neoliberalism, as a culture predicated on "market fundamentalism" that makes "the consuming citizen the guardian of her/his well-being" (Comaroff and Comaroff, 2006: 39). Neoliberal subjectivity seeks to extend an optimizing and maximizing market logic to most domains of human life (Harvey 2005), babushkas' care being one of them.

While the point of reference may remain the traditional babushka, the actual practices of a grandmother may not necessarily follow this romanticized ideal. Some women in their everyday practices and values are closer to an ideal of a liberal independent woman, being active in work and public life. For instance, Eleonora (born in 1960), married to a Finnish man, opened a hairdressing salon in Tampere. She takes pride in being financially independent and earning more than her husband does. Yet, this does not prevent her from expressing her babushka care toward her daughter's family that lives in Russia. She told me that her granddaughter is like a daughter to her (which also illustrates grandmothering as prolongation of youth, discussed earlier) and that her business success in Finland enabled Eleonora to help her daughter's family to purchase a three-room flat.

Anna (born in 1962), the youngest grandmother among my interlocutors, has a six-year-old granddaughter who is only one year younger than Anna's son. In addition, after remarrying she has also become a stepmother to two children. With her busy working life and being a mother of four, she admits that she is not particularly active in her role of a babushka, measuring her modest involvement by her childhood memories of her own babushka: "We are so lucky that our babushkas took care of us. Our children are not that lucky." Being a grandmother at this stage of her life is a minor part of her identity, as she rather focuses on her work, public activity, and nuclear family. Since her move to Finland, Anna has been actively involved in the Russian Club in Tampere.

96 *Tatiana Tiaynen-Qadir*

(Neo)traditional and (neo)liberal tendencies are not mutually exclusive; they may be intertwined in one babushka's practices and change across her life span. For instance, Elena (born in 1950) is an active transnationally mobile grandmother and an active member of the Center of Russian Culture in Tampere, regularly paying annual fees and participating in its gatherings and trips. She also values her "private life," dating a man in Finland and driving with him on a motorbike around the city.

Vesta, a grandmother of four, also carefully guards her "personal life," which includes dating. Work occupies a significant space in Vesta's narratives, which speaks of its importance in her identification as a working babushka (which is the case with most grandmothers in my study). Vesta was the head of a women's council at her workplace, and now she is currently involved in a women's NGO in Petrozavodsk.

It becomes clear that, alongside with grandmothering, public activity, once nourished by the Soviet gender culture, holds great prominence in women's current lives, particularly in Finland with its culture of civic associations and free-time activity. Salmenniemi (2008: 64) in her analysis of civic activism and democratization in Russia points out a "notable discursive shift" in women's activism from an individual's duty toward the state to the individual's responsibility for herself and society. This is also applicable when analyzing women's public activity in general. If during the Soviet period women's freedom and initiative were only possible within the grids of the Soviet ideology (of which women also often became channels), women's needs to be engaged in a public activity have been redirected for the women's individual and collective empowerment under new circumstances of migration and transnational mobility.

Networks of migrant women of a mature age are arranged around language courses or work practices. Midlife and elderly women are the most active members of the Russian Club, the Centre of Russian Culture, and Ingrian associations. Migrant and transnationally mobile grandmothers form social support networks on the premises of a Lutheran and Finnish Orthodox churches. To a certain extent, these women's networks can be also traced back to so-called babushkas' networks that used to be an integral part of the Soviet urban landscape (Novikova 2005).

On one hand, this kind of women's public involvement draws on a relatively new (in the Russian context as opposed to the Soviet one) liberal feminist idea of an independent, self-asserting, critical thinking woman with an ability to stand for her rights (Salmeniemi 2008). On the other hand, it also reproduces a particular discourse (evident in Soviet and Russian women's civic activism, according to Salmenniemi 2008) that constructs women's work in organizations as an extension of the private sphere, emphasizing women's altruistic agency—women's responsibilities for the home, family, and children—as a sphere of care for the society they live in. For instance, activists in the Center of Russian Culture are concerned with keeping traditional Russian culture alive and contributing to cultural interactions between Finland and Russia. These practices of women's networking and the active leading role of aging women in the women's groups illustrate a hybrid merger of the Soviet idea of women's public activity, women's care (babushka care), and liberal discourses of personal growth, individualism, and leadership.

The neoliberal aspect of grandmothering is evident in the commercialization of care (Zdravomyslova 2009), which affected babushka care in both Russian Karelia, and in a transnational context between Finland and Russia. As I have discussed elsewhere (Tiaynen 2013), a new practice, *babushka for reward*, emerged in postsocialist Karelia, when adult children started "paying" their mothers or other female relatives for child care. It has also become quite popular among well-to-do families to hire an elderly woman to take care of a child and carry out domestic work. Babushka care has started being marketed in local newspapers.

This phenomenon has also crossed the border, and found fertile soil in Finland with its more neoliberal understanding of care. Some midlife and elderly women are eager to provide child care for Russian migrants. Babushka care seems to be more appropriate and culturally familiar that "alien" babysitters. Russian migrants, when purchasing babushka care, are wittingly and unwittingly making use of the whole package of the babushka phenomenon, including love, warmth, "relativized" relationships, and trust. For instance, Elvira (born in 1950), before she became a grandmother herself, used to help other families with child care. One Russian mother, when going for a several days trip, felt at ease to leave her three-year-old daughter in Elvira's care, and the girl seemed to feel comfortable and enjoyed staying at Elvira's place during these days. This informal arrangement, based on trust and "relativized" relationships, would seem hardly possible with a babysitter employed through a company providing such services.

The market of babushka care as a social phenomenon and a hybrid practice illustrates how traditional (prerevolutionary/Soviet imagination of babushka) and neoliberal (post-Soviet, Western modernity, including market-economy thinking) can merge, producing new meanings and practices both in a postsocialist context and transnational Finnish–Russian context. The babushka as an imagined and lived Russian phenomenon is being turned into a specific marketable commodity in the mills of complex, "transnational cultural flows" (Appadurai 1996).

It seems that child care is also increasingly seen as work that should be rewarded. It is difficult to define precisely the sources of this neoliberal understanding of care among transnational babushkas. In part, market reforms and neoliberal transnational flows have influenced the content of care in the Russian context. Migrant grandmothers also seem to be influenced by the Finnish context, in which care has been understood for a longer time as a service provided by the Finnish welfare system. Informal and private arrangements of care also take place, but often in negotiation with the public care services (Zechner 2010).

98   Tatiana Tiaynen-Qadir

During one of my trips from Petrozavodsk to Tampere I discussed with a driver, Alexei, his working routine, routes, and passengers, and he mentioned that when he gets to Helsinki he stays at "one babushka's place." It turned out that the mentioned babushka was an elderly migrant woman from Petrozavodsk for whom the company, organizing minibus trips between Russian Karelia and Finland, pays for hosting drivers. Drivers usually have to spend a night in Helsinki to make a return trip the next day. In this case, again, the whole "babushka package" is expected to be delivered: homemade meals, warmth, and a cozy sleeping place, and "it is also cheaper than staying in a hotel," according to Alexei. This example again illuminates how the babushka phenomenon has crossed borders of traditional imagination on babushka and actual national borders.

TRANSNATIONAL FAMILIES

With all the discussed varieties in aging women's practices, family often remains the main site of their lives and identifications. It seems that in the midst of transnational mobility and odds of separation, women maintain their families across borders even more, as a source of stability and existential security for their members, including grandmothers themselves:

> "Family is like roots of a tree. A person is solidly standing on the ground, and knows that here his soul will be warmed when he encounters difficulties on his life path. (Vesta, born in 1943)"

The way family is talked of, imagined, and maintained by most grandmothers interviewed exceeds the boundaries of the nuclear family, as well as state borders, encompassing relatives "here" and "there," those alive and even those who passed away. Yet, in transnational grandmothering, specific means become especially important to sustain familyhood across borders. For instance, daily talking and discussing mundane, everyday life details, practices enabled by the new telecommunication technologies, are significant mechanisms for family routinization across borders. It has been convincingly discussed in various scholarship that the routine, something that often goes unnoticed or unarticulated, is, in fact, the basic element of day-to-day social activity, which lies at the "cyclical renewal" of everyday life (Blagojevic 1994: 470). The practice of "talking family," a "kind of social glue connections families" (Vertovec 2009: 56), is one of the essential means of maintaining family as a routine. This practice is necessarily enhanced by frequent visits, facilitated by geographical proximity, availability, and affordability of travel, as well as softened border regulations.

In old age, the narration of family histories and tales (not necessarily to a family member) becomes an essential mean for imagining and re-creating an extended family landscape that transgresses space and time. During one of my trips from Petrozavodsk to Tampere, I happened to share a seat with an Ingrian woman, Riita (born in 1932), and our conversation lasted almost ten hours until the woman reached her destination. She gave me a detailed description of every family member, their appearances, characters, and life situations. In her story she connected all these people into one family space, stretching across time and spanning different national contexts—Russia, Finland, Sweden, and Estonia. It included a complicated and tragic history of the moves of her family,[11] as well as the warm narrations of her beloved husband and her happy family and working life in Petrozavodsk.

Finally, one more "family member" who was often mentioned during our conversation was a cat, which is part of Riita's daily routine in Finland. This one trip and conversation with Riita left me with a feeling that the way she was narrating her family history, when the past was part of the present, and the present was linked to the past, was actually the contemporary family space that she lived in. I would suggest that narrating and imagining family histories become especially important means of sustaining family space when grandmothers grow older. At this stage of family life, babushkas can become those channels through which "family capital" and a sense of "familyhood" are transferred across generations. This role is strengthened in a transnational family space when the family becomes spatially dispersed.

Another important aspect of reproducing the sense of togetherness is a tangible recreation of familyhood (Vuorela 2002) through displaying pictures, pieces of arts made by family members, arranging a home altar to place all family members under God's protection, or keeping a room for a family member residing on the other side of the border. Likewise, praying and performing magic are applied by transnational grandmothers to reinforce their families and to protect their grandchildren and children.

I suggest that being a babushka also means having access to a subtle authority in intrafamily relations. Blagojevic (1994), analyzing everyday life and gender relation in Serbia, suggests the term *sacrificial micro-matriarchy* to mean the "structure of authority which gives power to women at the level of primary groups, when women achieve domination through self-sacrificing" (475). Likewise, the Russian babushka is often the "central figure of a grown, mature woman towards whom different generations and different needs converge" (Blagojevic 1994: 476). Russian babushkas, by being involved in the daily family routine of their children and grandchildren, daughters-in-law and sons-in-law, nieces and nephews, sisters and brothers, share access to hardly distinguishable, but vividly felt "micro-powers" (Foucault 1995: 222). The exercise of subtle power is often accomplished through "behavioral dominance" expressed through close monitoring of others' actions and direct and indirect criticism (Miller-Day 2004), particularly through "talking family" on Skype or phone, as well as long-term and short-term visiting. It seems that the powerful and celebratory representations linked to the imagination of the babushka in fact strengthen the position of micro-powers among grandmothers and may be

100 *Tatiana Tiaynen-Qadir*

wittingly employed by women. However, these micro-powers may go side by side with grandmothers' self-sacrifice, sometimes physical and emotional overexertion in their attempts to act as a babushka of the family.

Transnational family in grandmothers' narratives, lives, and selves emerges as an "imagined and real" community (Vuorela 2002). Family operates as something that grandmothers "make" (Carsten 2004) in their daily lives, an important site of production of mutual love, care, and support, based on the "solidarity" (Bender et al. 2012) of its family members. Thus, when grandmothers become old and frail, the transnational extended family usually makes specific arrangements (for instance, a grandmother lives permanently with a grandchild's family and/or a nurse is hired for hands-on care) to provide a daily care. The emotional support is mobilized through "talking family" and visiting. Yet, the detailed account of these practices would require another research inquiry, which I would see as an avenue of future research in this context.

CONCLUDING REMARKS

Based on an examination of the particular transnational context of Russian Karelia and Finland, I suggest that the practices and imaginations on the babushka qualitatively define women's aging strategies. Migrant, mobile, and staying put transnational babushkas are involved in family making across borders through child care, visiting, "talking family," tangible and imagined re-creating of transnational families, and religious practices. All these practices are greatly facilitated by geographical proximity and visa regimes.

In approaching the babushka as a strategy that mid-life and elderly women renegotiate in their lives, two major tendencies in the ways women see themselves and act as babushkas can be distinguished: (neo)traditional and (neo)liberal. The first one, rooted in Soviet family culture and Russian neofamilialism, manifests for instance in grandmothering practices as prolonged and postponed motherhood, babushka care expressed through religion, and women's attempts to raise their grandchildren as "cultural" individuals. The latter one, drawing on the Soviet legacy of women's public involvement and babushkas' gatherings, as well as neoliberal discourses, is evident in marketing babushka care, individualized strategies, and women's networks. These tendencies are not mutually exclusive but are easily combined in one woman's life and change across her life span.

The receiving context of Finland, with quite similar gender understandings of woman's work and motherhood duties, and its culture of civic associations, seemed to provide a fertile soil for these women's aging practices and strategies. Women's aging in this transnational context emerges as a diverse phenomenon, revealing not only their agency and micro-powers but also vulnerabilities in their self-sacrifice. Family solidarity and women's

Transnational Babushka 101

networks constitute the transnational social support that generates a comfort feeling of safe and dignified aging.

NOTES

1 The chapter draws on my doctoral research, which was financially and academically supported by the University of Tampere, the Russia in Europe Doctoral School in Border Studies at the University of Eastern Finland, and the Petrozavodsk State University (Program of Strategic Development of Scientific Research 2012–2016).
2 I apply the term *Russian Karelia* to mean mainly what is now called the Republic of Karelia, namely, Karelia on the Russian side of the border (except for the part that belongs to the Leningrad Oblast, the Karelian Isthmus) to distinguish it from Karelia (Karjala) located in Finland, the regions of South Karelian and North Karelia. A member of the Russian Federation, the region's official name is the Republic of Karelia.
3 Other grandmothers who do not have relatives living in Finland: I refer to these data when analyzing grandmothering practices in the context of postsocialist changes in Russian Karelia in my doctoral thesis (Tiaynen 2013)
4 In the seventeenth century, a large number of Finns from Savo and the Karelian Isthmus moved to and settled down in Ingria, the area that, nowadays, is the central part of Leningrad Oblast, near St. Petersburg.
5 From July 2011, people with an Ingrian background are no longer eligible to apply to move to Finland based on their ethnic Finnish belonging, because it is believed that those who wanted to apply to migrate had already done so.
6 This earlier retirement age for women in Russian Karelia was established in 1967. It was explained by Karelia being ranked as a "Northern region" with severe climate conditions and, therefore, more damaging for the people's health than in the rest of the Soviet Union.
7 In my thesis, I elaborate on this topic, suggesting a typology of translocal moves with various effects on grandmothers' individual and family lives (Tiaynen 2013).
8 For instance, child-care institutions accommodated only 23 percent of all preschoolers in 1965 (Lapidus 1978).
9 One can "relativize" into a family those people who are not necessarily blood relatives (Vuorela 2009).
10 Adopting this term from Krasnova (2000), I use it more inclusively and flexibly.
11 Ingrian Finns were subjected to discrimination policies and a chain of enforced moves during Stalinism.

REFERENCES

Appadurai, Arjun (1996): *Modernity at Large. Cultural Dimensions of Globalization*. Minneapolis: University of Minnesota Press.
Ashwin, Sarah (2000): Introduction: Gender, State and Society. In: Ashwin, Sara (ed.): *Gender, State and Society in Soviet and Post-Soviet Russia*. London/New York: Routledge, pp.1–29.
Baldassar, Loretta (2007): Transnational Families and Aged Care: The Mobility of Care and the Migrancy of Ageing. In: *Journal of Ethnic and Migration Studies* 33, 2, pp. 275–297.

102   Tatiana Tiaynen-Qadir

Baldassar, Loretta/Baldock, Cora V./Wilding, Raelene (2007): *Families Caring Across Borders. Migration, Ageing and Transnational Caregiving*. New York: Palgrave Macmillan.

Bender, Désirée/Hollstein, Tina/Huber, Lena/Schweppe, Cornelia (2012): Migration Biographies and Transnational Social Support—Transnational Family Care and the Search for "Homelandmen." In: Chambon, Adrienne /Wolfgang, Schröer/ Cornelia, Schweppe (eds.): *Transnational Social Support*. London, New York: Routledge, pp. 129–148.

Blagojevic, Marina (1994): War and Everyday Life: Deconstruction of Self/Sacrifice. In: *Sociology* XXXVI, 4, pp. 469–482.

Bryceson, Deborah/Vuorela, Ulla (2002): *The Transnational Family. New European Frontiers and Global Networks*. Oxford/New York: Berg Publishers.

Carsten, Janet (2004): *After Kinship*. Cambridge: Cambridge University Press.

Comaroff, Jean/Comaroff, John L. (2006): *Law and Disorder in the Postcolony*. Chicago: The University of Chicago Press.

Deneva, Neda (2009): The Young-Old Transnational Travellers: On the Transformation of Care Arrangements Among Bulgarian Muslim Migrants in Spain. In: *Migration. Focus on Central and Eastern Europe*. http://aa.ecn.cz/img_upload/ 6334c0c7298d6b396d213ccd19be5999/NDeneva_MigrationAgeingAndCare. pdf, accessed July 2009.

Dmitrieva, S. I. (1999): Traditsionnaya narodno-meditsinskaya praktika. In: Aleksandrov, V.A./I.V. Vlasova/N.S. Polishuk (eds.): *Russkie. Moskva: MAIK Nauka*, pp. 760–772.

Falzon, Mark-Anthony (2009): Multi-Sited Ethnography: Theory, Praxis and Locality in Contemporary Research. In: Falzon, Mark-Anthony (ed.): *Multi-Sited Ethnography*. Abingdon: Ashgate Publishing Group, pp. 1–23.

Fogiel-Bijaoui, Sylvie (2013): Babushka in the Holy Land: Being a Russian-Israeli Grandmother in Israel Today. In: *Journal of Comparative Family Studies* 44, 6, pp. 725–739.

Foucault, Michel (1995): *Discipline and Punish. The Birth of the Prison*. Westminster: Vintage.

Glickman, Rose L. (1991): The Peasant Woman as Healer. In: Clements, Barbara Evans/Barbara Alpern, Engel/Christene D. Worobec (eds.): *Russia's Women. Accommodation, Resistance, Transformation*. Berkeley: University of California Press, pp. 148–162.

Graney, Katherine E. (2004): The Gender of Sovereignty: Constructing Statehood, Nation, and Gender Regimes in Post-Soviet Tatarstan. In: Kuehnast, Kathleen/ Carol, Nechemias (eds.): *Post-Soviet Women Encountering Transition. Nation Building, Economic Survival and Civic Activism*. Washington, DC: Woodrow Wilson Center Press, pp. 44–64.

Harvey, David (2005): *A Brief History of Neoliberalism*. Oxford: Oxford University Press.

Hazleden, Rebecca (2011): Dragon-slayers and Jealous Rats: The Gendered Self in Contemporary Self-help Manuals.In: *Cultural Studies Review* 17, pp. 270–295.

Huttunen, Laura (2002): *Kotona, maanpaossa, matkalla. Kodin merkitykset maahanmuuttajien omaelämäkerroissa*. Helsinki: Suomalaisen kirjallisuuden seura.

Izuhara, Misa/Shibata, Hiroshi (2002): Breaking the Generational Contract? Japanese Migration and Old-Age Care in Britain. In: Deborah, Bryceson/ Ulla, Vuorela (eds.): *The Transnational Family. New European Frontiers and Global Networks*. Oxford: Berg Bublication, pp. 155–169.

Keinänen, Marja-Liisa (2002): Religious Ritual Contested. Anti-Religious Activities and Women's Ritual Practice in Rural Soviet Karelia. In: Ahlbäck, Tore (ed.):

Transnational Babushka 103

Ritualistics. Based on Papers Read at the Symposium on Ritualistics Held at Åbo, Finland, July 31–August 2, 2002. Åbo: The Donner Institute for Research in Religious and Cultural History, pp. 92–117.

Kelly, Catriona (1998): Popular Culture. In Rzhevsky, Nicholas (ed.): *The Cambridge Companion to Modern Russian Culture.* Cambridge: Cambridge University Press, pp. 125–158.

Krasnova, O. V. (2000): Babushki v sem'e. In: *Sotsiologicheskie issledovaniya* 11, pp. 108–116.

Lähteenmäki, Maria (1999): Responsibility Fosters Independence. In: *Women in Finland*, translated by Hildi Hawkins. Helsinki: Otava.

Lapidus, Gail Warshovsk (1978): *Women in Soviet Society. Equality, Development and Social Change.* California: University of California Press.

Marcus, George E. (1998): *Ethnography Through Thick and Thin.* Cambridge: Cambridge University Press.

Matossian, Mary (1992): The Peasant Way of Life. In: Farnsworth, Beatrice/Lynne Viola (eds.): *Russian Peasant Women.* New York: Oxford University Press, pp. 11–40.

Miller-Day, Michelle A. (2004): *Communication Among Grandmothers, Mothers and Adult Daughters. A Qualitative Study of Maternal Relationships.* Mahwah, NJ: Lawrence Erlbaum Associates.

Nesteruk, Olena/ Marks, Loren (2009): Grandparents Across Ocean: Eastern European Immigrants' Struggle to Maintain Intergenerational Relationships. In: *Journal of Comparative Family Studies* 40, 1, pp. 77–95.

Novikova, Irina (2005): "Riian "MUMMOKERHOT". Ikä ja valta venäjänkielisessä translokaalissa ympäristössä." In: Hirsiaho, Anu/Mari, Korpela/ Liisa,Rantalaiho (eds.): *Kohtaamisia rajoilla.* Tampere: Suomalaisen Kirjallisuuden Seura, pp. 71–91.

Parreñas, Rhacel Salazar (2010): Transnational Mothering: A Source of Gender Conflicts in the Family. In: *North Carolina Law Review* 88, pp. 1825–1856.

Plaza, Dwaine (2000): Transnational Grannies: The Changing Family Responsibilities of African Caribbean Born Women Resident in Britain. In: *Social Indicators Research* 51, 1, pp. 75–105.

Ries, Nancy (1997): *Russian Talk. Culture and Conversation during Perestroika.* Ithaca, NY: Cornell University Press.

Rousselet, Kathy/Agadjanian, Alexander (2010): Individual and Collective Identities in Russian Orthodoxy. In: Hann, Chris/Hermann, Holtz (eds.): *Eastern Christians in Anthropolgical Perspective.* California: University of California Press, pp. 311–328.

Salmenniemi, Suvi (2008): *Democratization and Gender in Contemporary Russia.* London: Taylor and Francis.

Semjonova, Valentian (1996): Babushki. Semeinye i sotsialnye funktsii praroditel'skogo pokoleniya. In: *Sud'by ludej. Rossiya XX vek. Biografii semei kak objekt sotsial'nogo issledovaniya.* Moskva: Institut Sotsiologii RAN, pp. 326–354.

Simic, Andrei (1983): Machismo and Cryptomatriarchy: Power, Affect, and Ambiguity in the Contemporary Yugoslav Family. In: *Ethos* 11, 1/2, pp. 66–86.

Solari, Cinzia (2010): Resource Drain vs. Constitutive Circularity: Comparing the Gendered Effects of Post-Soviet Migration Patterns in Ukraine. In: *Anthropology of East Europe Review* 28, pp. 215–238.

Temkina, Anna/Rotkirch, Anna (1997): Soviet Gender Contracts and Their Shift in Contemporary Russia. In: Temkina, Anna (ed.): Russia in Transition: *The Case of New Collective Actors and New Collective Actions.* Jyväskylä: Kikimora Publications, pp. 183–207.

104 Tatiana Tiaynen-Qadir

Tiaynen, Tatiana (2013): *Babushka in Flux. Grandmothers and Family-making between Russian Karelia and Finland*. Tampere: Tampere University Press.

Tilastokeskus (2013): *Lähes joka kymmenes 25–34-vuotias ulkomaista syntyperää*. http://www.stat.fi/til/vaerak/2012/01/vaerak_2012_01_2013–09–27_tie_001_ fi.html, accessed May 2014.

Tolstokorova, Alisa (2012): Zhdi i pomni menya': Ukrainskaya transnatsional'naya sem'ya kak objekt gendernogo analiza. In: *Diaspory* 3, pp. 6–24.

Vertovec, Steven (2004): *Trends and Impacts of Migrant Transformation*. http:// www.compas.ox.ac.uk/fileadmin/files/pdfs/WP0403.pdf, accessed January 2007.

Vertovec, Steven (2009): *Transnationalism*. London: Routledge.

Vullnetari, Julie/King, Russell (2008): "Does Your Granny Eat Grass?" On Mass Migration, Care Drain and The Fate of Older People in Rural Albania. In: *Global Networks* 8, 2, pp. 139–171.

Vuorela, Ulla (2002): Transnational Families: Imagined and Real Communities. In: Deborah, Bryceson/Ulla Vuorela (eds.): *The Transnational Family. New European Frontiers and Global Networks*. Oxford: Berg, pp. 63–82.

Vuorela, Ulla (2009): In the Olden Days We Kept Slaves. Layers of Memory and Present Practices. In: Larsen, Kjersti (ed.): *Knowledge, Renewal and Religion. Repositioning and Changing Ideological and Material Circumstances among the Swahili on the East African Cost*. Uppsala: Nordiska Afrikainstitutet, pp. 261–279.

Zdravomyslova, Elena (2009): Nyani: Kommertsializatsiya zaboty. In: Zdravomyslova, Elena /Anna, Rotkirch/Anna, Temkina (eds.): *Novyi byt v sovremennoi Rossii: gendernye sssledovaniya povsednevnosti*. Sankt-Petersburg: Izdatel'stvo Evropeiskogo universiteta v Sankt-Peterburge, pp. 94–136.

Zdravomyslova, Elena/Rotkirch, Anna/Temkina, Anna (2009): *Novyi byt v sovremennoi Rossii. Gendernye issledovaniya povsednevnosti*. Sankt-Peterburg: Izdatel'stvo Evropeiskogo universiteta v Sankt-Peterburge.

Zechner, Minna (2010): *Informaali Hoiva Sociaalipoliittisessa Kontekstissa*. Tampere: Acta Universitalis Tamperensis.

Part B

Migration in Later Life

Transnational Strategies and
Managing Risk in Old Age

5 Transnational Aging as Reflected in Germany's Pension Insurance

Ralf Himmelreicher and Wolfgang Keck

"Retiring abroad is becoming increasingly popular and the prospect of retiring in a new country can be extremely exciting for many people. After years of hard work it makes sense to seek out new experiences and moving to a new country can offer you a valuable opportunity to pursue new interests and an exciting lifestyle" (Expat Info Desk 2014). Expat Info Desk is a non-profit online resource specializing in international relocation guide services. It offers digital books that provide information about how to live in popular cities and destinations around the world. This web source exemplifies the growing trend of migration in old age. Several studies conclude that transnational migration in later life is on the rise (Kaiser 2011; O'Reilly 2000; Phillipson and Nilufar 2004). The object of this explorative chapter is to find an empirically based estimation of migration in old age related to Germany, by using the register data of the German Pension Insurance for retired persons who having lived in Germany for some time.

From a theoretical point of view, migration in later life comprises permanent return migration as well as circular migration. Permanent return migration can be based on very different intentions and motives (Currle 2006), such as the failure of economic or social integration or as a planned interim period abroad to build up the foundations for a new start in the country of origin. One important strand is remigration after retirement, that is, remigration at the beginning of the economically inactive phase, which sometimes starts at the age of 50 (Kaiser 2011). Having achieved a certain standard of living, for example, acquiring one's own home in the country of origin or wishing to be reintegrated into the culture of origin are strong drivers for such migration processes.[1]

Circular migration underlines the identity of migrants, which is connected with their biography, their way of life, and their social networks in the country of origin, as well as in the country of relocation. In consequence, transnational migrants are living in and between two or more national and cultural contexts and are moving backward and forward. If migration is not motivated by economic reasons, social (support) networks in both countries play a decisive role in establishing transnational migration flows (Dietzel-Papakyriakou 1999; Stepputat 2004). There are different types of transnational migration in later life according to the time the migrants spend in different places. The first type comprises the long-stay tourist who spends several weeks every year at the same destination but who remains a "permanent resident" of his or her country of origin. Most of these migrants rent accommodation abroad. The second type is the visitors who often own property in the destination country. Therefore, they are more flexible in planning when and for how long they will stay abroad, although they spent most of the year in the country of origin. The third type is the seasonal migrant, who stays abroad for several months, mainly during the (home) winter season. Most of them are also homeowners in the destination country. The fourth type is the permanent resident who has completely moved to the destination country and only sometimes visits his or her country of origin for a short time (King, Warnes and Williams 2000).[2]

From a historical perspective, migration in later life connected to Germany has three key sources.[3] The most important source is the large migration inflows of younger workers and their families, of resettlers (*Spätaussiedler*), and of refugees to Germany since the 1960s (see the following section). Most of the migrants to Germany maintain social ties in their countries of origin and keep two homes—one in Germany and one in the place where they grew up. A growing number of these migrants have reached retirement age and therewith dispose of free time to define and establish new living arrangements. Some of them either remigrate to their country of origin or keep their German residence but commute from time to time to their country of origin (Baykara-Krumme 2004).

A second source arises from the fact that many Germans have experienced growth of wealth, healthy aging, and educational expansion during the last decades. A large number of German people spend their vacations abroad. They experience other countries, improve their language skills, and, in a small but substantial number, undertake investments in property into those countries where they travel. Having achieved retirement age, this wealthy and healthy generation actively plans their third age abroad; this is the so-called lifestyle migration (O'Reilly and Benson 2009). In addition, a social infrastructure has been developed in the favored destinations that facilitates the migration of older German people (Kaiser 2011). Population aging boosts these migration processes because there are a growing number of elderly persons who are able to move abroad.

Finally, institutions matter. The process of Europeanization by extending and deepening the European Union (EU) has simplified migration within the EU member states (AEUV 2014, European Commission 2012). Relevant milestones in this process are the possibility to transfer social security claims between countries, the free movement of workers between EU countries, a common legal framework that fosters mutual trust, growing economic interdependence, and an increasing infrastructural homogeneity, for example, through the euro. The institutional processes of transnationalization

Migration in Old Age 109

trigger the transnationalization of life courses of individuals (Fligstein and Merand 2002; Gerhards and Rössel 2008; Roose 2010).

Although research on migration in old age and the social situation of migrants in later life has attracted more interest in recent years, the topic still tends to be sidelined compared to other migration issues, like the brain and care drain or migrant integration discourses (Gerhard et al. 2014). Most of the research is focussing on distinct national groups in a specific region. There is hardly any quantitative nationwide information about the phenomenon. For example, How many persons have moved to another country in later life? In which countries do they live? Do they stay permanently there or are they transnational commuters? The data to answer these questions is meager. On one hand, cross-national surveys have sample sizes that are too small to allow for in-depth analysis on migrants. On the other hand, polls on migrants in the destination countries are not representative of the population of migrants from the country of origin (Himmelreicher and Roose 2014).

In this study we made an attempt to estimate migration in later life to and from Germany. We made use of register data from the statutory German Pension Fund (Deutsche Rentenversicherung). Almost all German citizens are covered by pension insurance at least for some time during their professional life, and most of the migrants living in Germany for a longer time have paid pension contributions and so achieved pension claims. Once they reach the age of retirement and fulfill the eligibility criteria, they will receive a pension payment from the Germany Pension Insurance, which is paid even if the retiree lives in a foreign country. In 2013, more than 16 million people received an old-age pension from the German public pension system. Based on this data source, we addressed three research questions:

1. What is the extent of migration in later life?
2. In which way has migration in later life developed in the last twenty years?
3. What future trends can be expected?

Before introducing the data basis and presenting our empirical results, in the following section we provide an overview on migration flows from and to Germany since the 1950s, because a large part of transnational migration in later life is an outcome of past migration processes of younger individuals.

PRELIMINARY REMARKS: GERMANY MIGRATION HISTORY

The process of transnational aging depends on the development of in and out migration by foreigners to Germany and Germans in other countries. Work-related migration in younger years should influence transnational aging after the professional life. For understanding the development of

110 Ralf Himmelreicher and Wolfgang Keck

migration in later life, it is important to know the pathways of migration to and from Germany. For a rough approximation of various aspects of migration for the past 60 years, we show some migration statistics from the German Statistical Office. First, in Figure 5.1 we take a closer look at the migration of foreigners to former West Germany (1954–90) and since 1991 to Germany. In a quantitative historical classification we can distinguish five different phases (Hauschild, Himmelreicher and Keck 2013; Maier-Braun 2002; Münz, Seifert and Ulrich1997):

The first phase, from 1950 to 1961, is characterized by the immigration of people from the German Democratic Republic. In these 12 years, about 2.7 million people moved from the east to the west side of Germany. In 1961, this process ends abruptly with the construction of the Iron Curtain.

The second phase covers the beginning of the 1960s up to the economic crisis in 1973. The "economic miracle" in postwar Germany resulted in rapid economic growth and a shortage of labor supply at that time stimulated the German government to conclude migration agreements (*Anwerbeabkommen*) with several Mediterranean countries.[4] Workers from these countries were provided a job in Germany after having undergone a medical assessment. In particular, workers from Turkey, Italy, Spain, Greece, and Morocco moved to Western Germany. The initial idea was to have a system of rotating migration. Migrant workers could stay for a maximum of five years and then had to move back to their country of origin. Many of them did so, but employers wanted to keep their well-trained staff and the migrated employees asked to stay longer in Germany. As a consequence, the duration immigrant workers were allowed to stay in Germany was extended. In this period, approximately 8.7 million so-called *Gastarbeiter* (guest workers) moved to Germany.

This first generation of migrant workers reached the retirement age in the last ten years. Many of them are living in the region where they once started to live and work in Germany. There is a growing body of research on these migrant workers in Germany, in particular on the cultural specifics of care and social participation (Byakara-Krumme, Motel-Klingebiel and Schimany 2012). Another research focus is on remigrated workers and refugees who (have to) move back to their country of origin permanently (Ghosh 2000). There are also transnational commuters, most of them integrated both in the social and kinship networks both in Germany and in their country of origin (Baykara-Krumme 2013).

The third phase lasts from 1973 (the recruitment ban for foreign employees) until 1989 (the fall of the Iron Curtain). Guest workers returning to their countries of origin receive provisions (*Rückkehrhilfegesetz*) from different German institutions (Himmelreicher and Scheffelmeier 2012). Indeed, many guest workers move back to their country of origin, so the net migration in this period is negative for some years and the total volume of migration is relative low (Figure 5.1). On the other hand, in the 1970s new laws on integration provide migrant workers with better citizenship rights. They achieved a permanent resident status and children and spouses in the countries of origin receive residence permits. A large share of migrant workers has started to build up family networks in Germany in this period.

The fourth phase, from 1989 to 2000, was characterized by the fall of the Iron Curtain and the unification of Germany. The increase in immigration reached its peak in 1992 with 1.2 million migrants. Ethnic Germans (*Spätaussiedler*), individual asylum seekers from Southeast Europe, and refugees from former Yugoslavia moved to Germany in this period. In this phase, migration in later life concerns in particular ethnic Germans who settled (and resettled) in Eastern Europe and the Commonwealth of Independent States (CIS). After the fall of the Iron Curtain in 1989, many of them took the opportunity to move to Germany. Because of their German ethnic background, they could claim Germany citizenship and permanent residence rights. Whole families and communities moved to Germany in this phase, including large number of elderly people. Even though they did not pay contributions in the German statutory pension system, they received a pension according to their working history in the country of origin, regulated by a specific law called Fremdrentengesetz (FRG; see also the chapter by Sommer and Vogel in this volume).

The last and still evolving period (phase V) is characterized by EU enlargement and the associated influx of people between 2004 and 2007 from the ten new East European EU member states and by the ongoing network migration, in particular from Turkey. Figure 5.1 shows a high number of in-migrants to Germany and a rising level of out-migrations from Germany beginning with 2010, at the end of this period. In fact, after 2000, there were already signs that things started to turn around. Germany's new labor market miracle combined with the great crisis in some other European countries may have led to the increasing immigration of workers. In some years we can see whether this effect creates a new phase of migration in Germany. At the moment it does seem that, in net effect, more people get to Germany.

These two developments of increasing immigration and emigration are indications of Europeanization or transnationalism. Important for our analysis is the total volume of migration, shown in Figure 5.1, because this line potentially represents all the people with migration experience in Germany. Presumably they were or are employed subject to compulsory insurance in Germany, and with an account in the German social security system.

Compared with Figure 5.1, the migration movement from the Germans across borders shown in Figure 5.2 is quite low. The immigration is driven by ethnic Germans, in particular after the fall of the Iron Curtain in 1989.

In the period from 2004 through 2012, emigration from Germany is greater than immigrations, so net migration is negative (Erlinghagen, Stegmann and Wagner 2009). This development is also an indication of Europeanization or transnationalism. A growing number of Germans have moved abroad after reaching retirement age, most of them from the middle and upper classes who have been able to acquire property in Mediterranean countries. In some regions in Spain, Portugal, and Greece, Germans build the largest group of migrants and form their own inclusive communities with social and medical services, German-speaking newspapers, associations, and clubs. Research on this type of migration is scarce (Himmelreicher and Roose 2014; Kaiser 2011). Either they are seasonal commuters who escape the winter season in Germany but move back as soon as springtime is on the way, or they move permanently in their country of choice to spend their third age in a place of their choice. Most of the German migrants plan to return to Germany if they become frail and are in need of care, in order to be supported by their family in Germany and to receive the more generous social service provisions.

In summary, it can be said that transnational or European labor market integration is rising and that Germany has been an immigration country for a long time. But how does this development affect migration in older age?

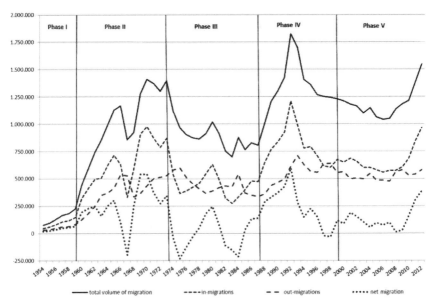

Figure 5.1 In- and out-migrations, net migration, and total volume of migration of foreigners in Germany (1954–2012)
Source: Statistisches Bundesamt (2013a), following Hauschild et al. (2013).

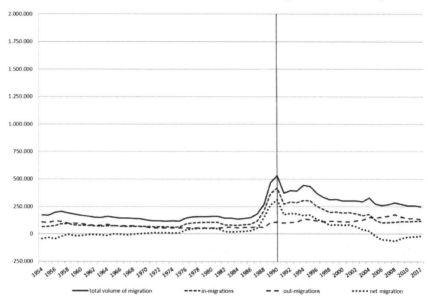

Figure 5.2 In- and out-migrations, net migration, and total volume of migration of Germans in Germany (1954–2012)
Source: Statistisches Bundesamt (2013a), following Hauschild et al. (2013).

DATA, VARIABLES, AND METHODS

The Research Data Centre of the German Federal Pension Insurance (FDZ-RV) supplies cross-sectional and longitudinal micro-data.[5] These data are process produced. In Germany, statutory pension insurance is mandatory for all employed persons in the private and public sector. In addition to this, contributions are paid out of unemployment insurance to those unemployed and out of health insurance in the event of long-term illness. So the majority of the population working in Germany—Germans and foreigners—comes into contact with the German Federal Pension Insurance, and the pension data cover more than 90 percent of the entire population. Not included are, for example, civil servants and most of the self-employed. The German Federal Pension Insurance is the biggest income source for people after retirement. Besides old-age pensions, another important function of the FDZ-RV is support for rehabilitation in the event of inability to work (Himmelreicher and Stegmann 2008).

Because of the lack of longitudinal information of migration in the FDZ-RV data, we focus on cross-sectional data. This framework of migration is used by different data sources of the German Federal Pension Insurance (see Himmelreicher and Stegmann [2008] for the entire data offer of the FDZ-RV). For different points on the spectrum from older to younger

114   *Ralf Himmelreicher and Wolfgang Keck*

people who were or are insured in the pension insurance, we can decide on some different cross-sectional data sources. First, there is the retirement stock data. These data include all recipients of pensions (invalidity, old-age, and survivor pensions) from the German pension insurance, regardless of nationality or the place of residence in a given year. Second, there is the retirement inflow data. These data include all recipients of new pensions from the German Pension Insurance in the year under review, regardless of whether it is invalidity, old-age, or survivor pensions, regardless of nationality or the place of residence in a given year. And third, there is a data set of all (active) insured persons in a reference period. Insured persons are working and paying contributions in the German pension insurance. They are educating kids and providing nursing care for family members, and they are normally in the labor force age of between 17 and 66 years. So, from the point view of migration, these three data sets allow us to analyze different periods of individual transnational working biographies.

In these three different data types, there are four variables dealing with the migration aspect (for details, see Himmelreicher and Scheffelmeyer, 2012):

- First, there is the nationality of the insured people. In 2012, the total population of Germany was 81.84 million. Of these, 9.1 percent (7.41 million) had a foreign nationality (Statistisches Bundesamt 2013b). In the FDZ-RV data, it is possible to identify whether people have German or any other nationality (for country and nationality codes, see Alda and Herrlinger 2005). Some have stateless status, others have nationality unknown or missing status (47,098 cases, or 0.2 percent, in the retirement stock data of 2013, old-age and invalidity pensions only). As usual, the nationality variable has some problems: for example, how to situate people born in Germany with a foreign nationality, naturalized foreign-born people, and dual citizenship (Burkert, Hochfellner and Wurdack 2012).
- The second important variable is the place of residence. This variable indicates whether the insured or retired people officially report living in Germany or in any other country. For Germany, small regions and federal states (*Bundesländer*) can be identified. All other countries have a specific country code, the same like the nationality code.
- Third and fourth variables are specific and indicate a transnational working sequence. The Act on Foreign Pensions (Fremdrentengesetz) compensates times of working in the German pension insurance for ethnic Germans who moved from former soviet countries to Germany (see Figure 5.2). The fourth variable is the Vertragsrente or contract pension, which indicates whether the pension falls under a transnational social security agreement with the EU or other countries, because of a transnational working sequence. Apart from the European Union (EU)/ European Economic Area countries and Switzerland, such bilateral treaties exist with countries such as Australia or the US. The data contain information on the last country where the person worked. There is

often no contract pension in the case of transnational firms if employees work in the same firm in a foreign country. However, in such cases the employee remains connected to the previous national pension account.

• This information on transnationality is not very well differentiated in the FDZ-RV data, but it can give a broad outline of the lower limit of transnational aging, because circular migration and other types of temporary migration are not covered. The main advantage of the data is the possibility to control for the work histories of the (former) insured persons and the large number of cases. With this approach we try to overcome national methodologism (Taylor 1994). Table 5.1 shows the interrelations of the four variables and possible strategy of analysis, with a focus on transnational aging.

Table 5.1 Framework of migration based on the data of the German Federal Pension Insurance

		Nationality			
		German		**Foreign**	
Place of residence 'retirement migration' 'stationary aging'	Living in Germany	Germans living in Germany	Transnational employment history no Transnational employment history yes: with contract pensions or Act on Foreign Pensions (FRG)	Foreigners living in Germany	Transnational employment history no Transnational employment history yes: with contract pensions or Act on Foreign Pensions (FRG)
	Living abroad	Germans living abroad	Transnational employment history no Transnational employment history yes: with Contract pensions or Act on foreign pensions (FRG)	Foreigners living abroad in country of origin or other country	Transnational employment history no Transnational employment history yes: with Contract pensions or Act on foreign pensions (FRG)

116 Ralf Himmelreicher and Wolfgang Keck

EMPIRICAL RESULTS

First, we replace the cells in Table 5.1 with results from the retirement stock statistics that partly reflect working phases from decades ago. Then we use the pension inflow statistics for the actual process of retirement. Finally, we analyze the statistics of the insured persons for the actual development of transnational working biographies.

In total, more than 17.5 million people received a full old-age pension from the German Federal Pension Insurance in 2013; their average age is 74.6 years. Most of them were living in Germany, but a share of about 7 percent of the pensioners, or more than 1.2 million people receiving a full old-age pension from Germany, was living in foreign countries (Table 5.2). In 2003, this proportion was less than 6 percent and in 1993 less than 5 percent (Deutsche Rentenversicherung Bund 2013). Thus, we see a slow increasing trend of German pensions being paid in foreign countries. Most of the pensioners who were living in foreign countries also had foreign nationality. Only 158,116 pensioners, or about 13 percent, of those living outside of Germany had German nationality. The majority of the older people living abroad were remigrants: 80 percent of the elderly Germans living in foreign countries had contract pensions, which also means transnational working biographies. And only fewer than 20 percent of those have no working history in foreign countries.

These results show that the mobility experiences of German employees in turn encourage transnational aging in other countries. In total, 1,754,964 pensioners (about 10 percent) had a foreign nationality in 2013. Roughly 40 percent of them were living in Germany, and the rest were living abroad. Only half the pensioners with a foreign nationality had transnational working biographies, so it seems that they had never worked in a foreign contract country as a legal employee. Maybe they were born with a foreign nationality in Germany or they immigrated in younger years. For elderly living outside of Germany we see a quite different picture. Nearly all of them have a transnational employment history. This shows that working mobility experiences by employees from foreign countries often leads to transnational aging in other countries. In other words, mobility in younger years encourages mobility in later years as well. But this mobility is limited, because the data show that most of the foreigners living abroad (80 percent) are living in the country of origin; therefore, transnational aging by foreigners becomes more of a two-country phenomenon. Our results are similar to Fassmann's (2012), who shows that former "guest workers" and their relatives have a higher drain quota than do Germans.

And in which countries do the elderly pensioners live? We looked at the data for Germans and foreigners separately and at the top five countries. Nearly 250,000 pensioners live in Italy, 150,000 live in Spain, more than 66,000 live in the US and Austria, and nearly 44,000 live in Canada. Of these, more than 20,000 older Germans prefer to live in the US and

Table 5.2 Migration in the stock statistics of the German Federal Pension Insurance 2013, pensioners with full old age pensions (people older than 60)

		Total		German	Foreigners
				Nationality	
Place of residence	Germany	16,461,951 (93.1%)	15,767,879 (99.0%)	% within* No trans-national employment 14,621,949 (95.7%) CONpen 726,950 (4.6 %) FRGpen 733,745 (4.7%)	% within* 694,072 (39.5%) No trans-national employment 345,063 (49.7%) CONpen 331,790 (47.8%) FRGpen 35,356 (5.1%)
	Abroad	1,219,008 (6.9%)	158,116 (1.0%)	% within* No trans-national employment 31,147 (19.6%) CONpen 126,428 (80%) FRGpen 3,542 (2.2%)	% within* 1,060,892 (60.5 %) No trans-national employment 22,092 (2.1%) In country of origin 1,017,902 (95.9%) — CONpen 1,038,528 (97.9%) In other country 42,990 (4.1%) — FRGpen 7,477 (0.01%)
Total		17,680,959 (100%)	15,925,995 (100%)		1,754,964 (100%)

Note: CONpen = contract pensions; FRGpen = Act on Foreign Pensions.
*Cases with both contract pensions and foreign pensions are possible, multiple answers are permitted, and therefore, percentages add to more than 100 percent.

Source: FDZ-RV pension stock statistics 2013, own calculation.

Switzerland. More than 14,000 live in Spain and Austria and 8,300 in Canada. With respect to the official return migration from foreigners back in their countries of origin, we see a wide variation. Nearly 98 percent of the former Italian guest workers live in Italy, 90 percent of the Spanish sub-population live in Spain, more than 80 percent of Canadians and Austrians returned to Canada or Austria, respectively, more than 70 percent of the Americans returned to the US, and only 3 percent of the elderly with a Turkish citizenship live in Turkey (see the appendix). In general, transnational

118   Ralf Himmelreicher and Wolfgang Keck

aging as reflected in the statistics of the Federal German Pension Insurance is largely the result of the immigration of guest workers in the last 50 years to Germany. We also see a growing number of Germans with transnational labor experience (Himmelreicher and Roose 2014) who are living as elderly in foreign countries (Horn et al. 2013).

The statistics on all old age pensions comprise a wide range of age cohorts, starting from 60 years of age up to 100 and older. It is a mapping of a broad time span, which covers different migration periods. Focussing on the new recipients of an old-age pension in the actual reporting year provides a more recent and narrow image of migration processes. The vast majority of new old age pensioners were aged between 60 and 65 years in 2013. They were born between 1948 and 1953. Most of the foreign pensioners in this group migrated to Germany as workers or as close family members in the late 1960s and 1970s.

As Table 5.3 shows, the share of new pensioners living abroad is higher than the share in the overall population of old age pensioners: 7.6 percent compared to 6.9 percent. This comes as no surprise because among the new old age pensioners in 2013, the share of foreigners is more than five percentage points higher than in the overall pensioner population, and foreign pensioners represent around 86 percent of the new pensioners living abroad. From those pensioners with foreign nationality who are living abroad, more than 95 percent move back to their country of origin. For foreign citizens remigration seems to be a dominant pattern.

The quota of new pensioners with a German nationality living abroad is 0.3 percentage points higher compared to all German old-age pensioners. However, the overall number remains small. Only 7,066 Germans who received an old-age pension for the first time in 2013 lived abroad, or 1.3 percent of all new pensioners with a German nationality. The most frequent destination countries are the US and Switzerland, with 11.4 percent of the new German old-age pensioners living abroad residing in each, followed by Spain (9.4 percent), Austria and France (each 8.2 percent), and Brazil (8.0 percent). Those pensioners who plan to move abroad sometime after they retire are not covered in this statistic.

Similar to the overall old age pensioner population, 98.5 percent of the new pensioners living abroad with foreign citizenship and 86.8 percent of the new German pensioners who are living abroad have gathered creditable periods for their German pension claims in another country. Most of the new old age pensioners living abroad experienced migration trajectories during their working lives. Unfortunately, there is no information on when those new pensioners moved abroad, but many of them receive considerable pensions payments—on average 280 euro for men and 204 euro for women. That means that a large share of pensioners living abroad has paid contributions in the German statutory pension scheme for years,[6] so we would assume that in most of cases emigration from Germany started in the second half of the working life or those pensioners have been transnational commuters for a long time.

Table 5.3 Migration in the pension inflow statistics of the German Federal Pension Insurance 2013, pensioners aged between 60 and 65 years with new full old-age pensions

		Total		German		Foreigners	
				Nationality			
		Total		German		Foreigners	
Place of resi-dence	Germany	606,405 (92.4%)	541,309 (98.7 %)	% within* No trans-national employment 505,711 (93.4%) CONpen 22,557 (4.2%) FRGpen 21,882 (4%)	65,096 (60.5 %)	% within* No trans-national employment 26,943 (41.4%) CONpen 36,962 (56.8%) FRGpen 2,825 (4.3%)	
	Abroad	49,575 (7.6%)	7,066 (1.3%)	% within* No trans-national employment 948 (13.4%) CONpen 6,097 (86.3 %) FRGpen 131 (1.9%)	in country of origin 40,714 (95.2%) in other country 1,795 (4.2%)	% within* No trans-national employment 667 (1.6%) CONpen 41,832 (98.4%) FRGpen 197 (0.5%)	
Total		655,980 (100%)	548,375 (100%)			107,605 (100%)	

Note: CONpen = contract pensions; FRGpen = Act on Foreign Pensions.
* Cases with both contract pensions and foreign pensions are possible, multiple answers are permitted, and therefore, percentages add to more than 100 percent.

Source: FDZ-RV pension inflow statistics 2013, own calculation.

The share of new pensioners who are living abroad increased marginally between 2003 and 2013, from 7.5 to 7.6 percent. The main reason for the stagnating percentage is that ten years ago in 2003 the first generation of migrants who had come in the late 1950s and early 1960s reached the age of retirement. We observe therefore a constant inflow of foreign pensioners in the last decade. Going back to 1993, the share of new pensioners living

120   Ralf Himmelreicher and Wolfgang Keck

Table 5.4   Number and total percent of insured persons of the German Federal Pension Insurance 2012 by place of residence and citizenship

	Germans	Foreigners	Total
Living in Germany	43,387,707 (82.4%)	7,695,031 (14.6%)	51,082,738 (97%)
Living abroad	411,551 (0.8%)	1,177,935 (2.2%)	1,589,486 (3%)
Total	43,799,258 (83.2%)	8,872,966 (16.8%)	52,672,224 (100%)

Source: Deutsche Rentenversicherung (2014), own calculation.

abroad was clearly lower than nowadays, as at that time around 6.2 percent were living outside Germany.

The statistical resources on pensioners living abroad reflect, to a large extent, migration and working histories from foreign citizens in Germany that date back 30 to 40 years. The statistics on insured persons of the German Pension Insurance provided more recent migration trajectories. Every person who has completed at least one month of a creditable period is registered by the German Pension Insurance. In total, there are more than 52.6 million accounts of recent or formerly insured persons, of whom around 1.6 million are living abroad (see table 4). This figure should be interpreted as a minimum number, because not all insured persons who have moved abroad indicated their change of residence to the German Pension Insurance.

Every three in four insured persons living outside Germany hold a foreign citizenship. Even though foreign citizens form the majority of insured persons living abroad, the share of 26 percent of insured Germans living abroad is much higher than among the pensioner population, which is 12 percent for all old age pensioners in 2013. At the same time, the share of foreign citizens is around 6.8 percentage points higher than in the population of old-age pensioners. Although some of these foreign citizens may have been born in Germany and never lived abroad, the figures indicate that transnational biographies are increasing for younger generations.

Taking into account our findings that living abroad at retirement age is closely associated with either foreign citizenship or insurance periods in other countries, we predict from the data on insured persons that migration in later life connected to Germany will be increasing in future.

CONCLUSION

Our analysis shows a growing number and share of transnational biographies among pensioners. More and more people with a foreign nationality have had regular employment in Germany, and more Germans have worked in foreign countries. Both effects indicate migration in particular across European countries. First, they perforate the "national container" (Taylor 1994), and second, they go hand in hand with an increasing number of elderly people living in foreign countries.

Migration in later life is characterized by a high level of mobility of the foreign population in Germany and in particular of former guest workers. Only little more than 1 percent of all retired Germans are living in a foreign country, and nearly 80 percent of them have worked in foreign countries, so we could assume that working mobility in younger years will influence the regional mobility in later life. In the pension stock statistics, the share of foreigners is only four percent. This share is rising to more than 16 percent of the population at working age who were insured in the German Pension Insurance in 2013. All in all, transnational aging will become more frequent in the future, especially when there is peace, stability, and shared prosperity in the countries of origin. If this is not the case, most older immigrants will probably stay in Germany.

The underlying data used for this analysis has some limitations. In most of the cases we only identify those pensioners who are officially registered in other countries as permanent residents. Various types of seasonal or long-stay migration are barely covered because the elderly people remain German residents in order to obtain full social security rights and avoid tax and inheritance penalties. Therefore, our empirical numbers represent only the upper threshold of the transnational aging. Moreover, the differentiation by nationality does not reflect double or multiple nationalities or the fact that a substantial share of (younger) foreigners was born in Germany. The data also do not contain information about the migration history of the insured person. What the data contain is some information about the working history of the (former) insured persons, and what we do see according to this information is a growing number of transnational migration in later life.

Migrants' settlement decisions seem to depend on the structural level of the host society, such as its laws, its economy, and its political, social, and cultural models. The quota of re-immigration in nations of peace, stability, and shared prosperity like Italy is quite high, but in other conditions it is low, like in Turkey. This result may also be due to the feasibility of commuting between two or more countries. It is, however, plausible to assume that remigration in risky regions is unlikely.

However, we know almost nothing about the cognitive–cultural orientation or the individual preferences of a transnational lifestyle. In this research field, we need further inquiries to understand the reasons why a person decides to move abroad after retiring, and for how long this decision will last. We assume that the observed growing number of transnational working biographies and the rising opportunities to move abroad to build a secure existence in a world with rising inequality will result in the increasing

122 Ralf Himmelreicher and Wolfgang Keck

numbers of transnational aging being seen as a kind of harsh discipline emerging at a time when elders feel relatively powerless.

NOTES

1 In practice, this objective turns out to be illusory because the migrants' standards change during the years abroad and social and cultural ties alter over the period the migrant is absent (Cassarino 2004).
2 Other authors describe similar typologies (see Kaiser 2011).
3 There are other pathways that lead to people moving into another country in later life, such as interethnic marriage. However, based on the numbers of migrants, these motivations to migrate are of minor importance in the German case.
4 Migration agreements were conducted with Italy (1955), Greece and Spain (1960), Turkey (1961), Morocco (1963), Portugal (1964), Tunisia (1965), and Yugoslavia (1968).
5 The Research Data Centre (FDZ-RV) was set up in 2004 as an integral part of the German Federal Pension Insurance (Deutsche Rentenversicherung). Since then, the FDZ-RV produced several cross-sectional and longitudinal datasets. These data are also available for researchers outside of Germany. For more information, see http://www.fdz-rv.de.
6 Model calculation: To achieve a pension claim in western Germany of 280 euro, a person has to have paid contributions at rate of an average income for approximately ten years.

REFERENCES

AEUV Artikel 21 (2014): *Vertrag über die Arbeitsweise der Europäischen Union.* http://www.aeuv.de/aeuv/zweiter-teil/art-21.html, accessed July 2014.
Alda, Holger/Herrlinger, Dagmar (2005): *Anlageband 1: Codepläne zum FDZ-Datenreport Nr. 7: LIAB-Datenhandbuch.* Nürnberg: Bundesagentur für Arbeit.
Baykara-Krumme, Helen (2004): Fortwährende Remigration: Das transnationale Pendeln türkischer Arbeitsmigrantinnen und Arbeitsmigranten im Ruhestand. In: *Zeitschrift für Soziologie* 33, 2, pp. 138–153.
Baykara-Krumme, Helen (2013): Returning, Staying, or Both? Mobility Patterns Among Elderly Turkish Migrants After Retirement. In: *Transnational Social Review* 3, pp. 11–29.
Baykara-Krumme, Helen/Motel-Klingebiel, Andreas/Schimany, Peter (eds.) (2012): *Viele Welten des Alterns. Ältere Migranten im alternden Deutschland.* Wiesbaden: Springer VS.
Burkert, Carola/Hochfellner, Daniela/Wurdack, Anja (2012): Ältere Migrantinnen und Migranten am Arbeitsmarkt. In: Baykara-Krumme, Helen/Motel-Klingebiel, Andreas/Schimany, Peter (eds.): *Viele Welten des Alterns. Alter(n) und Gesellschaft.* Vol. 22. Wiesbaden: Springer, pp. 77–100.
Cassarino, Jean-Pierre (2004): Theorising Return Migration: The Conceptual Approach to Return Migrants Revisited. In: *International Journal on Multicultural Societies* 6, pp. 253–279.
Currle, Edda (2006): *Theorieansätze zur Erklärung von Rückkehr und Remigration. Sozialwissenschaftlicher Fachinformationsdienst (soFid).* http://www.gesis.org/

fileadmin/upload/dienstleistung/fachinformationen/servicepublikationen/sofid/ Fachbeitraege/Migration_2006–2.pdf, accessed September 2014.

Deutsche Rentenversicherung Bund (2013): Rentenversicherung in Zeitreihen. *DRV-Schriften Band 22*. Berlin: in-house publication.

Deutsche Rentenversicherung Bund (2014): *Versicherte 2012. Statistik der Deutschen Rentenversicherung*. Vol. 195. Berlin: in-house publication.

Dietzel-Papakyriakou, Maria (1999): Wanderungen alter Menschen. In: Naegele, Gerhard and Schütz, Rudolf-Maria (eds.): *Soziale Gerontologie. Lebenslagen im Alter und Sozialpolitik für ältere Menschen*. Wiesbaden: Opladen, pp. 141–156.

Erlinghagen, Marcel/Stegmann, Tim/Wagner, Gerd (2009): Deutschland ein Auswanderungsland? In: *DIW Wochenbericht 39*, pp. 663–669.

European Commission (2012): *White Paper. An Agenda for Adequate, Safe and Sustainable Pensions*. COM 55, 2, Brussels.

Expat Info Desk (2014): *Retiring Abroad*. http://www.expatinfodesk.com/expat-guide/retiring-abroad/, accessed September 2014.

Fassmann, Heinz (2012): Ruhestandswanderung und stationäres Altern. In: Baykara-Krumme, Helen/Motel-Klingebiel/Andreas/Schimany, Peter (eds.): *Viele Welten des Alterns. Alter(n) und Gesellschaft*. Vol. 22. Wiesbaden: Springer, pp. 365–385.

Fligstein, Neil/Merand, Frederic (2002): Globalizitation or Europeanizitation? Evidence on the European Economy since 1980. In: *Acta Sociologica 45*, pp. 7–22.

Gerhards, Jürgen/Rössel, Jörg (2008): Zur Transnationalisierung der Gesellschaft der Bundesrepublik. Entwicklungen, Ursachen und mögliche Folgen für die europäische Integration. In: *Zeitschrift für Soziologie 28*, 5, pp. 325–344.

Gerhards, Jürgen/Hans, Silke/Carlson, Sören (2014): Transnationales Humankapital. Einleitende Bemerkungen zu Kontextbedingungen, Erwerb und Verwertbarkeit von transnationalen Kompetenzen. In: Gerhards, Jürgen/Hans, Silke/Sören, Carlsen (eds.): *Globalisierung, Bildung und grenzüberschreitende Mobilität*. Wiesbaden: Springer, pp. 7–19.

Ghosh, Bimal (ed.) (2000): *Return Migration. Journey of Hope or Despair?* Geneva: International Organization for Migration and the United Nations.

Hauschild, Matthias/Himmelreicher, Ralf/Keck, Wolfgang (2013): Die wachsende Bedeutung transnationaler Erwerbsbiografien und deren Auswirkungen auf die deutsche Rentenversicherung. In: *DRV 3*, pp. 199–221.

Himmelreicher, Ralf/Roose, Jochen (2014): Transnationale Erwerbsbiografien. Verbreitung und Spezifika untersucht mit Daten der gesetzlichen Rentenversicherung. In: Gerhards, Jürgen/Hans, Silke/Sören, Carlsen (eds.): *Globalisierung, Bildung und grenzüberschreitende Mobilität*. Wiesbaden: Springer, pp. 213–236.

Himmelreicher, Ralf/Scheffelmeier, Tine (2012): Transnationalisierung und Europäisierung der Altersrente? Entwicklung beim Zugang in Altersrente in Deutschland (1993–2009). *BSSE-Arbeitspapier Nr. 26*. Berlin: Freie Universität.

Himmelreicher, Ralf/Stegmann, Michael (2008): New Possibilities for Socio-Economic Research through Longitudinal Data from the Research Data Centre of the German Federal Pension Insurance (FDZ-RV). In: *Schmollers Jahrbuch 128*, pp. 647–660.

Horn, Vincent/Schweppe, Cornelia/Um, Seonggee (2013): "Transnational Aging—A Young Field of Research". In: *Transnational Social Review—A Social Work Journal 3*, 1, pp. 7–10.

Kaiser, Claudia (2011): *Transnationale Altersmigration in Europa*. Wiesbaden: VS Verlag für Sozialwissenschaften.

King, Russel/Warnes, Anthony M./Williams, Alan M. (2000): *Sunset Lives—British Retirement Migration to the Mediterranean*. Oxford/ New York: Berg.

Maier-Braun, Karl-Heinz (2002): *Deutschland, Einwanderungsland*. Frankfurt am Main: Suhrkamp Verlag.

124 Ralf Himmelreicher and Wolfgang Keck

Münz, Reiner/Seifert, Wolfgang/Ulrich, Ralf (1997): *Zuwanderung nach Deutsch land. Strukturen—Wirkungen—Perspektiven.* Frankfurt am Main: Campus Verlag.

O'Reilly, Karen (2000): *The British on the Costa del Sol—Transnational Identities and Local Communities.* New York: Routledge.

O'Reilly, Karen/Benson, Michaela C. (2009): *Lifestyle Migration: Expectations, Aspirations, Experiences.* Surrey: Ashgate.

Phillipson, Chris/Nilufar, Ahmed (2004): Transnational Communities, Migration and Changing Identities in Later Life: A New Research Agenda. In: Daatland, S. O. and S. Biggs (Eds.): Ageing and Diversity: *Multiple Pathways and Cultural Migration.* Bristol: The Policy Press, pp. 157–212.

Roose, Jochen (2010): *Vergesellschaftung an Europas Binnengrenzen. Eine vergleichende Studie zu den Bedingungen sozialer Integration.* Wiesbaden: VS Verlag für Sozialwissenschaften.

Statistisches Bundesamt (2013a): *Bevölkerung und Erwerbstätigkeit. Vorläufige Wanderungsergebnisse 2012.* Wiesbaden: in-house publication.

Statistisches Bundesamt (2013b): *Statistisches Jahrbuch 2013.* Wiesbaden: in-house publication.

Stepputat, Finn (2004): *Dynamics of Return and Sustainable Reintegration in a 'Mobile Livelihood' Perspective.* DIIS Working Paper 2004/10. Copenhagen: Danish Institute for International Studies.

Taylor, Peter (1994): The State as a Container. Territoriality in the Modern World-System. Progress. In: *Human Geography* 18, 2, pp. 151–162.

Appendix

Table A.5.1 Top five countries by numbers of pensions paid in foreign countries in the stock statistics of the German Federal Pension Insurance 2013, pensioners with full old-age pensions

	All		Germans		Foreigners/quota of remigration in the country of origin	
1	Italy	(253,943)	US	(20,629)	Italy	(249,191, 97.6%)
2	Spain	(164,950)	Suisse	(20,464)	Spain	(150,844, 90.4%)
3	US	(87,313)	Spain	(14,106)	US	(66,684, 72.7%)
4	Austria	(80,877)	Austria	(14,023)	Austria	(66,854, 80.3%)
5	Canada	(52.256)	Canada	(8,300)	Canada	(43,956, 81.5%)

Source: FDZ-RV pension stock statistics 2013, own calculation.

6 Maintaining Dual Residences to Manage Risks in Later Life
A Comparison of Two Groups of Older Migrants

Anita Böcker and Canan Balkir

In the Mediterranean region, two populations of older migrants from northern Europe are increasing in number: former labor migrants who return "home" on retirement and northern European retirees. At first sight, the two populations appear to be very different, in terms of ethnicity and previous migration experience and in terms of wealth or class. As Ackers and Dwyer (2002: 130–131) noted with regard to intra–European Union (EU) migrants, "[w]hile southern European returnee workers may be the nouveau riche in terms of some of their compatriots, they remain poor cousins when compared to many post-retirement migrants from northern Europe who have taken up residence beside them." However, there is also substantial diversity within both populations. The migration of northern European retirees to the Mediterranean was pioneered in the 1960s and 1970s by people with above-average incomes and education but has since become more broadly based socially. Likewise, not all former labor migrants were employed in blue-collar jobs, and some were able to build significant savings and investments during their working lives in northern Europe.

The two populations also share some similarities. Both groups have ties and resources in the country where they have spent their working lives. Migrants in both groups need to manage social and financial risks that are associated with later life, such as disease and disability, widowhood, loss of independence, and poverty. Moreover, both groups move from northern European to Mediterranean welfare states. In northern Europe, as well as in the Mediterranean, long-term care for persons who need assistance with daily living tasks is provided at least partly by (mostly female) relatives and other informal carers. However, in northern Europe, the state is also considered to have a responsibility. In the Mediterranean, the provision of long-term care is seen much more as a familial responsibility (Arts and Gelissen 2002; Esping-Andersen 1999). Because of (and reinforcing) these different "cultures of care," publicly provided or funded care services that are available to older people and their families in northern Europe are sparse or nonexistent in Mediterranean countries. Retirement migrants and retirement returnees (unless they have children or other close relatives in the home country) move away from family resources. Transnational families

126 *Anita Böcker and Canan Balkir*

may be able to exchange emotional and financial support across distance, but personal care requires proximity (Ackers and Dwyer 2002; Baldassar 2007). Finally, both groups may face challenges arising from how their home and their host countries respond to their mobility. National immigration rules and social security rules often impede or penalize international mobility, for example, by restricting the portability of welfare and pension rights or limiting newcomers' access to social rights.

This contribution examines how these features influence the migratory decisions of the two groups of older migrants. It can be assumed that, both because of their ties and resources in the country where they spent their working lives and the risks and vulnerabilities they face because of their age, many individuals in both groups prefer to migrate on a temporary or pendular—rather than a permanent—basis. However, different categories of older migrants are granted differential social and mobility rights. Therefore, it can also be assumed that the two groups—and individuals within them—face different challenges and opportunities in realizing their preferences.

The data for this contribution are drawn from a collaborative research project that compared retirement migrants and retirement returnees from the Netherlands in Turkey.[1] Traditionally known as an emigration country, Turkey has in recent years become a popular destination for European retirement migrants, particularly for German, British, Nordic, and Dutch pensioners (Balkir and Kirkulak 2009). Moreover, most of the Turkish labor migrants who moved to northern Europe in the 1960s and 1970s have become pensioners, and in recent years some of them have been choosing to retire in their home country.

MIGRATION IN LATER LIFE

For a long time, studies of international migration concentrated on migrants of working age and on onetime, permanent changes of residence. During the last 15 years, older migrants have received increasing research attention, and studies on transnationalism have shown that migration should be seen as a continuing process. Recent research shows that many retired labor migrants move back and forth between the country where they spend their working lives and their home country (Bolzman, Fibbi and Vial 2006; De Coulon and Wolff 2010; De Haas and Fokkema 2010; Krumme 2004). Studies on northern European retirement migrants show that many of them maintain dual residences (Casado-Diaz, Kaiser and Warnes 2004; King, Warnes and Williams 2000; O'Reilly 2000). These preferences for seasonal or pendular migration and for maintaining dual residences have been interpreted or explained in different ways.

Amenity maximization. In the literature on international retirement migration, seasonal migration is often described as a strategy for "residential

Maintaining Dual Residences to Manage Risks   127

amenity maximization," enabling migrants to enjoy the winters in warmer countries, for example, Spain, and the summers in northern Europe (Huber and O'Reilly 2004; King, Warnes and Williams 2000).

Extension of preretirement patterns. An interpretation which has been put forward both with regard to northern European retirees and former labor migrants is that postretirement migration patterns are a continuation or extension of preretirement patterns. For many northern Europeans, repeated holiday visits and the purchase of a second home act as stepping-stones to seasonal movement and then, perhaps, to permanent settlement (King, Warnes and Williams 2000: 110). The pendular migration of retired Turkish labor migrants has been described as a continuation, with changed time resources, of the transnationalism prevalent in their previous migration biography (Krumme 2004), and as a transformation of the original intention to return (Latcheva and Herzog-Punzenberger 2011).

Dual ties and transnational identities. Another interpretation draws attention to the duality of ties and resources and the transnational or "mixed" identities of the migrants. Many of the Swedish seasonal migrants interviewed by Gustafson (2001, 2008) claimed to be as much "at home" in Spain as in Sweden. Relatives and friends, especially children and grandchildren, were an important source of attachment to Sweden. Similar findings were reported in studies of retired labor migrants from the Mediterranean (Bolzman, Fibbi and Vial 2006). According to Krumme (2004), older Turkish migrants had developed feelings of national belonging that could not be classified as "either–or" but as "both–and" (or in some cases as "neither–nor"), and pendular migration enabled them to make use of social and other resources in both Germany and Turkey.

In this contribution, we examine whether and how increasing care needs or an awareness of future needs influence the migratory decisions of older migrants. Dwyer (2001) drew attention to the importance of what he called the "residency issue" for older intra-EU migrants. The EU free movement provisions grant mobility and social rights to citizens of EU member states who move to another member state for retirement. However, the EU is not itself a welfare state but merely affords to these mobile EU citizens the right to the same benefits as enjoyed by nationals of the host state. It does not entitle them to the same (standard and level of) benefits as they enjoyed in their home state. Therefore, the continued diversity of welfare states within Europe remains of crucial importance to these older migrants. Many of Dwyer's respondents wished to retain access to public health and care services in the countries where they spent their working lives. This and other studies also found that, partly for this reason, many intra-EU retirement migrants avoid being registered as residents in their southern European host state and maintain formal residency status in their northern European home state (Ackers and Dwyer 2002; Coldron and Ackers 2007; Dwyer 2001; King, Warnes and Williams 2000; Rodriguez, Lardies and Rodriguez 2010).

128   *Anita Böcker and Canan Balkir*

The residency issue may be even more important for older migrants who, like the Dutch and Turkish respondents in our research, cross the external EU border. The differences between the welfare states may be larger, and the portability of welfare rights from the home state and the migrants' access to social rights in the host state may be more restricted than within the EU. Moreover, for the Turkish migrants in our research, a longer stay in Turkey could lead to the loss of their residence rights in the Netherlands. In the Netherlands, as in most other countries, only citizens retain the right to return and re-obtain residency regardless of their length of stay abroad. A recent study of aging Moroccan migrants found that, partly to avoid losing their residence rights, many had adopted a pendular migration pattern (De Haas and Fokkema 2010).

METHODOLOGY AND RESEARCH POPULATION

The data for this contribution are drawn from a collaborative research project that examined and compared retirement migrants and retirement returnees from the Netherlands in Turkey. Interviews with migrants were the main data collection method. We wanted to capture different kinds of migratory movements, ranging from prolonged visits to permanent residence in Turkey. Particularly temporary movements are often not registered. This ruled out the possibility of recruiting a representative sample through a random sampling process (Balkir and Kirkulak 2009; Casado-Diaz, Kaiser and Warnes 2004: 354; King et al. 2004; O'Reilly 2003; Rodriguez, Lardies and Rodriguez 2010). Instead, we chose a qualitative approach with purposive sampling. Our main criteria for selecting respondents were that they were retired, in the sense that they had chosen or been required to give up paid work; that they had spent (a large part of) their working lives in the Netherlands; and that they were spending at least four months a year in Turkey. We attempted to include migrants with different migration patterns, family status, and health status in both samples.

We conducted 31 interviews with Turkish returnees and 19 with Dutch retirement migrants. Many of the interviews were with couples (12 Turkish and 10 Dutch couples), some were with male migrants (12 Turkish and 5 Dutch men), and a smaller number were with female migrants (4 Turkish and 4 Dutch women). Most interviews were conducted in Turkey, in the coastal provinces of Antalya, İzmir, and Aydın and in the neighboring inland provinces of Karaman and Denizli. Some respondents were interviewed in the Netherlands. We also conducted two focus groups in the Netherlands, one with a group of 10 retired Turkish men and one with a group of 11 retired Turkish women who lived part of the year in Turkey.

Most respondents had moved to Turkey (or were moving back and forth between Turkey and the Netherlands) together with their spouses. Most Dutch couples had done so (or started doing so) upon the husband's retirement. In most cases, the husbands had retired early (before the statutory retirement age of 65). The wives were often a few years younger; a few had given up paid work to retire together with their husbands. All the Dutch respondents had only Dutch citizenship. Among the Turkish respondents, a substantial minority had retired to Turkey at a younger age, around 50. A majority of these younger returnees had made use of the Dutch Remigration Scheme. This scheme offers older unemployed or disabled migrants the option of receiving a monthly benefit in their home country.[2] However, they have to leave the Netherlands for good. Those with long-term resident status lose this status; those with dual citizenship are required to renounce their Dutch citizenship. Most of our Turkish respondents had only Turkish citizenship; a minority were dual citizens.

MIGRATION PATTERNS AND MIGRATORY DECISION MAKING

Similar to the findings of studies on intra-EU retirement migrants (Gustafson 2008; King, Warnes and Williams 2000; O'Reilly 2002), the different migration patterns in both our Dutch and our Turkish samples cannot be mapped through a simple dichotomy of seasonal versus permanent migration. The picture becomes more complicated when we add information about the evolution of the respondents' migration patterns over time and about the respondents' intentions for the future, or when we compare the respondents' actual migratory behavior to their formal residency status in both countries. In this section, we present five case examples to give an overview of the decision-making processes and the resulting migration patterns of our Turkish and Dutch respondents.

Turkish Retirement Returnees

The first case is illustrative of the dilemmas faced by many of our Turkish respondents. They were able to invest in housing and other property in Turkey during the first half of their working lives in the Netherlands. Some also made payments to the Turkish state pension fund, so that they would be entitled to a Turkish old-age pension after their return.[3] They were pushed out of the Dutch labor market and came to depend on social benefits during the second half of their working lives. Many would have liked to spend longer periods in Turkey and utilize and enjoy their resources there but could not do so on pain of losing their (nonexportable) Dutch benefit or their Dutch residence permit or both.

Case 1: Settled Back in Turkey for Good (or Bad)

Mr. and Ms. Albayrak[4] settled back in Turkey three years ago, making use of the Dutch Remigration Scheme. They did not really feel at ease in the

Netherlands. Their life there became extra difficult after Ms. Albayrak had a stroke. The burden became too heavy for Mr. Albayrak, who had to work and do most of the housekeeping in spite of back problems. They thought life would be easier in Turkey, where they expected to be able to get by on the benefit they would receive from the Netherlands and the rental income of the apartments they owned in Turkey. Mr. Albayrak would not have to work, and they could pay someone to keep house for them. Nevertheless, it was a difficult decision, because it meant moving away from their (grand)children and losing the right to reside in the Netherlands, where they had lived for more than thirty years. Asked under what circumstances they would consider returning back to the Netherlands, Mr. Albayrak answered, "We don't have that option anymore, we are only allowed to make short visits." When he has left the room for a moment, Ms. Albayrak said she would not want to remain alone in Turkey. As a widow, she would want to go to her children: "Either that, or the children should come over to stay with me."

The Albayraks decided to make use of the Dutch Remigration Scheme because it guaranteed them a regular income for the rest of their life. However, they were required to give up their residence rights in the Netherlands. Respondents who had made use of the scheme found this requirement hard to accept. All of them said it had complicated their decision and caused them a lot of stress. Ms. Albayrak had found the decision even more difficult than her husband did, and she still seemed to have doubts. She was not an exception. Our female Turkish respondents tended to be less willing to return on a permanent basis than their husbands were. This may be, as Richter (2004) observed with regard to Galician migrant couples in Switzerland, because male migrants tend to link their social identity to the immovable goods they own "back home," whereas women's identity is built more around the family they have built in the host country. However, another reason may be that a permanent return carries higher risks for older women than for older men. Ms. Albayrak and other female Turkish respondents were aware that they were likely to become widowed at some point in the future, and they hoped to be able to fall back on their children for moral and other support when this risk materialized. Obviously, if one or more children live in Turkey, this may make the decision to return easier also for female migrants. However, as the next case illustrates, there are often other considerations against a permanent return.

Case 2: Spending the Summers in Turkey and the Winters in the Netherlands

Nine years ago, when Mr. Bulut reached Dutch state pension age, he and his wife started spending half the year in Turkey. They are financially able to do so because they own their house in Turkey and because Mr. Bulut receives a Turkish pension, which is just high enough to cover their remaining living costs in Turkey. In fact, Mr. Bulut would have preferred to settle back permanently in Turkey, but his wife was against it. A few years ago, when their son decided to move to Turkey, they considered returning together with him, but Ms. Bulut still did not want to return permanently and Mr. Bulut was not sure anymore. He explained: "We realized that we were not staying here [in the Netherlands] only for the children and the grandchildren. We like our life here just as well as our life in Turkey. Particularly my wife has many friends here. And the Dutch health care system is better than the Turkish system." He added, "I don't like having to move house all the time. I'm getting too old for carrying the luggage, but my wife has had a bypass operation and I don't want to upset her in any way. So we keep on traveling." He thinks they will continue to do so for as long as their health permits. However, if his wife were to die before him, he would stop traveling; in that case, he would settle permanently in Turkey.

Although Turkish migrants are the largest group of users of the Dutch Remigration Scheme, those who return to Turkey with a remigration benefit are a minority within the older Turkish population in the Netherlands. Many Turkish migrants wait until they become entitled to an (exportable) old-age pension. Then they start dividing their time between their home and their host country. Mr. Bulut's narrative suggests that this may be a strategy to enjoy and maintain their ties and resources in both countries, on one hand, and a compromise between husband and wife, between his wish to return home and her wish to stay in the host country, on the other hand. The case of the Buluts furthermore illustrates that migration decisions may evolve incrementally, in response to only partly predictable changes in personal circumstances (Ackers and Dwyer 2004). The Buluts anticipated that as pensioners, they would be able to spend longer periods in Turkey. Their son's decision to move to Turkey and Ms. Bulut's heart problems made them consider their options and preferences again. They decided to continue moving back and forth while being aware that they may not remain able to do so for the rest of their lives.

As Turkish citizens, the couples in the previous cases were subject to Dutch immigration law. However, older Turkish migrants in the Netherlands are a growing group of dual citizens; they have acquired Dutch citizenship without giving up their Turkish citizenship. The following case illustrates the significance of these migrants' Dutch citizenship for their migratory decision making.

Case 3: Spending a Trial Period 'Back Home'

About a year ago, Mr. Çankaya settled back in the town where he was born, after a 35-year stay in the Netherlands. His ex-wife and his children and grandchildren all live in the Netherlands. He returned because he was suffering from depression and hoped to recover in Turkey. Surrounded by relatives and old friends who "keep an eye on him," he actually feels much

132 *Anita Böcker and Canan Balkir*

better, less lonely than in the Netherlands. However, the decision to move away from his children took him years. Finally, the children took the decision from him, telling him that he should not stay for them and arranging all the paperwork for him. Mr. Çankaya does not own property in Turkey. He could return only because he was allowed to export his Dutch (disability) benefit and because he has Dutch citizenship. There is a risk that he would lose his benefit if he recovered completely. In that case, he would return to the Netherlands. "Otherwise, I would be on the street in Turkey," he said. He thought he may also miss his children and grandchildren too much. That could be another reason for settling back in the Netherlands. He explained: "Turkish people live for their children, for their family, that is our culture."

Unlike the couples in the previous cases, Mr. Çankaya cannot fall back on personal economic resources in Turkey to supplement or replace his Dutch benefit. His relatives and friends give him moral support, but he obviously does not (want to) count on them to provide for his subsistence. His Dutch citizenship is a source of security for him. It guarantees that he can re-obtain residency and access to (nonexportable) welfare benefits in the Netherlands if he loses his disability benefit, which is not, as a matter of fact, an imaginary risk; we interviewed several Turkish migrants who had returned to Turkey with a disability benefit but had seen it reduced or had lost it as a result of a reexamination.

Like Mr. Çankaya, several other respondents with dual citizenship stated that they would not have returned to Turkey without their Dutch passport. Particularly for female respondents—but also for Mr. Çankaya—this had to do not only with retaining access to Dutch welfare state provisions, but also and often primarily with maintaining family relations. Their Dutch passport ensured them of the easiest and most certain access to the country of residence of their children.

Dutch Retirement Migrants

The population of Dutch retirement migrants in Turkey is highly diverse in terms of income, wealth, health, and other characteristics. The couple in the first example below is relatively well-off and both spouses are in good health. They belong to a small but growing group of Dutch retirees who have settled permanently in Turkey.

Case 4: Settled in Turkey for an Indefinite Time, Perhaps Forever

Ten years ago, Mr. and Ms. Groen moved to Alanya. They think they were the first Dutch couple to settle there permanently and "officially." They notified their local council in the Netherlands of their emigration and applied for residence permits directly on their arrival in Turkey. It was not a difficult decision—they had lived all over the world because of Mr. Groen's work—and they have never regretted it. Asked when they would consider

Maintaining Dual Residences to Manage Risks 133

returning back to the Netherlands, Ms. Groen answered, "If our daughter would need support or care." Her husband said that they do not want to worry all the time about risks that may or may not materialize: "You don't know what will happen tomorrow anyway." Mrs. Groen added, laughingly, "When I get senile, he will simply put me on a plane to the Netherlands." Her husband continued: "It is simple, really. We still have our Dutch passports, so we can return to the Netherlands when we need provisions or services which are not available here." They think that, depending on the situation, they may also pay someone to care for them in Turkey.

The Groens and other Dutch respondents who settled permanently in Turkey experienced the decision-making process as exciting and pleasant. This was a striking difference from the permanent returnees among our Turkish respondents, most of whom looked back on the decision-making process as difficult and stressful. However, *permanent* had a different connotation for each groups. The Groens referred to their Dutch passports as a kind of insurance policy. Knowing that their decision was not irreversible—that they could return and re-obtain residency at any time—made it easier to relinquish their residency status in the Netherlands and the rights attached to it. For other Dutch respondents, their Dutch citizenship appeared to perform the same function. Contrary to our expectations, we found that the absence of free-movement rights between Turkey and the Netherlands had not complicated the respondents' decision making. "It does not make a difference if you are a pensioner, the only difference to moving to Spain is that you need a visa or a residence permit," Mr. Groen explained. Other respondents said the same. The need to "buy"—a rather telling word choice—a residence permit or tourist visas was perceived by most of our Dutch respondents as a practical nuisance rather than a requirement that made them feel uncertain about their legal position in Turkey.

For the Groens, their economic resources are, like their Dutch passports, a source of freedom and security. They may use their personal wealth to purchase private care in Turkey as an alternative to returning home to use Dutch public provisions if they start to need personal care or nursing care. They have a similar freedom of choice in case they need medical care. As nonresident citizens, they cannot access public health services in the Netherlands, but unlike many other respondents (and perhaps due to their preretirement migration history), they do not perceive this as an important disadvantage. They are entitled to Turkish public provisions on the basis of a bilateral agreement between Turkey and the Netherlands. As they have private insurance, they can access private (and English-speaking) doctors and hospitals. Migrants with poorer health (and less wealth) may not be able to obtain private health insurance because insurers generally charge higher premiums to individuals with preexisting and chronic conditions. We found that, both in our Turkish and our Dutch samples, respondents with chronic illnesses tended to attach greater importance to retaining access to

134　*Anita Böcker and Canan Balkir*

public services in the Netherlands. Ms. Bulut (case 2) and the couple in the following example are cases in point.

Case 5: Settled in Turkey, but Retaining a Base in the Netherlands

Mr. Huisman and Ms. Jansen (both widowed) used to spend their holidays in Alanya. Three years ago, they decided to settle there more or less permanently. An important reason was Mr. Huisman's health. He has rheumatism and arthritis. In Turkey, he has less pain and is much more mobile. They share a rented apartment in Alanya. They have both retained their homes (also rented) in the Netherlands. Ms. Jansen explains that they want to see their children and grandchildren regularly and that they intend to settle back permanently if their health deteriorates ("we hope to grow old here, but it is impossible to live here if you cannot walk and climb stairs"), or if one of them dies ("neither of us would want to live here alone"). She adds that Mr. Huisman had cancer a few years ago; he has to have a checkup twice a year, which is why they want to remain insured in the Netherlands. An added advantage of remaining registered in the Netherlands is that they continue to build Dutch state pension rights (they have not yet reached state pension age). Mr. Huisman says: "We both worked 35 years; we have contributed enough to the Dutch welfare state."

This case illustrates that lifecourse considerations may play a decisive role in older migrants' decision making. Both partners are aware that their circumstances may change suddenly. Anticipating a permanent return, they fly back to the Netherlands every three months for a few weeks stay. This enables them to preserve family and other ties and, moreover, to retain their residency status in the Netherlands. By flying back every three months, they also avoid having to apply for residence permits in Turkey. At the time of our fieldwork, a substantial group of Dutch retirement migrants were residing in Turkey on 90-day tourist visas. They had to leave the country when the visa expired but could obtain a new one on reentry. The main reason not to apply for a residence permit were the costs.[5]

This couple had retained their homes in the Netherlands and returned home several times a year. This appears to be a common pattern among Dutch retirement migrants in Turkey, though the number and duration of the stays in the Netherlands may vary. Some respondents alternated three months in Turkey with three months in the Netherlands. They wanted to spend time with their children and grandchildren and with friends; a few also referred to a parent who was still alive but frail. Several respondents added that they wanted to have "the best of both worlds." Like the Buluts (case 2), these respondents enjoyed living in both countries. Like Mr. Huisman and Ms. Jansen, they anticipated that they would (have to) settle back permanently in the Netherlands at some point in the future.

There was another group of Dutch respondents who were living permanently in Turkey and did not have a home in the Netherlands anymore (like the Groens in case 4), but who (unlike the Groens) had retained a postal address and formal residency in the Netherlands. These respondents wanted to keep their residency status in the Netherlands for similar reasons as Mr. Huisman and Ms. Jansen, that is, to retain access to public health and care services, and, if they had not yet reached pension age, to continue to build up pension rights in the Netherlands. Similarly to Mr. Huisman, several of them referred to the contributions they had paid during their working lives; they felt justified in maintaining formal residency in the Netherlands because of these contributions. Another respondent referred to recent changes in Dutch social security regulations that had been particularly disadvantageous for recipients of Dutch pensions living abroad.

PREFERENCES FOR AND OBSTACLES TO MAINTAINING DUAL RESIDENCES

Taken together, the five case examples show that our Dutch and Turkish respondents shared similar preferences. Many preferred to divide their time between Turkey and the Netherlands. Others lived more or less permanently in Turkey, but they preferred or would have preferred not to burn their bridges to the Netherlands.

The reasons or considerations behind these preferences were largely similar for both groups. In accordance with previous research, our interview data show that maintaining dual residences enables older migrants to have, as several Turkish and Dutch respondents put it, "the best of two worlds"; it facilitates enjoying and maintaining family and other ties to the country where the migrants spent their working lives; and may be a logical continuation of preretirement mobility patterns. In addition, for some of the Turkish couples in our research, pendular migration was a compromise between the husband's wish to settle back permanently in the home country and the wife's wish to stay in the host country.

However, our respondents' preference for maintaining dual residences (and retaining the option to settle back in the Netherlands) was also motivated by increasing care needs and an awareness of potential future needs.

Life-Cycle Considerations

Health care needs and preferences were a reason to maintain dual residences for migrants in both groups. Although they were not necessarily discontent with the health care services they could access in Turkey, most respondents preferred to retain access to public health care services in the Netherlands. In Turkey, many respondents preferred to make use of private health care services. This was possible by maintaining residency in the Netherlands (thus retaining access to public services in the Netherlands) and taking out additional private insurance (to obtain access to private services in Turkey).[6]

Respondents in both groups also realized—although they did not always like to talk about it—that their circumstances might change suddenly, that their health might decline, and that they might start to need assistance with daily living tasks. Nearly all pendular migrants expected to settle back permanently in the Netherlands when they would need long-term care, because of the availability of care services and/or family resources. The Dutch respondents more often referred to public (institutional or home-care) services. Turkish respondents, particularly Turkish women, more often referred to their children as potential sources of support. There were also respondents who thought they would prefer to stay in Turkey. A few Dutch couples who lived permanently in Turkey indicated that they would prefer to purchase private care and that this was less costly in Turkey. Several Turkish permanent returnees indicated that they had children or other close relatives in Turkey or that they would pay a neighbor or relative to keep house for them.

The loss of one's spouse is another risk that is distributed unequally across the life course. With increasing age, women are at greater risk of becoming widowed. Most Dutch respondents and many female Turkish respondents thought they would prefer to return to the Netherlands if they would become widowed because of the availability of family and other social ties. The Turkish respondents referred primarily to their children; the Dutch respondents often also referred to friends in the Netherlands as potential sources of support in widowhood.

For respondents who had not yet attained pension age, another advantage of maintaining dual residences was that they continued to build up Dutch state pension rights. The Netherlands has a residency-based old-age pension scheme. Fifty years of residence in the Netherlands are required for a full state old-age pension; each year of nonresidence leads to a 2 percent reduction on the full pension. Migrants who built no or very limited rights to supplementary pensions through occupational or private pension schemes may therefore remain dependent on supplementary (less or nonexportable) welfare benefits after reaching pension age.

Welfare Mixes

Thus, maintaining dual residences also helps older migrants to reduce or manage the social risks that are associated with later life. It enables them to maintain and retain access to a "portfolio" of resources in two countries for ensuring their wellbeing in later life. The concept of "welfare mix" has been applied mainly at the macro-level, to analyze the division of labor, responsibility, and costs between state, market, family, and the voluntary sector in the provision of welfare in a society. However, it can also be applied at the micro-level. Families, households, and individuals create their own welfare mixes by using and combining public, private, family, and other provisions. Their welfare depends on how well they manage to do this (Denton et al. 2001,2004; Esping-Andersen 1999; Klammer 2006).

Maintaining Dual Residences to Manage Risks 137

The preferred welfare mixes of our respondents were indeed complex, and the composition of the mix varied. Migrants in both groups preferred to combine public, private, and family provisions. Perhaps most notably, there were differences in how respondents referred to their children as potential sources of support. What types of care children were expected or hoped to give varied between the groups, between male and female respondents, and between individuals within each group and appeared to be influenced by family histories and personal relationships within families as well as by (highly gendered) cultural expectations (Baldassar 2007; Finch and Mason 1993).

Another difference was related to the respondents' ethnicity. The Turkish respondents attached much more importance to having provisions in Turkey in their portfolio than the Dutch respondents did. Some had paid voluntary insurance contributions to get a Turkish state pension when they retired. Private provisions were more common, however. Home ownership in Turkey was considered a source of security by all Turkish respondents. By contrast, some of the Dutch respondents tended to see it as a risk. These respondents felt more secure and free renting their homes in Turkey. Moreover, whereas the Turkish respondents valued their house and other property in Turkey also as a source of intergenerational wealth and security, several Dutch respondents feared that their children might encounter legal problems when claiming their inheritance in Turkey.[7]

Obstacles

Many of our Dutch and Turkish respondents shared a preference for maintaining dual residences and for retaining the option to settle back in the Netherlands, but the Turkish respondents clearly faced more legal obstacles to realizing their preferences. This was partly because they more often depended on means-tested, nonexportable income benefits in the Netherlands and partly because (unless they were dual citizens) they were subject to Dutch immigration law. The Dutch respondents were subject to Turkish immigration rules, but the impact on their daily lives was much less pronounced. As most of them did not depend on means-tested benefits, they were also less constrained by Dutch social security rules.

Their dependency on means-tested, nonexportable benefits meant that many Turkish respondents could stay only limited periods outside the Netherlands. Moreover, the wives were often not allowed to stay abroad for as long as their husbands because of their younger age. Our focus group interviews with Turkish seasonal migrants yielded many examples of couples where the husband had attained pension age and was allowed to stay outside the Netherlands for a longer time, but the wife was required to attend a language and integration course or had to comply with job search requirements in order to secure the couple's supplementary income support. These respondents experienced the effects of both policy reforms aimed at

138 Anita Böcker and Canan Balkir

formal gender equality in social security and increasing older workers' participation rates and the tightening of immigrant integration policies. Other respondents faced a dilemma because they received means-tested social benefits in the Netherlands while they owned a house or had purchased pension rights in Turkey. They felt they either had to break or evade Dutch social security rules (by failing to declare their property or income in Turkey) or forgo one of their income sources, which might make it too costly to continue moving back and forth between the two countries.

The Dutch respondents (unless they were dependent on means-tested benefits) faced hardly any legal obstacles when dividing their time between the Netherlands and Turkey. Moreover, they were able to retain formal residency in the Netherlands while living more or less permanently in Turkey. Most of our Dutch respondents could choose whether to deregister in the Netherlands or not, and they always retained the option to move back to the Netherlands and become residents again. Our Turkish respondents (unless they had dual citizenship) did not have the latter option, and nearly all the permanent returnees among them had been required (rather than had chosen) to deregister as residents of the Netherlands because they had applied for a Dutch remigration benefit.

Most research on international retirement migration to the Mediterranean has focused on intra-EU migrants. Our research focused on migrants who cross the external EU border and thus cannot take advantage of the EU free movement provisions. However, this made more difference for our Turkish respondents than it did for the Dutch respondents.

NOTES

1 The research was funded by MiReKoc (Migration Research Program at Koç University). For the research report, see Böcker and Balkir (2012) and Balkir and Böcker (forthcoming).
2 Turkish migrants are the largest group of users. Nearly 40 percent of all recipients of a remigration benefit (4,300 persons in 2009) live in Turkey (Kruis and Berkhout, 2009).
3 Turkey has special provisions for Turkish citizens who are working abroad. They can remain or become insured under the Turkish state pension scheme. Returning migrants can start receiving pension payments as soon as they have "purchased" the minimum number of insurance days required for becoming entitled to an old-age pension. These possibilities are provided in the Law on the Evaluation of the Periods Spent Abroad of Turkish Nationals Working Abroad with respect to Social Security. Permanent return is not required anymore for receiving pension payments, but the pensioner must not work abroad, must not receive unemployment benefits from abroad, and must not receive social aid based on residence abroad.
4 We have changed the names of all respondents to protect their privacy.
5 Dayir and Shah (2012) reported a similar finding for British migrants. Dutch and British citizens had to pay a relatively high fee for a residence permit. They paid much lower fees for tourist visas. This was the situation at the time of our

Maintaining Dual Residences to Manage Risks   139

fieldwork (in 2010). Since then, however, new visa regulations have made it impossible to stay in Turkey for more than 90 days in a 180-day period. In addition, the fees for residence permits have been lowered, so it can be assumed that most Dutch retirement migrants nowadays prefer to apply for residence permits.

6 Under the Dutch Health Insurance Act, all residents of the Netherlands are obliged to purchase a basic insurance package, and health insurance companies are obliged to accept everyone for the basic package at a flat-rate premium. All the Dutch and most of the Turkish seasonal migrants among our respondents had taken out additional health and/or travel insurance. This combination of public and private insurance gave them access to the widest range of health care services in both countries, including private doctors and hospitals in Turkey, for a relatively low cost.

7 See Bayir and Shah (2012: 11–12) on British migrants in Turkey.

REFERENCES

Ackers, Louise/Dwyer, Peter (2002): *Senior Citizenship? Retirement, Migration and Welfare in the European Union.* Bristol: Policy Press.

Ackers, Louise/Dwyer, Peter (2004): Fixed Laws, Fluid Lives: The Citizenship Status of Post-Retirement Migrants in the European Union. In: *Ageing and Society* 24, 3, pp. 451–475.

Arts, Wil/ Gelissen, John (2002): Three Worlds of Welfare Capitalism or More? A State-of-the-Art Report. In: *Journal of European Social Policy* 12, 2, pp. 137–158.

Baldassar, Loretta (2007): Transnational Families and Aged Care: The Mobility of Care and the Migrancy of Ageing. In: *Journal of ethnic and migration studies* 33, 2, pp. 275–297.

Balkir, Canan/Böcker, Anita (forthcoming): A Comparison of Residence, Social Security and Citizenship Strategies of Turkish Return Migrants and Dutch Retirement Migrants in Turkey. In: Tokat Karaçay, Altay B./Sert, Deniz/Gülru Göker/Zeynep (eds.): *Waves of Diversity: Socio-Political Implications of International Migration in Turkey.* Istanbul: Isis Press.

Balkir, Canan/Kirkulak, Berna (2009): Turkey, the New Destination for International Retirement Migration and Mobility in Europe. In: Fassmann, Heinz/Haller, Max/Lane, David (eds.): *Migration and Mobility in Europe.* Cheltenham: Edward Elgar, pp. 123–143.

Bayir, Derya/Shah, Prakash (2012): The Legal Adaptation of British Settlers in Turkey. In: *Transcultural Studies* 8, 1, pp. 43–76.

Böcker, Anita/Balkir, Canan (2012): *Migration in Later Life. Residence, Social Security and Citizenship Strategies of Turkish Return Migrants and Dutch Retirement Migrants in Turkey.* Nijmegen: Radboud University Nijmegen.

Bolzman, Claudio/Fibbi, Rosita/Vial, Marie (2006): What to Do After Retirement? Elderly Migrants and the Question of Return. In: *Journal of Ethnic and Migration Studies,* 32, 8, pp. 1359–1375.

Casado-Díaz, María/Kaiser, Claudia/Warnes, Anthony M. (2004): Northern European Retired Residents in Nine Southern European Areas: Characteristics, Motivations and Adjustment. In: *Ageing and Society,* 24, 3, pp. 353–381.

Coldron, Keleigh/Ackers, Louise (2007): (Ab)Using European Citizenship? EU Retired Migrants and the Exercise of Health Care Rights. In: *Maastricht Journal of European and Comparative Law* 14, 3, pp. 287–2007.

De Coulon, Augustin/Wolff, François-Charles (2010): Location Intentions of Immigrants at Retirement: Stay/Return or Go 'Back and Forth'? In: *Applied Economics,* 42, 26, pp. 3319–3333.

140 Anita Böcker and Canan Balkir

De Haas, Hein/Fokkema, Tineke (2010): Intra-Household Conflicts in Migration Decisionmaking: Return and Pendulum Migration in Morocco. In: *Population and Development Review* 36, 3, pp. 541–561.

Denton, Magaret A./French, Susan/Gafni, Amiram/Joshi, Anju/Rosenthal, Carolyn/ Webb, Sharon (2001): *Reflexive Planning for Later Life: A Conceptual Model and Evidence from Canada*. Hamilton: McMaster University.

Denton, Margaret A./Kemp, Candance L./French, Susan/Gafni, Amiram/Joshi, Anju/Rosenthal, Carolyn J./Davies, Sharon (2004): Reflexive Planning for Later Life. In: *Canadian Journal on Aging/La Revue canadienne du vieillissement* 23, 5, pp. 71–82.

Dwyer, Peter (2001): Retired EU Migrants, Healthcare Rights and European Social Citizenship. In: *Journal of Social Welfare and Family Law* 23, 3, pp. 311–327.

Esping-Andersen, Gøsta (1999): *Social Foundations of Postindustrial Economics*. New York: Oxford University Press.

Finch, Janet/Mason, Jennifer (1993): Negotiating Family Responsibilities. London/ New York: Tavistock/Roudledge

Gustafson, Per (2001): Retirement Migration and Transnational Lifestyles. In: *Ageing and Society* 21, 4, pp. 371–394.

Gustafson, Per (2008): Transnationalism in Retirement Migration: the Case of North European Retirees in Spain. In: *Ethnic and Racial Studies* 31, 3, pp. 451–475.

Huber, Andreas/O'Reilly, Karen (2004): The Construction of Heimat Under Conditions of Individualised Modernity: Swiss and British Elderly Migrants in Spain. In: *Ageing & Society* 24, 3, pp. 327–351.

King, Russel/Thomson, Mark/Fielding, Tony/Warnes, Tony (2004): *Gender, Age and Generations. State of the Art Report*. Amsterdam: IMISCOE.

King, Russel/Warnes, Anthony M./Williams, Allan M. (2000): *Sunset Lives: British Retirement Migration to the Mediterranean*. Oxford/New York: Berg.

Klammer, Ute (2006): Work Life Balance from the Children's Perspective. In: Lewis, Jane (ed.): *Children, Changing Families and Welfare States*. Cheltenham: Edward Elgar, pp. 220–242.

Kruis, Geerten/Berkhout, Abram (2009): *Profielonderzoek gebruikers remigratiewet*. Amsterdam: Regioplan Beleidsonderzoek.

Krumme, Helen (2004): Migration—Fortwährende Remigration: Das transnationale Pendeln türkischer Arbeitsmigrantinnen und Arbeitsmigranten im Ruhestand. In: *Zeitschrift für Soziologie* 33, 2, pp. 138–153.

Latcheva, Rossalina/Herzog-Punzenberger, Barbara (2011): Integration Trajectories: A Mixed Method Approach. In: Wingens, Michael/Windzio, Michael/De Valk, Helga/Aybek, Can (eds.): *A Life-Course Perspective on Migration and Integration*. Dordrecht/Heidelberg/London/New York: Springer, pp. 121–142.

O'Reilly, Karen (2000): *The British on the Costa del Sol: Transnational Identities and Local Communities*. London: Routledge.

O'Reilly, Karen (2002): Britain in Europe/The British in Spain: Exploring Britain's Changing Relationship to the Other through the Attitudes of its Emigrants. In: *Nations and Nationalisms* 8, 2, pp. 179–193.

O'Reilly, Karen (2003): When Is a tourist? The Articulation of Tourism and Migration in Spain's Costa del Sol. In: *Tourist Studies* 3, 3, pp. 301–317.

Richter, Marina (2004): Contextualising Gender and Migration: Galician Immigration to Switzerland. In: *International Migration Review* 38, 1, pp. 263–286.

Rodriguez, Vicente/Lardies, Raúl/Rodriguez, Paz (2010): *Migration and the Registration of European Pensioners in Spain*. Madrid: Real Instituto Elcano, ARI.

7 Pendular Migration of the Older First Generations in Europe
Misconceptions and Nuances

Tineke Fokkema, Eralba Cela, and Yvonne Witter

Migration to Europe is a well-established phenomenon, although the intensity, patterns, and composition of migration flows have varied greatly over time and across European countries. After World War II, decolonization triggered substantial migration flows to Europe. The largest groups came to France from its former colonies in North Africa and Indochina (1.8 million), to Portugal from its ex-colonies in Africa (about 1 million), and to the Netherlands from its former colonies Indonesia (300,000) and Suriname (350,000); smaller numbers arrived in the UK and Belgium from their ex-colonies in Africa and Asia (Emmer and Lucassen 2012; White 2006). Apart from political arguments, the main trigger for migration to the former colonial powers was to enjoy a higher standard of living and quality of life through better jobs and educational and public facilities (Oostindie and Schoorl 2011).

Labor was the second stimulus for migration to Western Europe. During the economic boom after World War II, most migration was the product of a spontaneous decision in response to labor demand. However, under the pressure of labor shortages, active recruitment was also carried out by several Western European countries, especially among unskilled and low-skilled workers. The so-called guest workers were recruited through bilateral agreements with low-wage countries belonging to the Mediterranean area (e.g., Italy, Spain, Turkey, Morocco, Tunisia, and Algeria) (Bousetta, Gsir and Jacobs 2005; Constant and Massey 2002; Hatton and Williamson 2005; Zimmermann 1995). They were considered temporary migrants and were granted temporary work permits accordingly. The general belief of EU governments was that return to the home countries was the natural outcome of the bilateral agreements: after a few years of working hard in the destination countries and saving enough money, guest workers would have achieved their migration targets and were therefore expected to go back home (White 2006). However, in order to keep guest workers during the economic boom, many companies and countries promoted and provided assistance with family reunification (Bousetta, Gsir and Jacobs 2005; Cottar, Bouras and Laouikili 2009; de Lary 2004). Moreover, the economic recession following the 1973 oil crisis did not result in large waves of return migration either. As a response to rising unemployment and decreasing demand for unskilled workers, stricter migration policies were implemented with the intention to reduce migration flows; labor migration was no longer encouraged and the recruitment schemes were stopped abruptly (Constant, Nottmeyer and Zimmermann 2012). Along with the halted policies, migrants were encouraged to return home through both in-cash and in-kind incentives (like vocational training) meant to facilitate their readaptation. But economic prospects in the home countries were not favorable either, and guest workers, especially those migrants from non–European Union (EU) countries for whom free mobility was not an option, feared they could never return to Europe if they left (Constant, Nottmeyer and Zimmermann 2012; De Haas and Fokkema 2010).

The result of these tighter migration policies was counterproductive; many guest workers ended up as permanent residents of their new countries, as testified by large-scale family reunification and family formation (Constant, Nottmeyer and Zimmermann 2012). Meanwhile, the direction of labor migration diverted to southern European countries and was characterized by a persistent demand for unskilled workers, especially in the widespread informal economy, but not by legislation on immigration (King 2000, 2002). The proportion of foreign-born residents in Western Europe increased from 1.3 percent in 1950 to 4.5 percent in 1990, excluding those who had been naturalized—those would have probably doubled this figure (Hatton and Williamson 2005). According to Eurostat, on January 1, 2012, there were 20.7 million foreign-born European residents (citizens of a country outside the EU-27), representing 4.1 percent of the EU-27 population.

The first generation of migrants in Europe has now reached or is approaching retirement age, and it is to be expected that the number of older migrants will continue to increase in the future: although retirement is a trigger of migration (Bolzman, Fibbi and Vial 2006; King 1986; King, Warnes and Williams 1998, 2000, 2006), and even though older migrants often still cherish the desire to return, most of them are likely to remain in the destination country (Bolzman, Fibbi and Vial 1999; Ganga 2006). Key reasons to stay include living close to children and grandchildren, retaining pension rights and residence permits, and having access to good health care services and social security (Bolzman, Fibbi and Vial 2006; De Haas and Fokkema 2010; Ganga 2006; White 2006). Making the decision to maintain official residence in the destination country does not mean, however, that older migrants cut or loosen the ties with their country of origin. On the contrary, free of work and daily responsibilities, older migrants have more time to strengthen such ties. Advances in communication and transport technology have definitely supported their transnational way of living (Bolzman, Fibbi and Vial 2006; Bolzman et al. 2004; Ganga 2006; Poulain and Perrin 2002; Warnes and Williams 2006).

Moreover, although official statistics are not available, an increasing number of older migrants seem to have adopted pendular strategies, that is, traveling back and forth and spending several months per year in their

Pendular Migration of the Older First Generations in Europe 143

country of origin (Baldassar and Merla 2013; Baykara-Krumme 2013; De Haas and Fokkema 2010; Ganga 2006; Hunter 2011; Warnes and Williams 2006). A 2003 Dutch survey among the largest groups of older migrants showed that 17 percent of the Surinamese, 28 percent of the Turkish, and 30 percent of the Moroccan respondents aged 65 and older had been in their home country in the previous year for more than three consecutive months (Schellingerhout 2004a). More recently, another study found that 25 percent of the older migrants from these three groups spent more than one time per year in their country of origin, with an average duration of stay of 9.5 week (Weltevrede, Seidler and De Boom 2013). In France, a large-scale survey of nonnationals, aged 45 and over in 2003 and who were not retired, found that 24 percent preferred the prospect of living part of the year in their home country (De Coulon and Wolff 2010). An even higher percentage—between 26 and 40 percent—was reported by those from African countries who migrated mainly in the late 1960s and 1970s as guest workers. A similar finding is observed among Italian and Spanish retired migrants in Switzerland: one-third expressed the intention to divide their time between their host country and their country of origin (Bolzman, Fibbi and Vial 2006).

Several stereotypes and common beliefs are prevalent in public and policy debates on this pendular behavior of older migrants. In this chapter we challenge four of them by providing a review of the existing literature, together with results from our own work. The first popular belief that prevails is that pendular migration is a temporary phenomenon, an intermediate stage between "staying" and "returning." The second stereotype is that pendular migration is a second-best option. The third is that older migrants' stay in their country of birth is a time of relaxing, enjoying the climate, and visiting family and friends. The final common assumption is that pendular migration is a private matter, with no connection to public support and no negative societal consequences. We elaborate on these four assumptions successively and confront them with research findings in order to find out to what extent they are supported by empirical evidence. A substantial part of the research findings stems from two of our own qualitative studies: (a) a survey conducted in 2011 with 22 Turkish and Surinamese persons 55 years or older, residing in the Netherlands but regularly traveling back and forth (Witter 2011), and (b) interviews in 2013 with 23 migrants aged 50 or older, of Moroccan and Albanian origin, carried out in the Marche region of Italy (Cela and Fokkema 2014).

STEREOTYPE 1: PENDULAR MIGRATION IS A TEMPORARY PHENOMENON

Pendular migration is commonly considered in public and policy debates as a temporary phenomenon. In EU policy reports, for instance, circular and temporary migrations are often placed side by side, as circular migration

144 *Tineke Fokkema, Eralba Cela, and Yvonne Witter*

in the member states "is often understood as a form of temporary migration, albeit repeated temporary migration, given that circular migration is often de facto included within the definition of temporary migration used by the member states" (European Migration Network 2011: 21). Moreover, in line with classical migration models, migrants are supposed to settle definitively in the country of origin or in the adopted country. While the neoclassical migration theory (Harris and Todaro 1970) predicts that "winners"—in terms of successful integration—settle and "losers" return (De Haas and Fokkema 2011), exactly the opposite is assumed by the more recent New Economic of Labor Migration—a new theoretical approach in migration research (Stark and Bloom 1985). Regardless of which one is more prevalent, however, return migration is commonly expected to be a prospect long contemplated, a transition prepared for by earlier return visits.

This general belief of a temporary pendular migration does not match with empirical findings. The oft-quoted phrase "there is nothing as permanent as a temporary migrant" (Hugo 2013: 3) is also true for the older first-generation migrants. Their cross-border commuting is generally neither a prelude to permanent return nor an indecisive situation between staying and returning. Rather, it appears to be a deliberate, long-term decision, different from that of permanent settlement at the destination or of a return to the origin. This is in line with Engelhard's (2006) argument that pendular migration is a distinct form of migration and, hence, that pendular migrants can be classified neither as settlers nor as returnees. Older migrants opt for the "back and forth" strategy as they like to live "here" and "there," which allows them to maintain resources and attachments in both the origin and adopted countries (Bolzman, Fibbi and Vial 2006), and which generates a personal idea of "home." Circularity becomes an integral part of their livelihood strategies, living some months in the host country and others in the home country, as expressed by these respondents:

> If we are retired, yes, I'd like to spend the spring there (Albania), a few days of winter, and summer here. This way of life would be a dream for me. Our life does not stop here. We also have a beautiful house there, we bought it. The wish is to live back and forth. (In the future, will you return to Albania?) Forever? No, I don't like to live forever in the same place. (Albanian man)
>
> When I retire I will go to Morocco from October to May and to Italy from May to October. I don't like winter, in Casablanca it's never too cold and there isn't the humidity we have here. I don't want to go just for the climate but especially because that's my homeland, my parents have lived there all their lives, I have a lot of childhood memories and the Moroccan mentality is different . . . I like to be there a little and here a little. Now that I have citizenship I can do that. I feel at home here in Italy too. (Moroccan man)

Pendular Migration of the Older First Generations in Europe   145

Most of the pendular migrants want to continue to travel back and forth, unless major life events and changes obstruct their pendular lifestyle. Significant deterioration of health is one of the most important life events in this respect, as good health is an important condition for cross-border travels. Traveling back and forth becomes routine for many older migrants and a way to cope with familiar and personal interests, unless it is no longer possible due to poor health. This is echoed by an Albanian woman:

> I think that when we aren't able anymore to travel back and forth we should settle down in Italy. Our children already want us to settle here and travel less, but now traveling has become for us the routine, our children don't want us to stay away that much and we can't stay here, away from our home for so long. (Albanian woman)

Besides travel difficulties, some of our respondents expressed that they do not want to be a heavy burden to others because of their poor health:

> I will stop traveling once I start having problems with my mobility. Otherwise I will be an albatross around their neck, causing inconvenience to others. (Surinamese woman)

A life change that may also hinder further pendular migration, or at least reduce its regularity, is a substantial deterioration of one's financial situation. This might not be exceptional, given the current, persistent economic crisis in Europe. Traveling is expensive, and therefore, it is not surprising that previous studies have found a positive relationship between one's income and the intention to move "back and forth" (Bolzman, Fibbi and Vial 2006; De Coulon and Wolff, 2010; Engelhard 2007). The travel costs of pendular migration are generally higher the longer the distance between the host and the home country. Those who have to travel a relatively short distance also need sufficient income, as people left behind often expect financial support or gifts. Even with their current income, many older pendular migrants live a sober lifestyle in the host country in order to be able to make the yearly trip to their homeland:

> I only have an old-age pension, you won't make a fortune out of it. Each year I have to save hard for my ticket to Suriname. I only wear cheap clothes from the market, I feel a bit ashamed about that. (Surinamese woman)

It is relevant to stress here that pendular migration is sometimes also a strategy for older migrants to cope with their limited financial resources (Baykara-Krumme 2013). Compared to their native peers, older migrants are often in a disadvantaged financial situation (Fokkema and Naderi 2013), because many rights to pensions and social assistance in old age are

146   Tineke Fokkema, Eralba Cela, and Yvonne Witter

dependent on migrants' history in the paid labor market of the host society. Those who migrate later in their lives will receive very low pensions after retirement. Hence, the lower costs of living in the home country attract older migrants to spend some months there, making pendular migration an income-optimization strategy:

> In Morocco I bought a house, so I don't have to pay rent when I go there and I can save some money. Unfortunately, I don't know if I will have a pension (in Italy) or how much I will get when I will retire. I have worked 17 years in Morocco and 20 in Italy. My Moroccan pension for those 17 years will be around 200 or 250 euros per month. (Moroccan man)

Another major life event that would make continuation of pendular migration difficult is the death of a spouse—at least this seems to be the case for women, especially from societies with strict, defined gender norms and roles such as Morocco and Turkey (Balkir and Böcker 2012; De Haas and Van Rooij 2010):

> I will only continue to visit Turkey if my husband travels with me. I can't and don't want to go alone, that would be too heavy. (Turkish woman)

Albanian women, even though they also come from a relatively traditional, patriarchal society (King, Castaldo and Vullnetari 2011; King, Dalipaj and Mai 2006; King and Vullnetari 2009), seem to be less reluctant to continue traveling back and forth after they are widowed; this is probably related to their higher level of education and urban origin. Migrants coming from urban areas express the will to travel back and forth "even alone," after the death of their husband. Surinamese women learn from an early age to take care of themselves and to live independently (Schellingerhout 2004a); therefore, they do not view traveling alone in the future, after the death of their husband, as problematic.

Such life events and changes will force many of the older migrants either to stay permanently in the host country or to return permanently to their home country. Which choice will prevail is a question for future research: most of the older migrants in Europe are still relatively young, living with their spouses, and their health is still good enough to travel. However, previous studies (Baykara-Krumme 2013; Bolzman, Fibbi and Vial, 2006; De Coulon and Wolff 2010) and our data suggest that the decision about the final destination later in life will generally favor the host country. There are more pull than push factors to stay permanently in the host country, including better social security and healthcare systems, as well as proximity to children and grandchildren. As one of our respondents commented,

Pendular Migration of the Older First Generations in Europe   147

After living in Italy for thirty years, it would be a radical change if I returned to Albania. If I go there my point of reference, which is my children, won't be in Albania. For them, life would become more difficult, also because if I needed them, they would have to take days off work to come over. As long as my health is good I will commute. (Albanian woman)

STEREOTYPE 2: PENDULAR MIGRATION IS A SECOND-BEST OPTION

Another type of evidence that pendular migration is a distinct form of migration comes from studies comparing older pendular migrants with returnees and/or stayers, concluding that characteristics are different from one group to another (Baykara-Krumme 2013; Bolzman, Fibbi and Vial 2006; De Coulon and Wolff 2010). The qualitative study of De Haas and Fokkema (2010) of older Moroccan pendular and return migrants shows that the two migrant groups differ mainly with respect to the location of their family members: while pendular migrants generally brought over their spouses and children in the 1970s and 1980s, most return migrants decided to leave their family in the country of origin. Several quantitative studies have also shown that, besides economic ties (e.g., business, property), social ties in the country of origin increase the likelihood that migrants (prefer to) return (De Haas and Fokkema 2011; Jensen and Pedersen 2007). With regard to older first-generation migrants in particular, the presence of children in the home country especially encourages a return, while children's residence does not seem to affect the "back and forth" option (Baykara-Krumme 2013; Bolzman, Fibbi and Vial 2006; De Coulon and Wolff 2010).

The main reasons why older return migrants did not reunify their families in Europe, although spouses and children often wanted to migrate, are related to: the belief that investment in the education of their children (i.e., sons) in the country of origin would bring better results, namely, good diplomas with an expectation to obtain a decent job without the humiliation they experienced in Europe, the burden of financial support if the whole family lived in Europe, and, last but not least, the fear of losing control over women and children, who would be "Westernized" in Europe (De Haas and Fokkema 2010). The decision not to reunify their families, as well as to return after their working life was over, was often taken unilaterally by the male migrant and not exclusively in the interest of the whole household. This is consistent with findings from other studies showing that households are not just a group of people sharing the same norms and interests and that participation in the family decision-making process depends on the person's role within family hierarchy, usually distributed along gender and generational lines (Hondagneu-Sotelo 1994; Hondagneu-Sotelo 2003; King, Castaldo and Vullnetari, 2011; Mahler and Pessar 2006; Pessar 1999).

148 *Tineke Fokkema, Eralba Cela, and Yvonne Witter*

Intra-household power relations did change, however, for those who reunified their families. In line with previous studies (Bolzman, Fibbi and Vial 2001; Itzigsohn and Giorguli-Saucedo 2005; Mahler and Pessar 2006; Pessar 1999; Richter, 2004), the migration experience strengthened the position of women and children, as did their coalition against a definitive return: while most male migrants persistently long to return after retirement as a way to regain status (Itzigsohn et al. 1999), their wives and children want to stay in the host country as a way to protect their social and economic achievements (e.g., freedom of movement, staying close to their children and grandchildren, better working conditions) and because of expected unfavorable (economic) prospects and problems with integration in their home countries. As a consequence, after their working life they adopt a pendular life (or want to), spending some months "here" and some months "there" as a compromise between conflicting intra-household desires. Respondents of our studies also confirm this finding:

> At first I only wanted to come (to Italy) for a few years. Then I brought my family here, that was a mistake because we had many problems here. Of course, having brought my family here means never going back to Morocco, because the children grow up here and become more and more Italian, and you can't just take them back to Morocco. (Moroccan man)
>
> For a moment, we thought of returning to Suriname after my retirement. But we have four children and seven grandchildren here. I wanted to go, but my wife absolutely not. (Surinamese man)

Given the preceding, at a first glance it seems—and is often assumed in public debate—that pendular migration is a second-best option, at least for male migrants. Some nuances are worth noting, however. The return decision is not always as simple and taken for granted as it may appear; it is not just a simple matter of "coming home," and many returnees face problems after they go back. Coming home for good is often a delicate moment of rearrangement in the family and can mark the start of family conflicts. De Haas and Fokkema's (2010) study, for example, showed that, because of the long absence abroad, return migrants often encountered problems of reintegration, even with their own family, because it was difficult to regain their predeparture position and authority within the family hierarchy. Moreover, there were regular conflicts between the returned father and the adult children (usually sons) because of the latter's resentment of the missed opportunity to join their fathers in Europe at a younger age. Most return migrants' children do obtain a high school diploma but are unemployed, as are many of their higher-educated peers in Morocco. Comparing their situation with their counterparts in Europe, they blame their father for his decision to not take the family to Europe. Now that their father finally returned, the way to Europe is blocked to them, and it is difficult to emigrate either legally

Pendular Migration of the Older First Generations in Europe 149

or illegally. Besides family problems, many returnees also experience more general readjustment difficulties at the origin. Once home, they realize that they are more "Westernized" than they thought and, accordingly, face disappointments about issues such as human relations, discrimination, bureaucracy, corruption, and quality of health care services.

Based on pendular migrants' reports from our study, it seems that most migrants are fully aware of the better health care system in the host country and their changed social norms and expectations during their permanence abroad. So for them the reluctance of their wife and children is usually not the only reason why they choose a pendular strategy instead of a definite return, as this awareness has made them change their plans accordingly:

> I don't want to live in Morocco (for good) anymore, it's okay to stay one month or two but then I want to escape. Life is better in Italy, even now during the crisis. Here with a normal salary you have a house, car, clothes, you live better. The health system is better here, in Morocco if you don't have the money you can't do anything. Social services are not there, the King occasionally helps the poor and that's it. If you have nothing in Morocco you can go to the hospital for free but the service is not like here, the nurses and the service are not good. (Moroccan man)
>
> (Do you want to return?) I don't think so. To me going back would mean a new migration. My children will not go back either. It doesn't make sense. Tirana is one hour away by plane, why to go back for good? Albania is nice for holidays, but everyday life is tough, you have to wish for yourself never to be in need to go to a public office, it's there where your dignity is trashed. For me, it would kill me. (Albanian man)
>
> I will never quit commuting, that is not possible for me. I can't do without, I long for Turkey, the contacts, my country and history. I'm always looking forward to going. But after staying four months in Turkey, I miss the Netherlands and especially the freedom of expression. (Turkish man)

STEREOTYPE 3: A STAY IN THE HOME COUNTRY IS A PERIOD OF RELAXATION

In public and policy debates, older pendular migrants are generally portrayed as taking advantage of the privileged position of their transnational life, by gaining the benefits of both societies: enjoying the climate and relaxed lifestyle of the home country while maintaining access to various social benefits and good health care services and staying close to their children, grandchildren, and other relatives in the host country. There is a strong one-sided view about the way pendular migrants spend their time when in the country of origin, namely, relaxing, enjoying the sun, and visiting families and friends.

150 *Tineke Fokkema, Eralba Cela, and Yvonne Witter*

This view is in line with the phenomenon of "sunset, lifestyle, amenity-seeking and retirement migration" (Huber and O'Reilly 2004; King, Warnes and Williams 2000; Warnes et al. 2004), for example, European retirees migrating to the south of the continent or American seniors to the Sun Belt states looking for new lifestyles, coastal resorts, spas (Casado-Díaz, Kaiser and Warnes 2004; Warnes and Williams 2006) and wonderful landscapes such as the Costa del Sol and Tuscany (King, Warnes and Williams 2000). This is far from reality of the majority of the older labor migrants (Božić 2006), who differ economically, physically, and socially from Western retirees and who often belong to the pool of the "most disadvantaged and socially-excluded of western Europe's older people" (Warnes and Williams 2006: 7). In addition, although most of the pendular migrants of the older first generations, including our respondents, go to their homeland for social and environmental reasons (Cela and Fokkema 2014; Weltevrede, Seidler and De Boom 2013; Witter 2011), some nuances of their stay should be mentioned. Contrary to common belief, not all older pendular migrants have a relaxed time during their stay in the home country. For instance, although they often enjoy meeting relatives and friends, visits are sometimes overloaded with expectations that create a burden of responsibilities and social obligations. This is why some of them even avoid going to their birthplace for holidays. Commitments in the home country seem to be gender specific: besides visiting their homeland for economic reasons (see Stereotype 1) and religious purposes (e.g., Ramadan; Hunter 2011), some men are involved in business, including transnational trade activities, housing improvements, and taking care of property:

> The last two times I went to Morocco not to rest but because I have started to build a house and I was very busy. The house is almost finished and this year we will go there. (Moroccan man)

Some female pendular migrants, on the other hand, are primarily driven by taking care of a family member or fulfilling their household duties and community responsibilities, like visiting relatives, friends, and neighbors for special events such as weddings, engagements, and funerals or the graveyards of their parents(-in-law) and other close ones.

> Every year I go for 3 to 6 months to Suriname to take care of my sister. She has Parkinson's disease. Of course, I'm also going to Suriname to enjoy the nice weather and to meet old friends. But the main reason is to take care of my family, to help my sister's children, to alleviate them a bit from their heavy care burden. (Surinamese woman)
>
> (What do you do when you go to Albania?) In theory I like to go for a holiday. But in practice I spend the time visiting relatives and friends. I go to the cemetery to see my loved ones. And that's how the holiday goes. I return more tired than I was before I left, and I always say that I need another week to recuperate. (Albanian woman)

STEREOTYPE 4: PENDULAR MIGRATION IS A PRIVATE MATTER

The final common notion in public and political debates is that pendular migration is a private matter without social consequences; hence, governments and other public agencies should not interfere in it. This notion is questionable for several reasons, as we illustrate with the case of the Netherlands. We chose the Netherlands not only because of author affiliation, but also because interference with and the social implications of pendular migration have recently been the subject of numerous discussions and several studies in that country.

First, governments already determine the possibilities and boundaries of pendular migration through migrant-oriented and social security legislation (Kilkey and Merla 2013). For instance, if non-Dutch nationals stay more than six months abroad per year, it is assumed that they have changed their main residence, and consequently, their residence permit expires. With regard to social security, in 2008 the Dutch government considerably expanded the opportunities for pendular migration for older migrants by removing important financial barriers (Witter 2011). Social security recipients exempt from the obligation to seek work and participation in a reintegration program are allowed to stay in their country of origin for a maximum of 13 weeks; this exemption was previously only provided for recipients older than 57.5 years without obligation to seek work. Moreover, those aged 65 or older who receive social benefit because of an incomplete old-age pension (which applies to the majority of the older migrants) were given permission to stay abroad for a maximum of 26 weeks. Since 2012, however, the maximum staying period has been shortened to 13 weeks (Kaptein 2013).

Second, older migrants who often travel back and forth may benefit from a greater involvement of public health organizations and insurance companies. Usually, not all medical care expenses incurred abroad are covered by health insurance. It is also likely that older pendular migrants will use the health care system in their home country more frequently if more facilities are available and good access to appropriate care can be ensured.

It is well known that older migrants are family-oriented and prefer informal to formal care; their use of institutional and home care services is low compared to their native peers (Albertsson et al. 2004; Bolzman et al. 2004; Ebrahim 1996; Hansen 2013). This is also the case in the Netherlands (Denktaş 2011; Gerritsen et al. 2006; Schellingerhout 2004b), even though many forms of formal care are covered by their medical insurance. The main reasons for the underrepresentation of older migrants in the formal health care sector are lack of knowledge about public care accessibilities and availabilities, language barriers, different expectations and norms about types of help and treatment, and a general mistrust of the Dutch health care system.

An increasing number of older migrants, however, come to realize that obtaining informal support (mainly provided by their daughters and daughters-in-law) is less assured than it would have been in their home country because of changed circumstances in terms of willingness and time

152   Tineke Fokkema, Eralba Cela, and Yvonne Witter

(Arjouch 2005; De Valk and Schans 2008; Lan 2002). There is uncertainty about whether their children will share their traditional views on providing care between the different generations (the elderly are to be taken care by their children or children-in-law in return for the care they themselves received as children) in the destination context, but these doubts are hardly discussed within the family. Although research has shown that younger-generation migrants place a lower value on family solidarity and internalize the cultural values of the host country more strongly than their parents do (Merz et al. 2009), most children still feel responsible and are motivated to take care of their parents or in-laws (Dykstra and Fokkema 2012). The conditions to take on the full responsibility for such care are more difficult in the host society context, though: it is less common for children to share a house with parents or in-laws, children are more likely to live farther away, and often both sons and daughters work and accordingly have less time to spend with their parents or in-laws. The pendular migrants we interviewed also acknowledged these less-favorable conditions and would rarely want to call on their offspring in old age if it meant them having to give up their jobs:

> (Do you hope that one of your children will take care of you?) (Man) Yes, I hope so. But I don't know if they will. (Woman) Because now things are different. Before, Moroccan women were always at home. They cooked and they looked after their family members. But now the women work, and this is no longer possible. (Moroccan couple)
>
> My children have their own clothing shop, which is not around the corner. Having your own business, you can't leave, I know as I had restaurants myself, it's a busy life. (Turkish man)
>
> The children will not care for us, they simply need to work. We understand this very well. I know how important it is to work and make money. They have their own lives and that's good. They do well and they are good children, but if we need care, we want to have it from professionals. They will continue to do the small tasks as long as they want. (Surinamese man)

Rather than being a burden to their children, several of our respondents, mainly those living in Italy, expressed the desire to make use of informal, foreign home caregivers (*badante*), usually from Eastern Europe. They were also reluctant to be institutionalized in the host country, unless ethnic or culturally specific long-term care facilities were present. Others, mainly living in the Netherlands, would like to make use of long-term care services in the country of origin, if available and especially designed for pendular migrants:

> If commuting is not physically possible anymore, then it stops. There will come a day that everything stops. In Suriname there are few

Pendular Migration of the Older First Generations in Europe 153

facilities, they don't have care services like here. If those facilities were there, I would make use of them. (Surinamese man)

In recent years, despite the lack of specific policies for pendular migrants, several Dutch health providers have operated (or attempted to operate) across borders. One of the biggest international initiatives is the care hotel in Paramaribo, the capital city of Suriname. It has been proved, however, that it is very difficult to develop cross-border projects, as the current legislation complicates activities outside the Netherlands. In addition, Dutch health care providers experience organizational barriers in these countries (e.g., noncooperative governments, difficulties obtaining a piece of land) and limited financial resources. As a result, only a few initiatives have been successfully implemented and maintained, and currently there is little interest among healthcare providers to be active internationally (Witter 2011).

Finally, there are actual and potential negative societal consequences of pendular migration that justify government intervention. One disadvantage of commuting may be that older migrants are not sufficiently prepared for their old age in the host country, so they delay for too long before seeking appropriate care and/or a suitable home. As mentioned earlier, although older migrants prefer to receive informal rather than formal care, it is not always certain that their children or other family members can meet this preference. Moreover, in some cases the family will not be able to meet their specific care needs, for example, when knowledge is lacking about conditions such as dementia. In such cases, despite all the good intentions of the family, the older migrants will not receive the care they need and this may result in social isolation and a reduced quality of life.

Another negative side of pendular migration is the long-term vacancy of pendular migrants' property or, when institutionalized, rooms in old-age homes. As noted by one of our respondents,

> Most of the elderly here are commuters, so for half a year it's very quiet. Only those who cannot travel stay, and they take care of the mail and the plants. That's very difficult for them, they are pretty lonely here. I feel at home here, but I couldn't live without going to Turkey. (Turkish man)

Besides possible negative impacts of a long-term vacancy on the viability of the neighborhood, the house is often unattended during the long stay abroad and pendular migrants pay rent unnecessarily. Dutch residents may lose their rooms in old-age homes if they are away for more than two weeks. So far, old-age homes are not experiencing major long-term vacancies, and they are accommodating toward those who stay for a longer period in their country of birth, as long as those residents keep paying rent for their rooms (Witter 2011). Nevertheless, given the shrinking number of places in old-age homes in combination with an aging population, there is an increasing resistance toward long-term vacancy and a lively debate about alternative forms of housing and residential care for older pendular migrants (Witter 2011).

A recent study among older pendular migrants aged 60 and older of Turkish, Moroccan, and Surinamese origin who live in subsidized rentals in the Netherlands shows that a substantial proportion of them is interested in a flexible form of housing that better fits with their pendular life (Weltevrede, Seidler and De Boom 2013). They are most in favor of a three-generation house where the kitchen is shared and the private space is smaller than in regular subsidized housing. Temporary rental of the house to third parties for the period they are away, as well as living in a house with age peers (preferably of same ethnic background and a small number of residents), are also relatively popular types of housing. Migrants are less enthusiastic about living in a short-stay accommodation—a sort of residential hotel with common areas and facilities (including a service counter, a restaurant, medical care, and guest rooms for visitors) where the residents do not need to pay rent during their stay abroad and are assured of a studio when they return.

CONCLUSION

This chapter focused on the pendular migration of the older first-generation migrants in Europe who periodically travel back and forth between their host and home countries. By reviewing existing research related to this topic, including findings from our own qualitative studies, four popular beliefs on pendular migration were challenged. The first, that pendular migration is a temporary stage between a permanent stay or a definite return, is not supported by empirical evidence: pendular migration is a distinct form of migration, and accordingly, pendular migrants can neither be classified as settlers nor as returnees. With regard to the size and frequency of pendular migration we can only speculate, as pendular migrants are not captured in migration statistics. No strong empirical evidence was found either for the second common belief that pendular migration is a second-best option. Even for the older male migrants, often cherishing for a long time a return to their country of birth, pendular migration seems to be the optimal choice, not only to meet the preferences of their wives and children but also to keep enjoying the benefits of official residence in the host country, such as access to social security benefits and health care.

The third popular belief, that pendular migration is a time for relaxation, enjoyment of the climate, and visiting family and friends, is largely confirmed by research. This, however, does not mean that pendular migrants are only having a good time during the stay in their homeland: relatives and friends are sometimes visited because of duty and responsibility, and while female pendular migrants sometimes take an active role in caring, their male

Pendular Migration of the Older First Generations in Europe 155

counterparts may be involved in business activities. Several contradicting arguments could be offered, too, for the final common belief we challenged, that pendular migration is a private matter with no role for government or other public organizations, and without societal consequences: existing legislation and availability of healthcare services, both "here" and "there," partly determine the boundaries of freedom to travel back and forth. Governments, health care providers, and public agencies can play an important role in ensuring a "good old age" for pendular migrants, whose number is likely to increase in the future.

Evidence for rejecting or supporting these four popular beliefs was mainly gathered from small qualitative studies among a limited number of migrant groups in a few European countries. Given the increasing number of aging migrants in Europe and their strong bonds with their countries of origin (Baykara-Krumme 2013; Bolzman, Fibbi and Vial 2006; Ganga 2006; Warnes and Williams 2006), more research, especially large-scale quantitative and mixed-method studies, is needed to ascertain whether our findings and conclusions are generalizable and hold true for large number of migrant groups and across Europe and to examine the phenomenon of pendular migration in old age more in depth.

REFERENCES

Ajrouch, Kristine J. (2005): Arab-American Immigrant Elders' Views about Social Support. In: *Ageing & Society* 25, 5, pp. 655–673.

Albertsson Marie/Albin Björn/Siwertson, Christina/Hjelm, Katharina (2004): Consuming Care and Social Services: Comparisons Between Swedish-Born Older People and Older People Born Outside Sweden. In: *Practice* 16, 2, pp. 99–110.

Baldassar, Loretta/Merla, Laura (eds.) (2013): *Transnational Families, Migration and the Circulation of Care: Understanding Mobility and Absence in Family Life.* New York: Routledge.

Balkir, Canan/Böcker, Anita (2012): *Migration in Later Life. Residence, Social Security and Citizenship Strategies of Turkish Migrants and Dutch Retirement Migrants in Turkey.* MiReKoc Research Projects 2009–2010. Nijmegen Migration Law Working Papers Series, no 2012/2. Nijmegen: Radboud University Nijmegen.

Baykara-Krumme, Helen (2013): Returning, Staying, or Both? Mobility Patterns Among Elderly Turkish Migrants After Retirement. In: *Transnational Social Review* 3, pp. 11–29.

Bolzman, Claudio/Fibbi, Rosita/Vial, Marie (1999): Les Italiens et les Espagnols proches de la retraite en Suisse: Situation et projets d'avenir [Italians and Spanish Residents Close to Retirement: Their Circumstances and Plans for the Future]. In: *Gérontologie et Société* 91, pp. 137–151.

Bolzman, Claudio/Fibbi, Rosita/Vial, Marie (2001): La famille: une source de légitimité pour les immigrés après la retraite [The family: A Source of Legitimacy for Immigrants After Retirement]. In: *Revue Européenne des Migrations Internationales* 17, 1, pp. 55–78.

Bolzman, Claudio/Fibbi, Rosita/Vial, Marie (2006): What to Do After Retirement? Elderly Migrants and the Question of Return. In: *Journal of Ethnic and Migration Studies* 32, 8, pp. 1359–1375.

156   Tineke Fokkema, Eralba Cela, and Yvonne Witter

Bolzman, Claudio/Poncioni-Derigo, Raffaella/Vial, Marie/Fibbi, Rosita (2004): Older Labour Migrants' Well-Being in Europe: The Case of Switzeraland. In: *Ageing and Society* 24, 3, pp. 411–429.

Bousetta, Hassan/Gsir, Sonia/Jacobs, Dirk (2005): *Active Civic Participation of Immigrants in Belgium.* Country Report prepared for the European research project POLITIS, Olderburg, http://www.uni-oldenburg.de/politis-europe.

Božić, Saša (2006): The Achievement and Potential of International Retirement Migration Research: The Need for Disciplinary Exchange. In: *Journal of Ethnic and Migration Studies* 32, 8, pp. 1415–1427.

Casado-Díaz, María/Kaiser, Claudia/Warnes, Anthony M. (2004): Northern European Retired Residents in Nine Southern European Areas: Characteristics, Motivations and Adjustment. In: *Ageing and Society* 24, 3, pp. 353–381.

Cela, Eralba/Fokkema, Tineke (2014): Il benessere degli anziani Albanesi e Marocchini in Italia: Come affronte la solitudine? [Well-being of Albanian and Moroccan Older Migrants in Italy: How Do They Cope with Loneliness Feelings?] In: *Rivista Italiana di Economia, Demografia e Statistica*, LXVIII, 1, pp. 85–92.

Constant, Amelie/Massey, Douglas S. (2002): Return Migration by German Guestworkers: Neoclassical versus New Economic Theories. In: *International Migration*, 40, pp. 5–38.

Constant, Amelie F./Nottmeyer, Olga/Zimmermann, Klaus F. (2012): *The Economics of Circular Migration.* IZA Discussion Papers 6940, Institute for the Study of Labor (IZA).

Cottaar, Annemarie/Bouras, Nadia/Laouikili, Fatiha (2009): Marokkanen in Nederland: De pioniers vertellen [Moroccans in the Netherlands: pioneers' narratives]. Netherlands: Meulenhoff.

De Coulon, Augustin/Wolff, François-Charles (2010): Location Intentions of Immigrants at Retirement: Stay/Return or Go 'Back and Forth'? In: *Applied Economics* 42, 26, pp. 3319–3333.

De Haas, Hein/Fokkema, Tineke (2010): Intra-Household Conflicts in Migration Decisionmaking: Return and Pendulum Migration in Morocco. In: *Population and Development Review* 36, 3, pp. 541–561.

De Haas, Hein/Fokkema, Tineke (2011): The Effects of Integration and Transnational Ties on International Return Migration Intentions. In: *Demographic Research* 25, 24, pp. 755–782.

De Haas, Hein/Van Rooij, Aleida (2010): Migration as Emancipation? The Impact of Internal and International Migration on the Position of Women Left Behind in Rural Morocco. In: *Oxford Development Studies* 38, 1, pp. 43–62.

de Lary, Henri (2004): Bilateral Labour Agreements Concluded by France. In: OECD and Federal Office of Immigration, Integration and Emigration (eds.): *Migration for Employment: Bilateral Agreements at a Crossroads.* Paris: OECD Publishing, pp. 43–54.

De Valk, Helga A. G./Schans, Djamila (2008): 'They Ought to Do this for Their Parents': Perceptions of Filial Obligations Among Immigrant and Dutch Older People. In: *Ageing & Society* 28, 1, pp. 49–66.

Denktaş, Semiha (2011): *Health and Health Care Use of Elderly Immigrants in the Netherlands: A Comparative Study.* Thesis, Erasmus University Rotterdam, Rotterdam, Netherlands.

Dykstra, Pearl A./Fokkema, Tineke (2012): Norms of Filial Obligation in the Netherlands. In: *Population* 67, 1, pp. 97–122.

Ebrahim, Shah (1996): Caring for Older People: Ethnic Elders. In: *British Medical Journal* 313, 7057, pp. 610–13.

Emmer, Pieter C./Lucassen, Leo (2012): *Migration from the Colonies to Western Europe Since 1800.* Mainz: EGO—Europäische Geschichte Online.

Pendular Migration of the Older First Generations in Europe   157

Engelhard, David (2006): Pendelen op je oude dag: Pendelmigratie en gezondheid bij oudere migranten [Commuting in Old Age: Pendular Migration and Health Among Older Migrants]. In: *Cultuur Migratie Gezondheid (Culture Migration Health)*, 3, 1, pp. 14–25.

Engelhard, David (2007): No Place Like Home? Return and Circular Migration Among Elderly Chinese in the Netherlands. In: *IIAS Newsletter* 45, pp. 20–21.

European Migration Network (2011): *Temporary and Circular Migration: Empirical Evidence, Current Policy Practice and Future Options in EU Member States.* Luxembourg: Publications Office of the European Union.

Fokkema, Tineke/Naderi, Robert (2013): Differences in Late-Life Loneliness: A Comparison Between Turkish and Native-Born Older Adults in Germany. In: *European Journal of Ageing* 10, 4, pp. 289–300.

Ganga, Deianira (2006): From Potential Returnees into Settlers: Nottingham's Older Italians, In: *Journal of Ethnic and Migration Studies* 32, 8, pp. 1395–1413.

Gerritsen A. A. M./Bramsen, I./Deville, W./Van Willigen, L. H. M./Hovens, J. E./Van der Ploeg, H. M. (2006): Use of Health Care Services by Afghan, Iranian, and Somali Refugees and Asylum Seekers Living in the Netherlands. In: *European Journal of Public Health*, 16, 4, pp. 394–399.

Hansen, Eigil Boll (2013): Older Immigrants' Use of Public Home Care and Residential Care. In: *European Journal of Ageing*. doi: 10.1007/s10433–013–0289–1.

Harris, John R./Todaro, Michael P. (1970): Migration, Unemployment and Development: A Two-Sector Analysis. In: *American Economic Review*, 60, 1, pp. 126–142.

Hatton, Timothy J./Williamson, Jeffrey G. (2005): *Global Migration and the Two Centuries of Policy and Performance.* London: The MIT Press.

Hondagneu-Sotelo, Pierrette (1994): *Gendered Transitions.* Berkeley: University of California Press.

Hondagneu-Sotelo, Pierrette (2003): *Gender and U.S. Immigration. Contemporary Trends.* Berkeley: University of California Press.

Huber, Andreas/O'Reilly, Karen (2004): The construction of *Heimat* under conditions of individualized modernity: Swiss and British elderly migrants in Spain. In: *Ageing & Society* 24, pp. 327-351.

Hugo, Graeme (2013): *What We Know About Circular Migration and Enhanced Mobility.* Policy Brief, No. 7. Washington DC: Migration Policy Institute.

Hunter, Alistair (2011): Theory and Practice of Return Migration at Retirement: The Case of Migrant Worker Hostel Residents in France. In: *Population, Space and Place* 17, 2, pp. 179–192.

Itzigsohn, José/Dore Cabral, Carlos/Hernandez Medina, Esther/Vazquez, Obed (1999): Mapping Dominican Transnationalism: Narrow and Broad Transnational Practices. In: *Ethnic and Racial Studies* 22, 2, pp. 316–339.

Itzigsohn, José/Giorguli-Saucedo, Silvia (2005): Incorporation, Transnationalism, and Gender: Immigrant Incorporation and Transnational Participation as Gendered Processes. In: *International Migration Review* 39, 4, pp. 895–920.

Jensen, Peter/Pedersen, Peder J. (2007): To Stay or Not Stay? Out-Migration of Immigrants from Denmark. In: *International Migration* 45, 5, pp. 87–113.

Kaptein, G. (2013): *AOW en Pensioenen* [AOW (General Old Age Pensions Act) and Pensions]. Utrecht: NOOM.

Kilkey, Majella/Merla, Laura (2013): Situating Transnational Families' Care-giving Arrangements: The Role of Institutional Contexts. In: *Global Networks*. doi: 10.1111/glob.12034.

King, Russel (1986): *Return Migration and Regional Economic Problems.* London: Croom Helm.

158 Tineke Fokkema, Eralba Cela, and Yvonne Witter

King, Russel (2000): *Southern Europe in the Changing Global Map of Migration.* In: King, R./Lazaridis, G./Tsardanidis, C. (eds.): *Eldorado or Fortress? Migration in Southern Europe.* London: Palgrave Macmillan, pp. 1–26.

King, Russel (2002): Towards a New Map of European Migration. *International Journal of Population Geography* 8, 2, pp. 89–106.

King, Russel/Castaldo, Adriana/Vullnetari, Julie (2011): Gendered Relations and Filial Duties along the Greek-Albanian Remittance Corridor. In: *Economic Geography* 874, pp. 393–419.

King, Russel/Dalipaj, Mirela/Mai, Nicola (2006): Gendering Migration and Remittances: Evidence from London and Northern Albania. In: *Population, Space and Place* 12, 6, pp. 409–434.

King, Russel/Vullnetari, Julie (2009): The Intersection of Gender and Generation in Albanian Migration, Remittances and Transnational Care. In: *Geografiska Annaler: Series B, Human Geography* 91, 1, pp. 19–38. doi: 10.1111/j.1468-0467.2009.00304.x.

King, Russel/Warnes, Anthony M./Williams, Allan M. (1998): International Retirement Migration in Europe. In: *Population, Space and Place* 4, 2, pp. 91–111.

King, Russel/Warnes, Anthony M./Williams, Allan M. (2000): *Sunset Lives: British Retirement Migration to the Mediterranean.* Oxford/New York: Berg.

Lan, Pei-Chia (2002): Subcontracting Filial Piety: Elder Care in Ethnic Chinese Immigrant Families in California. In: *Journal of Family Issues* 23, 7, pp. 812–835.

Mahler, Sara J./Pessar, Patricia (2006): Gender Matters: Ethnographers Bring Gender from the Periphery Toward the Core of Migration Studies. In: *International Migration Review* 40, 1, pp. 27–63.

Merz, Eva-Maria/Özeke-Kocabas, Ezgi/Oort, Frans J./Schuengel, Carlo (2009): Intergenerational Family Solidarity: Value Differences Between Immigrant Groups and Generations. In: *Journal of Family Psychology* 23, 3, pp. 291–300.

Oostindie, Gert/Schoorl, Jeannette (2011): Postkoloniale migratie [Post-Colonial Migration]. In: Jennissen, R. P. W. (ed.): *De Nederlandse migratiekaart: Achtergronden en ontwikkelingen van verschillende internationale migratietypen [The Dutch Migration Map: Backgrounds and Developments of Different Migration Types].* The Hague: CBS/WODC/BJU, pp. 251–285.

Pessar, Patricia (1999): Engendering Migration Studies: The Case of New Immigrants in the United States. In: *American Behavioral Scientist* 42, 4, pp. 577–600.

Poulain, Michel/Perrin, Nicolas (2002): The Demographic Characteristics of Immigrant Populations in Belgium. In: Haug, Werner/Compton, Paul Alwyn/Courbage, Youssef (eds.): *The Demographic Characteristics of Immigrant Populations.* Strasbourg: Council of Europe, pp. 18–57.

Richter, Marina (2004): Contextualizing Gender and Migration: Galiciun Immigration to Switzerland. In: *International Migration Review* 38, 1, pp. 263–286.

Schellingerhout, Roelof (2004a): *Cijferrapport allochtone ouderen* [Statistical Report of Older Migrants]. The Hague: Sociaal en Cultureel Planbureau.

Schellingerhout, Roelof (ed.) (2004b): *Gezondheid en welzijn van allochtone ouderen* [Health and Well-Being of Older Ethnic Minorities]. The Hague: Sociaal en Cultureel Planbureau.

Stark, Oded/Bloom, David E. (1985): The New Economics of Labour Migration. In: *American Economic Review* 75, 1, pp. 191–196.

Warnes, Anthony M./Friedrich, Klaus/Kellaher, Leonie/Torres, Sandra (2004): The Diversity and Welfare of Older Immigrants in Europe. In: *Ageing & Society* 24, 3, pp. 307–326.

Warnes, Anthony M./Williams, Allan (2006): Older Migrants in Europe: A New Focus for Migration Studies. In: *Journal of Ethnic and Migration Studies*, 32, 8, pp. 1257–1281.

Pendular Migration of the Older First Generations in Europe 159

Weltevrede, A. M./Seidler, Y./De Boom, J. (2013): *Transnationaal wonen onder oudere migranten* [Transnational Living Among Older Migrants]. The Hague: FORUM.

White, Paul (2006): Migrant Populations Approaching Old Age: Prospects in Europe. In: *Journal of Ethnic and Migration Studies* 32, 8, pp. 1283–1300.

Witter, Yvonne (2011): *Ik woon niet waar ik ben geboren: Een onderzoek naar pendelen door ouderen migranten, het beste van twee werelden. . . . .* [I Do Not Live Where I Was Born: A Study of Commuting by Older Migrants, the Best of Two Worlds. . . . .]. Master Thesis, Vrije Universiteit, Amsterdam.

Zimmermann, Klaus F. (1995): Tackling the European Migration Problem. In: *Journal of Economic Perspectives* 9, 2, pp. 45–62.

Part C

Facets of Old-Age Care in a Transnational World

Traveling Institutions, Boundary Objects, and Regimes of Inequality

8 "Moving (for) Elder Care Abroad"
The Fragile Promises of Old-Age Care Facilities for Elderly Germans in Thailand

Vincent Horn, Cornelia Schweppe,
Désirée Bender, and Tina Hollstein

Care for the elderly is one of the key challenges of almost all European countries, a challenge that is often referred to as the "old-age care crisis." So far, strategies to address this challenge have given rise to two broader processes: the movement of migrant care workers into households and the recruitment of foreign labor by the old age care sector. However, alongside these processes of "moving carers in," a process of "moving care out" can increasingly be observed, that is, the migration of older people from Western countries to old-age care facilities abroad. This development also applies to Germany, from where older people in need of care move to facilities established specifically for them and other German-speaking elderly, primarily in Eastern Europe and Southeast Asia. Until now, very few academic studies have been examining the underlying factors of this development and the organization and provision of care in these facilities. This research gap is addressed by our project "Moving Elder Care Abroad," which focuses on the (transnational) processes through which these facilities are created and organized and the living conditions and concepts of care and aging arising in this context.

In this chapter we first analyze the sociopolitical context of old-age care in Germany as an important background to these facilities. We argue that the so-called old-age care crisis and the transnational opening of the social security systems in German-speaking countries constitute two important sociopolitical conditions leading to the development of old-age care facilities abroad. We show that this development is linked to an old-age care system that shifts a large part of costs and responsibilities to the families and, at the same time, tends to downplay the deficits of old-age homes in the country. Second, we describe the ambivalence of old age care facilities abroad, designed as promising structures for care and support. More precisely, we address the following research questions: Through which promises do these facilities position themselves as attractive alternatives to old age homes in Germany? and In what ways are these promises kept or remain unfulfilled? We seek to answer these questions by analyzing the homepage of an old-age care facility in Thailand and by providing insights from empirical research carried out in different facilities in this country.

164　*Vincent Horn, et al.*

THE SOCIOPOLITICAL CONTEXT OF OLD-AGE CARE IN GERMANY

Germany, as virtually all industrialized and increasingly also "developing" countries, is faced with severe social, economic and political challenges due to demographic change and increasing longevity. According to the Organisation for Economic Development and Co-operation (OECD; 2013), Germany will soon become one of the countries with the highest proportion of people older than 80 in its population. While 5 percent of its population belongs to this demographic group today, the OECD estimates that this will grow to 15 percent by 2050, a share that will only be surpassed by Japan. Consequently, a rapidly increasing demand for old-age care is expected because of this demographic group experiencing multimorbidity and mental illness. The Bertelsmann Foundation (2012), for example, estimates that the number of elderly German citizens in need of care will increase from around 2.5 million today to 3.4 million in 2030.

The main political response of the German government to this demographic change has been the introduction of a compulsory long-term care insurance (LTCI) in 1995 (Landenberger 1995).[1] Its main goal is to mitigate the risk of dependency by providing coverage for the physical, mental, and financial burdens resulting from care needs in old age. However, unlike health insurance, LTCI only offers basic provision "and must be supplemented by either the family's resources or social assistance" (Da Roit and Bihan 2010: 291). A further goal of LTCI is to facilitate caregiving at home. According to the principle of "home care before institutional care," inpatient care is only eligible if home care cannot or can no longer be provided, such as in the case of intensified long-term care needs. For home care, LTCI offers benefits both in cash and in-kind. The first can be used to pay nonprofessional caregivers, and the second, to hire professional home care providers. A mix of nonprofessional and professional care providers is also possible. If care is provided in an old-age home, beneficiaries only receive in-kind benefits.

The amount of LTCI benefits depends on both the level of care needed by the elderly person and the type of care provided.[2] Cash benefits are lowest if home care is provided by family members or friends, ranging from 235 to 700 euro a month. If a professional home care provider is engaged, a minimum of 450 euro to a maximum of 1,550 euro are paid per month. For inpatient care, monthly benefits start at 1,023 euro and can reach 1,550 euro (in hardship cases this can go up to 1,918 euro). Given that old-age home costs have reached a monthly average of between 2,700 and 3,000 euro, and are much higher in the case of intensive, round-the-clock care, LTCI only covers a part of the overall expenses. As a consequence, the private-to-public ratio expenditure for long-term care in Germany is among the highest within the European Union (EU; Lipszy, Sail and Xavier 2012).

Indeed, as shown by Lipszy and colleagues (2012), copayments and out-of-pocket payments make up one third of the expenditure on long-term care in Germany, compared to 0.6 percent in France, 10 percent in Sweden, and 16.8 percent in Austria. Therefore, it is not surprising that 59 percent of German people think of old age homes as not affordable, and only 12 percent think the opposite (EC 2007). Public expenditure for long-term care in Germany is low: measured as a percentage of the grand domestic product, Germany (1.4 percent) spends less than the EU average (1.8 percent) and far less than other high-income countries such as Denmark (4.5 percent), Sweden (3.8 percent), France (2.1 percent), or Italy (1.9 percent; Lipszy, Sail and Xavier 2012).

The high copayments and out-of-pocket payments partly explain why families still shoulder the bulk of elderly care in Germany. Thus, of the current 2.5 million older people in need of care, 70 percent are cared for at home, of which two-thirds receive care exclusively from family members (Statistisches Bundesamt 2013). In a comparative study of long-term care in the EU, Bettio and Verashchagina (2012) emphasize the strong role of family caregivers in Germany. By measuring the extent to which old-age care in Germany is outsourced to home and residential care, this study reveals a close affinity between Germany and countries with a familistic welfare regime such as Italy and Spain. This is, of course, not to say that at home care is not the preferred option for elderly care among German people. As indicated by the Eurobarometer (EC 2008), the majority prefers that elderly persons in need of care are cared for in their home (57 percent) or in one of their children's homes (25 percent). In contrast, only 8 percent consider an old-age home the best option. At the same time, however, care within private households involves considerable structural problems. Numerous studies show the enormous strain put on the family members who provide elder care. The social, emotional, psychological, physical, and financial pressures have often been identified (Schneekloth 2005, 2006, 2007; Schweppe 2013). Moreover, serious errors and care gaps can also be found in the case of family care (Schneekloth and Wahl 2009).

Apart from the financial aspect and rather strict eligibility criteria, the reluctance to use residential care in Germany can also be explained by widespread doubts about the quality of old-age homes. In response to this, the German government established a quality management system in 2011. Since then, annual audits are carried out by the Medical Advisory Services of the Health Insurance Funds to assess the quality of approximately 11,000 old-age homes based on the German school grade system (e.g., 1 is *very good* and 6 is *poor*). The policy goals of this measure were to stimulate competition among professional care providers and enhance transparency for care-seeking elderly persons and their family members. However, old-age homes in Germany are overwhelmingly positively assessed (Uken 2014), with an average grade of 1.2, making it difficult to detect quality differences between them. These results stand in contrast not only to the public

166   *Vincent Horn, et al.*

opinion about the quality of old-age homes in Germany but also to many reports and newspaper headlines about care scandals and deficits in these facilities (Focus 2012; MDS 2012; Contanzo 2011). In addition, critiques of the German LTCI address not only inpatient care but also ambulatory care provision. Many discrepancies have been identified between the structures, offers and billable services in inpatient and ambulatory old-age care, on one hand, and the actual needs and necessities of dependent older people and their relatives, on the other hand (Karl 2009; Schweppe 2012).

According to these studies, apart from the high costs, a central structural problem of old-age care in Germany is the precarious staff situation. Both public and private care providers are struggling with significant labor shortages when trying to meet the needs of health and long-term care. The German Association of Private Care Providers estimates that there is a present gap of about 30,000 care workers in the country (BPA 2012). This situation is expected to get worse in the near future as the number of elderly persons in need of care increases. The Bertelsmann Foundation (2012) projects a gap of almost half a million care workers in Germany by 2030. The precarious staff situation is also reflected in the working conditions: low pay accompanied by heavy workloads and rising demands, a lack of social recognition, and fast-paced schedules, with little chance to satisfy people's individual needs for care resulting in relationships that work according to principles of rationality and a high turnover.

The political response to the shortage of care workers has been to reduce the skill requirements for staff in old-age homes and to launch recruitment programs for qualified care workers especially from Southern Europe, Romania, Serbia, and recently from China, the Philippines, and Vietnam. The first measure broadens the pool of potential care workers and allows employees to hire (less-qualified) staff at lower costs but is likely to have negative effects on the quality of care provided. The second measure still needs to prove its efficiency. However, it is doubtful that the recruitment programs will pull enough care workers into the country to satisfy the rapidly growing demand. In brief, the two measures do not represent a forward-looking solution for the major structural problems of old-age care in Germany and will not solve the aforementioned structural challenges concerning the precarious staff situation.

Critiques of old-age care in Germany also refer to the dominance of the medical paradigm in care, the lack of focus on lifeworlds, and a dearth of individual care and support structures. The introduction of LTCI in Germany (see the following discussion) is a particularly clear example of the medical paradigm becoming firmly established in (billable) care (Jansen and Klie 1999; Schweppe 2005, 2012). Because the benefits system recognizes the need for care as resulting only from illness and disability, both residential and nonresidential care are mainly related to somatic aspects and hygiene. Accordingly, social or emotional aspects are rarely taken into account. Another point of criticism is that the term *care*, when based on medical criteria, creates a normative framework which excludes other understandings of care, and which

"*Moving (for) Elder Care Abroad*"   167

ignores the fact that care can be understood as something negotiated by those involved in care relationships (Jansen and Klie 1999; Schweppe 2005). Strict stipulations for the services that can be billed, according to which activities such as feeding or bathing are calculated on a per-minute basis, are a particularly striking illustration of the standardization of care.

Accordingly, fierce criticism is leveled at the fact that organizational rationalities outweigh individuality, ensuring that institutional procedures run smoothly but leaving them unable to satisfy individual needs and necessities. In many ways, care for the elderly is shaped by its focus on organizational efficiency, daily routines that are often not based on individual needs for care, a lack of participation, the right for residents to exert their free will and maintain their own temporal rhythms and opportunities for action, and a lack of private spaces and single rooms, as well as the use of restraints. Correspondingly, Schneekloth and Wahl (2009: 11, translation by the authors) show "that care tends to be provided in a conventional manner rather than by means of new standards based on prevention and rehabilitation or self-determination and independence."

These structural problems and the negative image of old-age care in Germany are important reasons why individuals and families search for alternative solutions abroad. This search, in turn, is inextricably linked to the gradual transnational opening of the German social security system, which allows for receiving certain social benefits while residing in another country. This process can be observed with regard to all three pillars that are especially relevant in old age: the old-age pension, the health care system, and LTCI. Table 8.1 shows the different degrees to which benefits from these three systems can be received abroad. Old-age pension shows the highest degree of cross-border portability, with pensions being transferred to more than 150 countries in the world (DRV 2014). According to German old-age insurance (DRV) statistics, an increasing number of German citizens receive their pensions abroad. In 2013, 221,166 German citizens made use of this transfer compared to 191,739 in 2008 and 160,706 in 2003 (DRV 2003, 2008, 2013). After old-age pension, health care insurance shows the next highest degree of cross-border portability: it can be transferred to EU countries and to several other countries with which Germany signed bilateral agreements. In the case of LTCI, the portability of benefits is more restricted, both financially and geographically. German citizens who reside in another EU country can only receive cash benefits up to a maximum of 700 Euro, but are not eligible for the higher in-kind allowances.[3] In contrast, those who reside in a country outside the EU are not eligible for any kind of LTCI benefit.[4] Thus far, the number of elderly Germans who receive benefits from LTCI in another EU country is very small, only 5,000 or 0.2 percent of the total LTCI beneficiaries (Mihm 2013). However, there is a considerable data gap for this group (Kaiser 2011), and a higher number of Germans receiving long-term care abroad can be assumed than reflected in the official figures.

168   *Vincent Horn, et al.*

Table 8.1   Elder care and the portability of social benefits*

Type of Insurance	Portability within EU**	Portability outside EU
Old Age Pension	Yes	Yes***
Health Insurance	Yes****	No
Care Insurance	Yes for cash (235–700€) No for allowances in kind (1,023–1,500€; in hardship cases 1,918€)	No

*Only refers to the public social security system that covers about 90 percent of the German population.

**Applies also to countries that have signed bilateral agreements with Germany: Iceland, Norway, Switzerland, Liechtenstein, Israel, Turkey, Croatia, and Tunisia.

***Depending on the country, deductions are possible, for example, because of exchange rate losses.

****Does not apply if the person is also entitled to pension benefits in the hosting country.

MOVING ELDER CARE ABROAD

The field of old-age facilities abroad directed toward the care needs of elderly Germans[5] is highly complex, confusing, and dynamic. The majority of these facilities have been established during the last three to five years. Since then, some have closed (and sometimes reopened), while new ones are constantly emerging. What adds to the complexity is the enormous heterogeneity of these facilities, which are serving a wide spectrum of elderly people with different needs of care or support and offering a broad range of care arrangements and costs. Although no accurate numbers on these facilities exist, we can gain an approximate idea by looking at the Internet portal "Wohnen im Alter" ("living-in-old-age"; http://www.wohnen-im-alter.de), Germany's biggest information platform for the search of care options for the elderly. According to these non-exhaustive figures, the number of offers for old age care facilities abroad increased considerably within only one year (2013–2014).This trend was particularly strong for facilities in Spain (+11) and Poland (+7) but also notable in Thailand and the Czech Republic (both +3). Altogether, the Internet portal currently provides offers from 150 facilities in more than 20 different countries located in Asia, Africa, Europe, and Central America. A clear concentration of facilities can be observed in Eastern Europe (48) and Thailand (21).

Although these facilities quickly received media exposure and extensive reporting, so far they have been given only scant academic attention. This gap is addressed by the research project "Moving Elder Care Abroad" at the University of Mainz (Germany). The central focus of this research project is on the (transnational) processes by which these facilities are created and organized. Of particular interest are the care concepts (and the implicit understandings of aging and old age) and the living conditions of their residents. The study uses an ethnographic approach to gain insights into these processes. Guided interviews carried out with key actors (facility operators, residents if possible, family members, and staff) and observations of everyday life at the facility are used as central methods of data collection, supported by media reports on television, in the print media, and on the Internet. The data analysis is informed by grounded theory methodology, following Strauss and Corbin (1996).

The study is being carried out in facilities in Thailand and Poland. These two countries were chosen because of the relatively large number of facilities in both countries and the differences in these facilities between the two countries The most obvious differences are the geographical distances from the old people's countries, the facility size, the levels of staff qualification, the pricing levels, the portability of social benefits, and the spectrum of support and care services provided. In both countries, the facilities offer a wide range of services. However, in Poland the facilities are primarily directed to the elderly with physically and/or mentally impediments whereas the facilities in Thailand cover a wider range, offering support and care both for people with only few support or care needs and those in need of full-time care.

Although the facilities generally cost less in both countries than in Germany, the prices in Poland tend to be below those in Thailand: a nursing home in Poland costs between 1,000 and 1,500 euro a month depending on the level of care and the type of accommodation, sometimes even less. There are facilities that calculate the monthly costs for those in need of care, accommodated in four-bed rooms, at 700 euro.[6] Full-time care at the facilities in Thailand, meanwhile, costs between 2,000 and 2,800 euro per month. When less care is required, there is a wider range of costs, starting at 800 euro.

The two countries also differ in terms of the portability of old-age benefits: as has been described, only pensions can be transferred to Thailand, whereas both pensions and benefits from the German LTCI and health insurance system can be transferred to Poland. Accordingly, further cost savings can be expected at the facilities in Poland. Altogether, the facilities for the elderly Germans in Thailand and Poland thus cover a wide spectrum, allowing for a finely nuanced, contrastive investigation of the questions raised by the project.

PROMISES: THE CONSTRUCTION OF ATTRACTIVENESS

What do these old-age care facilities promise that attracts elderly people and their family members? Based on our analysis of the facilities in Thailand, we show that, in addition to lower costs, they project alternatives to other existing problems in the care for the elderly provided in Germany. Based on

170   *Vincent Horn, et al.*

the example of the homepage of a facility in Thailand aimed at the elderly suffering from dementia, we show what and how constructions are made to present these facilities as promising alternatives.[7]

The institution offers a 1:1 care 24 hours a day. Every resident is allocated three individual carers. According to the homepage, this care structure permits carers to concentrate all their efforts on the individual resident, allowing for individually arranged structures and daily programs (including individual menus and mealtimes) depending on the residents' needs and preferences. Care structures of this kind not only promise individualized care but also offer "answers" to specific problems that, so far, have remained largely unsolved in Germany. For example, the homepage explicitly refers to the problem of falls among elderly people. Old people have a higher risk of falls, and when falls occur the hazards are also considerable. The risk of falls can become an insurmountable problem, especially if people who are physically frail or suffering from dementia wish to remain mobile, but the help required to stay active is not available, not asked for, not accepted, or no longer within their understanding because of cognitive restrictions. What are often desperate final attempts on the part of carers (family members or professionals) to prevent falls, for example, by attaching rails to the bed, frequently also prove unsuccessful, not only because of legal barriers or moral reservations regarding personal liberty but also because of vehement rejection on the part of those in need of care. In the Thai facility, this difficult problem is solved by using a special practice: "At night one of the three carers lies next to the bed of each guest, on standby. If their sleep is disturbed, the carers are there and can take care of the guest. All trips to the toilet are of course accompanied by the carer."[8]

In addition to individualized care, emphasis is also placed on the special quality of care and the relationship between the carers and residents. In this regard, the cultural naturalization of Thai people is of especial importance. Mention is made of the status allocated to old people and their treatment in Thai society: "Frail, elderly people are held in high regard in Thai society and deserve respect and good affectionate care." It is assumed that this status held by old people affects the carers' work: "Caring for the elderly is considered a meaningful, merciful task and is highly valued among the population. As a result, people in Thailand are highly motivated to care for elderly people." Correspondingly, the central characteristic of care among Thai staff is described as follows: "One outstanding quality of the care provided by the Thai staff is the warm-hearted, tender way they deal with elderly, dependent people: they are physically close and respectful." Thus, the culturally ascribed relational qualities of Thai staff are stressed as a specifically desirable capacity for elderly care. Thais are considered as naturally possessing relational qualities that are desirable among those caring for the elderly. It is noteworthy that the attributes mentioned as signs of quality largely revolve around certain personality traits and attitudes. No reference is made to specific (professional) knowledge or skills.

Opening to the community is also important for the facility. "In our village, we are known and valued as an institution caring for elderly people. Our facility has the acceptance and support of the community: We take part in celebrations and temple ceremonies, spurred by a wish to actively experience the surroundings and environment." Finally, the reasonable cost of care is mentioned. Though costs are always calculated on an individual basis, it is mentioned that they are generally only half the price of services in Germany.

Interestingly, the homepage implicitly adopts a kind of external view by picking up and responding to possible problems with and criticism of these facilities. This practice is illustrated with the following two examples concerning the weather and the language.

The Example of the Weather

The warmer and nicer climate in Thailand is emphasized as another advantage of the facility. Compared to Germany, however, the climate is not just warmer but is, in fact, quite hot and with high humidity. Doubts or critical queries as to whether old people might struggle with this extreme heat and humidity are met first with medical arguments. It is argued that, thanks to the warm climate, people suffer from colds and influenza less often. Second, pragmatic, everyday arguments are developed to show the positive effects of the weather on the old people: "The people in need of care do not need to be 'bothered' with lots of clothes. Depending on their level of illness, dressing and undressing can be very complicated. As they can basically stay outside all day long, activities and excursions can take place more frequently and spontaneously." In some cases, the argument is even put forward that the climate and familial atmosphere at the facility can allow people to stop taking medicine they previously needed and that it is not unusual for their health to improve.

The Example of the Language

The carers generally speak no German, or just a "minimum number of important German expressions." This "lack" is dealt with by first relativizing the importance of verbal communication with people suffering from dementia, and second suggesting that the avoidance of verbal communication could hold positive potential with dementia sufferers, creating more positive and less conflict-prone relationships between residents and carers. Thus, it is claimed that

> [p]eople with dementia often look for other ways to communicate, particularly through body language, especially as they may have more difficulty expressing themselves and speaking as the illness progresses. The search for new forms of communication can both bring to light

172 *Vincent Horn, et al.*

new resources and hide existing deficits. . . . Experience shows that
when relatives or carers who speak the same language have frictions
with dementia sufferers, they often become defensive and argue with
them. This can lead to both sides making accusations. This problem can
be reduced considerably when carers communicate non-verbally or in
another language.

Ultimately, the arguments of these two examples not only address potential sources of difficulty or problems for the facility in Thailand but are also used positively in solving specific sets of problems encountered in elderly care in Germany. Potential criticism is deflected by looking at possible sources of difficulty in care for the elderly in Germany and addressing by reference to the specific conditions in Thailand.

To summarize, according to the homepage, the facility offers an individualized, 24-hour, 1:1 care arrangement with an emphasis on respect, love, tenderness, and physical closeness, along with integration into the community, at prices that are generally much lower than in Germany. In terms of the professional discourse and public opinion in Germany regarding desirable care for the elderly in Germany (which can be derived from the earlier-mentioned criticism leveled at old-age homes in Germany), the homepage projects a care arrangement that comes very close to meeting the criteria that are not put into effect in Germany. It implicitly builds on the discontent with old-age homes in Germany and develops a model that meets the criteria of what is considered as "good care" in Germany. In other words, the concepts and ideas of "good care" are "exported" to Thailand (along with the old-age home as an institution, a rarity in Thailand) and attempts are made to implement these ideas by referring to specific structural conditions (low costs of living and low wages), cultural stereotypes and climatic conditions.

However, when concepts of desirable care developed in Germany are merged with Thai "resources," the original "ideal construct" necessarily changes or takes on certain connotations. The criticism and doubt potentially produced by these specific connotations are deflected by implicitly addressing and depicting them as an advantage or a solution to other difficulties. This is passed on to the beneficiaries in the form of attractive promises along with cultural stereotypes about constantly friendly, polite Thai women. In this way, the facilities can take advantage of the long-established Thai tourism from Germany and other German-speaking countries in Europe by using it in their advertising strategies (e.g., by using the slogan of "Thailand, the country of smiles").

A DIVERSE AND UNREGULATED FIELD

These promises, however, prove to be ambivalent. The following quotation taken from an interview with a facility operator in Thailand identifies a central structural condition under which these facilities are created and developed:

> I: How is it actually possible to open a facility like this in Thailand? Can anyone do it? Are there requirements or something?
> A: Not so many requirements, I mean in fact you have to make the requirements yourself.
> I: I mean (. . .) for example in Germany, there's a million rules that an institution like this has to follow. Isn't there anything like that here?
> A: No, no, I actually do all that alone, whether it's the toilet door handles or this or that because obviously, otherwise it's extremely dangerous for the people living here.

This illustrates the unregulated field, with little preexisting structure and hardly any legal regulation, in which facilities for the elderly are established in Thailand. There are no regulations on the qualifications of the operators or staff, architectural stipulations, medical treatments or monitoring, and so on. The quote above shows that it is up to the operators to "make the requirements themselves." In this unregulated field, the operators of these facilities, usually Swiss or Germans with long-term living and working experiences in Thailand are the central, powerful actors and decision makers who determine the orientation and nature of the facility. This power is accentuated by the fact that there are hardly any controls on either them or the facility.[9] The main requirement on the part of the Thai authorities refers to the employment of Thai staff and the compliance with Thai working conditions in these facilities. Inquiries of Thai authorities *may* occur in the form of a request for an autopsy in the case of a resident's death. The family, who sometimes serves as an instance of control in old-age care facilities in Germany, takes a backseat as potential monitors in the facilities in Thailand because of geographical distance, little time spent in the facility, and a lack of information. The virtual absence of regulations and quality measurements carries the risk of abuse, neglect, and precarious living conditions. Nevertheless, at the same time it opens a space for innovative and unconventional approaches to old-age care.

Accordingly, our data show a wide range of very different types and quality of care in the facilities in Thailand, very different ways in which care and support are delivered and very different implicit care concepts. In our observations, we come across the 24-hour care described in the homepage analysis in some facilities, where the carers do stay with the residents during the night. We were able to observe highly individualized care arrangements with lots of attention given to individual needs and with facility operators aiming to maintain quality of life in different spheres of everyday lifeworlds. *Time* is a crucial resource in these facilities, compared to Germany. We experienced caring scenes in some facilities that are rarely or never part of

174   *Vincent Horn, et al.*

the everyday practices in German old-age homes, for example, the initiative of carers to look at and talk about the photograph album belonging to a bedridden, severely ill resident suffering from dementia; physical closeness when talking or other communication forms are no longer possible; varied activities, such as playing the residents' favorite games; looking at German magazines together; or taking walks hand in hand with the carers or playing games together during which the residents' own reality is followed. Moreover, strong body-oriented practices such as hairdressing, manicures, pedicures, and massages can also be observed as regular services.

However, we also discovered that, because of precarious contractual arrangements, for instance, some residents have to leave the facility on short notice, without consideration of their difficulties to relocate to another facility or to return to Germany. Other residents feel they "go mad" and "get ill" due to the remoteness of the home, the monotony of everyday life, lack of communication and unbearable boredom. We also learned about staffing concepts that do not distinguish between the staff members' duties: they take care of the garden as well as of the residents' bodies. Similarly, we learned about cleaners who are responsible for controlling the resident's daily medication intake and operators without medical training who decide on whether and how much medicine the residents will take—ultimately making decisions on life and death, as they sometimes decide on life-prolonging measures.

However, despite this heterogeneity—no two facilities are alike—all facilities share a common approach insofar as they clearly react to the conditions and structures of old age care in Germany. As shown by our homepage analysis, the facility contrasts the shortcomings of old age care in Germany with apparently better conditions in Thailand. All facilities have in common a reference to deficits in old-age care in Germany and the advantages of old-age care in Thailand. In this respect, the lack of regulation does not imply complete freedom and arbitrariness for the operators to set up their facilities, if they want to be successful in the long run. In order to recruit future clients and to ensure long-term sustainability in the market, it is necessary to take measures to mark the differences from facilities in Germany. For this reason, the unregulated field is not completely free from regulatory influences, while at the same time it leaves open a wide range of options and risks.

CONCLUSION

In this chapter we argued that old-age care facilities for elderly Germans increasingly emerge in Thailand and other countries with lower wages and living costs. The main reasons and structural preconditions for this development are the so-called old age care crisis in Germany and the gradual transnational opening of its social security system. As revealed by our empirical research, these facilities emerge as a response to the old-age care crisis, with old-age care facility operators referring explicitly to the central criticisms of long-term care in Germany. In doing so, the facilities are constructed as both affordable and qualitatively better alternatives to old-age homes in Germany. However, whether the promise of better care is redeemed or remains unfulfilled cannot be answered easily.

According to our empirical research in Thailand, some facilities deliver on this promise better than others. On the one hand, this outcome reflects the diversity of facilities now available. On the other hand, these differences are related to the capacity, resources, motivations, and willingness of the operators who are not held accountable for their actions due to the absence of regulations and quality measurement. While these circumstances open the door for abuse and maltreatment of residents, they also offer the chance for care concepts that break with or go beyond the medical paradigm by putting a stronger emphasis on the individual, as well as the social and emotional, needs of elderly people.

This wide range of arrangements and practices makes it difficult to draw simple conclusions about whether these facilities keep their promises and to make assumptions about the quality of care delivered. Indeed, the variety of approaches requires careful case-by-case analysis to scrutinize whether and how the residents' aging experiences are positively and/or negatively affected by their new environments.

NOTES

1 LTCI replaced the hitherto means-tested long-term care system that was managed by regional governments (the Länder) and local authorities.
2 The care level is defined by the Medical Advisory Services of the Health Insurance Funds according to the applicants' evaluated need for basic care, including personal care, nutrition, and mobility.
3 The European Court of Justice recently strengthened the German position of not co-financing residential care abroad when it decided against an action of the European Commission which argued that the German regulation would be a discriminatory limitation of the freedom of services within the EU (Info-Curia 2014). A further point that prevents German LTCI from establishing deals with old-age care facilities abroad is that quality checks are difficult.
4 The favorable portability of benefits within the EU can be explained by the freedom of movement, which is one of the constituting elements of the single European market. According to EU law, European citizens are allowed to settle in any member state as long as they do not rely upon social transfers or pose a risk to public health and order.
5 The facilities in Thailand also serve elderly people from Switzerland and other German-speaking countries in Europe.
6 This information is based on Internet research into homes for German elderly people in Poland, carried out on the homepages http://www.carefinder24.de; www.pflegeheim-in-polen.net; http://www.pflegeheim-osteuropa.de; and http://www.wohnen-im-alter.de, which give an overview of these care facilities in German.

176   Vincent Horn, et al.

7 All quotations from the homepage were translated from German and anony-
   mized by the authors of this chapter.
8 This quotation inevitably raises questions and concerns about the situation of
   the care workers in these facilities. However, due to our focus on the recipients
   we do not further discuss this issue here.
9 Note that this lack of control refers primarily to the relationship between caregivers and care receivers in these facilities and less to the employer–employee
   relationship that is regulated by Thai employment legislation. The extent to
   which the rights of the care workers are actually respected, however, deserves
   our further attention, as well as do the care workers' specific experiences in
   this type of elder-care arrangement.

REFERENCES

Bertelsmann Foundation (2012): *Themenreport "Pflege 2030": was ist zu erwarten—
   was ist zu tun?* Bielefeld: Matthiesen Druck.
Bettio, Francesca/Verashchagina, Alina (eds.) (2012): *Long-Term Care for the Elderly. Provisions and Providers in 33 European Countries.* Luxembourg: Publica-
   tions Office of the European Union.
BPA (Bundesverband privater Anbieter sozialer Dienste) (2012): *Zehntausende
   Pflegefachkräfte fehlen und die Arbeitsagentur streitet mit den Ländern.* http://
   www.bpa.de/Aktuelles.112.0.html?&no_cache=1&tx_ttnews[tt_news]=502&c
   Hash=f07251b690e83a999f64fdbca75cf00f, accessed October 2014.
Costanzo, David: TZ München (2011): *Der alltägliche Pflegeskandal.* http://
   www.tz.de/muenchen/stadt/alltaegliche-pflege-skandal-1289370.html, accessed
   November 2014.
Da Roit, Barbara/Le Bihan, Blanche (2010): Similar and Yet So Different: Cash-for-
   Care in Six European Countries' Long-Term Care Policies. In: *Milbank Quarterly*
   88, 3, pp. 286–309.
DRV (Deutsche Rentenversicherung) (2003): *Rentenbestand am 31.21.2003.* Statis-
   tik der Deutschen Rentenversicherung. Berlin.
DRV (Deutsche Rentenversicherung) (2008): *Rentenbestand am 31.21.2008.* Statistik der Deutschen Rentenversicherung. Berlin.
DRV (Deutsche Rentenversicherung) (2013): *Rentenbestand am 31.21.2013.* Statis-
   tik der Deutschen Rentenversicherung. Berlin.
DRV (Deutsche Rentenversicherung) (2014): *Zahlung ins Ausland.* http://www.
   deutsche-rentenversicherung.de/Allgemein/de/Inhalt/1_Lebenslagen/05_Kurz_
   vor_und_in_der_Rente/02_Fuer_Rentner/06_zahlung_ins_ausland.html;jsessioni
   d=7F883A2EB2F360FF01163BD96F057230.cae01, accessed October 2014.
EC (European Commission) (2007): *Health and Long-Term Care in the European
   Union.* Special Eurobarometer 283/ Wave 67.3 —TNS Opinion & Social.
Info-Curia (2014): Action for Failure to Fulfil Obligations — Article 56 TFEU —
   German Legislation Regarding Care Insurance. In: *Case C-562/10.* http://curia.
   europa.eu/juris/document/document.jsf?doclang=EN&text=&pageIndex=0&
   part=1&mode=lst&docid=124987&occ=first&dir=&cid=434150, accessed
   November 2014.
Focus (2012): *Pflegeskandal weitet sich aus. Heimleitung wusste von Behandlung
   und tat nichts.* http://www.focus.de/panorama/welt/pflegeskandal-weitet-sich-
   aus-heimleitung-wusste-seit-februar-von-misshandlung_aid_772158.html, accessed November 2014.
Jansen, Birgit/Klie, Thomas (1999): Häuslichkeit. In Jansen, Birgit/Karl, Fred/Rade-
   bold, Hartmut/ Schmitz-Scherzer, Reinhard (eds.): *Soziale Gerontologie.* Wein-
   heim/Basel: Beltz, pp. 521–539.

"*Moving (for) Elder Care Abroad*" 177

Kaiser, Claudia (2011): *Transnationale Altersmigration in Europa: Sozialgeographische und Gerontologische Perspektiven.* Wiesbaden: VS Verlag.

Karl, Fred (2009): *Einführung in die Generationen- und Altenarbeit.* Opladen/Farmington Hills.

Landenberger, Margarete (1995): Pflegeversicherung—Modell für sozialstaatlichen Wandel. In: *Gegenwartskunde* 1, pp. 19–31.

Lipszy, Barbara/Sail, Etienne/Xavier, Ana (2012): *European Economy. Long-Term Care: Need, Use and Expenditure in the EU-27.* Economic Papers 469. Brussels: Directorate-General for Economic and Financial Affairs.

MDS (Medizinischer Dienst des Spitzenverbandes Bund der Krankenkassen e.V.) (2012): *Qualität in der ambulanten und stationären Pflege.* Köln: asmuth druck + crossmedia gmbh & co. kg.

Mihm, Andreas: FAZ (Frankfurter Allgemeine Zeitung) (2013a): *Kein "Oma-Export" nach Osteuropa. Der Deutsche lässt nur ungern im Ausland pflegen.* http://www.faz.net/aktuell/wirtschaft/menschen-wirtschaft/kein-oma-export-nach-osteuropa-der-deutsche-laesst-nur-ungern-im-ausland-pflegen-12031697.html, accessed November 2014.

OECD (Organization for Economic Cooperation and Development) (2013): *Historical Population Data and Projections Database.* Paris: OECD.

Schneekloth, Ulrich (2005). Entwicklungstrends beim Hilfe- und Pflegebedarf in Privathaushalten—Ergebnisse der Infratest-Repräsentativerhebung. In: Schneekloth, Ulrich/Wahl Hans Werner (eds.): *Möglichkeiten und Grenzen selbständiger Lebensführung in privaten Haushalten (MuG III).* München: TNS Infratest Sozialforschung, pp. 55–98.

Schneekloth, Ulrich (2007): Entwicklungstrends beim Pflegebedarf in Privathaushalten—Ergebnisse der Infratest-Repräsentativerhebung. In: Schneekloth, Ulrich/Wahl, Hans-Werner (eds.): *Möglichkeiten und Grenzen selbständiger Lebensführung in stationären Einrichtungen (MuG IV).* München, TNS Infratest Sozialforschung, pp. 57–102.

Schneekloth, Ulrich/Wahl, Hans Werner (2009): *Pflegebedarf und Versorgungssituation bei älteren Menschen in Heimen: Demenz, Angehörige und Freiwillige, Beispiele für "good practice".* Stuttgart: Kohlhammer.

Schweppe, Cornelia (2005): Soziale Altenarbeit. In: Thole, Werner (ed.): *Grundriss Soziale Arbeit. Ein einführendes Handbuch.* Opladen: Verlag Barbara Budrich, pp. 331–348.

Schweppe, Cornelia (2012): Altenarbeit: Altenhilfe, Altenpflege, Altenbildung. In: Krüger, Heinz-H./Rauschenbach, Thomas (eds.): *Einführung in die Arbeitsfelder des Bildungs- und Sozialwesens, Fifth edition, thoroughly revised and expanded revision.* Opladen: Verlag Barbara Budrich, pp. 187–208.

Schweppe, Cornelia (2013): Familiale Generationenbeziehungen: solidarisch, aber belastet. In: Popp, Reinhold/Garstenauer, Ulrike/Reinhardt, Ulrich/Rosenlechner-Urbanek, Doris (eds): *Zukunft. Lebensqualität. Lebenslang.* Wien/Berlin/Münster: LIT Verlag.

Statistisches Bundesamt (2013): *Statistisches Bundesamt: Pflegestatistik 2011.* Pflege im Rahmen der Pflegeversicherung. Deutschlandergebnisse.

Strauss, Anselm L./Corbin, Juliet (1996): *Grounded Theory: Grundlagen Qualitativer Sozialforschung.* Weinheim: BeltzPVU.

Uken, Marlies: Zeit Online (2014): *Zwischen Alten- und Aktenpflege.* http://www.zeit.de/wirtschaft/2014–07/altenpflege-pflegeheime-bewertung-auswertung, accessed November 2014.

9 Traveling Institutions as Transnational Aging
The Old-Age Home in Idea and Practice in India

Sarah Lamb

Studies of transnational aging have focused on the movement of people, and the nature and workings of mobility and absence in contemporary family life.[1] Yet it is not only people who travel. Circulating institutions and the ideas embedded in them also play a vital role in constituting the experience of aging in the current transnational era. This chapter focuses on the concept and practice of the old-age home as a key institution constituting transnational aging, with a focus on the burgeoning role of the old-age home in contemporary India.

Historically, institutional care for the elderly has been predominantly a Western phenomenon, developing in Western Europe and North America beginning in the mid-1800s and gradually coming to be very widespread and normal, although never practiced universally, in these nations (Haber 1993; Lamb 2009). Over the past several decades, the elder-care institution has increasingly spread around the globe, taking on a particularly striking role in many Asian nations, where such institutions are widely interpreted as signs of pervading processes of Westernization, globalization, or modernity contrasting historically traditional family-centered care practices (e.g., Brasor and Tsubuku 2014; Lamb 2009, Lee, Woo and Mackenzie 2002; Liu et al. 2012; McMillan and Danubrata 2012; Toyota and Xiang 2012). Yet old-age homes are not merely globally ubiquitous sites for making families and societies "modern" but, rather, are unique local institutions creatively forged and interpreted, critiqued and expanded, opposed and embraced by local actors. This chapter probes how a focus on the circulating institution of the old-age home[2] helps us understand the nature and experience of aging and the mobilities of care institutions in India today. It further asks how a concept of "traveling institutions" can enhance our understandings of transnationalism and aging more generally. Moving into an old-age home entails profound shifts in forms of personhood, moral orders, daily habitus,[3] and gendered care cultures. As such, the experience of both living and working in an old-age home in a nation such as India involves the creative, often fraught, blending of more familiar and newer, more local and global, lifeways. I suggest that the interpenetration of competing lifeways in such traveling institutions of elder care constitutes a fundamental part of how transnational aging is fashioned and experienced today, because the institution itself and the modes of aging fostered by the institution both become transnational.

Research for this project concentrated on the major Indian metropolis of Kolkata and its environs and was conducted over a period of over ten years, from 2003 through 2014. Over this period, I located 71 old-age homes in and around Kolkata, most of which had been established just over the past one to fifteen years. Among these 71 homes, there were five homes—of varying sizes and degrees of fanciness—that I spent extended time in during my fieldwork trips, participating not only in formal interviewing and life-story gathering but also in the kinds of everyday conversations, sharing of tea and meals, poring over each other's family photos, and exchanging of small gifts and letters that make up the core research methodology anthropologists call "participant observation." I analyzed taped and transcribed interviews and fieldwork notes by searching for common themes as well as variation across class, caste, gender, life-circumstance, and personal-outlook differences. I interviewed in total 100 residents (all Hindu), while also speaking with the paid caregivers, proprietors, and founders of the homes, including soliciting founders' stories of how and why they came up with the idea to establish an elder-care institution in India. On occasion, I was also able to speak with family members who had arranged for their elders to reside in such an institution rather than to follow the much more familiar living arrangement in India of lifelong intergenerational reciprocity and co-residence in a multigenerational family home.[4]

CONCEPTUALIZING TRANSNATIONAL AGING

For many people worldwide, processes and experiences of aging are increasingly being configured in a transnational context. Transnational aging involves both the ways care is exchanged among family members living across two or more nations, as well as the mobilities of ideas, goods, practices, and services—regarding moralities of elder care, contrasting policy regimes, and ideologies of how to live and age well—in a globalized world (e.g., Baldassar, Baldock and Wilding 2007; Baldassar and Merla 2014; Lamb 2002, 2007, 2009, 2014; McDaniel and Zimmer 2013; Sokolovsky 2008; Sun 2012; Toyota 2013).

Scholarship on transnational aging has concentrated most extensively on the family. Increasingly commonly, family networks are dispersed transnationally across two or more nations, entailing profound shifts in the ways aging and caregiving practices are configured—especially for those from communities where multigenerational co-residence has long been the norm. Loretta Baldassar and Laura Merla (2014) and contributors to their edited volume examine the intricate ways family members today—including elders and adult children, grandparents and grandchildren, those who move

180 *Sarah Lamb*

and those who stay—care for each other through processes of reciprocal exchange across and despite distance. Writing of transnational families as "contemporary family forms," they "propose that a focus on the disparate trajectories of care circulation helps us better understand mobility and absence in family life" (2014: 6), making a case for regarding "caregiving and its management as constitutive of transnational family life" today (2014: 7). In Lamb (2002: 300), I explore how a central concern among immigrants from India in the United States is "how to maintain intimate family relations in a world of flowing borders and moving populations." Ken Sun (2012) focuses on changing practices of geriatric care within transnational Taiwanese–US families to examine the processes through which family ideologies of reciprocity travel, change, and operate across worlds, in the context of family separation and dislocation.

In the growing body of work on transnational aging, relatively less attention has been directed to the notion of the traveling institution. Jonathan Xavier Inda and Renato Rosaldo define globalization, of which transnationalism is a part,[5] as entailing a mobility or cultural flow "of capital, people, commodities, images, and ideologies—through which the spaces of the globe are becoming increasingly intertwined" (2008: 4). Institutions could be productively added to such a list of mobile entities constituting global and transnational lifeways. The institution of the old-age home is connected to other circulating forms, certainly. It involves circulating ideologies (of moralities of care, visions of personhood, notions of appropriate and inappropriate in/dependence); in addition, the institution is made necessary often due to the mobility of people (such as adult children moving abroad leaving a vacuum in conventional home-based caregiving systems); and it can involve circulating capital, as when "Western-style" retirement-living facilities are pursued by multinational corporations as fledgling business opportunities in burgeoning overseas markets (e.g., McMillan and Danubrata 2012), or when elders from wealthier nations purchase residence in more affordable retirement homes abroad (e.g., Connolly 2012; Toyota and Xiang 2012). The traveling institution of the old-age home or senior residential facility, especially in nations where such facilities did not previously exist, involves novel caregiving arrangements and profound, complex changes in the daily habitus of residents. At the same time, such institutions—although around the globe interpreted as "Western style"—take on unique local forms, at once international yet without being examples of mimicry.

A focus on the old-age home as a transnational institution and an institution of transnational aging offers a productive means to trace some of the profound ways ideologies and practices of aging are being constituted and experienced today. By exploring the notion of the traveling institution of the old-age home in India, this chapter seeks to counter simplistic arguments about "Westernization" and "traditional identity" both in India and around the world, as it examines how those involved with old-age homes are creating unique Indian cultural versions of the modern, globally widespread

Traveling Institutions as Transnational Aging   181

institution of the retirement facility. Those participating in India's new old-age homes are innovatively striving to maintain older needs, desires, and values, while also producing and fulfilling new ones, wrestling strategically with what they see as the changing conditions of their society and lives.

INTRODUCING OLD-AGE HOMES IN INDIA

Until the 1990s and early 2000s, residences for elders scarcely existed in India, save for a handful established by Christian missionaries during the British colonial era catering largely to the Anglo-Indian community and the very poor (Andrews 2012; Lamb 2009). Now, old-age homes number nearly 1,000 or more across India's urban centers, with new institutions continuing to spring up at a fast pace (Kalavar and Jamuna 2008; Lamb 2009, 2013a; Liebig 2003; Sawhney 2003). The first old-age home in India was established in Kolkata (then Calcutta) in 1882 by the Little Sisters of the Poor, an international congregation of Roman Catholic women serving the elderly poor in more than 30 countries across the world. Recently refurbished, this home still exists in bustling central Kolkata, accompanied now by numerous additional large and small old-age homes dotted across the city and its suburbs, catering largely to the Hindu middle- and upper-middle classes. Narratives by proprietors and founders of these new institutions often describe being specifically inspired by models of elder living in Western Europe and the US, encountered sometimes while traveling abroad; and the public as well interprets India's emerging old home homes as "Western"-originating and "Western"-style institutions.

Mr. R. N. Roy[6] was the man behind the founding of Kolkata's first major old-age home for the middle and upper-middle classes, an upscale three-story institution established in 1985 on the outskirts of Kolkata surrounded by verdant rice fields and mango groves, and funded by the multinational Aditya Birla Group. R. N. Roy and his wife had travelled abroad to Europe and the United States about 10 to 12 times, his widowed wife later narrated, and they had encountered old-age homes there. At first the idea of founding one in India did not enter their minds, but gradually her husband began to notice changes in his society. Where once children looked after their parents in multigenerational homes, now (his wife told me) families were breaking down, and sons and daughters-in-law did not wish to live with their parents. Furthermore, parents were not getting along with their children; many were educated themselves and did not want to mind their children's ways. Many children were moving abroad for work, too, and even elders with plenty of sons and daughters-in-law living right nearby were not being looked after. "Thinking about all this," Mrs. Roy recalled, "my husband got it into his idea that he would establish an old-age home right here in India like they have in the West." He approached a friend within the Birla group who liked the idea, and they went to work establishing the home. Later it became her

182 *Sarah Lamb*

husband's dying wish that another old-age home be established in his name; he left this wish and money for the project in his will, and so a second home for middle-class residents living apart from children was founded.

Another founder of one of the larger early old-age homes in Kolkata, a member of the Indian business conglomerate the Peerless Group, reflected as follows, first contrasting India with the US, where I am from:

> In your country, you have the system of old-age homes. Here, this is a very new idea. But necessary. If you visit our home, you'll see so many residents who are practically *deserted* by their families, though they are all highly placed. But in spite of that, they are not looked after by their families. Earlier we had the joint family system, but now modern families are taking hold. That is the problem in India these days; people don't care for their aged parents.

To this institution founder, the neglect of caring for elders by families makes old-age homes a necessary and, he felt under the circumstances, attractive new option for living.

The discourse of old-age-home residents similarly highlights an image of the elder residence as a Western-originating and Western-style institution. One gentleman resident reflected:

> The whole world is undergoing a major transformation. . . . Now American civilization is spreading throughout the world.[7] For that reason, self-centeredness is growing. Now no one wants to or has the time to look after others. . . . Like before when parents used to send their children to a hostel for better education, now if the [adult] children are busy, and if they can find a good [old-age] home, then they will place their parents there.

Retired psychiatrist and old-age home resident Dr. Ranjan Banerjee asserted to me: "Old age homes are not a concept of our country. These days, we are throwing away our culture. The U.S. is the richest nation in the world and therefore has won us over." Soumil Chowdhury, a retired engineer who had just made plans, with mixed feelings, to move into an old-age home with his wife, similarly narrated:

> We are experiencing a clash between the Indian era and the Western era. We [Indians] want to live jointly, amidst our relatives, not alone. . . . In European culture, everyone does want to live separately. *We* don't want old-age homes. We want joint families—sisters and brothers, daughters and sons, granddaughters and grandsons, all together. . . . This is Indian culture.

Public media discourse as well frequently interprets the rise of elder residences as an alien, Western-inspired phenomenon: "Old Age Homes Against Our Culture," reads one representative newspaper headline (*The Hindu Staff*

Traveling Institutions as Transnational Aging 183

Reporter 2004). More positively, a piece on "The New-Age Old-Age Homes" in *The Times of India* observes that "[r]etirement homes, a popular concept in the West, [are] beginning to find a market in India. Changing social dimensions, fading joint families and financial independence are some factors that are contributing to the trend. It offers independence, community and security" (Mukherjee 2012). In nearby Nepal, one news story reads, "The situation here resembles some Western countries where parents have to go and live in the old-age homes . . . when they become old and helpless" (Pokharel 2014).

Yet the elder homes in the region are very profoundly also "Indian" institutions—complex, intriguing examples of the localization of global phenomena. There is nothing so new conceptually about this argument; many scholars have analyzed the complex cultural processes by which apparently global phenomena become taken up, refashioned, reinterpreted, indigenized, or made local within particular social-cultural contexts.[8] It is nonetheless worth looking closely at the Indian old-age-home case through such a lens—in part because such non-family-based elder-care institutions are multiplying, not only in India but elsewhere around the globe as well. International development discourses frequently depict the availability of state and market-based programs for old age security beyond the family as "progress"—the sign of a developed rather than developing nation.[9] Yet it is worth understanding, through careful critical analysis, how such institutions are not examples of a uniform march of modernity, as they are locally interpreted, fashioned, and experienced.

MAKING LOCAL A GLOBAL INSTITUTION: APPROPRIATE DEPENDENCE AND THE SPIRITUAL FOREST

To grasp differences in the ways elder-care institutions are understood, one must consider more general notions of personhood and valued forms of living in late life in varied social-cultural settings. In North America as in Western Europe, tremendous emphasis is placed on independence as key to social personhood, and a central aim of many elders is to maintain their independent personhood (Buch 2013; Lamb 2014). A strong ideal is to remain living "independently" in one's own home (Rowe and Kahn 1998; Sixsmith et al. 2014), with a spouse or alone and, if necessary, with the assistance of hired in-home care (Buch 2013; Twigg 1999). In such a context, to enter a nursing home signifies a failure of independence and a threat to social personhood, although moving to an activities-, peer- and convenience-focused "retirement" home or "independent living" facility does not necessarily pose so strong a threat. At the same time, most North Americans and Western Europeans do not wish to depend on one's family for full emotional, financial and bodily support (Lamb 2014). Anthropologist Andrei Simic observes that "[w]hat the American elderly seem to fear most is 'demeaning dependence' on their children or other kin" (1990: 94); and Margaret Clark's (1972) research found that many Americans think of

184   *Sarah Lamb*

fully depending on younger relatives destructive to their sense of dignity and value as a responsible person.

In India, in contrast, by far the most common, expected and valued form of living in late life is in a multigenerational family home (Brijnath 2012; Lamb 2013a; Rajan and Kumar 2003). Despite the recent rise of old-age homes in the nation, prevalent perceptions across India are that the family has for generations been the most normal, natural and familiar site of aging and elder care for Indians. When I ask US elders in retirement homes why they chose to move in,[10] almost none mention the alternative of the family. Yet, *all* in India do: They each must explain why they are there and not with the family—perhaps their kids are abroad, or they do not get along with their children, or they have only daughters and no sons,[11] or they have no children at all; perhaps they were never married, or perhaps their only son is deceased. All experience residing in an old-age home in the context of absence from family.

Yet living in an old-age home apart from the conventional family, for those in India who have made such a move, is not unequivocally narrated as a loss. In a cultural context where it is appropriate as a senior adult to be dependent on the family or on family-like relations (just as those in North America envision a child to be appropriately dependent on his or her parents), moving to an old-age home to be the recipient of care can be experienced as more normal and desirable than the possible alternative of living alone. Residents commonly say to me, "It's not possible to live alone" (*eka to thaka jae na*), or "Because of being alone, I had to come here," or "I couldn't stay alone [in my son's house when they were all out at work and school], so I had to come here," or "There was no one there at home to serve [or provide care, *seva*]." One woman, Mayadi, praised the loving and caring proprietors of her chosen home, a husband and wife pair who had founded a modest, ten-person old-age residence in an ordinary middle-class flat on the outskirts of Kolkata: "Gautam is very dutiful and very good; Pushpa, too. They treat all boarders as their mother. *That* was my attraction. That he is not my own stomach's son (*peter chele nae*) but that he cares so much—I have sons, but that a non-blood boy/son (*chele*) would do all this." She and her roommates listed all that Gautam and Pushpa offer: bed tea in the morning, meals and snacks delivered, mosquito nets hung, oil massaged into hair, and loving and respectful companionship. "It's for *them* that I came here." Another woman resident reflected, "Old age homes are highly necessary these days. Everyone's children are moving abroad, and not everyone can live alone. The most difficult thing for us is that living alone is not possible. Here [in the old age home], everyone is together. We talk, we watch TV, they serve us and bring all our meals." In this way, old-age homes are being experienced by some in India as offering not simply a new form of modern abandonment but rather a new site for *appropriate dependence* in a changing society (Lamb 2013b).

Supporting such an image of the old-age home as a novel venue for appropriate dependence is the traditional Hindu Indian notion of *seva* or service to and respect for the aged. Complementing their narratives of being inspired by old-age homes in the West, proprietors and founders of Kolkata's homes tell of being motivated to offer *seva* or respectful care to their society's deserving elders in need. *Seva* is a central component of traditional Hindu notions of elderhood, and many Indian old-age homes centrally figure the concept of *seva* in their names, mission statements, and marketing materials. Quite a few, in fact, are simply named *Seva*. Other similarly evocative names include *Sraddhanjali* (Offering of Reverence) and *Gurujan Kunja* (Garden Abode for Respected Elders). The manager of Gurujan Kunja explained the home's name: "It indicates the home's purpose: to serve and honor the old people living here. You see, they are all revered people living here." Although offered by hired staff and proprietors rather than one's own junior kin (a not insignificant distinction), residents nonetheless tell of greatly appreciating and enjoying the receipt of *seva*—in the form of the faithful arrival of 5 a.m. bed tea, meals served, feet massaged, mosquito nets hung, bath water warmed and delivered, and respectful affection offered. Resident Sri Ashok commented effusively, "There's something you should know: We are living here *completely* without worry. *Everything* we need, we receive: the giving of food, tea, warm bath water—*whatever* we need, we receive. *Truly*, there are no worries! At *precisely* the right time, the tea comes, the food comes! Be there a strike, or a storm, whatever there is, *still* the food comes at just the right time." To date, the majority of old-age home residents I have encountered in India are, by North American standards, quite "young" both in chronological years and degrees of fitness—often in their sixties and seventies, and quite physically capable of performing activities of daily living on their own. But as most residents and staff view late life as an appropriate period for receiving attentive care from juniors, elders are pleased to be able to receive care from staff.

Elder residents also comment that old-age-home living offers a familiar "joint-family-like" feel and sociality, less alien than living alone—reminding residents of their childhood days in overflowing households, where (in both settings) all eat food cooked from the same hearth, people sleep in groups of two to six to a room, and one almost never has to be alone. Some speak of the proprietors as if are they sons or nephews, and the proprietors and caretakers call the elder residents by kin terms—aunt and uncle, grandmother and grandfather. In these ways, in contrast to North American and European conceptualizations, the old-age home serves not as a failure of independence but as one novel way to practice appropriate dependence. Although the old-age home can be interpreted as a marked alternative to family care and co-residence, at the same time it is experienced by some as an instantiation of family values and *seva*.[12]

Another conventional Hindu Indian value and vision of personhood highlighted in many of India's elder residences involves the Hindu notion

186   Sarah Lamb

of *vanaprastha* or spiritual "forest dwelling"—the life phase long presented in Hindu texts as appropriate for older age, where one purposefully loosens ties to family and the world in order to pursue spiritual realization. Hindu texts present four life stages: that of the student, the householder, the forest dweller, and the wandering renouncer (*sannyasi*). Of these, the final two comprise older age, and many older Hindus find resonance in particular with the notion of *vanaprastha*—the idea of retiring from the hubbub of family-household life in later years to a physical or metaphorical "forest," while focusing on spiritual development and loosening worldly ties in preparation for the myriad transitions of dying. Many old-age home proprietors have taken up the forest-dwelling image in the missions of their institutions, with names such as the Forest-Dweller (*Vanaprastha*) Ashram (this is a fairly common name for elder residences across India), Bairag (Renunciate), Prasanti (Absolute Peace), Abasar Malancha (Retirement in a Garden of Flowers), Tapovan (a hermitage for religious practice, usually off in the countryside or a mountaintop), and Milan Tirtha (a place of pilgrimage or of crossing from worldly to spiritual planes). Most provide temples where residents, especially women, may spend hours each day praying and singing hymns.

The Vrindavan Vanaprastha Ashram along the banks of the Karmana River among lush green coconut groves in Kerala declares on its website,

> Our ancient culture calls for four phases or Ashramas [shelters, stages] of one's life: Brahmacarya [student], Garhasthya [householder], Vanaprastha [forest-dweller], and Sannyasa [renouncer]. Vrindavan—the Home for the Aged—is inspired by this concept of the Vanaprastha Ashrama. Vrindavan offers a spiritual haven for us, away from the strife and toil of daily life and routines . . . , to offer a unique opportunity for those who are above fifty to live independent lives, to bring out their latent talents and above all to lead a life of spiritual solace and security.[13]

One of the managers of an old-age home situated on a small lake and surrounded by gardens on the outskirts of Kolkata reflected:

> This particular old-age home was built on the idea of *vanaprastha ashram* [the forest-dwelling life phase]. Now the practice of *vanaprastha* varies from person to person, boarder to boarder. It is expected, but I cannot say that all religiously follow it. But most of us like at least the serenity, calmness and environment of the place. There is always a spiritual rhythm.

Resident Monisha Mashi invoked *vanaprastha* or forest dwelling—the third phase of life and beginnings of older age—in her narrative about choosing life in an old-age home: "People ask me, 'Huh?! Staying in an old-age home? No! Don't joke! You are so happy-go-lucky!' " alluding to the prevailing public sentiment that old-age-home living is for the despondent and rejected.

> But *I* say, "I have everything." We sold our house and car: I came there [to the home] in the midst of full health. I don't own anything anymore. But I received everything: everything out of nothing. The idea of *vanaprastha* is to forsake everything, and *then* to enjoy—to enjoy your life *through* abandonment [*tyag*]. I have everything I need living there!

Another gentleman resident commented, "This home is sort of like the Indian idea from earlier times of the forest-dweller [*vanaprastha*]. People used to go to the forest. This is a modern form of that practice."

The theme of spiritual retreat and tranquility contrasts quite strikingly with the "active aging" agenda promoted in public policy and contemporary retirement homes in Western nations (Katz 2000; Lamb 2009; Lassen and Moreira 2014). However, some of the most elite Indian homes are taking up the international active aging message—promoting activities, hobbies, exercise, travel, fun, lifelong learning, and self-development in their missions, such as the recently established Aamoksh One Eighty, which claims to be "the first International brand of Retirement homes in India."[14] Aamoksh targets the "active and spunky" seniors who "have been part of a generation which saw India emerge to achieve great heights and . . . were at the center of the revolution," offering opportunities for "activities, travel, dining, exercise, everything."[15] At the same time, this institution has chosen the important Hindu concept of *moksh*—spiritual "release" from worldly life—to figure in its name. Replying to my e-mail inquiry regarding the significance of the name choice, a director replied,

> The reason we did this is to reflect our values about ensuring that our customers, seniors who will live in our centres, can renounce all their worldly worries, having taken care of their careers, settled their children and taken care of most of their responsibilities, and settle down to do things that they wanted to do. Be it learning music, dancing, traveling, writing a book or whatever that it may be, they should be able to focus on only doing things that they really like to do, hence attaining Moksh [release] or should we say "Aamoksh"[16] in life.

Striving to integrate the salient international schema of active aging with older more "Indian" ideals of spiritual release in later life, this upscale institution offers a very transnational vision for aging.

The use of *seva*, the forest and "release" as tropes to make sense of elder residences in India is an interesting example of appropriating aspects of Indian tradition in constructing locally the global institution of the old-age home. Indians are incorporating some very different—one could say

188 Sarah Lamb

uniquely Indian—interpretive frames, meanings and aspirations into their emerging elder residences, support for prominent views of late life as a time of both receiving care and cultivating spirituality. So the elder institution becomes not simply a Western invasion but, rather, in certain respects, a uniquely Hindu Indian way of ordering the life course.

GENDER IN CONVENTIONAL AND UNCONVENTIONAL WAYS

India's old-age homes are also, in some similar ways, syncretic sites of both promoting change and upholding convention regarding gender roles. On one hand, old-age-home living involves quite a significant transformation of gender and personhood, especially for women, of both senior and junior generations. On the other hand, in the homes I have witnessed around Kolkata, old-age-home living can uphold some very conventional notions of women as fundamentally tied to and needing the protection of men and families.

In what many regard as a traditional Indian family living arrangement for old age, elder parents reside with and are cared for by their sons and daughters-in-law. Common conceptualizations are that children care for aging parents out of a profound sense of love, respect, and moral, even spiritual, duty to attempt to repay the unerasable "debts" (*rn*) they owe their parents for all the effort, expense, and affection their parents expended to produce and raise them. Although the discourse is that "children" care for their parents, in practice it is sons and in-marrying daughters-in-law who shoulder core parental care responsibilities. A common sentiment is that it can be very difficult for the young daughter-in-law in her in-laws' home. Older women in conventional multigenerational households also tend to have relatively little autonomy compared to men. For instance, it is men—husbands and sons—who tend to control a household's major finances, with property and bank accounts in the males' names.

It is against this context of a conventional family home that some older women residing in India's new elder residences are finding opportunities to break free from certain patriarchal strictures. Renuka Biswas, at age 89, is a lively widow with four married sons who has resided for 15 years in a 40-person home for elders with a lovely central Hindu temple and an expressly spiritual mission. She claims with conviction to be enjoying her independent (*svadhin*) life in the home. Her husband had been a domineering man, and while he was alive, she had had no knowledge of money and could make no important household decisions. After he passed away and she became a widow, she decided to move to the home, taking with her the pension she received as a government employee's widow. She reported that her sons—whom she continues to visit—all love her very much and objected to her coming to the home. But if she had remained living with them, she would not have been able to control her pension. She relishes her novel financial

Traveling Institutions as Transnational Aging 189

independence, with which she pays the old-age-home fees, travels to visit family members, and puts aside money to buy special food items for her and her roommates. Other pension-receiving widows in elder homes are also enjoying a financial freedom, autonomy, and independence that they had never experienced before, finding the old-age home to be a creative new cultural space not only in which to age but also to rework facets of gender. Some also (selflessly, it seems) speak of old-age-home living as a better, easier and more egalitarian option for their daughters-in-law, recalling their own difficult years of submissively serving mothers-in-law in a joint family home. Some women, too, enjoy living amid a group of peer friends for the first time in their lives, comparing the elder abode to what they imagine life in a college hostel to be like. One resident—who shared a cozy room with three other women—told me, "I said to my daughter, 'I'm having my hostel life now. I always thought it would be fun to live in a hostel.'" Additionally, old-age homes are offering a few younger unmarried women (never married, divorced or separated) a safe, convenient place to stay, one of the rare sites available for women to live outside the family in Kolkata.[17] Moving to an old-age home can thus involve significant transformations of gendered selfhood.

Yet at the same time I have been struck by how many of the homes I encounter in Kolkata uphold very conventional patriarchal notions that women need protection, are fundamentally tied to men and families, and should not be independent. These notions appear in explicit and implicit ways. One is that although most all male residents were the ones to make the decision to move into elder residences themselves, fewer than half of the 75 women I studied had made their own decisions, with many of the remaining ones being placed in the homes by male kin (Lamb 2009: 95). Another circumstance is that although male residents tend to move freely in and out of the homes—for daily walks and errands and on longer trips to visit relatives—women residents tend to go out only when accompanied by male kin who have come to get them. In one all-women's home, Sraddhanjali, this is an explicit policy: The brochure for the residence provides a list of rules; number 18 reads, "If on any occasion the boarder wants to go out of the Home to her relative's house or anywhere else, either her guardian or her recognized relative will have to accompany her." I asked about this rule; the "guardian" can be either male or female, although in most cases the women residents have a male kin—most commonly a son or a nephew—appointed as the formal guardian. When I broached the possibility one day of taking Kalyani-di, a woman resident of a different home, out to the movies, or on a shopping trip—as she had been complaining of feeling like a "prisoner" in her home—she and her roommates, and the ayahs or caretakers present, did not really feel that she could go out without her son's permission. Yet she maintained almost no contact with her estranged son and so was stuck in the home, although she was physically fit and had previously been quite independent as a widowed single mother raising three children and working outside of the home for 40 years.

190   Sarah Lamb

Once I attempted to visit Gauri-di, a close family friend of my research assistant Hena, who had moved with her ailing husband to an old-age home after their only beloved son had passed away. I had been to the home only once before, accompanied by Hena, and had phoned Gauri-di earlier this second day to ask if I could come again. Gauri-di warmly invited me. Later that evening I titled my field notes "The Guarded Guard and the Importance of Husbands" and provide an excerpt here to illustrate the theme of conventional mores regarding the nonindependence of women as it played out in Gauri-di's elder residence:

As upon our first visit, although this time during the official 4:30–7:00 PM "visiting hours," I rattled the large locked metal gate. A guard appeared, a slight middle-aged man dressed in a deep blue button-down shirt, opening the gate just a crack. I told him that I was there to visit Gauri Chattopadhyay, and he replied that there was no one there by that name. I assured him that indeed there was, that I had come and met with her earlier and had even phoned her this morning, and that she was expecting me. He asked to see the small red notebook that I had out, to scrutinize what address was written there. Indeed, I had the correct name and address, he seemed disappointed to ascertain. "And you're coming to a *briddhabas* [home for elders]?" he asked skeptically. "Yes! A *briddhabas*. I'm coming to see Gauri Chattopadhyay. I believe she resides in Room 216." "Hmm. Well. Does she have a husband?" "Yes. Yes, she does. She lives here with him." "OK, then. Why didn't you say? What is her husband's name? Is her husband a doctor?" "Yes, her husband *is* a doctor!" I was pleased that he seemed to have figured out whom I was talking about. "But I'm sorry," I added. "I don't recall his name. He is bedridden, and he can't speak well any more. So when I met him, I didn't learn his name well." "Well, this is our system, you must understand. Unless you tell me her husband's name, you can't come in. His name has to be written in the visitor's book." Still unperturbed, I was finding the conversation somewhat entertaining and instructive, confident that I would eventually manage to gain entry. I told the guard, "Well, Gauri-di is expecting me. I have her mobile number here and could call her right now if you would like. I regret that I never did get to be properly introduced to her husband, as he was [I repeated] bedridden when I visited last and couldn't speak well at all." Then I added, questioning softly, "Now, what would happen in the case of a widow? In that case, would one be able to visit without knowing the husband's name?" "A widow is a different matter!" the guard retorted indignantly. "In *this* case, the husband (*uni*) *is* still alive!" But at this, he went over and reluctantly pulled out the visitor's book, instructing me to write down my name, the date, time, and name of the person I was visiting. There, as I began to enter "Gauri Chattopadhyay," he told me to write down "Dr. Samiran Chattopadhyay—*that* is the husband's name," while muttering under his breath disparagingly, "*Aschurjo*! [astounding!] Not knowing the husband's name!"

A month or so after this visit, Gauri-di's husband died. When I visited her again the first time after his passing, I felt almost like I should please the guard by telling him that I was there to see "the widow of late Dr. Samiran Chattopadhyay," now that I had well learned the husband's name. But I thought it would be more interesting to try saying simply that I wished to visit *her*, Gauri Chattopadhyay. I did, and the guard let me in with no problems at all, asking me simply to write her name and my name down in the visitor's register. I jotted in my notebook: "I guess the woman as widow finally gains a name and identity of her own."

We see, then, that just as the old-age homes in Kolkata offer novel contexts for some women to break free from gendered strictures in family life, in other ways these institutions have become new sites for reproducing very conventional Bengali Indian gendered mores. Certainly outside of old-age homes, in various contexts of everyday life, women are often pressed to define themselves in terms of male kin and family. When sending letters to married women friends in Bengali villages, for instance, I must address the envelopes to their husbands. In the Laws of Manu—a foundational work of Hindu law and society compiled and written about 200 CE and still widely cited by Hindus—is found a well-known set of lines which many Indians pronounce in daily conversation, even if they do not see themselves as agreeing with the lines. They go like this: "A girl, a young woman, or even an old woman should not do anything independently, even in (her own) house. In childhood a woman should be under her father's control, in youth under her husband's, and when her husband is dead, under her sons.' She should not have independence" (Manu V.147–48, 1991:115). Such conceptualizations are evident in the practices of some of India's old-age homes, providing another example of the intricate ways traveling institutions are configured in terms of local practices and meanings.

AN EMERGING TRANSNATIONAL RETIREMENT INDUSTRY

To grasp the nature of the traveling institution of the old-age home, one must look not only at nations such as India where the budding retirement homes cater to local elders but also at what can be called an emerging transnational retirement industry (Toyota and Xiang 2012) involving traveling retirees from wealthier nations seeking more affordable and attractive care homes abroad. Newspapers and scholars have begun to report on this trend of "exporting" elderly from wealthy nations such as Japan and England to retirement and nursing homes in less-developed nations of Southeast Asia and Eastern Europe, where care is less expensive and, some report, of higher quality than that offered at home (e.g., Bender et al. 2014; Connolly 2012;

192   *Sarah Lamb*

Innes 2014; Toyota 2013; Toyota and Xiang 2012). One premise behind the notion of higher-quality care is the image of a traditional "culture" of looking after the elderly in the receiving nations. In a piece in the *Mail Online* headed "The Families Sending Relatives [from the UK] to Nursing Homes in Thailand: Care Is 'Cheaper and Often Better in Asia,'" they say," Emma Innes reports that

> [w]ith the average cost of care in a UK nursing home exceeding £28,000 a year, many families worry about how they will look after their elderly relatives. Now, an increasing number of families are sending their loved ones to more affordable care homes 8,000 miles away in Asia, it has been reported. While nursing care in Asia is much cheaper, it is also often of higher quality than that offered in the UK, families say. . . . In the UK, a string of abuse scandals have left people afraid of entering a nursing home. However, *in Thailand there is a culture of looking after the elderly* and care is often excellent. (Innes 2014, emphasis added)

The piece concludes by invoking contrasting cultural mores of personhood, family, and care: "Ironically, many of the Thai carers who look after Europe's elderly say they would not consider putting their own parents in such a home. Instead, they expect to look after them at home. While this situation sounds idyllic, it is not feasible for most people in Europe." Yet the fact that Japan is one of the sending nations in such transnational care arrangements (Toyota 2013; Toyota and Xiang 2012) complicates notions of "Asians" as better at caring for their older people, and reveals ways in which economic and cultural forces intersect.

The 2012 British comedy-drama film hit *The Best Exotic Marigold Hotel* features British pensioners who decide to "outsource" their retirement to less-expensive, seemingly exotic, and reverent-of-elders India. In the novel inspiring the film, *These Foolish Things*, the wheeler-dealer founder of the transnational retirement home proclaims to the relocated UK clientele:

> By opening your hearts to the hospitality of my country you have shown that in the twenty-first century the world has no borders. . . . Throughout the centuries my country has enjoyed a unique bond with yours. . . . I hope our modest venture will be the start of a whole new export market—no longer cotton, but people! . . . I would like to inform you that I propose to wind down my other commitments and devote my energies to this enterprise, for *here in my country we have a tradition of reverence of older people.* (Moggach 2004: 259, emphasis added)

Although to date no such elder-care institutions catering to an international clientele have been established in India, *The Best Exotic Marigold Hotel* and *These Foolish Things* playfully display circulating images regarding cultures and economies of aging flowing across India and the UK.

Traveling Institutions as Transnational Aging   193

Highlighting one's national-cultural penchant reverential elder care can be a "development" strategy for receiving nations. The Philippine Retirement Authority (PRA), a government-owned and -controlled corporation established in 1985, is one association promoting the Philippines as a retirement and elder-care destination. Partnered with industry stakeholders both locally and offshore, the PRA "hopes to offer an excellent opportunity for foreign investors to venture in setting up a global retirement facility that would showcase the country's retirement industry. An investment in this facility that would bring our world-class medical services and care to the retirees aims to boost the country's image as the premiere retirement destination."[18] Positioning the Philippines as a "premiere retirement destination" resonates with the nation's strategy of exporting Filipina women domestic workers promoted as possessing exceptional care-taking values and skills (Parrenas 2001) and is an example of the ways nations may market their people and institutions in a transnational context, where values are held out as part of the "value" the international employer or consumer receives.

Constituted of both traveling institutions and traveling retirees, the emerging transnational retirement industry involves an intricate admixture of values and aims, national and cultural projects, and visions of what makes a good late life—as elders, their families, policy makers, and entrepreneurs make and remake ways of aging across borders.

CONCLUSION

This chapter has focused on how residents, kin, and proprietors within India are creating unique cultural versions of the traveling institution of the modern old-age home. Yet the local configuration of elder-care institutions must happen wherever there are elder homes—so that the Chinese ones become, in part, Chinese; the Thai ones catering to the British, both Thai and British; the Puerto Rican ones, Puerto Rican; and so on, although such processes have not yet been given much scholarly attention. Even in the West, old-age homes that were made in the 1880s under specific cultural-historical contexts have been remade in the 2000s to instantiate new values—such as the independent living, active aging, and prolongation of midlife scripts promoted in US retirement communities today (Lamb 2009; McHugh 2000).

I have argued that the old-age home as a traveling institution plays an important role in constituting aging itself in a transnational way. Both the institution as well as the modes of aging fostered by the institution become transnational—as those involved with India's homes, even when physically remaining in their homeland, find themselves selecting some ideas, values and lifeways from what they perceive to be one nation/culture (of India), and some from another (often, "the West"), making their daily lives and ways of aging across national-cultural worlds.

194 *Sarah Lamb*

For those most intimately involved in India's old-age homes—in particular for residents who had been unaware earlier in their lives of the existence of such institutions, having always imagined that they would age and die right within multigenerational family homes—the impact on ways of living and aging is profound. However, even for those who do not reside in such institutions themselves (current estimates are that less than one percent of India's elders live in old-age homes[19]), public discourses and debates regarding India's old-age homes impact broader cultural imaginaries. Television serials, films, newspaper articles, policy debates, and everyday talk are replete with deliberations on the merits, demerits, and societal significance of India's emerging old-age homes. Indians are grappling with discerning not only what the old-age homes signify regarding modes of aging per se but also what they mean for Indian society, social mores, and national-cultural identity at large (Lamb 2009). In part, it was the rise of old-age homes that motivated India's Maintenance and Welfare of Parents and Senior Citizens Bill, passed in 2007 and implemented into law in 2009, stipulating that it is now not only morally but also legally obligatory for children to care for their aging parents. In the preface to the Bill, the legislators articulate straightforwardly: "It is an established fact that *family* is the most desired environment for senior citizens/parents to lead a life of security, care and dignity."[20] Indian film director Jayaraj's award-winning *Pathos* (*Karunam*) portrays an aging Kerala couple, abandoned by their children who have settled in America. The couple eagerly plans for a visit from their sons, cleaning the house, preparing food, and putting up a swing in the garden for the grandchildren. Then the news comes: the children have canceled in favor of a trip to the Niagara Falls. Worse yet, the sons arrange to sell the ancestral property and place their parents in an old-age home. Director Jayaraj comments on his motivations in making the film: "In Europe, it may be normal that children leave home. But in our society, we have roots, and suddenly, all these families have started sending their children abroad; the children lose contact with their past; they forget to come home" (in Dupont 2000; Lamb 2009). Yet other Indian gerontologists and policy makers argue that Indians *should* become more open-minded about living in old age homes and begin striving to practice forms of self-reliance beyond the family (such as savings, pension plans, and exercise), as to rely on the family alone has become backward (e.g., Rajan, Mishra and Sarma 1999).

We see in the case of the rise of India's old-age homes, as elsewhere in the emerging transnational retirement industry, a burgeoning array of images about how to live and age well, about movements of people and social trends, about gendered care cultures and visions of personhood, about contrasting policy regimes, and about new business opportunities. Cultural and economic factors involving both sending and receiving nations, and the interplay between national and transnational forces, come together to create the historically situated institution of the old-age home in unique contexts. At the same time, and in part *through* the forging of the transnational elder-care institution, visions of how best to live in late life become fashioned and refashioned in profoundly transnational ways.

NOTES

1 See, for instance, Baldassar and Merla (2014) for an analysis of existing literature and rich ethnography of aging and circulating care in the context of contemporary transnational family life.

2 In India, the English term *old-age home* is commonly used to refer to residential facilities for elders—widely regarded as Western-style and Western-originating institutions—even when conversers are speaking local languages such as Bengali or Hindi. Thus, I often continue to use the term *old-age home* in this chapter, although in my home nation of the US, more euphemistic labels such as "independent living," "retirement community," and "senior housing" are customary, and it is often considered socially and politically incorrect to refer to persons as "old."

3 Habitus refers to the values, dispositions, expectations and lifestyle of particular social groups that are acquired through the activities and experiences of everyday life (Bourdieu 1977; Mauss, 1979 [1935]).

4 I describe the earlier phases of this fieldwork, as well as the rise, nature, and intricate daily experiences of those living in Kolkata's old-age homes, in much more detail in chapters 3 through 5 in Lamb (2009).

5 "Transnational" refers to ties and movements extending across two or more specified nations, whereas "globalization" entails more dispersed, encompassing, worldwide flows.

6 To protect their privacy, I use pseudonyms throughout when referring to my research subjects, even when (in cases like this) the subject is somewhat of a public figure.

7 In my research, "America" was frequently invoked as the national-cultural force generating Westernization today, surpassing the role that the UK earlier played in India during and just after the British colonial era.

8 Appadurai (1996), Hannerz (1996), Lynch (2007), Sahlins (1999), and others provide rich ethnographic examples and analyses of these sorts of processes, sometimes termed the "indigenization of modernity," or the "customization" or "localization" of global phenomena. Inda and Rosaldo (2008) provide a perceptive summary of some of this literature.

9 See Lamb (2009, 2013) for a critical analysis of such development discourse.

10 Since January 2013 I have begun to conduct formal comparative anthropological research among North Americans in the Boston and California areas, some living in "retirement communities"; I report on some of this early research in Lamb (2014).

11 Most families in India (except in some regions in the south) find it highly inappropriate for older parents to reside with a married daughter. Conventionally sons and in-marrying daughters-in-law live with and care for the senior parents, most traditionally in the family home in which the sons were raised.

12 Lawrence Cohen (1998: 115) similarly describes a "retirement ashram" he visited in North India as a "locus of *seva*," fashioned as an "equivalent space to the family."

13 http://www.sambodh.org/NEW/2002/vana/vana.htm, accessed June 2014.

14 http://www.aamoksh.com/, accessed June 2014.

15 http://www.aamoksh.com/, accessed 10 June 2014.

196 Sarah Lamb

16 Inserting *aa* before a term signifies "until" or "as long as"—in this case (*aamoksh*) implying until one attains release (*moksh*), or as long as one lives.

17 While doing research on Kolkata's old-age homes from 2004 to 2014, I have encountered three such young women choosing to live in old-age homes. My new research focuses on single, unmarried women in India, where it is widely regarded as morally inappropriate, sexually unsafe, and simply strange for women (and even to some extent men) to live independently.

18 http://investphilippines.gov.ph/en/incentives/philippine-retirement-authority/, accessed June 2014.

19 The vast majority of India's seniors continue to live with family members. According to a 2005 United Nations report titled "Living Arrangements of Older Persons Around the World," more than 80 percent of elders in India live with a child or grandchild, 8.2 percent live as a married couple, and only 3.3 percent live alone (United Nations 2005). Figures for old-age-living are not included in this report; however, popular estimates reported in news stories and by gerontologists are that the percentage remains very low.

20 The text of the 2007 bill is available at http://www.prsindia.org/uploads/media/1182337322/scr1193026940_Senior_Citizen.pdf (accessed July 2012, emphasis added). Note that the bill does also advocate for the establishment of old-age homes in cases where family members are not available to provide parental elder care. See Brijnath (2012) and Lamb (2014) for discussions of this bill.

REFERENCES

Andrews, Robyn (2012): Anglo-Indian Residential Care Homes: Accounts from Kolkata and Melbourne. In: *Journal of Cross-Cultural Gerontology* 27, pp. 79–100.

Appadurai, Arjun (1996): *Modernity at Large. Cultural Dimensions of Globalization*. Minneapolis: University of Minnesota Press.

Baldassar, Loretta/Baldock, Cora/Wilding, Raelene (2007): *Families Caring Across Borders. Migration, Ageing and Transnational Caregiving*. New York: Palgrave Macmillan.

Baldassar, Loretta/Merla, Laura (eds.) (2014): *Transnational Families, Migration and the Circulation of Care. Understanding Mobility and Absence in Family Life*. New York: Routledge.

Bender, Désirée/Hollstein, Tina/Horn, Vincent/Huber, Lena/Schweppe, Cornelia (2014): Old Age Care Facilities and People in Need of Care on the Move. In: *Transnational Social Review: A Social Work Journal* 7/8, pp. 290–293.

Bourdieu, Pierre (1977): *Outline of a Theory of Practice*. Translated by Richard Nice. Cambridge: Cambridge University Press.

Brasor, Philip/Tsubuku, Masako (2014): *Retirement Homes Come of Age in Booming Market*. In: *The Japan Times*, Community section, January 6. http://www.japantimes.co.jp/community/2014/01/06/how-tos/retirement-homes-come-of-age-in-booming-market/#.U3vH5PldV1Y, accessed June 2014.

Brijnath, Bianca (2012): Why Does Institutionalised Care Not Appeal to Indian Families? Legislative and Social Answers from Urban India. In: *Ageing and Society* 32, 4, pp. 697–717.

Buch, Elana D. (2013): Senses of Care: Embodying Inequality and Sustaining Personhood in the Home Care of Older Adults in Chicago. In: *American Ethnologist* 40, 4, pp. 637–650.

Clark, Margaret (1972): Cultural Values and Dependency in Later Life. In: Cowgill, Donald O./Holmes, Lowell D. (eds.): *Aging and Modernization*. New York: Appleton Century Crofts, pp. 263–274.

Traveling Institutions as Transnational Aging 197

Cohen, Lawrence (1998): *No Aging in India. Alzheimer's, the Bad Family, and Other Modern Things.* Berkeley: University of California Press.

Connolly, Kate (2012): Germany's Far-Flung Pensioners Living in Care Around the World. *The Guardian*: World section, December 28. http://www.theguardian.com/world/2012/dec/28/germany-pensioners-living-care-world, accessed June 2014.

Dupont, Joan (2000): An Indian Director's Stirring Vision of Old Age. In: *International Herald Tribune*, January 28. http://www.nytimes.com/2000/01/28/style/28iht-fest.t.html accessed June 2014

Haber, Carole (1993): Over the Hill to the Poorhouse: Rhetoric and Reality in the Institutional History of the Aged. In: Schaie, K. Warner/Achenbaum, W. Andrew (eds.): *Societal Impact on Aging: Historical Perspectives.* New York: Springer Publishing Co., pp. 90–113.

Hannerz, Ulf (1996): *Transnational Connections: Culture, People, Places.* London: Routledge.

Hindu Staff Reporter (2004): *Old Age Homes Against Our Culture: Vaiko.* Hindu, September 14. http://www.hindu.com/2004/09/14/stories/2004091405490300.htm, accessed July 2014.

Inda, Jonathan Xavier/Rosaldo, Renato (eds.) (2008): *The Anthropology of Globalization: A Reader*, 2nd ed. Malden, MA: Blackwell.

Innes, Emma (2014): The Families Sending Relatives to Nursing Homes in Thailand: Care Is 'Cheaper and Often Better in Asia', They Say. In: *Mail Online*: Health section, January 9. http://www.dailymail.co.uk/health/article-2536580/The-families-sending-relatives-nursing-homes-THAILAND-Care-cheaper-better-Asia-say.html, accessed June 2014.

Kalavar, Jyotsna M./Jamuna, Duvvuru (2008): Interpersonal Relationships of Elderly in Selected Old Age Homes in Urban India. In: *Interpersona: An International Journal on Interpersonal Relationships* 2, 2, pp. 193–215.

Katz, Stephen (2000): Busy Bodies: Activity, Aging, and the Management of Everyday Life. In: *Journal of Aging Studies* 14, 2, pp. 135–152.

Lamb, Sarah (2002): Intimacy in a Transnational Era: The Remaking of Aging Among Indian Americans. In: *Diaspora: A Journal of Transnational Studies* 11, 3, pp. 299–330.

Lamb, Sarah (2007): Aging Across Worlds. Modern Seniors in an Indian Diaspora. In: Cole, Jennifer/Durham, Deborah (eds.): *Generations and Globalization. Family, Youth, and Age in the New World Economy.* Bloomington: Indiana University Press, pp. 132–163.

Lamb, Sarah (2009): *Aging and the Indian Diaspora. Cosmopolitan Families in India and Abroad.* Bloomington: Indiana University Press.

Lamb, Sarah (2013a): Independence, Intergenerational Uncertainty, and the Ambivalent State: Perceptions of Old Age Security in India. In: *South Asia: Journal of South Asian Studies*, n.s., 36, 1, pp. 65–78.

Lamb, Sarah (2013b): Personhood, Appropriate Dependence, and the Rise of Elder-Care Institutions in India. In: Lynch, Caitrin/Danely, Jason (eds.): *Transitions and Transformations. Cultural Perspectives on the Life Course.* New York: Berghahn.

Lamb, Sarah (2014): Permanent Personhood or Meaningful Decline? Toward a Critical Anthropology of Successful Aging. In: *Journal of Aging Studies* 29, pp. 41–52.

Lassen, Aske Juul/Moriera, Tiago (2014): Unmaking Old Age: Political and Cognitive Formats of Active Ageing. In: *Journal of Aging Studies* 30, pp. 33–46.

Lee, Diana T. F./Woo, Jean/Mackenzie, Ann E. (2002): The Cultural Context of Adjusting to Nursing Home Life: Chinese Elders' Perspectives. In: *The Gerontologist* 42, 5, pp. 667–675.

198 *Sarah Lamb*

Liebig, Phoebe S. (2003): Old-Age Homes and Services. Old and New Approaches to Aged Care. In: Liebig, Phoebe S./Rajan, Sebastian I. (eds.): *An Aging India. Perspectives, Prospects and Policies.* New York: Haworth, pp. 159–178.

Liu, Guangya/Dupre, Matthew E./Gu, Danan/Mair, Christine A./Chen, Feinian (2012):Psychological Well-Being of the Institutionalized and Community-Residing Oldest Old in China: The Role of Children. In: *Social Science and Medicine* 75, 10, pp. 1874–1882.

Lynch, Caitrin (2007): *Juki Girls, Good Girls. Gender and Cultural Politics in Sri Lanka's Global Garment Industry.* Ithaca, NY: Cornell University Press.

Manu (1991): *The Laws of Manu.* Translated by Wendy Doniger, with Brian K. Smith. New York: Penguin.

Mauss, Marcel (1979 [1935]): Body techniques. In: *Sociology and Psychology: Essays.* Translated by B. Brewster. London: Routledge and Kegan Paul, pp. 97–123.

McDaniel, Susan A./Zimmer, Zachary (eds.) (2013): *Global Ageing in the Twenty-First Century. Challenges, Opportunities and Implications.* Burlington, VT: Ashgate.

McHugh, Kevin E. (2000): The "Ageless Self"? Emplacement of Identities in Sun Belt Retirement Communities. In: *Journal of Aging Studies* 14, 1, pp. 103–116.

McMillan, Alex Frew/Danubrata, Eveline (2012): *Old Age in China Is a Fledgling Business Opportunity.* In: *New York Times*: Global Business Section, October 1. http://www.nytimes.com/2012/10/02/business/global/old-age-in-china-is-a-fledgling-business-opportunity.html?pagewanted=all&_r=1&, accessed June 2014.

Moggach, Deborah (2004): *These Foolish Things.* London: Chatto and Windus.

Mukherjee, Saswati (2012): The New-Age Old-Age Homes. In: *The Times of India*, May 15. http://timesofindia.indiatimes.com/city/bangalore/The-New-Age-old-age-homes/articleshow/13144171.cms, accessed June 2014.

Parreñas, Rhacel Salazar (2001): *Servants of Globalization. Women, Migration, and Domestic Work.* Palo Alto, CA: Stanford University Press.

Pokharel, Yogesh (2014): *Elderly People Get New Lease of Life at Pashupati Briddhashram.* In: *The Rising Nepal.* Friday Supplement section, June 6. http://www.gorkhapatra.org.np/detail.php?article_id=18196&cat_id=4, accessed June 2014.

Rajan, S. Irudaya/Kumar, Sanjay (2003): Living Arrangements Among Indian Elderly: New Evidence from National Family Health Survey. In: *Economic and Political Weekly* 38, pp. 75–80.

Rajan, S. Irudaya/Mishra, U. S./Sarma, P. Sankara (1999): *India's Elderly. Burden or Challenge?* New Delhi: Sage Publications.

Rowe, John W.,/Kahn, Robert L. (1998): *Successful Aging.* New York: Pantheon Books.

Sahlins, Marshall (1999): What Is Anthropological Enlightenment? Some Lessons of the Twentieth Century. In: *Annual Review of Anthropology* 28, pp. i–xxiii.

Sawhney, Maneeta (2003): The Role of Non-Governmental Organizations for the Welfare of the Elderly. The Case of HelpAge India. In: Liebig, Phoebe S./Rajan, Sebastian I. (eds.): *An Aging India: Perspectives, Prospects and Policies.* New York: Haworth, pp. 179–191.

Simic, Andrei (1990): Aging, World View, and Intergenerational Relations in America and Yugoslavia. In: Sokolovsky, Jay (ed.): *The Cultural Context of Aging: Worldwide Perspectives.* 2nd ed. New York: Bergin and Garvey, pp. 89–108.

Sixsmith, J., A./Sixsmith, Fange/Malmgren, A./Naumann, D./Kucsera, C./Tomsone, S./Haak, M./Dahlin-Ivanoff, S./Woolrych, R. (2014): Healthy Ageing and Home: The Perspectives of Very Old People in Five European Countries. In: *Social Science and Medicine* 106, pp. 1–9.

Sokolovsky, Jay (ed.) (2008): *The Cultural Context of Aging: Worldwide Perspectives.* 3rd ed. Westport, CT: Praeger.

Sun, Ken C. (2012): Fashioning Reciprocal Norms of Aging in the Transnational Social Field: A Case of Immigrants in the U.S. and Their Parents in Taiwan. In: *Journal of Family Issues* 33, 9, pp. 1240–1271.

Toyota, Mika (2013): Japan: Elderly Care in a Transnational Context. In: Li, Yushi (Boni) (ed.): *Global Aging Issues and Policies: Understanding the Importance of Comprehending and Studying the Aging Process*. Springfield, IL: Charles C. Thomas, pp. 91–108.

Toyota, Mika/Xiang, Biao (2012): The Emerging Transnational "Retirement Industry" in Southeast Asia. In: *International Journal of Sociology and Social Policy* 32, 11/12, pp. 708–719.

Twigg, Julia (1999): The Spatial Ordering of Care: Public and Private in Bathing Support at Home. In: *Sociology of Health and Illness* 21, 4, pp. 381–400.

United Nations (2005): *Living Arrangements of Older Persons Around the World*. Department of Economic and Social Affairs. http://www.un.org/esa/population/publications/livingarrangement/covernote.pdf, accessed July 2014.

10 Negotiating the Potato
The Challenge of Dealing With Multiple Diversities in Elder Care

Karin van Holten and Eva Soom Ammann

This chapter discusses current debates on migration and elder care in nursing homes and in home health care in Switzerland, reflecting health care provisions in an increasingly diversified society. In the context of care, migration is relevant both from a personal care need and a health care provider perspective. On one hand, care services are challenged by providing for an increasingly heterogeneous population with respect to socioeconomic background, lifestyles, religious beliefs, supportive networks, and migration. On the other hand, an increasing number of care workers migrate to Switzerland to deliver nursing and caring services in nursing homes and private households. Therefore, locally based care settings and daily caring practices are shaped by potentially transnational dimensions, since these local settings emerge as a consequence of transnational strategies of the involved agents. In other words, they become potentially transnational because they involve diverse social practices consisting of, for example, labor markets and financial exchanges transgressing national boundaries as well as keeping up transnational personal relationships, which also shape how people act and are perceived within the local care settings. Focusing on food and feeding as elementary caring activities, we intend to show how debating proper food for the cared-for both transcends and essentializes ideas of national belonging. Empirical insights into two fields of elder care are outlined. They illustrate how migration may matter in caring relationships and how debates about quality of care refer to it, thereby manifesting transnational dimensions in local social practice.

The data presented are based on two current research projects focusing on different institutional points of view: the private household and the nursing home. The first project, based at Careum Research,[1] focuses on care arrangements with migrant home care workers, mainly from Central and Eastern Europe, who are employed in Swiss households of frail elders. The second project, conducted by the Institute of Social Anthropology, University of Bern,[2] explores nursing homes and their strategies of dealing with the diversity of their staff and residents in end-of-life care.

Both projects investigate the complex processes of interpreting what is adequate care in a diversified social context. We are interested in understanding the dimensions of diversity that are relevant in these two settings, and how they are linked to debates about quality of care. We try to illustrate the dynamics and interrelations of the concepts "diversity" and "quality of care" by presenting some empirical data referring to negotiations about food and meal styles. Both settings, the household and the nursing home, require strategies for negotiating quality of care and quality of life, ideally resulting in good outcomes for those in need of care. The question of what kind of food is provided in what way seems to be a "hot potato" in debating both diversity and quality of care in the two care settings. What emerges from our data is that transnational dimensions of care intersect with concrete localities and everyday practices of care, thereby showing very complex, multilayered meanings of diversity.

This chapter focuses on the Swiss context. We therefore start with a short introduction to long-term elder care and migration in Switzerland and the relevant theoretical concepts we refer to in this chapter. We then use empirical insights to discuss how negotiating differences is a way to negotiate quality of care as well.

LONG-TERM ELDER CARE IN SWITZERLAND

The transnational dimensions of care settings outlined here need to be discussed in light of national care policies. Similar to most European societies, the current Swiss elder care system is challenged by demographic developments, cost calculations, and increasingly diversified lifestyles. As a guiding principle of health care policy, "outpatient rather than inpatient" has established itself in terms of living with care needs. Home care—especially in the context of long-term care—is regarded as a "cost effective way of maintaining people's independence" (Genet et al. 2011: 1). Furthermore, concepts of self-determination and the request to ensure individualized care services are at the basis of the individual preference for home care settings (van Holten, Jähnke and Bischofberger 2013). Accordingly, home care plays an increasingly relevant role in long-term care. Nearly 45 percent of the Swiss population aged older than 65 years who are in need of care live at home are cared for by their relatives or by professional home care providers, the so-called Spitex[3] (Bayer-Oglesby and Höpflinger 2010).

In Switzerland, long-term care is regarded as "an individual and family responsibility" (OECD 2011). Compared to other European countries, there is a very high amount of private funding of home care services (Colombo 2011). Furthermore, the supply of home care services has not yet fully adapted to the rising demand and the requirements of private households, that is, support with instrumental activities, around-the-clock caring, and so on (van Holten, Jähnke and Bischofberger 2013). Hence, families are at present extremely challenged by organizing and financing stable long-term home-care arrangements (Bischofberger 2011a, b; Levine et al. 2010).

202   *Karin van Holten and Eva Soom Ammann*

In addition to the relevance of home care, nursing homes play an important role in providing care for the elderly. Especially when extensive caring and nursing is required or when persons suffer from advanced dementia, caring arrangements in the private household may fail or become too expensive. Due to the current primacy of living at home and organizing home care, persons moving to the nursing home tend to be of advanced age and suffer from multimorbidity. While 90 percent of people in the 80–84-years age group still live at home, the probability to move to a nursing home rises with increasing age, and in the age group of 95-plus, 45 percent are living in a nursing home (Höpflinger et al. 2011). Therefore, nursing homes are increasingly changing from institutions of providing a convenient living to institutions of administering the end of life.

Whereas being cared for in the private household is assumed to enable self-determination, the setting in the nursing home is characterized by a basic dilemma of modern "total social institutions" (Goffman 1961), that of balancing autonomy and institutional control (Kostrzewa and Gerhard 2010). On one hand, nursing homes claim to enable a self-determined life for care receivers. On the other hand, they also have to subordinate individuals to institutional rules and necessities. Home care also may be affected by issues of power and its abuse, since it is characterized by low hierarchical structures and a variety of actors with specific interests periodically entering and leaving the setting.

MULTIPLE DIVERSITIES IN ELDER CARE

The term *diversity* is used to refer to the heterogeneity of societies, historically always present, but in the past decades increasing considerably. Societal diversity is increasing due to growing global mobility and societal changes characterized by the individualization of identities and lifestyles and the pluralization of values and roles, for example, with reference to gender or age. The increasing diversity within contemporary societies demands strategies to deal with diverse categories of social difference in everyday life, and it has produced manifold scientific debates about adequate theoretical concepts (see, e.g., Heite 2008). While political concepts tend to focus on the nation state, its mechanisms of inclusion and exclusion (see, e.g., the debates about the concept of "citizenship"), and the challenge of establishing social justice within a pluralistic, nationally defined society (see, e.g., the redistribution/recognition/representation debate in Fraser and Honneth 2003), organizational concepts have taken up the economic notion of "diversity management." "Diversity" in this understanding is a concept focusing on how to deal productively with "cultural" differences within a globalized field of customers and workforce (Heite 2008; Purtschert 2007). This notion of diversity and the idea of an organizational need for "diversity management" have also been adopted by public and nonprofit institutions

Negotiating the Potato   203

to provide equal opportunities and prevent discrimination (Ehret 2011). Within this context, diversity has to be understood as a conceptual basis for institutional practice, indicating that individual differences in gender, age, socioeconomic status, educational background, sexual orientation, family status, religion, and (dis)ability, among others, are not to be regarded as fixed attributes but rather as constructed in different situations and contexts with reference to the respective constellations of power (Ehret 2011). By stressing that diversity has to be regarded as being associated with power imbalances, the contemporary literature on the concept of diversity is reacting to severe critiques, mainly articulated from feminist positions, that the discourse on diversity tends to shift the focus from inequalities to heterogeneities and therefore may avoid questions of social injustice and structural discrimination (Knapp 2005).

We decided to use the term *diversity* to refer to the multifaceted and subtle notions of difference structuring the caring interactions we are studying. When applied to those settings, the concept allows us to discuss the agents' practices of negotiating difference, which also have to be associated with questions of power and inequality. Caring relationships are by definition asymmetrical, because they evolve around a dependent individual in need of care; therefore, we hold the position that validating, questioning, or negotiating this asymmetry is an integral part of all caring interactions.

The Nursing Home as a Place of Multiple Diversities

Contemporary nursing homes in Switzerland are characterized by nationally diversified residents: the number of aging migrants is still small among elder and frail persons, but it is growing. Up to now, migrant aging in Switzerland has been characterized by the history of the "guest worker" migration regime, with mainly Italian guest workers getting older and entering the nursing homes. Because of their number and the relatively strong influence of their interest groups (migrant associations, Catholic missions, trade unions), the first so-called Mediterranean departments have been established in three larger cities of Switzerland. However, the nursing homes are now becoming more pluralistic lifeworlds, because of more individualistic generations getting old. For instance, persons with cosmopolitan lifestyles and diversified religious or spiritual frames of reference increasingly enter the nursing home.

Moreover, the staff in nursing homes shows increasing national diversities: both the highly qualified nursing staff and the lower-qualified caring personnel include a high percentage of migrants. Figures are not available for nursing homes, but they are estimated to be even higher than in Swiss hospitals, where 34 percent of the workforce has a non-Swiss nationality (Jaccard Ruedin and Weaver 2009). In addition, a considerable part of staff holding Swiss nationality has a migrant background (e.g., second generation, married to a Swiss citizen). Two main reasons lead to this overrepresentation of

204 *Karin van Holten and Eva Soom Ammann*

a migrant background in the institutional long-term-care workforce. First, there is a general shortage of highly qualified staff in the health sector, and an estimated 120,000 to 190,000 additional nursing staff will be needed until 2030, both in hospital and long-term care (Jaccard Ruedin and Weaver 2009). The need for qualified staff is currently met mainly by recruitment abroad, for example, in the neighboring countries (mostly Germany) but also in Eastern Europe (e.g., Romania) and Asia (India, Philippines). Second, there is a considerable demand for unqualified labor in the long-term care sector (Vangelooven, Richter and Mezenthin 2012). In this way, the nursing home is an entrance gate to the labor market for migrants with very diverse nationalities, migration histories, and educational skills (ibid.). Thus, the nursing home is also a highly diversified place regarding the socioeconomic stratification among staff, with highly qualified nurses holding a university degree on one end of the spectrum and personnel with very low (or unrelated) professional education at the other end.

The Household as a Place of Multiple Diversities

Similarly, home care arrangements are increasingly diverse. Multiple agents with very different professional, national, and socioeconomic backgrounds are involved in home health care. In the family-oriented Swiss care regime, family caregivers often are the most relevant agents shaping the setting—be it as informal caregivers themselves or by organizing and coordinating stable long-term home care (Bischofberger 2011a). Furthermore, professionals such as home health care nurses, physiotherapists, podologists, and physicians, among others, enter the setting to provide their functionally specialized services. This makes clear that—in contrast to the dominant perception of the household as a comparatively homogeneous unit—the home care setting involves multiple agents with different backgrounds, interests, and responsibilities. Managing this heterogeneous set of actors is challenging with regard to responsibilities, cooperation, and communication, especially as it has to be integrated into the atmosphere of "privacy" of the household, often without defined hierarchies or responsibilities of the different agents (Jähnke and van Holten 2013).

In order to ensure the stability of long-term home care, there is a growing demand for individualized caring services around the clock and "from one hand." Such services are hardly affordable when paid and organized as a regular employment relationship according to the Swiss labor rights. Therefore, one of the upcoming strategies is to engage migrant carers, working for lower wages, into the private household (Schilliger 2012; van Holten and Bischofberger 2012). These migrant care workers are mediated either through informal personal networks or through professional agencies (Truong et al. 2012). Switzerland is a partner in the EU free-movement-of-persons agreement. Therefore, migrants from the new EU countries in Central and Eastern Europe have access to the Swiss labor market (Medici and Schilliger

2012). The extent of care migration into Swiss households is not reliably reflected by existing statistics because of short-term stays and circular migration patterns, but as the increasing number of recruitment agencies indicates, this phenomenon is growing considerably. Migrant care workers for private households seem to come mainly from Poland but also from East German federal states, the Czech Republic, Slovakia, Romania, and Hungary (Jähnke, van Holten and Bishofberger 2012; van Holten, Jähnke and Bischofberger 2013). Therefore, home care also becomes an increasingly diversified setting with transnational dimensions.

FOOD AND FEEDING IN ELDER CARE

The academic discussion of food in old age generally focuses on the physical issues of nutrition, that is, on energy and nutrients intake, which is essential for human survival, and on its decrease in old age, leading to malnutrition and the so-called anorexia of old age (Volkert 2013). Studies have shown that malnutrition rates are especially high in geriatric hospitals and rehabilitation facilities, but also considerably high in nursing homes (14 percent of all residents); in private or community-living settings, malnutrition rates are relatively low (5 percent) (Kaiser et al. 2010). Therefore, research has focused on the physical aspects of nutrition. However, malnutrition in old age is a complex problem that involves not only diseases and malfunctioning bodies but also emotional, mental, and social components, as shown by research on the symbolic meaning of meals (Bundgaard 2005) or the social behavior at mealtime in institutional care (Curle and Keller 2010). Because of easily measurable bodily parameters, however, mal-/nutrition has become one of the central indicators for quality of life and quality of care: calories, drinking protocols, and body weight measurements have become standard instruments in professional care. However, these indicators often leave out other important dimensions of food associated to the quality of life of dependent elder individuals: emotional, mental, and social aspects of food intake seem to be central to feelings of quality of life, whereas body weight is not a useful indicator for this (Agbih et al. 2010). Therefore, food and feeding are increasingly getting the attention of care researchers. Successful interventions, as Volkert (2013) argues, build on attentive and affectionate relationships between care receivers and caregivers. In institutional care, the focus on caring relationships is accompanied by an increasing focus on understanding meals as social events that can be framed by enabling structural contexts (see, e.g., Nijs et al. 2006). The literature on how mealtimes can be organized in the nursing home setting to meet the residents' needs for individual and social care reflects an implicit or explicit orientation toward the ideal of the mealtime setting of families in the private household (Carrier et al. 2009; Nijs et al. 2006; Philpin 2011). Furthermore, attempts to improve mealtime experiences in institutional care are understood to make

206 *Karin van Holten and Eva Soom Ammann*

references to individual biographical experiences, personalities, and identities, and therefore are acknowledged as occasions both for the performance of individuality and autonomy and for the construction of a sense of belonging and community (Agbih et al. 2010; Bundgaard 2005; Merell et al. 2012; Palacios-Ceña et al. 2012; Philpin 2011). The role of the caregivers in this setting is characterized by the provision of person-centered and attentive care (Volkert 2013) but also holds the potential to be paternalistic and restrict individual autonomies (Agbih et al. 2010; Merell et al. 2012).

Dimensions of Diversity in Food and Feeding

Considering the preceding—increasingly individualized and diversified Western societies with ever more transnational dimensions as well as long-term elder care within those societies relying heavily on migrant workers—it becomes obvious that food, feeding, and preparing dishes deserve attention with respect to issues of diversity and belonging in long-term elder care. Food and the ways of preparing dishes are closely linked to (sub)cultural practices as well as to conceptions of health (Helman 2007). Because of its considerable symbolic power, food reflects cultural and social affinities. As Gabaccia (1998: 8) points out, "[h]umans cling tenaciously to familiar foods because they become associated with nearly every dimension of human social and cultural life. . . . humans share particular foods with families and friends, they pursue good health through unique diets, they pass on the food lore, and create stories and myths about food's meaning and taste." Therefore, food, the preparation of dishes, and the ingredients used also represent powerful criteria in negotiating the quality of care in the nursing home and the private household. However, meanings of food may be different in relation to social and cultural contexts, so what may be estimated as an indicator for good caregiving from one perspective may be criticized from another point of view. Accordingly, what is considered as healthy in one context may be seen as damaging to one's health elsewhere.

NEGOTIATING DIFFERENCE AND QUALITY OF CARE: EMPIRICAL INSIGHTS

Observations that came up while working on two independent research projects in progress, one dealing with diversities in institutional elder care and the other in home care, provide us with insights into practices of negotiating difference in concrete interactions of care. Analysis of our data was still in progress while writing this chapter and the findings presented here focus on a detail not addressed directly within the research projects. Nevertheless, we have observed in our data that negotiating difference seems to be closely linked to discussions about the quality of care. Quality of care, both in the literature and in everyday practice, is often debated with reference to

Negotiating the Potato 207

issues of professionalism. A second topic, which is specifically debated in caring contexts involving agents with a migrant background, is that of language and communication. We would like to focus on another topic, which appears to be a "hot potato" in shaping and negotiating care arrangements in the context of diversity, namely, food.

To illustrate this, we have chosen a short excerpt from each data set—one on the nursing home and one on the private household—to exemplify how diversity issues come up when food and eating are at stake. In debating food issues as issues reflecting diversities referring to the migrant background of the involved agents, the empirical data excerpts show multilayered dynamics of negotiating ethnicity, nationality, and belonging as well as dependency and power inequality. This may show up in the form of strategies to strive for autonomy or to communicate expectations regarding good care, as shown in the following.

Case A: The Nursing Home

The first empirical example stems from a research project focusing on nursing homes and their "doing diversity" while "doing death." As nursing homes are increasingly becoming institutions of end-of-life, they are facing the challenges of "doing death" in a societal context in which definitions of what a "good death" means are becoming ambiguous. Because nursing homes are confronted with growing diversities and individualities of their resident population, developing everyday strategies of negotiating and interpreting a "good" end of life is requested. This is especially important for when residents are not able to express their needs and wishes, be it due to morbidity (e.g., dementia) or restricted language competency (e.g., when residents or caregivers are of migrant background). One way of dealing with diversity and its consequences for adequate care in nursing homes is to establish departments grouping together residents with supposed common characteristics, for example, the newly emerging "Mediterranean departments" for Italian migrants in Switzerland. This research project has included one such department into the study. By exploring how processes of "doing diversity" shape stationary elder care, the research project aim for a better understanding of processes of negotiation of "good dying" within caring arrangements.

These issues are examined by following an ethnographic research strategy, that is, by doing participant observation in an urban nursing home with 11 wards. Each ward is organized as a community of ten to twelve residents living in single rooms and sharing a common eat-in kitchen and a living room. One of the wards is a designated "Mediterranean" department. It has been established to offer specific care to former guest workers from Italy who migrated to Switzerland in the post–World War II years. When getting old, this group tends to be characterized by low socioeconomic resources and underaverage health, and their local social networks tend to be small,

208 Karin van Holten and Eva Soom Ammann

concentrating on family and migrant communities (Hungerbühler and Bisegger 2012; Soom Ammann 2011). The Mediterranean department tries to offer them an ethno-specific service in the institutional frame of a regular nursing home, grouping residents with Italian migrant background and hiring caring personnel with Italian language skills. Furthermore, the department runs a culturally adapted social program (mainly organized by the Italian Catholic Mission and migrant associations) and attempts to create a Mediterranean atmosphere during mealtimes. In this context, the following field note was written during a participant observation in the eat-in kitchen.

Setting: Observations of Eva Soom Ammann, the field researcher, while working as a care assistant in the Mediterranean department

> Today I am working in the kitchen, in charge of preparing lunch for the residents. It is the first week of a new menu planning which is supposed to bring more Mediterranean food on the tables. When the box with today's groceries arrives, team leader Mariella[4] comes in and has a look at it. She vigorously picks out a plastic bag with potatoes and throws it into the outgoing box. "Potatoes again! When will they understand that we do not need any potatoes here, they are not good for our residents, they're not used to it. We will send those potatoes back right away." Later on, while I am busy cooking the pasta for lunch, care assistant Laura comes in and looks into the cooking pot. "Put the heat up, this has to cook properly, otherwise the pasta will get sticky, and you know that Italians like their pasta 'al dente,' don't you?" Eager to do everything right, I prepare the salad with the Balsamico vinegar I found in the cupboard, not with the white vinegar, which is standing there as well. When lunch is served, I note that Mrs. Vuillemier puts sugar on her salad, and I ask her if there is something wrong. She answers that she simply hates this cursed Italian vinegar.

Mrs. Vuillemier, who migrated from Northern Italy as a young unmarried factory worker and had been married to a Swiss for more than 40 years, regularly discusses food issues with her friend Mrs. Moretti sitting next to her. They both, as the staff members say, complain about the food all the time. This is also why the team leader instructed the staff to note every comment Mrs. Vuillemier and Mrs. Moretti are giving on the new Italian food plan we had this week. The two ladies are thus used as a barometer to measure the quality of menu planning and cooking: serving food that receives their approval must be good and appropriate food for the residents in this department.

But why is the regular food, prepared and eaten in the other wards of the nursing home, not good for this specific department? As the previously described scene suggests, serving potatoes instead of pasta seems to be a problematic issue, because potatoes are "not good," but pasta is—at least when it is prepared properly, that is, "al dente," not soft and sticky. Potatoes and pasta show up here as markers of the difference of this department compared to other departments in the nursing home. One could say that the staff is defending the borders of the Mediterranean department by defining what is "real" in terms of Mediterranean-ness and how it has to be done. By essentializing the food preferences of the residents and by defining what is "good" for them (e.g., the al dente pasta) and what is not (e.g., potatoes), they construct ethnic belonging as the central element of the household unit studied here. Also the vinegar comes up as a marker of difference. I, as a researcher with Swiss background, speaking a little Italian and presently working as a care assistant, also get involved in the constructions of difference by consciously using the Italian vinegar, which is my strategy to comply with the ethnical markers stressed by the staff. My strategy to construct sameness, however, is undermined by Mrs. Vuillemier when she puts sugar on her salad. By doing this and telling me that she hates Italian vinegar, she undercuts my attempts to care well by "doing italianità" for her. Her complaining about food can be seen as an opposition to the "doing Mediterranean-ness" by the staff, thereby contesting the assumed Mediterranean ascriptions used by the staff. Her use of sugar on the Italian-style salad may also be interpreted as a strategy to claim her uniqueness as an individual in a setting that stresses community and homogeneity, thereby she uses her limited scope of action to negotiate power relations in the nursing home, where the relationship between residents and caregivers is extremely asymmetric. Complaining about food and questioning our attempts to "do it right" is her way to oppose ascriptions and strive for autonomy in a setting characterized by dependency. Furthermore, it may also be interpreted as a means to question the efforts of the staff to care well, that is, provide a culturally adapted care that is supposed to be better than the standard care of the nursing home, as they are not good enough to get the approval of Mrs. Vuillemier and Mrs. Moretti. Refusing to be contented may also be seen as a strategy to increase the efforts of staff to care well.

Preparing Mediterranean food is one of the main issues of caring in a unique Mediterranean way for the migrant residents, as the field note shows. And caring well in this sense is not based on professional qualification but, rather, on the habitual knowledge that is associated with "being Italian" or "knowing about Italian lifestyle." Nursing aide Laura obviously has this qualification while the staff are not yet sure if I, the Swiss researcher working as a care assistant, have it. In this respect, the example also illustrates that "caring well" refers to diverse qualifications, not only of a formal nature, and in this sense it transgresses conventional hierarchies of professional staff.

Furthermore, the department does not only have to do its caring right for the residents, such as cooking the right food for Mrs. Vuillemier. Above all, it has to prove its uniqueness within the organization and thereby legitimize caring for Italian migrant residents as different from caring for Swiss residents. While the other ten living communities share identical menu plans and get identical groceries, the Mediterranean department has its own menus, its own grocery orders, and its own serving sequence of courses. By attempting to get confirmation from the residents that this effort is appreciated, the nursing team negotiates its specific status within the organization. This is also the reason why Mariella sends the potatoes back immediately, instead of keeping them for the traditional evening soup (the "minestrina"), and uses the pasta from the cupboard instead. Sending back the potatoes is a statement of the uniqueness of the department and its residents, aimed toward the domestic economy department. The attempts of the caring personnel "to do it right" also offer the residents a possibility to negotiate diversity, by implicitly questioning the caring personnel's success to care well. Mrs. Vuillemier's and Mrs. Moretti's chatting on the quality of the food, the composition of dishes, and the question of whether they were prepared properly, as well as their overt complaints about it when they are asked, can be interpreted as questioning that they are cared for properly. This seems to be a strategy both to get more attention from the caring personnel and to claim individuality and autonomy in a setting that explicitly stresses community and ethnic commonalities.

Case B: The Household

The following empirical data stem from a research project focusing on home health care arrangements involving migrant home care workers, mainly from the new EU countries. Based on 11 in-depth interviews, the project "Care Migration—Transnational Care Arrangements in the Private Household" reconstructs the experiences of family caregivers who hired migrant care workers into the household of their relatives in need of care. As mentioned before, caring needs of the private household are not sufficiently satisfied through the existing professional nursing and caring services delivered by the Spitex. Elderly people living at home often need nursing services as well as lower-level care related to instrumental activities of daily living (IADL), such as domestic help, administrative support, or social contact (OECD 2011). On one hand, these supportive services of lower-level care are not comprehensive in Switzerland; on the other hand, because of the system of financing home health care, they mostly have to be paid out-of-pocket by the household; that is, they may become very expensive, especially in the context of long-term care. This is one of the main reasons why migrant home care workers are hired (van Holten, Jähnke and Bischofberger 2013). They mainly deliver services related to IADL, such as feeding, bathing, dressing, grooming, homemaking, and leisure. Furthermore, they ensure daily social contact and deliver a specific form of attention in the caring arrangements, which distinguishes their caring services significantly from the services of the Spitex (ibid.).

Food preparation turned out to be one of the vital factors of satisfaction with the caring arrangement. In all of the 11 cases, the preparation of food

Negotiating the Potato 211

is part of the basic duties of the migrant home-care worker. In several interviews, the way of preparing the dishes, the groceries used, and even issues regarding the kind of food (e.g., freshly prepared or convenience) were vividly discussed by the relatives.

The following quote is taken from an interview with a Swiss blue-collar worker talking about his experiences with a Polish live-in care worker looking after his Japanese wife, who has been suffering from dementia for two years:

> At the beginning, she cooked potatoes the whole week. Because the Polish eat a lot of potatoes, potatoes and meat. Then, the whole week, she cooked potatoes. I mean, the Japanese, as you may know, are a rice people. Well, I like potatoes. But when she prepared potatoes for the fourth time, I said: "Elena, I got a headache." I had to say that sometimes, when I eat too much potato, I get a headache. One has to tell things this way. I could have come home and say: "Why the hell did you prepare potatoes again? I told you several times . . ." However, one has to approach this gently. This, at least, I seem to have learned the last few years. And then, we both laughed. And finally, we had pasta again. And this is, as I already mentioned, it works well like this.

In contrast to the example from the institutional context discussed above, in this quote the potato is not a marker for Swissness, but for Polishness. This illustrates how food as a cultural symbol depends on the specific contexts and interpretations of those who use it to ascribe belonging and mark difference. Thus, not only the food itself is relevant as a marker of belonging, but a kind of commonness of certain foods also seems to be relevant. Swiss people eat potatoes more often than Italians do, as documented in the first example. The second example illustrates that the Polish eat more potatoes than the Swiss do. Hence, concepts of belonging seem to be based on certain stereotyped imaginations of a culturally specific cuisine, pointing to the eating habits of the others. The food preferences of the Swiss worker's Japanese wife, however, are associated with "belonging to a rice people." The term *rice people* illustrates in a very condensed way how food is used to construct ethnicity. The rice people are those who eat rice. In fact, almost everybody eats rice. But Japanese (as other Asians) are supposed to eat more rice than "we" do. Therefore, *they* are "a rice people." In this way, the consumption of specific food serves as a marker of difference by ascribing national belonging. These widespread concepts of specific cooking rites make clear how the intersections of ethnic or national ascriptions and food are commonly used to mark the belonging of "us" and "the others."

The quote points not only to these powerful markers of differences. It furthermore illustrates how appropriate food is assumed to be linked to one's health and well-being. The way in which the husband communicates his expectations on appropriate cooking refers to—real or symbolized—physical distress (i.e., the headache) and the ability of proper food to heal this. He is thereby explicitly linking cooking with good or bad care. Even if we consider the husband's headache to be a socially accepted way to express his dissatisfaction symbolically, as a strategy to avoid conflicts when communicating critique on the migrant care worker's cooking, communication of physical distress serves here as incentive to optimize care services, namely, more variety in daily cooking. To cure *his* (real or symbolic) headache, the migrant home-care worker needs to cook something else than potatoes. At the very least, the groceries used for the meals should be diversified.

However, good care in this case has to be delivered not only to the wife suffering from dementia but also to the husband who gets a headache when eating too many potatoes. We may suppose that the wife is not able to communicate her well-being on her own because of her advanced stage of dementia. Nevertheless, this also shows that the caregiver hired for the wife has to care for the husband as well. As the Polish care migrant is a live-in worker in a private household, she is in this respect also supposed to partially take over the role of the wife. Another example for this is the fact that the husband feels disturbed when the Polish care worker leaves the lunch table after ten minutes and starts to wash the dishes, because he, as he told me in the interview, would prefer to have some company at the table. Aside from different manners of eating as a cultural practice, this illustrates the blurring of boundaries between employment and personal relationship inherent in the private household as a workplace. On one hand, the husband would prefer a quasi-private relationship, symbolized by having lunch together and talking to each other while eating (the way he was used to have lunch with his wife). On the other hand, the husband is clearly positioning himself as the employer who needs to say how things have to be done. From his point of view, the "laughing together" suggests a successful negotiation of good care within the employee–employer hierarchy. Nevertheless, the complaint about the headache the husband gets as one consequence of the migrant care worker's cooking also could be seen as a strategy to avoid direct complaints about the migrant home-care worker's quality of care. Obviously, he does not want to offer critique on the quality of care too overtly. This illustrates the complex dynamics of power relations within the private household.

What remains open here is this: How much is good care for the husband also good care for the wife with dementia? In the end, to get rid of his headache, the "Swiss" husband gets "Italian" pasta instead of "Polish" potatoes, but we do not know if the Japanese wife is content with having to eat pasta instead of rice.

NEGOTIATING THE POTATO

The preceding examples illustrate ways of negotiating difference in food preferences. The potato plays an important and distinct role in both

Negotiating the Potato 213

examples. To conclude this chapter, we focus on this role of the potato as a marker of difference and its relevance in negotiating good care within settings of long-term elder care.

The potato—one might call it a "transnational" vegetable that migrated a long time ago and spread into various national contexts—shows its symbolic power to express and to ascribe belonging, which is articulated with reference to categories of nationality. It seems that food, the preparation of it, and its consumption are cultural techniques and therefore markers of belonging. At the same time, the groceries (in this case, the potato), and the way they are prepared, serve as indicators for the quality of care. The example of the potato and how it is used to negotiate belonging make debates about diversity and quality of care visible. Paradoxically, the transnational dimensions of local care settings not only transcend national categories, but also seem to foster essentializations of national belonging.

The potato in our examples is a symbol for food in general, and when it comes to care, food has two components. First, giving food is feeding, an integral part of keeping somebody alive. In this respect, food is a way of caregiving in the strict sense. Second, food is also a symbolic act of giving attention and empathy, which is care in the sense of "taking care of" or "caring about" somebody (see Fisher and Tronto 1990). Both aspects, the giving of care necessary to survive and the giving of attention and empathy, are elementary dimensions of care. Therefore, debating food is also debating quality of care in a general way.

The negotiation of diversities is inherent in all caring constellations but shows up more clearly when migration is involved because differences tend to be more obvious. Furthermore, as our examples show, if differences occur, their explicit articulation seems to rely on clear-cut categories of ascription—in our case, national ascriptions. In this sense, we interpret the discussions about the potato as characteristic for the debating of care quality in caring settings involving dimensions of difference.

Research on transnational aging in the past tended to focus on issues of care in the context of informal family caring across borders. But caring also has a considerable local dimension, especially when hands-on care is needed. Both our research projects look at local settings of care involving agents with migrant backgrounds. That is, we are dealing here with local agency within a frame of reference involving transnational dimensions. Our goal in this article was to provide an insight in our work in progress by illustrating the complexities of differences, as well as the complexities of power issues inherent in caring arrangements. Close examinations of concrete social settings and the agents involved in them reveal the complexity of handling aging and old-age care involving transnational dimensions. There are indeed multiple differences at stake, and good caring requires that these differences be debated.

The conclusion that negotiating differences is a basic element in the efforts to strive for a common understanding about what good care is seems to be

214 *Karin van Holten and Eva Soom Ammann*

a simple truth. However, just as the potato, which is a well-known staple food, evolves very complex symbolic qualities when becoming a metaphor for appropriate care, this alleged simplicity develops fascinating symbolic complexities reflecting the manifold nuances of debates about "good care" in daily practice.

NOTES

1 The research project "Care Migration—Transnational Care Arrangements in the Private Household" is conducted by Careum Research, Kalaidos University of Applied Sciences, Department of Health Sciences, Zurich, in cooperation with the Swiss Health Observatory (Obsan). The research team includes Prof. Dr. Iren Bischofberger; Anke Jähnke, MA, MPH; and Karin van Holten, MA. For details, see http://www.careum.ch/care-migration.

2 The research project " 'Doing Death' and 'Doing Diversity' in Nursing Homes" is located at the Institute of Social Anthropology of the University of Bern and funded by the National Research Program No. 67 "End-of-Life" (http://www.nfp67.ch). The research team includes Prof. Dr. Heinzpeter Znoj, Dr. Corina Salis Gross, Dr. Eva Soom Ammann, and Gabriela Rauber, MA. For details, see http://www.anthro.unibe.ch/content/forschung/forschungsprojekte/lebensende/.

3 This is an abbreviation of "Spitalexterne Pflege," which can be translated as "out-of-hospital care."

4 All names are pseudonyms.

REFERENCES

Agbih, Sylvia/Gerling, Anne/Giese, Constanze/Heubel, Friedrich/Hildebrandt-Wiemann, Hella/Hofmann, Irmgard/Koch, Christian (eds.) (2010): *Essen und Trinken im Alter. Mehr als Ernährung und Flüssigkeitsversorgung.* Berlin: Cornelsen.

Bayer-Oglesby, Lucy/Höpflinger, François (2010): *Statistische Grundlagen zur regionalen Pflegeheimplanung in der Schweiz: Methodik und kantonale Kennzahlen.* Obsan Bericht No. 47. Neuchâtel: Schweizerisches Gesundheitsobservatorium Obsan.

Bischofberger, Iren (2011a): Angehörige als wandelnde Patientenakte: Ausgewählte Ergebnisse aus einem Projekt zur Klärung der Rolle der Angehörigen. In: *Care Management* 4, 5, pp. 27–29.

Bischofberger, Iren (2011b): Rücksicht nehmen auf pflegende Angehörige: Eine moderne Familienpolitik umfasst auch Familien und Paare mit pflegebedürftigen Personen. In: *Care Management* 4, 6, pp. 6–9.

Bundgaard, Karen Marie (2005): The Meaning of Everyday Meals in Living Units for Older People. In: *Journal of Occupational Science* 12, 2, pp. 91–101.

Carrier, Nathalie/West, Gale/Oellet, Denise. (2009): Dining Experience, Foodservices and Staffing Are Associated with Quality of Life in Elderly Nursing Home Residents. In: *The Journal of Nutrition, Health & Aging* 13, 6, pp. 565–570.

Colombo, Francesca (2011): *Help Wanted? Providing and Paying for Long-Term Care.* Paris: OECD.

Negotiating the Potato 215

Curle, Lea/Keller, Heather (2010): Resident Interactions at Mealtime: An Exploratory Study. In: *European Journal of Ageing* 7, pp. 189–200.

Ehret, Rebebba (2011): Diversity—Modebegriff oder eine Chance für den strukturellen Wandel? In: van Keuk Eva/Ghaderi Cinur/Joksimovic Liliana/David Dagmar M. (eds.), *Diversity. Transkulturelle Kompetenz in klinischen und sozialen Arbeitsfeldern*. Stuttgart: Kohlhammer, pp. 43–53.

Fisher, Berenice/Tronto, Joan (1990): Toward a Feminist Theory of Caring. Theoretical Issues. In: Abel, Emily K./Nelson, Margaret K. (eds.): *Circles of Care. Work and Identity in Women's Lives*. Albany, New York: State University of New York Press, pp. 35–57.

Fraser, Nancy/Honneth, Axel (2003): *Umverteilung oder Anerkennung?: Eine politisch-philosophische Kontroverse*. Suhrkamp Taschenbuch Wissenschaft: Vol. 1460. Frankfurt: Suhrkamp.

Gabaccia, Donna R. (1998): *We Are What We Eat: Ethnic Food and the Making of Americans*. Cambridge, MA: Harvard University Press.

Genet, Nadine/Boerma, Wienke G. W./Kringos, Dionne S./Bouman, Ans/Francke, Anneke L./Fagerström, Cecilia et al. (2011): Home Care in Europe: A Systematic Literature Review. In: *BMC Health Services Research* 11, p. 207.

Goffman, Erving (1961): *Asylums: Essays on the Social Situation of Mental Patients and Other Inmates*. Garden City, NY: Doubleday.

Heite, Catrin (2008): Ungleichheit, Differenz und 'Diversity'—Zur Konstruktion des professionellen Anderen. In: Böllert, Karin/Karsunky, Silke (eds.): *Genderkompetenz in der Sozialen Arbeit*. Wiesbaden: VS Verlag für Sozialwissenschaften, pp. 77–87.

Helman, Cecil G. (2007): *Culture, Health and Illness*. 5th ed. London: Hodder Arnold.

Höpflinger, François/Bayer-Oglesby, Lucy/Zumbrunn, Andrea (2011): *Pflegebedürftigkeit und Langzeitpflege im Alter. Aktualisierte Szenarien für die Schweiz. Buchreihe des Schweizerischen Gesundheitsobservatoriums*. Bern: Huber.

Hungerbühler, Hildegard/Bisegger, Corinna (2012): *"Und so sind wir geblieben. . ." Ältere Migrantinnen und Migranten in der Schweiz* (Materialien zur Migrationspolitik). Bern: Eidgenössische Kommission für Migrationsfragen EKM.

Jaccard Ruedin, Hélène/Weaver, France (2009): *Ageing Workforce in an Ageing Society. Wie viele Health Professionals braucht das Schweizer Gesundheitssystem bis 2030?* Careum Working Paper No. 1. Neuchâtel: Schweizerisches Gesundheitsobservatorium Obsan.

Jähnke, Anke/van Holten, Karin (2013): Care-Migration: verschiedene Akteure im Privathaushalt: Lokale Zusammenarbeit und globale Vernetzung. In: *NOVAcura*, 44, 9, pp. 32–35.

Jähnke, Anke/van Holten, Karin/Bischofberger, Iren (2012): Befragung der Spitex zur Situation in Privathaushalten mit Care-Migrantinnen: *Schlussbericht Teilprojekt im Rahmen des Projekts «Arbeitsmarkt Privathaushalt» der Fachstelle für Gleichstellung der Stadt Zürich*. Zürich: Fachstelle für Gleichstellung der Stadt Zürich.

Kaiser, Matthias J./Bauer, Jürgen M./Rämsch, Christian/Uter, Wolfgang/Guigoz, Yves/Cederholm, Tomy et al. (2010): *Frequency of Malnutrition in Older Adults: A Multinational Perspective Using the Mini Nutritional Assessment*. In: *Journal of the American Geriatric Society JAGS* 58, 9, pp. 1734–1738.

Knapp, Gudrun-Axeli (2005): "Intersectionality"—ein neues Paradigma feministischer Theorie? Zur transatlantischen Reise von "Race, Class, Gender". In: *Feministische Studien* 1, pp. 68–81.

Kostrzewa Stephan/Gerhard, Christoph (2010): *Hospizliche Altenpflege*. Bern: Huber.

216 Karin van Holten and Eva Soom Ammann

Levine, Carol/Halper, Deborah/Peist, Ariella/Gould, Daniel A. (2010): Bridging Troubled Waters: Family Caregivers, Transitions, and Long-Term Care. In: *Health Affairs* 29, 1, pp. 116–124.

Medici, Gabriela/Schilliger, Sarah (2012): Arbeitsmarkt Privathaushalt—Pendelmigrantinnen in der Betreuung von alten Menschen. In: *Soziale Sicherheit CHSS* (1), pp. 17–21.

Merell, Joy/Philpin, Susan/Warring, Joanne/Hobby, Debra/Gregory, Vic (2012): Addressing the Nutritional Needs of Older People in Residential Care Homes. In: *Health and Social Care in the Community* 20, 2, pp. 208–215.

Nijs, Kristel A. N. D./Graaf, Cees de/Kok, Frans J./van Staveren, Wija A. (2006): Effect of Family Style Mealtimes on Quality of Life, Physical Performance, and Body Weight of Nursing Home Residents: Cluster Randomised Controlled Trial. In: *BMJ British Medical Journal*, published online May, 5, 2006, pp. 1–5.

OECD (2011): *Switzerland. Long-term Care: Country Notes and Highlights.* Country Notes, from http://www.oecd.org/els/health-systems/47878092.pdf.

Palacios-Ceña, Dominga/Losa-Iglesias, Marta E./Cachón-Pérez, José M./Gómez-Pérez, Daniel/Gómez-Calero, Cristina/Fernández-de-las-Peñas, César (2012): Is the Mealtime Experience in Nursing Homes Understood? A Qualitative Study. In: *Geriatrics & Gerontology International* 13, 2, pp. 482–489.

Philpin, Susan (2011): Sociocultural Context of Nutrition in Care Homes. In: *Nursing Older People* 23, 4, pp. 24–30.

Purtschert, Patricia (2007): Diversity Management: Mehr Gewinn durch weniger Diskriminierung? Von der Differenz im Umgang mit Differenzen. In: *Femina Politica Zeitschrift für feministische Politikwissenschaft* 1, pp. 88–96.

Schilliger, Sarah. (2012): "Polinnen sind günstig und fürsorglich": Ethnische und geschlechtliche Segregation des Arbeitsmarktes für 24h-Betreuung. In: *Tangram—Bulletin der Eidgenössischen Kommission gegen Rassismus* 29, 6, pp. 68–70.

Soom Ammann, Eva (2011): *Ein Leben hier gemacht. Altern in der Migration aus biographischer Perspektive.* Italienische Ehepaare in der Schweiz. Bielefeld: transcript.

Truong, Jasmine/Schwiter, Karin/Berndt, Christian (2012): *Arbeitsmarkt Privathaushalt.* Charakteristika der Unternehmen, deren Beschäftigungsstruktur und Arbeitsbedingungen: Eine Studie im Auftrag der Fachstelle für Gleichstellung der Stadt Zürich.

van Holten, Karin/Bischofberger, Iren (2012): Globalisierung im Privathaushalt. In: *NOVAcura* 43, 4, pp. 45–47.

van Holten, Karin/Jähnke, Anke/Bischofberger, Iren (2013): *Care-Migration—transnationale Sorgearrangements im Privathaushalt.* Obsan Rapport No. 57. Neuchâtel: Schweizerisches Gesundheitsobservatorium Obsan.

Vangelooven, Christa/Richter, Dirk/Mezenthin, Petra (2012): *Zugewandertes Pflegeassistenzpersonal und Brain Waste I: Quantitative Daten zur Soziodemografie, Qualifikation und berufliche Motivation.* Obsan Dossier No. 20. Neuchâtel: Schweizerisches Gesundheitsobservatorium Obsan.

Volkert, Dorothee (2013): Malnutrition in Older Adults—Urgent Need for Action: A Plea for Improving the Nutritional Situation of Older Adults. In: *Gerontology*, published online February 8, 2013, pp. 1–6.

11 More Than Demand and Demographic Aging
Transnational Aging, Care, and Care Migration

Susan McDaniel and Seonggee Um

Transnational aging, although a young field (Horn, Schweppe and Um 2013), has rapidly expanded into an area of strong research interest. Google Scholar, for example, reveals 2,580 hits for "transnational aging" from 2013 alone (April 2014 search). Although numerous topics are covered under the rubric of transnational aging, the research focus has been largely on the micro-level, on the lives of family members and paid care workers who care for, or arrange the care for, older people across boundaries, on dyadic relations of carer with care recipient (see, e.g., Baldassar and Merla, 2013; Wall and Bolzman 2013). A second research focus has been on caregiver/caregiving policies within and across countries (e.g., Yeates 2012; Zhou 2013a).

Less a focus of research thus far has been the macro-level, for example, on the supply of *potential* caregivers in relation to demographic and economic forces or on the broad political economy of care. This focus is not absent, of course (Bakan and Stasliulis 2012; Grundy, Tomassini and Festy 2006; Tronto 2013; Williams 2010; Yeates 2009), just leaving room for additional research and insights. What macro-level research exists tends to focus on the increasing *demand* for elder care as a function of population aging and the lesser availability of familial care as more women globally join the paid labor force. These factors are mentioned in virtually every study of elder care and the growth of care demand. Little research thus far has looked extensively at the meso-level, how structural changes in societies, intersect with the work of care and care migration.

This chapter seeks to examine the interconnections of population aging, transnationalism, and socioeconomic inequalities through the lens of the care work and care migration. The standard script of aging and transnational care work has tended to be linear. The conjunction of population aging with more women in the paid workforce, changing families, and increased transnational mobility together, it is argued, lead directly to increased demand for elder care. This results in what is referred to in the literature as a care deficit and creates, it is argued, greater demand for transnational caregivers. Of course, this linear script is, in part, true. We ask here, however, if there may be more complexity in the relation of care work, particularly transnational care migration, and population aging. Specifically, we ask what role

218   Susan McDaniel and Seonggee Um

growing income inequalities, both within countries and among them, may play in contributing to increasing the supply of potential care workers and in changing patterns and dynamics of care migration. We ask how inequalities may be embedded in the relation of population aging and the work of care and care migration in multiple, complex ways.

CONTEXT

Centre stage in current policy concerns of more-developed countries (MDCs) is population aging and intergenerational issues (Grundy, Tomassini and Festy 2006; Zimmer and McDaniel 2013). This is particularly true in European Union countries where challenges of demographic aging have been elevated recently in policy circles (European Commission 2012). Heightened concern in Europe is a consequence of the shift to the lowest low-fertility regimes in several countries combined with substantial improvements in longer life expectancies. The latter has meant growth in both numbers and proportions of the oldest old, those most likely to be in need of care and support. This demographic pattern and concern are also apparent in some countries in East Asia, most notably Japan, but are also increasingly in Taiwan, South Korea, and Singapore, where there are considerable policy concerns. Canada has similar concerns, as does Australia, although both have less-aged populations than the eldest countries in Europe or in East Asia. With a higher birth rate in the US than most other MDCs, population aging is slower there and its population less aged. The relatively higher birth rate in the US combined with greater inequalities make the US an interesting case study, as we discuss.

Population aging trends and concerns have led to a preoccupation in policy circles with anticipated escalating demand for elder care. It is a status quo linear script, argued to be exacerbated by the increasing movement of women into the paid labor force. Thus, so this script goes, the supply of familial carers for elderly relatives is diminishing at the same time as need or demand for care is accelerating. The combination of factors is said to result in increased demand for paid care workers, many of whom will be transnational migrants. In this chapter, we argue that this linear script, while true to a degree, may oversimplify the cause-and-effect relationship of population aging with care demand.

Paralleling policy concerns about population aging and care deficits/ demand has been growing attention to the social and other implications of growing income inequalities. Inequalities, always of sociological interest although seldom given much attention until recently by the popular media, the public, or policy makers, are now on everyone's lips. Headline after headline expresses worry about growing inequalities and what they mean to societies, to well-being, to life chances, to economies, to dreams and ideologies, and even to democracy and political stability (see Banting and Myles

More Than Demand and Demographic Aging 219

2013; Stiglitz 2012). The subtitle of Nobel laureate Joseph Stiglitz's 2012 book is "How Today's Divided Society Endangers our Future." Topping the best-seller list and the media interview circuit in 2014 is Thomas Piketty's heavy (700-page) tome *Capital in the Twenty-First Century* (2014). Who would think that an economic treatise that is lengthy and chock-full of data and graphics focused on inequalities would be a best seller? This is certainly indicative of how prominent public concerns about income inequalities have become. As a recent OECD report (2014a: 1) suggests, "[i]nequalities and policies to restore equal opportunities have moved to the forefront of the political debate in many countries." More complex factors, we suggest, may be involved in the interconnections among transnationalism, aging, and the work of care in the contextual backdrop of growing inequalities. Many of the factors we outline are embedded in, and work through, growing inequalities and the hardening of inequality regimes.

HOW THE INEQUALITY FACTOR WORKS

The role of inequality in relation to fertility and care work was unearthed in the United States, spurring us to widen the analysis to look at other ways inequality may be a factor in care work. The puzzle of higher United States birthrates in the absence of substantial welfare state policies to support childbearing, parenting, or child care has long perplexed researchers. Conventional wisdom, based on empirical analyses across MDCs agrees that income and fertility are negatively correlated. This relationship has been found in most countries, both MDCs and less-developed countries (LDCs), at both aggregate and family levels. As countries increase their average incomes, and as women's incomes increase, fertility tends to fall. The long-standing phenomenon is typically correlated with growth in women's education. Women or couples with higher incomes and education tend to have lower fertility.

Not so in the United States, however, where a U-shaped fertility curve is apparent (Hazan and Zoabi 2011). Women with higher education and higher income tend to have higher fertility than those with middle levels of education or income. To add further complexity to the puzzle, more highly educated American women tend to work more hours, on average, in the paid labor force than those with less education. The perplexing question is how to explain this pattern, which diverges from patterns found elsewhere. How does the higher US birthrate among highly educated women continue in the face of more limited welfare state supports than in other MDCs? Hints of an answer open the door to possibly explaining how *supply* of potential caregivers, rather than only demand and demographic aging, may be a factor in transnational migration of care workers and in the work of care. Hazan and Zoabi (2011) find that it is the large supply of potential in-home caregivers in the US as a result of income inequalities that enables

220 *Susan McDaniel and Seonggee Um*

high-income women and couples to have inexpensive child care and thus achieve their desired family sizes.

THE US AS A CASE STUDY

Three characteristics of the US relevant to our focus, taken together, distinguish the US from most other MDCs. First is that the US is positioned on the extreme minimal end of liberal welfare states. Although the US is, at times, categorized with Canada among liberal welfare regimes (Esping-Andersen 1990), when one zooms in, the comparability fades. Canada has a much more developed set of welfare states policies and programs than does the US. In the US, there are few welfare state supports for care of any sort. Childbearing/child-rearing and parenthood leave policies are rare, and the state (neither federal nor the states) offers nothing but very minimal leaves for pregnancy or new parenting, if it offers any leaves at all. Most all other MDCs offer varying degrees of parental leaves. Canada offers up to a full year of parental leave provided the applicant has accumulated the requisite number of hours of eligible paid work. This is specified as 600 hours of insurable employment (under Employment Insurance) in the 52-week period before the leave (Canada 2012). Child care in the US, of course, exists but is often private and costly, with long waiting lists. Child care places for newborns are not plentiful either, with child care focused on older preschool children.

Second, the highly charged politics of immigration in the US, particularly intense with respect to undocumented US residents who lack official papers to be lawful residents, reveal how sociopolitical contexts matter to options and life chances without documentation. Gonzales (2011) reveals, in heartbreaking detail, how the life hopes and chances for the children of undocumented parents, who may not realize that their parents and thus they themselves are undocumented, rapidly close down as they attempt to gain acceptance to postsecondary institutions, or to obtain driver's licenses. Without documented evidence of legal US residency, even the brightest of youth and adults are relegated to working on the fringes, where their undocumented status may be less readily detectable.

In some jurisdictions, for example, in Arizona, where state law permits anyone who looks Hispanic to be stopped on the street and asked for their papers, racial surveillance works to keep migrants and immigrants, whether documented or not, on edge and in the margins (McDowell and Wonders 2009/10). Arizona laws, more draconian than in other states, nonetheless are revelatory in how the politics and policies of immigration in the US can work to exacerbate inequalities and create a group of people who are fearful of public spaces. Borders have become fortified, literally and socially, against the foreign "other," even if that "other" is legitimately a refugee, an immigrant or even native-born. The US is not alone in this tendency.

The research of McDowell and Wonders (2009/2010), among others, shows how the constant gaze of surveillance in Arizona shapes the behavior and aspirations of racialized minorities. The "stop and search" powers given to New York City police are similar in targeting racial minorities in poorer neighborhoods. Through enforcement rituals—immigration raids on workplaces, neighborhood sweeps, detentions, and general harassment in public places—racialized minorities curtail their public activities. Respondents in the McDowell/Wonders study mentioned that they did not feel free to travel to other cities or to travel out of Arizona. They also express reluctance to take their children to public parks or libraries. Those interviewed reported practicing "tactics of evasion" by not driving, not leaving the house, not socializing, and avoiding seeking medical assistance.

Another dimension of the politics of immigration and regimes of inequality is revealed in a case study of the daughter of a live-in maid for a wealthy family in Los Angeles (Romero 2011). The daughter, "Olivia," is followed over a period of 20 years, her life experiences textured and contextualized by interviews with other children of domestic workers. Romero shows how the political climate surrounding Hispanic immigrants in the US matters greatly to creating a tension between identity creation for these children of live-in maids/caregivers and deeply held American ideals. Selection of domestic workers itself is laden with gender, class, and ethnic stereotypes and socializes children into scripts of inequality. Those scripts are reproduced through care work.

Domestics and their offspring learn deference to employers, so that children living with their care-working mothers learn to assume the care worker role. Living simultaneously in the world of the upper-class employer in whose home she lives yet also in experiencing working-class, ethnic minority status makes class and ethnic hierarchies vivid to these children. In essence, care workers and their offspring learn that "passing" is required for mobility—leaving behind one's own ethnicity and class is needed to seek acceptance and social mobility, yet this is difficult with low-pay and limited mobility options. The inherent contradictions and tensions in the American Dream of mobility with hard work are called into sharp contrast with the lessons learned by care workers and their children.

Third, among the largest income inequalities among MDCs are found in the US. A recent Organisation for Economic Co-operation and Development (OECD) study found that among 34 OECD countries, the US had the fourth-highest income inequality, only after Turkey, Mexico, and Chile. As of 2012, the Gini coefficient in the US (0.39) was much higher than the OECD average (0.32; OECD 2014b). This, together with the US having the most rapidly growing inequalities among MDCs, creates a particular circumstance for considering the supply side of care work. Vast and growing income disparities means a large pool of precariously employed people in the bottom rungs of the distribution (see Standing 2011, 2012). Whatever the causes, vastly growing income inequalities are apparent in many MDCs.

222 *Susan McDaniel and Seonggee Um*

Through marital homogamy, highly educated, high-earning women and men live in dual-income families. This parallels a growing class of people stuck on the margins. Thus, the potential pool of cheaply hired care workers is large and is deemed a rational solution to child care for high-income couples.

Inequalities have been found to be a key factor in explaining why the American birth rate is higher among more highly educated women, a pattern not apparent in other MDCs (Hazan and Zoabi 2011), as mentioned earlier. In the absence of child-care options, dual high-income couples find that child-care workers are readily available for low cost. The addition to the pool of the undocumented increases to the potential supply of care workers, particularly since they may have no choice but to take home-based, low-wage employment where they can be sheltered from surveillance. Inequalities work in such a way then to diminish the costs, both financial and social, of employing care workers for high-earning couples. Highly educated women can then more often attain their desired family size, which is large enough that these women have a higher birth rate than less well-educated women have. Inequality is a key factor explaining this unusual fertility pattern. This leads us to ask how inequality may be a factor in the potential care-worker supply in other ways and contexts, and how this might work.

GLOBAL INCOME INEQUALITY AS A FACTOR

Global income inequalities, or income inequalities across countries, can influence transnational care migration. For example, low costs for care services or that can be provided by unpaid labour of family members in LDCs, relative to the rates of pay for care work in MDCs may be a factor encouraging care migration. As outlined in Hochschild's *global care chain* approach, global inequalities in the costs of care create "a series of personal links between people across the globe based on the paid or unpaid work of caring" (Hochschild 2000: 131). In a typical global care chain, according to Hochschild's description, "an older daughter from a poor family in a third world country cares for her siblings while her mother works as a nanny caring for the children of a nanny migrating to a first world country who, in turn, cares for the child of a family in a rich country" (ibid.).

This migration of women for care work can also work to help LDCs with trade deficits through deliberate policies of exporting care workers, who then provide remittances as in the case of the Philippines. Remittances significantly shore up the domestic economy of that country. In the Philippines, remittances account for 11 percent of the national economy and cash remittances from overseas Filipinos reached a record high of US$22.9 billion in 2013, according to the central bank of the Philippines (BSP 2014). This is another dynamic of global income inequality working in the supply side of

More Than Demand and Demographic Aging   223

transnational care migration. Since the government of the Philippines first adopted labor export as a development policy in 1974, migrant women have been celebrated as "new national heroes" for their work abroad and in sending remittances home (Rodriguez 2005).

Income inequality at the global level or among countries can also lead older people in LDCs or in regions without solid welfare states or with high costs of living to migrate to MDCs or regions as *labor migrants*. There are some indications that older women from former Eastern Bloc countries without good pensions after the demise of their state structures are migrating as elder-care workers to Western Europe (Bauer and Österle 2013; Lutz and Palenga-Möllenbeck 2010; Schwenken 2013; Shutes and Walsh 2012). This inequality gap between Eastern and Western Europe is contributing to a pool of transnational care workers.

Labor migration among older women is also found in the Asian context, in which retired women in poorer regions move to find employment opportunities in richer regions. For instance, the rising wage gap between China and South Korea triggered the migration of many retired Korean Chinese women (ethnic Koreans residing in China) into Korea's expanding care market. Previous studies have found that Korean Chinese women in their 50s and 60s are increasingly taking care and domestic work, often in live-in positions. Korean families prefer these women for such jobs given their maturity, shared language and culture, and, most important, their willingness to work for low pay and in poor working conditions. For many older migrants, care labor migration to Korea is their postretirement strategy to boost their incomes and savings for their families (Lee 2004; Um forthcoming).That the pool of potential care workers is not limited by age is evident in this dimension of transnational care work and aging.

Inequality at the global level can also be a factor in older people in MDCs moving transnationally between their home country and an LDC country, seeking warmer weather, lower living costs, and less expensive personal care services (e.g., East Asian older people migrating to South Asian countries, Western Europeans to southern Europe, Canadians and Americans to Mexico and the Caribbean). Although still a relatively new area of research, transnational late-life migration of those seeking affordable care is attracting growing scholarly interest. A case study of Japanese retirees in Thailand by Toyota (2006: 530) finds one of the main reasons for later-life migration among Japanese is to "stretch the value of their limited savings or pension and to seek care." In other studies of foreign retirees in Malaysia, cheaper living costs and availability of elder-care facilities are also pointed to as motivating retirement migration (Ono 2008; Wong and Musa 2014). Low costs of living and care services in LDCs are appealing to pensioners who are seeking more affordable living and care options not only within their home country but also globally.

State policies also play an active role in driving elder migration flows. Toyota and colleagues (2006) explain that increasingly unified European Union

224 Susan McDaniel and Seonggee Um

laws have facilitated pensioners' mobility in Europe. In Asia, there have been growing initiatives to promote the movement of pensioners from richer countries around the globe. The governments of Malaysia, Thailand, the Philippines, and Indonesia have all developed specific programs to promote foreign pensioners' migration. For example, under the current "Malaysia My Second Home" program, launched in 2002 and updated several times, the Malaysian government grants a renewable ten-year multi-entry visa to foreign retirees who comply with certain financial conditions (e.g., retirees are required to show proof of receiving a pension from the government of RM 10,000 per month, equivalent to US$2,800). These countries see late-life migration of foreign pensioners as "an opportunity to restore local economies after the Asian economic crisis" (Toyota et al. 2006: 30). There are hints of entrepreneurial efforts in some LDCs to create communities specifically for old migrants seeking care, where the language and cuisine of the home country are provided but, of course, in a warmer climate and at a lower cost than in the homeland. Examples are found in Korean and Japanese communities in the Philippines (Financial News 2006).

Global inequalities at the most fundamental level motivate people from LDCs to migrate to where they see opportunities. This means various pools of transnational migrants moving largely, but not exclusively, from LDCs to MDCs. Some may move for specific occupational opportunities. One such pool is sex workers, a popular occupational category recruited in Canada. Others may move intending to be nurses, doctors, lawyers, social workers, or another occupation but find that their occupational credentials are unrecognized in the destination country. There is some evidence, although not much as yet, that many who do the work of care and are transnationals do not enter the country as care workers but in some other immigration category (Atanackovic and Bourgeault 2013; Walton-Roberts 2012).

A primary category of such transnational care workers, according to the scant evidence that exists, is family migrants. They migrate with a family member and are not able to find work or sometimes are ineligible to work for pay. They thus may seek work in the underground economy, as cash-paid care workers. Others may be imported as brides who then care for the aging in-laws. Evidence shows a thriving migration in brides from South Asia to East Asia, particularly Korea and Taiwan. In patriarchal East Asian societies, a growing number of working-class families choose international marriages as a deliberate strategy to bring the affordable and docile reproductive labor of foreign brides often from Southeast Asia (Wang 2011). Families in richer regions, such as Taiwan and South Korea, expect that foreign brides should shoulder the care for their parents-in-law (Lu 2008; Um 2013).

On the other hand, older persons may participate in transnational migration if requested to care for their grandchildren—the children of dual-income immigrant families—often in MDCs. A few studies have documented this pattern of *transnational grandparenting*: Zhou (2013b) on

Chinese grandparents in Canada and Da (2003) on Chinese grandparents in Australia. While not care workers in the paid economy, they are doing transnational care for the aged or children nonetheless. Migration as brides or grandparents is also strongly driven by global inequalities that motivate migrants or migrants' children to move abroad hoping for better lives. Our point here is to illustrate that the boundaries between various classes of transnational migrants are permeable and shaped by income inequalities that contribute to pools of potential care workers.

CONCLUSION AND CONTRADICTIONS

Various contradictions come into play when examining the many interconnections of transnationalism, aging, and the work of care. For example, as the focus of neoliberal social policy moves to a "just in time" workforce through selective immigration policies and the goals of economic competitiveness, the care needs of both domestic, and transnational families are lost. Restrictions on family-class migration in Canada, as one example, increase difficulties for immigrant working families who may rely on informal child-care networks (such as grandparents) to balance paid and unpaid work. As well, transnational migration is becoming increasingly market-based, relegating caring to the background as incompatible with economic, capitalist needs. In parallel, there are social policy initiatives aimed at activating labor participation of all, including older people, but without much attention to the care needs of working families. Yet, in LDCs, those unable to "live up to" expected activation in the market may be relegated to transnational caring of one type or another. They are stuck as "noncitizens" in the social sense, in both their home countries and their destination countries; as "transnational citizens," a precarious designation in a security-sensitive world; or as "other" (neither here nor there). Thus, the quest for socially cohesive and inclusive societies through activation policies turns on itself as more transnational care workers become marginalized. They may even contribute to population aging in the receiving countries as they age but without having reached their own desired family size to contribute to "de-aging" of the population of the adopted country because their own families are left behind in their homelands. Contradictions and complexities in transnationalism, aging, and the work of care abound.

REFERENCES

Atanackovic, Jelena/Bourgeault, Ivy Lynn (2013): The Employment and Recruitment of Immigrant Care Workers in Canada. In: *Canadian Public Policy* 39, 2, pp. 335–350. http://0muse.jhu.edu.darius.uleth.ca/journals/canadian_public_policy/v039/39.2.atanackovic.html.

226 Susan McDaniel and Seonggee Um

Bakan, Abigail B./Stasliulis, Daiva (2012): The Political Economy of Migrant Live-In Caregivers: A Case of Unfree Labour. In: Lenard, Patti Tamara/Straehhle, Christing (eds.): *Legislated Inequality. Temporary Labour Migration in Canada.* Montreal & Kingston: McGill-Queen's University Press, pp. 202–226.

Baldassar, Loretta/Merla, Laura (eds.) (2013): *Transnational Families, Migration and the Circulation of Care. Understanding Mobility and Absence in Family Life.* London/New York: Routledge.

Bangko Sentral ng Pilipinas (BSP) (2014): *Overseas Filipinos' Remittances.* http://www.bsp.gov.ph/statistics/keystat/ofw.htm, accessed August 2014.

Banting, Keith/Myles, John (2013): Canadian Social Futures: Concluding Reflections. In: Banting, Keith/Myles, John (eds.): *Inequality and the Fading of Redistributive Politics.* Vancouver: University of British Columbia Press, pp. 413–427.

Bauer, Gudrum/Österle, August (2013): Migrant Care Labour: The Commodification and Redistribution of Care and Emotional Work. In: *Social Policy and Society* 12, 3, pp. 461–473.

Canada (2012): *Employment Insurance Maternity and Parenting Benefits.* http://www.servicecanada.gc.ca/eng/ei/types/maternity_parental.shtml#eligible, accessed March 2014.

Da, Wei Wei (2003): Transnational Grandparenting: Child Care Arrangements Among Migrants from People's Republic of China to Australia. In: *Journal of International Migration and Integration* 4, 1, pp. 79–103.

Esping-Andersen, Gøsta (1990): *The Three Worlds of Welfare State Capitalism.* London: Polity Press.

European Commission (2012): *The 2012 Ageing Report: Economic and Budgetary Projections for the 27 Member States (2010–2050).* Brussels: European Union. http://ec.europa.eu/economy_finance/publications/european_economy/2012/pdf/ee-2012-2_en.pdf, accessed July 2014.

Financial News (2006): *Constructing a Retirement Community for Koreans in the Philippines.* Interview with Lee Jong Bae. Published on September 25, 2006. http://www.fnnews.com/view?ra=Sent0701m_View&corp=fnnews&arcid=06 0925190208&cDateYear=2006&cDateMonth=09&cDateDay=25, accessed August 2014.

Gonzales, Roberto G. (2011): Learning to Be Illegal: Undocumented Youth and Shifting Legal Contexts in Transitions to Adulthood. In: *American Sociological Review* 76, 4, pp. 602–619. http://0-asr.sagepub.com.darius.uleth.ca/content/76/4/602.full.pdf+html.

Grundy, Emily/Tomassini, Cecilia/Festy, Patrick (2006): Demographic Change and the Care of Older People. In: *European Journal of Population* 22, pp. 215–218.

Hazan, Moshe/Zoabi, Hosny (2011): *Do Highly Educated Women Choose Smaller Families?* Discussion Paper no. 8590London, UK: Centre for Economic Policy Research. http://www.cepr.org/pubs/dps/DP8590.asp.

Hochschild, Arlie (2000): The nanny chain. In: *American Prospect* 11, 4, pp. 32–36.

Horn, Vincent/Schweppe, Cornelia/Um, Seonggee (2013): Transnational Aging: A Young Field of Research. In: *Transnational Social Review* 3, 1, pp. 7–10.

Lee, Hye-Kyung (2004): Foreign Domestic Workers in Korea. In: *Korea Journal of Population Studies [Hankook Ingoohak]* 27, 2, pp. 121–153. [In Korean]

Lu, Melody Chia-Wwen Lu (2008): Commercially Arranged Marriage Migration. Case Studies of Cross-Border Marriages in Taiwan. In: Palriwala, Rajni/Uberoi, Patricia (eds.): *Marriage, Migration and Gender.* New Delhi: Sage, pp. 125–151.

Lutz, Helma/Palenga-Möllenbeck, Ewa (2010): Care Work Migration in Germany: Semi-Compliance and Complicity. In: *Social Policy and Society* 9, 3, pp. 419–430.

McDowell, Meghan G./Wonders, Nancy A. (2009/10): Keeping Migrants in Their Place: Technologies of Control and Racialized Public Space in Arizona. In: *Social Justice* 36, 2, pp. 54–72.

More Than Demand and Demographic Aging 227

OECD (2014b): *Inequality*. Paris: OECD. http://www.oecd.org/social/inequality. htm, accessed August 2014.

OECD (2014a): *Rising Inequality: Youth and Poor Fall Further Behind*. Paris: OECD. http://www.oecd.org/els/soc/OECD2014-Income-Inequality-Update.pdf, accessed June 2014.

Ono, Mayumi (2008): Long Stay Tourism and International Retirement Migration: Japanese Retirees in Malaysia. In: Yamashita, Shinji/Minami, Makito/Haines, David W./Eades, Jerry S. (eds.): *Transnational Migration in East Asia Senri Ethnological Reports 77*, pp. 151–162.

Piketty, Thomas (translated by Arthur Goldhammer) (2014): *Capital in the Twenty-First Century*. Cambridge, MA: Harvard University Press.

Rodriguez, Robyn M. (2005): *Domestic Insecurities: Female Migration from the Philippines, Development and National Subject-Status*. Working Paper 114. San Diego: The Center for Comparative Immigration Studies. University of California. http://ccis.ucsd.edu/wp-content/uploads/WP_114.pdf, accessed August 2014.

Romero, Mary (2011): *The Maid's Daughter. Living Inside and Outside the American Dream*. New York: New York University Press.

Schwenken, Helen (2013): Circular Migration and Gender. *The Encyclopedia of Global Human Migration*. Oxford: Blackwell Publishing, pp. 1–5.

Shutes, Isabel/Walsh, Kieran (2012): Negotiating User Preferences, Discrimination, and Demand for Migrant Labour in Long-Term Care. In: *Social Politics: International Studies in Gender, State & Society* 19, 1, pp. 78–104.

Standing, Guy (2011): *The Precariat: The New Dangerous Class*. London: Bloomsbury Academic.

Standing, Guy (2012): The Precariat: From Denizens to Citizens? In: *Polity* 44, pp. 588–608. http://www.palgrave-journals.com/polity/journal/v44/n4/abs/pol201215a.html.

Stiglitz, Joseph E. (2012): *The Price of Inequality: How Today's Divided Society Endangers Our Future*. New York: W. W. Norton and Company.

Toyota, Mika (2006): Ageing and Transnational Householding: Japanese Retirees in Southeast Asia. In: *International Development Planning Review* 28, 4, pp. 515–532.

Toyota, Mika/Böcker, Anita/Guild, Elspeth (2006): Pensioners on the Move: Social Security and Trans-Border Retirement Migration in Asia and Europe. In: *IIAS Newsletter*, #40, Spring 2006. http://www.iias.nl/nl/40/IIAS_NL40_30.pdf, accessed August 2014.

Tronto, Joan C (2013): *Caring Democracy. Markets, Equality and Justice*. New York/London: New York University Press.

Um, Seonggee (2013): The Migration of Asian Women for Elder Care: Governing the Movement of Carers in South Korea. In: *Transnational Social Review* 3, 2, pp. 155–172.

Um, Seonggee (Forthcoming): Struggling to Make Time for Family: Korean-Chinese Migrant Workers in the South Korean Long-Term Care Market. In: Kontos, Maria/ Bonifacio, Glenda Tibe (eds.): *In the Dark: Family Rights and Migrant Domestic Work*. London, UK: Palgrave Macmillan, Chapter 12.

Wall, Karin/Bolzman, Claudio (2013): 'Mapping the New Plurality of Transnational Families: A Life Course Perspective. In: Baldassar, Loretta/Merla, Laura (eds.): *Transnational Families, Migration and the Circulation of Care: Understanding Mobility and Absence in Family Life*. London/New York: Routledge, pp. 61–77.

Walton-Roberts, Margaret (2012): Contextualizing the Global Nurse Care Chain: International Migration and the Status of Nursing in South India. In: Global Networks 12, 2, pp. 175–194.

Wang, Hong-zen (2011): Immigration Trends and Policy Changes in Taiwan. In: *Asian and Pacific Migration Journal* 20, 2, pp. 169–194.

228 Susan McDaniel and Seonggee Um

Williams, Fiona (2010): Migration and Care: Themes, Concepts and Challenges. In: *Social Policy and Society* 9, 3, pp. 385–396.

Wong, Kee Mun/Musa, Ghazali (2014): Retirement Motivation Among 'Malaysia My Second Home' Participants. In: *Tourism Management* 40, pp. 141–154.

Yeates, Nicola (2009): *Globalizing Care Economies and Migrant Workers. Explorations in Global Care Chains.* New York: Palgrave Macmillan.

Yeates, Nicola (2012): Global Care Chains: A State-of-the-Art Review and Future Directions in Care Transnationalization Research. In: *Global Networks* 12, 2, pp. 135–154.

Zhou, Yanqui Rachel (2013a): Toward Transnational Care Interdependence: Rethinking the Relationships Between Care, Immigration and Social Policy. In: *Global Social Policy* 13, 3, pp. 280–298.

Zhou, Yanqui Rachel (2013b): Transnational Aging: The Impacts of Adult Children's Immigration on Their Parents' Later Lives. In: *Transnational Social Review: A Social Work Journal* 3, 1, pp. 49–64.

Zimmer, Zachary/McDaniel, Susan A. (2013): Global Ageing in the Twenty-First Century. In: McDaniel, Susan A./Zimmer, Zachary (eds.): *Global Ageing in the Twenty-First Century: Challenges, Opportunities and Implications.* Farnham, Surrey, UK: Ashgate, pp. 1–12.

Part D

Social Protection and Transnational Aging

The Circulation of Ideas and the Role of Nongovernmental Actors

12 Older Persons' Rights
How Ideas Travel in International Development

Carmen Grimm

According to the United Nations' definition, an older person is a person aged 60 or older (United Nations Population Fund and HelpAge International, 2012). The worldwide proportion of this group of people is growing considerably: while in 1990 older people formed a 9.2 percent share globally, by 2013 the percentage had increased to 11.7 percent, with projections predicting 21.1 percent by 2050 (UNDESA 2013). The effects of population aging are already quite visible in some countries, while other countries will face the highest ratio at some point in the future. For example, countries such as Peru will undergo a phase with a demographic dividend[1] in the near future (INEI 2009). The topics of demographic change on societal levels and aging on an individual level are now discussed extensively in politics and science. Additionally, they have gained more and more importance in international development (Lloyd-Sherlock 2011).

This chapter argues that age-related concepts or ideas develop and travel in the transnational field of development cooperation. It shows that such concepts are not static but that they change over time and distance and between different actors that employ age-related ideas. A theoretical background that builds on the assumptions of actor-network theory and conceptualizes the exchange and adoption of concepts as *traveling ideas* will serve as the basis for the arguments developed. After an introduction into the formation of the area of age-centered international development, the example of a German nongovernmental organization (NGO) is presented. Focusing on this particular NGO and a few concepts employed by it, I show that older people have been important in international development for quite a while. Through international discourse centered on the United Nations, they have become a target group perceived to have specific needs and rights. This attention to age-related problems in international development has given urgency and legitimacy to aid projects directed at the group of persons aged 60 or older.

Older persons, old age, and aging are traveling ideas or, rather, conglomerates of different ideas and assumptions from very different places and subject areas. For example, concepts from science and broader politics shape the way ideas are discussed in international cooperation. They are

232 *Carmen Grimm*

transported transnationally when institutions and individuals work together on projects that are financed in the so-called global North. They all have in common the fact that they transgress borders: this is the case when development organizations implement programs based on methodologies, concepts, and ideas developed in the global North and put into practice in the global South. In addition, ideas return from the ground to influence international debates and policy. In this chapter, I want to stress the multidirectionality and complexity present in the travel of ideas. In order to describe how transnational exchange works in general or in international development specifically, one has to be careful not to simplify exchange processes. Simplification can occur if, for instance, one assumes that processes only flow from the North to the South or that ideas have a traceable origin, typically, again, in the global North. This chapter also stresses the importance of actors working in international cooperation: partner organizations in developing or transitional countries, NGOs in funding countries, and governmental or international organizations. All of them are engaged in constant exchange. They continuously adapt and reshape concepts and ideas by putting them into action.

The insights presented in this chapter are the result of a multisited ethnographic research conducted by the author from 2013 to 2014 and focused on German NGOs that support age-related projects in developing countries. In order to capture the field of age-related development cooperation in Germany as holistically as possible, different methods were combined. Documents produced by NGOs and international organizations were analyzed. Participant observations with German NGOs and expert interviews with their employees were conducted in Germany. However, NGOs cannot be considered in isolation. One has to "follow the metaphor"[2] (Marcus 1995: 108) in order to be able to understand its implications and transformations in different contexts. In 2014, I conducted a five-month field research in Peru, observing and participating in the work of NGOs and interviewing both NGO employees and older persons. This chapter presents the example of the NGO Caritas Germany and its cooperation with Latin American and Caribbean Caritas organizations, and builds on interviews with former and current employees from Germany and Peru who were and are involved in projects for elder persons in Latin America and the Caribbean.

HOW IDEAS TRAVEL

Development cooperation is transnational or international. It is a field that connects people, ideas, and objects from ideologically and locally distant places. These connections can be described as a kind of chain (Rottenburg 2002). This chain leads from practice and discourses in so-called developing or transitional countries to practices and discourses in developed countries or even at subnational levels, and vice versa. Various actors take up different

Older Persons' Rights 233

spots—nodes—in this chain of transnational cooperation and assume different roles. They might be nongovernmental or governmental institutions and, in some cases, individuals. These actors, although they might have quite unique expectations, interests, points of view, and languages, nevertheless, refer to the same generalized concepts and ideas and adapt them to particular environments. How can we conceptualize this transnational exchange of ideas and, consequently, of practices? How does the adaptation of ideas at the nodes of the chain work?

According to Cziarniawska and Joerges (1996), in contexts where there is transnational exchange, certain ideas *travel*. They originate from one place and are turned into actions or objects in other places. Ideas are

> images which become known in the form of pictures or sounds (words can be either one or another). They can then be materialized (turned into objects or action) in many ways. . . . Their materialization causes change: unknown objects appear, known objects change their appearance, practices become transformed. (Cziarniawska and Joerges 1996: 20)

Since they travel across distance and sectors, ideas are *boundary objects* (Star and Griesemer 1989): they link contexts that are otherwise unrelated. They are usually abstract and generic; thus, they can be transmitted and appropriated more easily (Feldmann 2011).

The term *to travel* allows us to go beyond the one-directionality implied in other constructionist approaches. For example, *diffusion* has also been used to explain the spread of ideas to other places (Best 2001). Using this concept for our example, however, confronts us with limitations. First, ideas do not necessarily travel from " 'more satiated' to 'less satiated' environments" (Cziarniawska and Joerges 1996: 23). Second, ideas usually do not have a fixed origin, temporal or spatial. Instead, they take form over time and combine elements or ideas that have existed for a while already. They do not simply travel in one direction but, rather, travel forth and back; they circulate, thus enriching and changing constantly. Latour (2000), discussing *transformation* processes between things and words or representations, also stresses the reversibility of such processes.

Although ideas usually do not have a clear-cut origin, they are often symbolically associated with a specific time and place. This gives them authenticity and ideological convincibility (Peck and Theodore 2010: 170). Cziarniawska and Joerges (1996: 26) put it as follows:

> When the translation of ideas into actions is well advanced, the actors involved feel a need to mythologize by dramatizing origins. . . . It might well be that, in the reconstruction of the past, an event is chosen or invented because it is rhetorically convenient . . . Alternatively, the incidental and disruptive character of the initial events is stressed to

234 *Carmen Grimm*

demonstrate the incredible touch of luck in the idea's timely arrival. Both types of memories serve the same purpose: to tie, meaningfully, the arrival of an idea to present problems experienced by people in organizations or attributed to the organizations themselves.

As should have become clear by now, ideas are not static, and the chain of translation processes cannot be considered independent of outside factors. During translation processes, a traveling idea integrates assumptions and thoughts from neighboring discourses and institutions. The idea is changed and adapted constantly.

Ideas are disseminated into other contexts with the help of intermediaries. Such intermediaries might be texts, technical objects, embodied practices, or money (Tait and Jenssen 2007). In their new context, abstract ideas are translated into concrete action. In international development, this becomes obvious when projects that have been decided on in one place are put into practice in another. All four intermediaries mentioned earlier are crucial: texts may exist in the form of documents; technical objects may play an especially important role in aid projects of technical cooperation, for example, in the field of agriculture; embodied practices may concern the actual approach of NGOs in the field; and money is a central component of all development cooperation. In the highly cross-linked field of international development, the process of transmission or traveling can be particularly complex:

> Development projects and technology transfers to so-called developing countries present particularly intricate cases of idea materialization. Ideas are turned into things, then things into ideas again, transferred from their time and place of origin and materialized again elsewhere. (Czarniawska and Joerges 1996: 18)

Thinking of ideas and policies applied in international development as traveling ideas provides us with a useful approach to understanding the relations between the actors involved and the misunderstandings between them. In what follows, the field of development and old age is presented, together with new concepts adopted in the last couple of years that have shaped the implementation of development projects.

THE SUBJECT AREA OF INTERNATIONAL DEVELOPMENT CONCERNED WITH OLD AGE

Demographic change and the growing number of older persons have been discussed for more than half a century in both academic discourses and national politics in the global North, with attention clearly rising during the last decades (Baltes and Mittelstraß 1992). Although developing countries

Older Persons' Rights 235

have not completely ignored the topic, it is only recently that demographic change has been recognized as an issue of concern for nations worldwide (Leisering 2011). Clearly, there are huge differences concerning when, in what pace, and under which conditions countries all over the world will face demographic aging (Lloyd-Sherlock 2011).

In the discussion about demographic aging, a distinction is drawn between developing and developed countries (Lloyd-Sherlock 2011). Developing countries, the assumption goes, may require more financial support and advice. Their social security and health systems are often insufficient, and several nations of the global South may face additional problems such as AIDS and general poverty (Lloyd-Sherlock 2010; United Nations Population Fund/HelpAge International 2012). This support can be given through international cooperation. Over time, voices were raised that addressed the existing disregard of broader aid provision for the specific age-related needs of older persons in developing countries, for example, needs arising from physical impairments (Walker, Gorman and Bünte 2011).

International organizations, particularly the United Nations, have been important actors creating and maintaining an age-related global developmental discourse. While at the first World Assembly on Aging in 1982 the focus still lay on so-called developed countries, subsequent decisions and conferences addressed aging more and more as a global issue (United Nations 1982). The United Nations Principles for Older Persons were adopted in 1991, arguing for recognition of human rights for older persons (United Nations 1991). In 2002, a second World Assembly on Aging took place in Madrid, where the emphasis shifted to older people in developing countries (Sidorenko and Walker 2004). In the nongovernmental sector, old age gained importance as well (Walker, Gorman and Bünte 2011). For example, in 1983 several NGOs joined to found HelpAge International in London, UK, which has since grown into a worldwide network. It funds development projects that specifically focus on older persons and works as a mediator between older persons and political institutions (HelpAge International 2012).

Generalized ideas about the characteristics of older persons and the implications of societal aging are discussed in age-related global developmental debates. These debates always draw on or react to assumptions of what I called earlier neighboring discourses, such as wider economic and developmental debates. Income security in old age serves as an example here: it is an issue that has been discussed for years by the World Bank. In a World Bank study about pension reform, demographic aging is presented as an "old age crisis" and income security as a "worldwide problem" (World Bank 1994). The topic of pensions has now been taken up in international developmental discourse on aging. In fact, income security has become one of the most debated issues (Walker, Gorman and Bünte, 2011: 399). However, another solution to the worldwide "crisis" of aging is promoted here. Since many older persons in developing countries live in poverty and do not have access to pensions, the United Nations and NGOs such as HelpAge International advocate universal, noncontributory pensions. Another idea enters the debate here, which I will come back to later: the claim to social pensions is seconded by referring to values, namely, older persons' rights (Walker, Gorman and Bünte 2011; see also the chapter by Fröhlich in this volume).

Just like the discourse on aging in general does (Göckenjan 2000), developmental debates employ polarized views of older persons (Lloyd-Sherlock 2011). On one side are the rather negative ideas of aging and older people: as in the case of debates on pensions or older persons' rights, older persons are regarded as a vulnerable and marginalized group, which is what makes transnational support necessary in the first place. On the other side are quite positive statements stressing older persons' value for and their contribution to society. Findings or key assumptions of gerontological research provide an important basis for this. In scientific writing, positive aspects of aging and old age have been highlighted for many years, as a response to supposedly negative stereotypes prevailing in society (Cohen 1994). For example, the potential of older persons has been an important concept in gerontological writing (Kruse 2010), and the report of the Second World Assembly on Aging in Madrid repeatedly refers to older persons' potentials as well (United Nations 2002). Such potential can be realized through the use of older persons' knowledge or by way of voluntary work (United Nations 2002). Another example is the promotion of active aging, which serves as a concept in gerontological theory (Katz 2000) and is used as a keyword in international development as well, for example, in the Madrid Plan of Action on Aging (United Nations 2002).

Thus, during the last decades, older persons have become a target group with associated specific needs, problems, and qualities. They have now been established as a target group next to classic vulnerable groups such as women, disabled persons, or children (BMZ 2013). It is not at all the aim of this chapter to allege that the needs, problems, and qualities of older persons are only constructed. International institutions and NGOs do employ generic ideas and concepts, which are necessary to make communication and cooperation possible. At the same time, they also make simplifications and generalizations about quite diverse conditions and should therefore be discussed critically. Ideas employed and transferred in the development context comprise, in their totality, a complex net of assumptions, keywords, and thoughts. In the following section, one particular concept closely associated with older persons—human rights—shall serve as an example of a traveling idea in international development. I discuss next how one NGO that has worked in the field of aging for many years employed this traveling idea.

THE ROLE OF NGOS IN THE TRAVEL OF IDEAS

The German Caritas Association (Deutscher Caritasverband) has shaped and at the same time been shaped by the international discourse on aging in

Older Persons' Rights 237

development cooperation. By following ideas associated with older persons and old age employed by Caritas Germany over the years, we can point out how thoughts from other subject areas shaped discussions and prioritizing. Since the conference in Madrid in 2002 is recognized as a milestone in the field and considered very important by the NGO in question, the first part of the section focuses on this event. In the second part, I look at how ideas materialize into action in terms of concrete project work and consider the role that NGOs play in this context.

Before Madrid

For many decades, charity organizations have provided care for elderly people. This has not been restricted to national charity work. International development aid has also been directed at elderly people since the second half of the past century, at the same time or even before the United Nations included the topic on its agenda. One of few examples is Caritas Germany, which, through bilateral cooperation within the worldwide Caritas network, has directed funding for elderly related projects to Caritas organizations in Latin America and the Caribbean since the 1970s (Schreck 2012).

Caritas Germany, through its experience in doing social work for and with older people in Germany, had expert knowledge on how to train people working with older persons. This knowledge was transmitted to different Caritas organizations in Latin America, for example, Peru, by means of consultants. A consultant that worked in the area during the time explains how this type of cooperation started:

> There was the earthquake [2001 in Peru]. Then Caritas Germany says: We would like to support Caritas Peru in the area of senior citizens, in the earthquake region. And they respond: We would like to do that, but we have never done this so far. And then they [Caritas Germany] say: We have a consultant, we will send her.[3] (Int 1)

Such cooperation turned Caritas Germany employees into experts in the field of social work with older persons, which made them sought after when new cooperation projects started in other Latin American countries or regions.

In 1999, the Latin American Network of Gerontology (Red Latinoamericana de Gerontología, RLG) was founded. It is a virtual network that aims to share and exchange information on the topic of gerontology and works on building a positive image of older persons. They receive financial support from Caritas Germany and, until today, have maintained a close association with the German Caritas (Red Latinoamericana de Gerontología 2014).

Using its experience in Latin America, Caritas Germany became involved in the preparations for the Second World Assembly on Aging in 2002 and the resulting document. Although in a generalized way, the Plan of Action

238   *Carmen Grimm*

on Aging draws on experience in the field and on priorities that developed through actual practice. Civil organizations played an important role in providing that kind of information.

In March 2002, Caritas Germany submitted a statement regarding experiences and concepts of social work with older persons in Latin America and the Caribbean, with recommendations drawing on more than 20 years of experience in social work with older persons (Deutscher Caritasverband 2002). The statement demands (a) that attention is given to the impacts of aging, (b) that the topic is integrated into developmental discussions, and (c) that senior citizens are included in these discussions. Caritas Germany could claim expertise and a leading and pioneering role, since they were one of few development organizations working in this area for a long time: "This is unusual in international cooperation, particularly as for a long time no connection between the poverty of senior population in countries of the South and the developmental problems of these countries has been recognized"[4] (Deutscher Caritasverband, 2002: 4).

Caritas Internationalis, an international confederation of national Caritas organizations (Caritas, 2014), also participated in the World Assembly in Madrid. Before that, in 2001, the coordinator of the Latin American Network of Gerontology (RLG) had spoken in New York on the occasion of the seventh annual meeting of the International Day of Older Persons, sharing the panel on "Global NGOs" with HelpAge International, among others (Bezrukov de Villalba 2009).

After Madrid

The conference in Madrid strengthened, if not created, what Escobar calls the "institutionalization of development" (Escobar 1988: 431), or, in this case, of a subfield of development. What during the 1970s and 1980s, when Caritas Germany began financing social work for older persons in some Latin American countries, had been no more than a part of social work, now became a small but growing particular subject area of development cooperation: work directed at older persons. What had developed over the years was a network of actors involved in age-related development. This network exhibits typical characteristics (DiMaggio and Powell 1983): (a) involved actors refer to the same concepts and phrases, (b) actors are familiar with each other and cooperate or exchange information to a certain extent, and (c) some actors play a leading role and are considered experts. For example, HelpAge International plays an important role through many publications and research on the topic, partly together with United Nations institutions (United Nations Population Fund and HelpAge International 2012).

In spite of all the reports published, the work done, and other reunions held before the conference in Madrid,[5] it seems to be that this particular event gives legitimacy and recognition to the topic of older persons in development cooperation. Thus, many publications refer to the conference in Madrid or the Plan of Action on Aging (Equipo de Coordinación del PRAM 2012; United Nations Population Fund and HelpAge International 2012). The discussion of demographic change as a worldwide challenge gives urgency to the topic (for instance, see United Nations 2002). Although the Plan of Action on Aging only provides recommendations for governments and has been criticized on that score, it serves as a basis of argumentation for civil organizations when trying to press policies or receive funding.

In the case of Caritas Germany, the 2002 conference served as a trigger in two ways. First, according to Caritas Germany employees, it evoked the "desire to work together more" and to work more "in this area" among the Caritas organizations in Latin America and the Caribbean and the German Caritas. The topic had gained importance and international recognition of this importance. Second, for Caritas Germany it became possible to receive governmental funding for a project explicitly directed at the target group of older persons. A financial tool for development politics of the German ministry that has existed since the 1960s could now be used for a program directed at the new target group of older people.[6] A Caritas employee remembers that Caritas Germany asked Latin American Caritas organizations "who was interested in working in this thematic area now, since we saw that funding could be achieved for this."

Caritas Germany successfully applied for funding, and starting in 2004, a project[7] was formed that operated in its first phases in six[8] locations in Latin America and the Caribbean (Schreck 2012). The implementation of the project was facilitated to a great extent by the international conference in Madrid and its resulting report. However, further criteria affected the choice of the project's thematic focus. The program aimed at "improvement of quality of life and full respect for human rights of older persons"[9] (DCV and BMZ 2004–2012). This focus, centering on human rights for older people, differed in many ways from the work in Latin America funded by Caritas Germany during the previous decades. While the work done before was characterized by provision of short-term, mostly material aid (*asistencialismo*), the new cooperative project wanted to work with "groups that get active" and that are "protagonists of their own lives." The most important factors influencing the choice of the project's specific orientation are as follows:

1. Caritas intern: Many years of work with older persons in different Latin American and Caribbean countries provided experience as to what were main issues. The different Caritas organizations involved also tried to find common concerns. A Caritas Germany employee states: "These topics were brought up because experience had shown that these were main issues."
2. Reference to the international developmental discourse on aging: In order to have "major impact," the project not only had to comply

240 *Carmen Grimm*

with the goals and viewpoints set by Caritas but also those set by the
United Nations Aging Report (Müller 2008: 5).

3. The idea of participation in development cooperation in general: In
the 1990s, partly as a response to criticism of development cooperation, participation became the main approach used in aid projects. If
you let people on the ground co-decide and participate, goes the assumption, development projects have more sustainability in the long
run (Mosse 2003; Schreck 2012).

4. Funding: Participation is also a requirement of the financial tool used
for the project (see note 5; AGS 2004).

5. Gerontological thought: In academic discourse about older persons,
appeals to more positive images of elderly people have been made
for decades. Such appeals have slowly but steadily entered the political discourse as well. In order to sustain a more positive image, the
participation of older persons in and their contributions to society are
stressed (Carls 1996; Cohen 1994).

In the program financed through Caritas Germany, the human rights of
older persons are a central thought. The idea of particular rights for older
persons is not that recent. Latin American countries have been addressing
the issue for many years (Mendonça 2012). Countries such as Argentina
were pioneers in their struggle for a UN convention for older persons' rights
as early as 1949 (Secretaría Nacional de Niñez, Adolescencia y Familia
2011). An important reunion on Latin American ground was the follow-up
to the Second World Assembly, held in 2007 in Brazil, where one plea was
that "legal frameworks and monitoring mechanisms be created to protect
the human rights and fundamental freedoms of older persons" (ECLAC
2007: 3). Globally, the topic was addressed in the 1991 United Nations
Principles for Older Persons mentioned earlier. In 2010, an open-ended
working group on aging was established by a United Nations resolution in
order to "consider the existing international framework of the human rights
of older persons and identify possible gaps and how best to address them"
(UNDESA 2014).

The specific focus of the Caritas program was thus in line with not
only international but also Latin American discourses. The development
of the idea of older persons' rights attests that thoughts do not travel
one-directionally from the global North to the global South but that there
is constant exchange and reshaping. The Caritas focus of older persons'
rights developed out of long experiences in social work, including in Latin
America. Today, it is one of the most important issues in the field of international development and aging and shapes the way older persons are talked
about to a great extent.

Before providing some examples for materializations of the idea of older
persons' rights, I briefly discuss how the concept of rights relates to a neighboring concept. Both in international discourse and within the Caritas

project of 2004, the idea of rights for older persons is strongly associated with another concept: that of dignity. Dignity is a concept that is central both in broader human rights discourse and within Caritas itself. Human dignity is inherent to all human beings (Deutscher Caritasverband 1997). In the Caritas project discussed here, human rights and dignity are interdependent: older persons have the right to dignity. And since dignity is human and universal, every person should have their rights fulfilled. This line of argumentation implicates certain images about older persons. It also influences how concrete work with and for older persons is organized in the different participating countries.

Materialization of ideas

First of all, what images of older persons are entailed? What makes intervention and the project necessary in the first place is the initial assumption that rights and dignity are not yet guaranteed in old age. They are, on the contrary, violated. The elderly that the Caritas organizations work with are thus considered a vulnerable target group. However, it is also assumed that older persons have the potential to stand up for their rights. Once supported, they can become active themselves. In this duality between vulnerability and potentials, similarities to general discourses in international development and academic writing can be recognized.

How, then, does the idea of rights affect practice on the ground? Three areas of intervention are presented. First, in the work with older persons, it is stressed that older people should stand up for their own rights. They have the potential to speak and fight for themselves, and this potential should be used. Such an approach is also in line with the general participatory orientation of the project. However, if you want to stand up for your rights, you have to know them first. Since many older persons are not aware of their rights, they first have to be sensitized. Education is of importance here. Capability courses and group work therefore comprised a great part of the practical work of the Caritas program (Schreck 2012: 26–29). The second area of intervention concerns relations between different generations. Recognition of older persons' right to dignity means that other age groups respect older persons and value their role in society. Disrespect and violation of rights can be changed by concretely improving images of old age in the different Latin American countries and cities (DCV/BMZ 2004–2012). Most of all, younger generations have to feel and show more respect and esteem for older persons. Accordingly, the Caritas project aimed at improving images of old age and involved intergenerational work, for example, in Peru (Quispe Chura 2012). A third area of intervention is on the political level. General rights involve the right to a life in dignity and to dispose of sufficient material means. Thus, the topic of older persons' rights enters social policy debates. Part of the work conducted in the Caritas program focused on sensitizing and lobbying for the improvement of pensions or

242 *Carmen Grimm*

for the implementation of universal, noncontributory pensions in the Latin American countries involved (Mendonça 2012).

Many actors in international development, including Caritas organizations, advocate for legislation protecting older persons' rights. The most pronounced claim is the one for a proper UN convention of the rights of older persons, comparable to the United Nations convention on children's rights (ECLAC 2007). In 2014, the idea of rights for older persons materialized in the appointment of an International Special Correspondent through the United Nations Human Rights Council. The Special Correspondent will give more legitimacy and authority to the topic and reunite organizations and people all over the world working for a convention (United Nations Office of the High Commissioner for Human Rights, 2014). Furthermore, even in Europe, where in many countries violations of rights are not considered a pressing issue, the topic is now being discussed. In Germany, for example, the Working Group of Senior Organizations (BAGSO) addressed the issue in 2012. Two arguments are made: In developing countries, rights are violated in areas of social security, health, or AIDS. Although older persons in Germany are not directly affected, attention should be given to the issue on grounds of transnational solidarity. Regarding Germany itself, the topic of rights is addressed as well. However, it is put into a national context and focuses on violations of rights of older persons in need of care or persons with dementia (BAGSO 2012). The political debate about the idea of rights again shows the complexity of transnational relations that traveling ideas create and maintain.

In all of this, NGOs are central points of intersection. Caritas Germany's role in the project is pivotal: financial and narrative reports of the Latin American and Caribbean Caritas organizations are collected at the offices of Caritas Germany, where the information is translated, harmonized, and then forwarded to the German Ministry for Economic Cooperation and Development. Thus, the NGO holds the position of broker between the different Caritas organizations in Latin America and the Caribbean and the governmental financial institution.

Caritas Germany, as many other NGOs, serves as a kind of "eye of a needle" and fulfills its role as translator of ideas about older persons and aging—in both directions. Thus, for example, they have to pass on information from international levels to individuals. This is done by means of educating elderly in groups or strengthening rights in intergenerational relations. However, this also involves difficulties because of the high degree of abstractness of the concept of older persons' rights. On a local level, for example, diocesan Caritas organizations in Peruvian cities addressed older persons' rights in group talks with older persons or in intergenerational encounters, for example, by means of games, *juegos recreativos* (Quispe Chura 2012: 206). In capability courses in Peruvian towns, the concepts of rights and dignity of older persons are discussed and made comprehensible on a personalized level, using questions such as "Have you ever been mistreated?" and "What is respect and how is it shown?" (Quispe Chura 2012: 209). At the same time, it is challenging for the NGO to provide commensurable evidence for effects at individual levels, which, however, is what the governmental financial institution is interested in: "We realized that, in this very broad discourse of rights on the level of the United Nations, it is quite arduous to actually account for effects on individual levels of older persons."

CONCLUSION

During the last decades, the issues of older people have attracted attention in international development. This chapter argued that certain ideas about older people, old age, and aging move transnationally in age-related development cooperation. Concepts such as older persons' rights are associated with the general idea of older persons as a target group in international development. Thus, they carry a certain image of older persons who are vulnerable to a certain extent because their rights and dignity are not sufficiently recognized. At the same time, these concepts generate expectations, for example, that older persons get active themselves. By referring to such established concepts and connecting them to age-related issues, arguments become stronger and more accessible. For instance, referring to universal rights of older persons serves as argumentative basis in the campaign for a universal pension. As the example of the Madrid Plan of Action on Aging illustrates, symbolic associations with a place—in our case the conference in Madrid—also helps to legitimize and reinforce an idea, for example, when trying to receive financial support for projects.

What is more, the example of Caritas showed that ideas do not only travel from the global North (or international levels) to the Global South. Both the development of the Madrid Plan of Action on Aging and the discussion about older persons' rights reveal the importance of work and experience in Latin America in shaping ideas. Not only in age-related cooperation but also in international development in general, relations and exchange processes of ideas are complex. When describing transnational fields such as international development, we have to be aware that movements usually are not one-directional. Instead, there is multidirectional, continual exchange of concepts and practices. This exchange is not only transregional but also passes different areas or discourses. It is important to recognize such multiple connections and multidirectional flows and to be careful with oversimplification. Also, NGOs as intermediaries should ideally be aware of this and be reflective in their use and transmission of concepts.

NOTES

1 Demographic dividend denotes a period after demographic transitions with low fertility and mortality rates. During these decades, working age population grows rapidly, which leads to a decreased old-age dependency ratio. The

244   *Carmen Grimm*

high rate of working-age population provides an opportunity for economic growth and family welfare.

2   The term *to follow* is used here in reference to methodological approach and is not meant to imply one-directionality of metaphors or ideas. To follow an idea thus means that the researcher, rather than determining her sites of research beforehand, is open trace an idea during the research process to multiple sites where it is put into practice.

3   The quotes are from interviews with former and current Caritas Germany employees conducted by the author between October 2013 and February 2014. They were carried out in German and translated into English by the author.

4   Translation from German by the author.

5   To name but a few, the United Nations conference in Vienna (United Nations 1982), the United Nations Principles for Older Persons (United Nations 1991), and the foundation of HelpAge International in 1983 (HelpAge International 2012). For a detailed list see also Leisering (2011).

6   It is a tool for development policy by the German Federal Ministry for Economic Cooperation and Development (BMZ) for furtherance of social structure. It promotes the participation of disadvantaged population groups (AGS 2004).

7   Programa Regional de Cáritas a favor de las Personas Adultas Mayores de América Latina y el Caribe (PRAM; Equipo de Coordinación del PRAM 2012).

8   Seven if you count the headquarters of the RLG in Uruguay as "location."

9   Translation from Spanish by the author.

REFERENCES

Arbeitsgemeinschaft Sozialstruktur (AGS) (2004): *Grundsatzpapier zur Strukturförderung.* Online Resource: http://www.sozialstruktur.org/de/files/Grundsatzpapier_zur_Sozialstrukturfoerderung.pdf, accessed August 2014.

Baltes, Paul B./Mittelstraß, Jürgen (1992): Vorwort. In: Baltes, Paul B./Mittelstraß, Jürgen (eds.): *Zukunft des Alters und Gesellschaftliche Entwicklung.* Berlin/New York: Walter de Gruyter, pp. VII–XIV.

Best, Joel (2001): Introduction. The Diffusion of Social Problems. In: Best, Joel (ed.): *How Claims Spread. Cross-National Diffusion of Social Problems.* New York: Aldine de Gruyter, pp. 1–18.

Bezrukov de Villalba, Lila (2009): Expectativas que las ONGs de Todo el Mundo Albergan Sobre los Resultados de la 2a Asamblea Mundial del Envejecimiento, su Importancia y la Esperanza que su Impacto Pueda Tener en la Vida de las Personas de Edad Avanzada a Nivel Mundial. In: RLG (ed.): *En Homenaje a Lila Brezukov de Villalba.* Montevideo: RLG, pp. 5–10.

Bundesarbeitsgemeinschaft der Senioren-Organisationen (BAGSO) (2012): *Erklärung der BAGSO anlässlich des Internationalen Tages der älteren Menschen am 1.* Oktober 2012. http://www.bagso.de/fileadmin/Aktuell/News/Erklaerung_der_BAGSO_zum_1.10.12.doc, accessed July 2014.

Bundesministerium für wirtschaftliche Zusammenarbeit und Entwicklung (BMZ) (2013): *Katastrophenvorsorge für Alle.* Berlin: BMZ.

Caritas (2014): *Who We Are.* http://www.caritas.org/who-we-are/, accessed July 2014.

Carls, Christian (1996): *Das "neue Altersbild". Interpretationen zur Inszenierung: "Wissenschaftliche Aufgeklärtheit in vorurteilsumnachteter Gesellschaft".* Münster: Lit.

Older Persons' Rights 245

Cohen Lawrence (1994): Old Age: Cultural and Critical Perspectives. In: *Annual Review of Anthropology* 23, 1, pp. 137–158.

Czarniawska, Barbara/Joerges, Bernward (1996): Travels of Ideas. In: Czarniawska, Barbara/Sevón, Guje (eds.): *Translating Organizational Change*. Berlin/New York: Walter de Gruyter, pp. 13–48.

Deutscher Caritasverband (DCV) (1997): *Leitbild des Deustchen Caritasverbandes*. Freiburg: Deutscher Caritasverband.

Deutscher Caritasverband (DCV) (2002): *Projektarbeit Altenhilfe. Erfahrungen und Konzepte in Lateinamerika und Karibik*. Freiburg: Deutscher Caritasverband.

Deutscher Caritasverband (DCV)/Bundesministerium für Wirtschaftliche Zusammenarbeit und Entwicklung (BMZ) (2004–2012): *Programa Regional Cáritas: Trabajo Social a Favor del Adulto Mayor en América Latina y el Caribe: Unidos abriendo rumbos*. Brochure published by Deutscher Caritasverband/BMZ.

DiMaggio, Paul J./Powell, Walter W. (1983): The Iron Cage Revisited: Institutional Isomorphism and Collective Rationality in Organizational Fields. In: *American Sociological Review* 48, 2, pp. 147–160.

Economic Comission for Latin America and the Caribbean (ECLAC) (2007): *Brasilia Declaration of the Second Regional Intergovernmental Conference on Ageing in Latin America and the Caribbean. Towards a Society for all Ages and Rights-based Social Protection*. Report of the Conference at Brasilia 2007, ECLAC, December 4–6, 2007: http://www.un.org/esa/socdev/ageing/documents/regional_review/Declaracion_Brasilia.pdf, accessed July 2014.

Equipo de Coordinación del PRAM (2012): Introducción. In: *PRAM: Envejecimiento con Dignidad y Derechos. Desafío de Cáritas*. Lima: MV masideas SAC, pp. 13–15.

Escobar, Arturo (1988): Power and Visibility: Development and the Invention and Management of the Third World. In: *Cultural Anthropology* 3, 4, pp. 428–443.

Feldman, Gregory (2011): If Ethnography Is More Than Participant-Observation, Then Relations Are More Than Connections: The Case for Nonlocal Ethnography in a World of Apparatuses. In: *Anthropological Theory* 11, 4, pp. 375–395.

Göckenjan, Gerd (2000): Altersbilder und die Regulierung der Generationsbeziehungen. Einige systematische Überlegungen. In: Ehmer, Josef/Gutschner, Peter (eds.): *Das Alter im Spiel der Generationen: Historische und sozialwissenschaftliche Beiträge*. Wien: Böhlau, pp. 93–108.

HelpAge International (2012): *Who We Are*. http://www.helpage.org, accessed November 2012.

Instituto Nacional de Estadistica e informatica (INEI) (2009): *Estado de la Población Peruana 2009. Situación de la Mujer*. Lima: INEI.

Katz, Stephen (2000): Busy Bodies: Activity, Aging, and the Management of Everyday Life. In: *Journal of Aging Studies* 14, 2, pp. 135–152.

Kruse, Andreas (2010): *Potenziale im Altern. Chancen und Aufgaben für Individuum und Gesellschaft*. Heidelberg: AKA.

Latour, Bruno (2000): *Die Hoffnung der Pandora. Untersuchungen zur Wirklichkeit der Wissenschaft*. Frankfurt am Main: Suhrkamp.

Leisering, Lutz (2011): Die Entdeckung der Alten. Die Globale Altenfrage. In: Leisering, Lutz (ed.): *Die Alten der Welt. Neue Wege der Alterssicherung im Globalen Norden und Süden*. Frankfurt am Main/New York: Campus, pp. 13–41.

Lloyd-Sherlock, Peter (2010): *Population Ageing and International Development. From Generalisation to Evidence*. Bristol: Policy.

Lloyd-Sherlock, Peter (2011): Ageing and International Development. A Critical Review. In: Leisering, Lutz (ed.): *Die Alten der Welt: Neue Wege der Alterssicherung im Globalen Norden und Süden*. Frankfurt am Main/New York: Campus, pp. 144–161.

Marcus, George E. (1995): Ethnography in/of the World System: The Emergence of Multi-Sited Ethnography. In: *Annual Review of Anthropology* 24, 1, pp. 95–117.

246 *Carmen Grimm*

Mendonça, Jurilza (2012): Los Caminos para una Convención en Defensa de los Derechos de las Personas Adultas Mayores. In: *PRAM: Envejecimiento con Dignidad y Derechos: Desafío de Cáritas*. Lima: MV masideas SAC, pp. 35–46.

Mosse, David (2003): The Making and Marketing of Participatory Development. In: Van Quarles Ufford, Philip/Giri, Ananta K. (eds.): A Moral Critique of Development: *In Search of Global Responsibilities*. London/New York: EIDOS/Routledge, pp. 43–75.

Müller, Oliver (2008): Prólogo. In: Wasiek, Christel et al. (eds.): *Cáritas Alemana: Desafíos y Oportunidades del Envejecimiento en América Latina y el Caribe: Experiencias desde el Programa Regional Cáritas a favor de los Adultos Mayores*. Brasil: Unisind Gráfica Ltda, p. 5.

Peck, Jamie/Theodore, Nik (2010): *Mobilizing Policy: Models, Methods, and Mutations*. Geoforum 41, pp. 169–174.

Quispe Chura, Rafael (2012): Encuentros intergeneracionales con Personas Adultas Mayores en el sur del Perú. In: PRAM (ed.): *PRAM: Envejecimiento con Dignidad y Derechos. Desafío de Cáritas*. Lima: MV masideas SAC, pp. 203–213.

Red Latinoamericana de Gerontología (RLG) (2014): *Quienes somos. Sobre la RLG*. http://www.gerontologia.org/portal/about.php, accessed July 2014.

Rottenburg, Richard (2002): *Weit Hergeholte Fakten. Eine Parabel der Entwicklungshilfe*. Stuttgart: Lucius & Lucius.

Schreck, Dorothea (2012): El Programa Regional de Cáritas a favor de las Personas Adultas Mayores. In: PRAM (ed.): *Envejecimiento con Dignidad y Derechos: Desafío de Cáritas*. Lima: MV masideas SAC, pp. 17–31.

Secretaría Nacional de Niñez Adolescencia y Familia, Dirección Nacional de Políticas para Adultos Mayores (2011): *Carta de Derechos de las Personas Mayores*. Buenos Aires: Secretaría Nacional de Niñez, Adolescencia y Familia.

Sidorenko, Alexandre/Walker, Alan (2004): The Madrid International Plan of Action on Ageing: From Conception to Implementation. In: *Ageing and Society* 24, 2, pp. 147–165.

Star, Susan Leigh/Griesemer, James R. (1989): Institutional Ecology, 'Translations' and Boundary Objects: Amateurs and Professionals in Berkeley's Museum of Vertebrate Zoology, 1907–39. In: *Social Studies of Science* 19, 3, pp. 387–420.

Tait, Malcolm/Jensen, Ole B. (2007): Travelling Ideas, Power and Place: The Cases of Urban Villages and Business Improvement Districts. In: *International Planning Studies* 12, 2, pp. 107–128.

United Nations (1982): *The Vienna International Plan of Action on Aging*. New York: United Nations.

United Nations (1991): *United Nations Principles for Older Persons*. Resolution 46/91, United Nations, December 16, 1991. http://www.un.org/documents/ga/res/46/a46r091.htm, accessed July 2014.

United Nations (2002): *Report of the Second World Assembly on Ageing. Report of the Conference at Madrid 2002*, United Nations, April 8–12, 2002. http://daccess-dds-ny.un.org/doc/UNDOC/GEN/N02/397/51/PDF/N0239751. pdf?OpenElement, accessed September 2013.

United Nations Department of Economic and Social Affairs (UNDESA) (2013): *World Population Ageing 2013*. New York: United Nations.

United Nations Department of Economic and Social Affairs (UNDESA) (2014): *Open-Ended Working Group on Ageing for the Purpose of Strengthening the Protection of the Human Rights of Older Persons: Who We Are*. http://social. un.org/ageing-working-group/, accessed July 2014.

United Nations Office of the High Commissioner for Human Rights (2014): *Human Rights Bodies: Nomination, Selection and Appointment of Mandate Holders*. http://www.ohchr.org/EN/HRBodies/SP/Pages/HRC25.aspx, accessed July 2014.

United Nations Population Fund/HelpAge International (2012): *Ageing in the Twenty-First Century. A Celebration and a Challenge*. New York/London, UK: United Nations Population Fund.

Walker Bourne, Astrid/Gorman, Max/Bünte, Michael (2011): Non-Governmental Organisations. HelpAge International as a Global Actor. In: Leisering, Lutz (ed.): *Die Alten der Welt. Neue Wege der Alterssicherung im Globalen Norden und Süden*. Frankfurt am Main/New York: Campus, pp. 395–425.

World Bank (1994): *Averting the Old Age Crisis: Policies to Protect the Old and Promote Growth. A World Bank Policy Research Report*. New York: Oxford University Press.

13 From Alms to Rights

Boundaries of a Transnational Nongovernmental Organization Implementing an Unconditional Old-Age Pension

Katrin Fröhlich

People in most developing countries are getting increasingly older. Among the older population, the proportion of persons aged 80 years or older is the fastest-growing segment of the world population. Rapid increases in this group are also expected in the less-"developed" regions (UN 2011a). While in 1950 a 65-year-old person from sub-Saharan Africa had an average remaining life expectancy of 10 years, this number is expected to double by 2100 (see UN 2011b). HIV/AIDS and increasing urbanization are leading to a decline of informal protection systems like the family or community and leave older people to care for themselves and, in many cases, for their grandchildren, too (see Leisering, Buhr and Traiser-Diop 2006; OPM 2010). Thus, many old people in developing countries probably need to support others while they are at risk of being unreliably supported themselves (Nabalamba and Chikoko 2011). Eventually, the "burden of care is increasingly being shifted to those least able to afford it" (Nabalamba and Chikoko 2011: 10). But a lack of care is not the only challenge considering the circumstances of older people in many developing countries. Increasingly unable to earn their own income (be it in cash or in-kind), old people do not only become more dependent on care but also need to rely on some form of regular income, like a pension.

As is shown in this chapter, pensions need not be and are not paid only by the state. Against the backdrop of decreasing family care and insufficient public and private social protection strategies in many developing countries,[1] this chapter elaborates on "transnational aging" from the angle of transnational social protection for older people. More specifically, the chapter analyzes a transnational nongovernmental organization (TNGO) delivering a pension through social cash transfers (SCTs) on an institutionalized and thereby regular and reliable basis. Various studies have examined the impact of SCTs at the micro- and macro-levels, with different research focuses such as the design and implementation of SCT programs (Samson, van Niekerk and Mac Quene 2006), the efficiency and positive outcomes of SCTs (Hanlon, Barriantos and Hulme 2010; Schubert 2005), or the changing social structures due to SCTs (Wietler

From Alms to Rights   249

2007). This study supplements the current state of research by examining in more detail the meso-level, namely, the implications of a pension project for the TNGO itself. After a brief introduction of the conceptual framework of global social policy, the role of TNGOs within that policy field, and SCTs in general, the chapter exemplifies the challenges of TNGOs implementing SCTs through a case study. The conclusion looks at how expanding the TNGO's role to an advocate for pensions can be an approach to deal with the TNGO's own institutional limitations as a service provider of pensions.

CONCEPTUAL FRAMEWORK

Global Social Policy—Actors Beyond the State

Social pensions come out of the concept of social protection. Unlike the concept of social security, social protection is not and does not necessarily need to be solely implemented by the state (ILO 2011; Loewe 2003; Standing 2010). Within a welfare mix, social protection is provided by different actors beyond the state, such as the family, the community, or the economy. According to the different concepts of governance based on Rosenau's (1992) approach of "governance without government," the state does not naturally have to be the only one containing and controlling the political and social sphere. Nongovernmental actors are especially seen as important actors in policy making (Seifer 2007). Referring to social protection, German social anthropology stressed the importance of nongovernmental actors especially in developing countries already in the 1980s. Because of the different impact of public social protection schemes within developed and developing countries, anthropologists (Benda-Bekmann 1988; Zacher 1988) claimed that the concept of the welfare state needs to be adapted to the situation on the ground. Rather than social security strategies of a state, they emphasized the importance of "informal" or "traditional" protection strategies, like religious or familiar rights and obligations (Benda-Beckmann et al. 1988: 12).[2] But it took another ten years, until the end of the 1990s, for the concept of social protection to be adopted by international organizations such as the International Labour Organization (ILO) and the World Bank (Holzmann and Jorgenson 1999; World Bank 2001).

In the meantime, the research paradigm of global social policy was "developed" and reached a broad international audience. In 1997, Deacon used the term to highlight the global impacts of social policy. According to him, "we have witnessed the globalization of social policy" (i.e., global dimensions of social problems), as well as "the socialization of global politics" (i.e., issues of social policy getting on the agenda of international organizations) for the last three decades (Deacon 2009: 3). National policy is

250 *Katrin Fröhlich*

not considered to be necessarily sufficient to ensure local social protection on the ground anymore (ibid.). The list of global agents and levels of social protection is supplemented by Gough and Wood (2008), in accordance with this global social policy paradigm. They enlarge Esping-Andersen's (1990) triangle of state, market institutions, and the family to a quadrangle by adding the civil society on a domestic level. They also add an international or transnational level, which is especially important for developing countries (Gough and Wood 2008). There are transnational social protection strategies beyond the state as well as inter- or supranational organizations related to social protection. Those transnational social protection strategies focus on actors crossing national borders but who do not belong to the public sphere, like multinational corporations (MNCs), TNGOs, and migrants (see also Table 13.1).[3]

Usually, studies about transnational actors within that welfare mix focus on individuals and the matter of care. Social protection on a transnational level is barely researched as a matter of income security or (re)distribution. If it is, income security strategies are mainly known as remittances by migrants. However, some TNGOs also provide support based on SCTs. In opposition to unique donations, SCTs are reliable, regular, and expectable. That is why some studies consider only the state to be able to deliver SCTs (Leisering, Buhr and Traiser-Diop 2006) financed by taxes. However, this article shows that a TNGO also can, and does, deliver SCTs on a regular, reliable, and institutionalized basis, even though its program is not on a national scale.[4] In doing this, however, the TNGO has to cope with different structural limitations. Before those limitations and the coping strategies of the TNGO are shown, further aspects of legitimization and positioning within the field of social protection are briefly presented next.

Table 13.1 Social protection strategies

	Domestic	**Inter-, Supra-, and Transnational**
State	Domestic governments	Inter- and supranational organizations, national donors
Market	Domestic markets	Global markets, multinational corporations
Community	Civil society, nongovernmental organizations (NGOs)	Transnational NGOs (TNGOs)
Family	Households	International household strategies

Source: Table based on Gough's (2008: 30) "institutional responsibility matrix."

From Alms to Rights 251

TNGOs as Actors of Social Protection: Positioning and Legitimization

TNGOs, especially TNGOs delivering services and not simply engaging in advocacy work, have to face the criticism of undermining the state (Lewis and Kanji 2009), indirectly supporting failing states, and/or not being adequately legitimized:

> Structures of the civil society as well as democratic structures can be weakened if it is not the state but developmental donor institutions taking over the responsibility for social protection in a country. Because who is deciding how social protection is organized, which benefits are included and who is benefiting; the possibly democratically elected government or the donor(s)? (Javad 2011: 4; author's translation)

In most discussions about welfare mix and governance theories, it is still the state that is often seen as the only responsible and legitimized actor for social protection. That is why this chapter focuses on the question of how the TNGO positions itself with regard to the aforementioned other actors of social protection (see Table 13.1), especially the state and family.[5] Closely related to the question of positioning, this chapter also focuses on how the TNGO legitimizes its actions. Although TNGOs take over services that might be of public interest, they have no direct democratic input legitimization for those actions:

> INGOs[6] frequently claim to be the spokespeople of global civil society, acting as much-needed representatives for disenfranchised groups such as the poor, the sick, and the oppressed. There can be a significant tension between such claims, however, and the realities of INGOs' working practices. Unlike democratic governments, INGOs are not legally bound to act in the 'public interest', and neither can they claim that their actions are somehow legitimized by formal democratic procedures. (Collingwood and Logister 2005: 175)

Thus, apart from the discussion of whether TNGOs should be democratically legitimized, legally they do not necessarily need this kind of legitimization (Hurrelmann, Schneider and Steffek 2007). Going beyond the question of the aforementioned normative criteria of a democratic legitimization, this research is focused on the empirical or descriptive legitimization of TNGOs. Based on Max Weber, the empirical understanding of legitimization is not about political or legal rules that should constrain the power of actors. Instead, the question is about what the actors themselves perceive to be justified (Collingwood and Logister 2005; Hurrelmann, Schneider and Steffek 2007).

Notably, individual and organizational donors are very relevant for the economic survival of TNGOs (Altvater and Brunnengräber 2002: 12). In the end,

252   *Katrin Fröhlich*

TNGOs have to gain support to be able to support others in turn. In order to "deserve" that support, they necessarily have to adapt to the norms, values, and beliefs of their environment (Troyer 2007: 1). Looking at TNGOs offering unconditional SCTs, as in the following case study, norms, values, and beliefs are not per se existent and might have to be established. While SCTs, especially social pensions and conditional cash transfers, are receiving more and more international acceptance (Leisering 2010), unconditional SCTs are still highly controversial.[7] That is why this research puts special emphasis on the question of legitimizing a highly controversial matter of social policy: unconditional SCTs.

Social Cash Transfers as a "Southern Revolution"

The income of older people in most developing countries is or was mainly irregular, unreliable, or nonmonetized, and just a small number of older people could contribute to and eventually benefit from formal public or private insurance systems (Holzmann, Robalino and Takayama 2009; Leisering et al. 2006; van Ginneken 2009). Contributory (private and public) pension systems might work in most developed countries,[8] but they are inappropriate for the majority of the population in developing countries, as long as the majority of the people cannot regularly pay private insurances or benefit from protection systems for public employees (Holzmann, Robalino and Takayama 2009; Leisering, Buhr and Traiser-Diop 2006; van Ginneken 2009). Against the backdrop of a changing international discourse on social protection systems since the beginning of this century,[9] noncontributory SCTs are considered as an instrument to protect people and combat poverty in many developing countries and are even called a "southern revolution" by some social scholars (Hanlon, Barrientos and Hulme 2010). All over sub-Saharan Africa, there are already 20 public SCT schemes, 13 of which are social pension schemes (see Barrientos, Nino-Zarazúa and Maitrot 2010; HelpAge International 2011).[10] But not all of those schemes are implemented nationwide. Some of them are just regional pilot projects executed together with other actors, mainly international donors. Other pension systems are limited because of the measurement of means testing but can still cover up to 83 percent of the older generation (people older than 60 years; see HelpAge International 2011). Finally, six countries have implemented a (even) universal and nationwide social pension scheme (Botswana, Lesotho, Namibia, Mauritius, Seychelles, and Swaziland; ibid.), still leaving many other countries without sufficient social security schemes for older people.

CASE STUDY

A TNGO Giving Money Without Conditions to Older People

In opposition to the previously mentioned countries, to this day there is no public noncontributory system of social security for people who cannot make a living because of age, unemployment, or illness in Tanzania. Since the end of the 1990s, people working in the formal economy or public sector have been able to contribute to different types of insurance, such as old-age pension (implemented in 1998), disability pension (implemented in 1998), work injury (implemented in 2002), or cash maternity benefits (implemented in 1997). But most Tanzanian businesses are not formally registered and belong to the informal economy. According to ILO (2008), 91 percent of all people who are employed (including those in agriculture) work in an informal economy. People are either self-employed or contribute unpaid labor within their families. This is why income is irregular for the majority of Tanzanians, unreliable or nonmonetized, and less than one percent of the population can actually contribute to and gain from formal insurance systems of the state (ibid.).

Against this backdrop, the TNGO of this case study, called "For Older People/FOP,"[11] is implementing a social pension in a selected region in Tanzania. FOP itself is based in a European country and is situated in Tanzania. Since 2003, it provides an unconditional SCT to older people in Tanzania. Today more than 1,000 older people, mostly women, receive this social pension.[12] They have to be older than 65 years and receive 8,000 Tanzanian shillings (approximately US$5) per month without any condition on what to do for or how to use the money. If they care for children within their household—mostly HIV/AIDS orphans of their own children—they get another 4,000 Tanzanian shillings per month and child. All in all, the TNGO is providing its targeted and unconditional SCT on a regular and institutionalized basis to approximately 1,600 people. Even if the amount of the pension is extremely small—according to the TNGO itself, one can buy a food basket consisting of some fish, salt, and rice, as well as several kilograms of cornmeal, kerosene for cooking and lighting, and schoolbooks for the children (as of January 2011)—for some of the older people it is the only cash they receive and is therefore essential for making ends meet.[13]

Field Access, Data Collection, and Data Analysis

Finding an unconditional SCT project like the pension project of FOP was a challenge, because most of the SCT projects (conditional or not) are implemented by national or international public actors, rarely by private TNGOs. But with the help of a gatekeeper of a main German development organization, it was finally possible to gain an in-depth overview over existing SCT projects in general and to get access to relevant stakeholders of TNGOs. Not all of the TNGOs are implementing SCT projects themselves; some of them are "just" financially supporting and advocating SCT projects within their portfolio. That is why FOP, as a TNGO implementing a social pension in Tanzania, as well as financing and advocating for it from Europe, was selected for this research.

254 Katrin Fröhlich

The following results are based on a qualitative empirical research about this SCT project. Following the principles of grounded theory (Strauss and Corbin 1996), results are based on a theoretical saturated analysis of semistructured interviews with experts (chairperson and executive directors) from the implementing TNGO and a closely connected TNGO supporting them. In addition to the interviews, public documents of the TNGOs such as flyers and annual and project reports have been analyzed. Besides positioning and justification strategies within the interviews, those public documents are an essential supplement of producing legitimization (Sandhu 2012) toward their individual and organizational donors.

Empirical Results: Foundation of the Project—Charity in a Situation of Emergency

The TNGO was founded by a European citizen who lived and worked in Tanzania for many years. When he became a pensioner some years ago, he started giving money to old people he knew in the surroundings of the Tanzanian village where he was living. The founding of the organization was prompted by an awareness of a situation of emergency, in combination with the personal situation of the founder and his ability to help, as this quote from the interview shows:

> The realization of the situation, a state of emergency of those old people was more or less random because Albert [*the founder*, author's note] gets increasingly confronted in his work with orphans living with their grandmothers in very, very difficult and disastrous living conditions. And some of those women, grandmothers he got to know. At the same time, because he became 65 years old, he received his own pension and thought that he could provide a part of it for those cases of emergency. (FOP chairperson; author's translation)

Furthermore, as the European chairperson said, at the beginning there was no long-term development of concepts behind the project. No one was an expert about pension projects. There was barely any information about SCT projects at all:

> When the project started in 2003, there were hardly any lessons learned from other organizations to refer to and many of the policy discussions about cash transfers or social pensions only reached a wider audience in recent years. (evaluation report by FOP et al.)

The intervention is legitimized as a beneficent act of emergency help within a special structure of opportunities, that is, getting to know the living conditions of old women and receiving one's own (European) pension, which is big enough to share and help. The pensions are alms given for charity's

From Alms to Rights   255

sake. Referring to the founding report, social protection for the elderly by the state, the families, or other organizations is insufficient. Thus, FOP positions itself as a unique actor that has realized the alarming situation of old people and that is able to help them.

Although the beginning of the project is based on a voluntaristic approach of individuals, the efforts are soon institutionalized by founding a TNGO based in Europe and Tanzania:

> ... FOP started "without blueprints or log frames" but "developed" by learning from the realities of the people and an attitude of flexibly adapting its methods to these realities. (evaluation report by FOP et al.)

Considering missing "blueprints or log frames" as openness and flexibility, FOP is transforming those organizational weaknesses into its own strength and legitimizes its process of growing. Within the first five years of its existence, FOP contacted a variety of actors in Europe and Tanzania. Because of its growing network, FOP has increasingly been receiving more publicity, getting more financial support from individuals and organizations. Having had no lessons learned from other organizations to build on at the beginning of their own project, one highlight of its organizational growth is FOP's own role as a reference for a public study in Tanzania. After being used as the example in a Tanzanian study about the feasibility of a nationwide social pension system, FOP starts to see itself not only as emergency help, but as an example for "The Meaning of Pensions for Fighting Poverty" (title of project study by FOP). However, despite the financial growth and their increasing political impact, FOP still has to cope with different boundaries within its role as a service provider who is implementing pensions.

Financial Boundaries and the Question of Selectivity of SCTs

First of all, FOP cannot reach all the persons it wants to help. Even in the village where the pension program was started, the TNGO cannot support every old person it wants to support. FOP decided to give support to the neediest and introduced means testing by different actors (i.e., community mapping by local experts) to find out who needed the money most. But FOP is neither convinced by the procedure of targeting nor by the result. Reflecting on its own limitations, the FOP, in its brochure, quotes a grandchild of a recipient:

> Yes, we receive a pension in our village, but there are others who don't get it. I don't know why they are not supported. Maybe the computer didn't choose them. (brochure of FOP; author's translation)

FOP shows how unintelligible the targeting is. The child considers that others in the village should actually get a pension too, blaming a machine—the

256   *Katrin Fröhlich*

computer—for not doing it. Even if the TNGO is criticizing its own targeting with those quotes, financial boundaries force them to stick with and legitimize the concept of selectivity.

Even the growth of its financial means does not lead to a solution to this problem. Instead, it has to face another dilemma. FOP becomes aware of more needy people just outside the "borders" of the initial project region. Confronted with the question of eligibility, the organization could either widen the project region now or include more people from the initial village. But who is it responsible for? Unlike a state, which is primarily responsible for its own citizens on a normative basis and has obligations on a legal basis too, a TNGO has to negotiate and decide by itself for what it assumes responsibility. Thus, its financial growth does not solve the problem of targeting but leads back to "financial boundaries in space"—limitations that come up because of the unavoidable local focus of the project:

> For a long time we had our focus in X [village in Tanzania] until we realized that in villages that are a bit further away there are some people who partially are much poorer, thus there is bigger misery. Why should you give 100 more people a pension here if 14 or 20 kilometers away there are many more "ultra poor"? (chairperson of FOP; author's translation)

Thus, a decision had to be made within the TNGO whether it should spread the money to more people at all. Instead of increasing the number of recipients, FOP could also increase and secure the pensions it already pays.

Financial Boundaries and the Question of Durability of SCTs

By giving pensions to elderly people, FOP has taken over a long-term responsibility, which prolongs with every new recipient. The cash transfer is originally not considered as a stimulus for growth, like a singular micro credit. The responsibility to care for the recipients stays as long as the recipient is part of the special category of people. In the case of child support, for example, children are supported until they reach a certain age, depending on the society's view about the ability and necessity of a child to earn his or her own income. In case of a pension system, old people are never considered as able or as having to earn their own income anymore. In general, once receiving a pension, older people are supposed to be supported until their death. Hence, a pension project is always open-ended and long-term.

Because of that, FOP also has to cope with its "financial boundaries in time"—limitations that come up because of the necessary durability of an old-age pension. In giving a pension, FOP aspires to guarantee the cash flow for an uncertain period, while at the same time its own funding is barely secured for several years. Looking for long-term funding, the organization has to realize that "no one likes long-standing obligations" (chairperson of FOP; author's translation). One reason for that might be that any kind of long-term funding of a project is problematic because it contradicts the principle of a regular "upward accountability" from an organization to its own funders and donors. Another aspect mentioned by FOP emphasizes the desire of organizations to be and remain flexible:

> No one likes it if you always have to pay such-and-such much money for ten years. They want to be flexible and address new needs or new projects. (chairperson of FOP; author's translation)

Thus, FOP does not have the same options as its recipients have. After the old person is selected, he or she is supposed to receive the money all his or her life. However, FOP itself, in contrast to its own recipients, has to justify its actions regularly and request for funding.

Images of Old Age as a Chance for Legitimizing Unconditional Cash Transfers

Paying a pension to old people can offer an easier justification of the unconditionality of cash transfers. FOP decided against conditions because it did not believe in expecting old people to give something in return:

> What do you want to demand from 70–80 years old women and men in return, as work or service delivery? This question did not come up. (chairperson of FOP; author's translation)

As long as FOP is referring to old people not being able to give something in return, old people can more easily be supported without any kind of condition. Besides, it is the picture of the innocent and deserving poor—those who became poor through no fault of their own—which can be more easily painted with old people than with middle-aged persons. In social policy discourse, people who are in their working age and cannot socially protect themselves are more readily blamed for not earning an income on their own. Based among others on the ideas of the British poor laws introduced in the sixteenth century, only those who could not work through no fault of their own (including old and ill people as well as children) actually deserved support (Hanlon, Barrientos and Hulme 2010). Until today, middle-aged people are rather supposed to help themselves and SCTs are more often based on a "life circle" approach than on a needs-based approach (for South Africa, see Weible and Leisering, 2012).

In general, negative images of old people[14]—showing them as being neglected, as in need of protection, and as having a weak agency—depict old people as innocent victims who deserve support and who got into that unfair situation because of circumstances they could not change or improve: "Many of them are left alone by their families" (project flyer by FOP et al.;

258   *Katrin Fröhlich*

author's translation). The impact of HIV/AIDS is emphasized as the main reason for the shortfall of the caring middle generation: "The rapid prevalence of HIV/Aids . . . puts them into a big misery" (project flyer by FOP et al.; author's translation), while old people are shown as helplessly watching their children becoming ill, dying, or migrating for improving their living conditions and leaving alone their old parents and probably even their own children. It is a consequence of HIV/AIDS and impoverishment and not the fault of an individual that "informal" support structures are declining.

In contrast to that controversial image of old people, being (positively) innocent, on one hand, and (negatively) weak and passive persons on the other, there is another clearly positive image of them. Illustrated as "lifesavers" or "silent heroes" in project flyers and brochures, FOP and another supportive TNGO refer to their role as caring grandmothers for the HIV orphans of their own children. At first glance, this might not fit the image of old people as poor, helpless, and passive victims. But their concurrent role as "lifesavers" underlines even more that they deserve support. They deserve it because they save other people's lives and do not just use the pension to help themselves. It is a gesture of altruistic behavior that is pictured. Portrayed as "silent" or "unsung heroes," they are shown at the same time as unacknowledged heroes. The pension is not just a social cash transfer and an opportunity for the donor to distribute his or her money anymore. It is also a kind of gratification every donor gives to the "unsung" heroic deeds of the old people. Besides emphasizing the children within the concept of "unsung heroes," it is also an opportunity for the TNGO to make clear that money is never "lost." Focusing on the fact that the pension is also used for the grandchildren, improving their nutrition and health, as well as their schooling facilities, the pension can be seen as an investment in the upcoming generation, too.

Boundaries of Legitimizing Unconditional Cash Transfers

The negative, as well as positive, images of old age turn out to be helpful for legitimizing an *unconditional* social pension. But there are also limitations for justifying conditional SCTs. In its brochures, the TNGO uses narrations of old people that show how their lives changed positively and that the money is not just used altruistically but also efficiently and results in poverty reduction. It is even emphasized that the money is not misused for alcohol: "The increasingly few cases of abuse, e.g. if alcohol is used, are exceptions that confirm the rule of a sensible use of the money" (brochure of FOP; author's translation).

Even though there is no condition attached to the pensions and people should be allowed to do whatever they want to do with the money, FOP is nevertheless emphasizing how the pensioners use the money. It tries to convince the public that SCTs are something worthy of support by showing outputs of an effective and sensible use of the money. There are no milestones in

From Alms to Rights 259

FOP's documents beside its general aim to support old and especially poor people in the project region mainly with pensions. Even if FOP gives the money without any condition, the organization has to show that it fulfills its aim. The "positive" individual stories of the old persons are an opportunity for FOP to compensate for the missing milestones other development projects actually have. The organization has to cope with a boundary that is an intrinsic part of every unconditional cash transfer project; while the recipients do not have to justify how they use the money, the TNGO has to do it—at least as long as it focuses on an "output legitimacy" for its project.

A Pension as a Human Right: Giving the Responsibility Back

At the time of its founding, FOP was solely acting in cases of emergency, increasingly becoming a service provider paying an unconditional pension on a regular and institutionalized basis. FOP blamed the state and families for their insufficient protection strategies and decided to pay pensions to help. Unconditional pensions were chosen because of the negative image of old people. No one in the organization expected old people to give anything in return, and old people could easily be legitimized to receive the money as "deserving poor." Thus, unconditional pensions were chosen for pragmatic reasons; they fit the target group of FOP. But as time goes by, the pension itself is not just seen as an appropriate cash transfer but also as a human right:

> It came up with the years, for us too, the idea, that pensions are a right. This idea that actually everyone should not be only supported somehow but that they have an entitlement—as existing in our legal system—an entitlement to this support. (chairperson of FOP; author's translation)

Based, among other, on the International Covenant on Economic, Social and Cultural Rights (UN 1966, 2007, 2008), FOP claims a human right for social protection,[15] supporting social pensions as an adequate way of implementing it. By claiming that social protection is a human right, the responsibility for social protection is given (back) to the state, which has the obligation to respect, protect, and fulfill human rights. TNGOs might respect and protect human rights, too, but in a legal understanding it is not their obligation to fulfill them.[16] Against the background of this international discourse, FOP might give itself a normative responsibility to fulfill human rights, but the state is seen as the only actor who can and has to guarantee these rights. In this way the organization can also legitimize its own "boundaries in time and space," which evolve out of its role as a service provider trying to implement a human right for social protection by paying a pension to some older people. As long as the primary responsibility for guaranteeing the social pensions comes with the state, the boundaries of the TNGO are justified. The state is seen as the only one who can solve

260   *Katrin Fröhlich*

its problems of eligibility and who should guarantee a nationwide, durable, and even universal pension:

> Yeah, in the meantime it is clear. It [the pension] should be a measure within the social budget of the state. That is for sure. We cannot, we are very small. . . . Sure, the best solution for the durability would be a national program. That has to be the final goal, the middle- or long-term objective. (chairperson of FOP; author's translation)

By claiming a human right, FOP is not only a service provider anymore. It has become an advocate, basing its work on human rights and claiming a human right for the social protection of older people, too. Its long-term objective is a national pension, implemented by the state, not by itself. At the same time, it gives back the responsibility for social protection not only to the state but also to the recipients: FOP teaches them that they have a right to receive support from the state and encourages them to demand that right too:

> In those times, two or three years before, we raised that topic in talks, group talks with the old people and of course that was an idea which was very, very far away from them at that time. To have rights at all. They grew up in a totally different tradition, but I think today it would be slightly different. (chairperson of FOP; author's translation)

IN SUMMARY: EXTENSION FROM A SERVICE PROVIDER TO AN ADVOCATE AS OPPORTUNITY

In summary, the TNGO is widening its work from a needs-based approach in which they act as a service provider for some people to a rights-based approach for (at least in theory) all people. People in a rights-based approach do not just need and deserve support. They have an entitlement to that kind of social protection. A service provider, the state is seen as an actor who failed to protect its inhabitants. The TNGO becomes a "duty-bearer" (Harris-Curtis, Marleyn and Bakewell 2005: 15), legitimizing its intervention as an act of emergency help and charity. In a rights-based approach, the state must assume an active role because the state finally has to guarantee the right. The positioning of FOP is therefore changing as well. While the state is not supposed to be passive anymore, the individuals are also not just passive victims anymore, who need and receive help. Being rights holders, the recipients actively have to claim that right as well (see Table 13.2).

Nevertheless, the unconditional SCT itself is publicly barely legitimized within that rights-based approach. Giving the pension without any conditions is justified with pragmatic decisions based on the images of old people and an "output-legitimacy." On one hand, they can be seen as the helpless and innocent victims who deserve support (and cannot give anything

From Alms to Rights   261

Table 13.2   Model of a needs-based and rights-based approach of the TNGO

	Needs-based approach	Rights-based approach
Legitimizing the mode of social protection	Unconditional social cash transfers as alms for charity's sake	Unconditional social cash transfers as an obligation based on human rights
Positioning toward the recipients	Victims who need and deserve support	Rights bearers who have an entitlement to receive support and who have to claim it themselves
Positioning toward the state	State who failed to protect is people	State who has to guarantee a right
Role of the TNGO	Service provider	Advocate

Source: Table based on Harris-Curtis, Marleyn and Bakewell (2005: 16).

in return). On the other hand, they are often labeled as "unsung heroes" who deserve tribute, always using the money effectively, sensibly, and even sustainably. A strategy of justification solely focusing on a human right for social protection does not seem to be enough for getting support.

Coming back to "transnational aging," we can ask, "How does a 'transnational social protection'—in this case a pension paid by a TNGO—influence the life of older people?" Apart from impacts on the micro-level by changing the living conditions of old people, the long-term impact might rather be on a macro-level, the national level. Advocating a human right for an old-age pension, which already exists in international law but is neither implemented globally nor stipulated as noncontributory and unconditional, the TNGO engages old people to become active right bearers. As such, they again have to claim this right from the state and might get the chance of changing social policy themselves. But especially in cases where TNGOs are primarily focusing on the duty of the state, different cultural and political backgrounds might also lead to too much of a focus on "welfare state systems" of developed countries. As seen in the case of FOP, the responsibility for social protection of old people is considered a task of the state. In this sense, old people become right bearers of the state. Other actors such as "informal" support systems are considered to be dissolving and are therefore neglected in their role as "duty bearer," although the human rights charter of the African Union (Banjul Charter; 1981) says that caring for older people is not just a duty of the state. Exceptionally, the Banjul Charter is referring to the family as a duty bearer, too. Thus, transnational actors can also influence the point of views about the issue of responsibilities and duty bearers.

262 *Katrin Fröhlich*

NOTES

1 For Tanzania see also ILO (2008), ISSA (2011), OPM (2010), and Spitzer, Rwegoshora, and Mabeyo (2009).

2 Referring to the term *traditional* it has to be mentioned that these so-called traditional actors might be more recent, relevant, and less static to many people than the meaning of the term *traditional* suggests.

3 In this study, transnational social policy is defined as a part of global social policy, which relates to transnational actors only. In an etymological sense the term *transnational* is understood as border-crossing and *transnational actors* (distinct from supra- and international actors) as nongovernmental border-crossing actors.

4 It must be pointed out that states do not automatically guarantee national SCTs. Especially in African countries, many SCT programs are still pilot programs, which are neither implemented nationally nor by national public actors alone (e.g., "Pilot Cash Transfer Schemes" in Zambia; data are based on Barrientos and colleagues [2010] and HelpAge International [2011]).

5 The PhD project, which is the source of the results presented in this chapter, has shown that in this case study the TNGO barely took other actors of the economy and civil society into account.

6 The abbreviation INGO stands for international nongovernmental organization. Unlike INGO, the TNGO is preferred in this chapter to emphasize the criteria of "nongovernmental" organization. Finally, in international law, the term *international* in international organizations stands for organizations consisting of different states. On the contrary *transnational* emphasizes actors beyond the state (see note 3).

7 Arguments about advantages of conditional SCTs can be found in statements and programs of international organizations such as the World Bank (see Fiszbein, Schady and Ferreira, 2009). Basic arguments (mainly based on SCT projects without conditions) against conditionalities are summarized by Hanlon and colleagues (2010).

8 For critical analyses of private fund systems in Europe see Casey (2012).

9 Especially the ILO could internationally push for their favored system of public social pensions financed by taxes within their campaign on "coverage for all" and their recent campaign on "social protection floors" (ILO 2001).

10 Countries having implemented a social old-age pension in sub-Saharan Africa include Botswana, Cape Verde, Kenya, Lesotho, Mauritius, Mozambique, Namibia, Nigeria, Seychelles, South Africa, Swaziland, Uganda, and Zambia (see HelpAge International, 2011).

11 All names of persons and organizations and other identifying details have been changed to preserve anonymity (Hopf 2004).

12 According to FOP, the recipients are mainly women because there are more old women living in the project region than men. Besides, women tend to be in a worse economic situation than men because of the traditional inheritance law, which is discriminating against them by favoring male heirs (FOP project study).

13 In comparison to other pension programs in low-income countries of sub-Saharan Africa, the public programs are sometimes even less (US$4 in Mozambique) or just slightly higher (US$9 in Uganda; US$12 in Zambia; US$13–18 in Kenya; HelpAge International 2011).

14 Images of old age are understood as individual and social (cultural) ideas about old age, aging, or old people themselves. Every individual and every society has multiple images of old age, which can form the public discourse

From Alms to Rights 263

(macro-level), can be reproduced and institutionalized by organizations on the meso-level, and influence the personal interactions and individual perceptions on a micro level. They are "negative" or "positive," relating to individual or societal normative expectations of what should be or should not be, thereby images of old age are always evaluative (Bundestag 2010; Rossow 2012).

15 Based on the national character of human rights law, the state has the main responsibility for respecting, protecting, and fulfilling human rights (Krennerich, 2013: 101ff.). That is why social protection is seen as a public duty and is named as a social security (UN 1966, Article 9) in human rights law. Nevertheless, the term *social protection* is still preferred here to emphasize that social security is and can be implemented by different actors beyond the state.

16 For the latest legal discussion on state obligations on economic, social, and cultural human rights not just within but also beyond its borders, see also the Maastricht Principles on Extraterritorial Obligations of States in the area of Economic, Social and Cultural Rights (2012).

REFERENCES

Altvater, Elmar/Brunnengräber, Armin (2002): NGOs im Spannungsfeld von Lobbyarbeit und öffentlichem Protest. In: *Aus Politik und Zeitgeschehen (APuZ)*, B 6–7/2002, pp. 6–14.

AU (African Union, formally OAU/Organization of African Unity) (1981): *African Charter on Human and Peoples' Rights (Banjul Charter)*. Adopted 27 June 1981, OAU Doc. CAB/LEG/67/3 rev. 5, 21 I.L.M. 58 (1982), entered into force 21 October 1986.

Barrientos, Armanda/Nino-Zarazúa, Miguel/Maitrot, Mathilde (2010): *Social Assistance in Developing Countries Database. Version 5.0*. Manchester: The University of Manchester/ Brooks World Poverty Institute.

Benda-Beckmann, Franz v./ Benda-Beckmann, Keebet v./Bryde, Brun/Frank, Otto (1988): Introduction: Between Kinship and the State. In: Benda-Beckmann, Franz v./Benda-Beckmann, Keebet v. (eds.): *Between Kinship and the State. Social Security and Law in Developing Countries*. Dordrecht: Foris, pp. 7–20.

Bundestag, Deutscher (2010): *Sechster Bericht zur Lage der älteren Generation in der Bundesrepublik Deutschland: Altersbilder in der Gesellschaft und Stellungnahme der Bundesregierung*. Drucksache 17/3815. Berlin: Deutscher Bundestag.

Casey, Bernard H. (2012): The Implications of the Economic Crisis for Pensions and Pension Policy in Europe. In: *Global Social Policy* 12, 3, pp. 246–265.

Collingwood, Vivien/Logister, Louis (2005): State of the Art: Addressing the INGO 'Legitimacy Deficit'. In: *Political Studies Review* 3, pp. 175–192.

Deacon, Bob (2009): *Global Social Policy and Governance*. Los Angeles: SAGE.

Esping-Andersen, Gøsta (1990): *The Three Worlds of Welfare Capitalism*. Princeton: Princeton University Press.

Fiszbein, A./Schady, Norbert-R./Ferreira, Francisco H. G. (2009): *Conditional Cash Transfers. Reducing Present and Future Poverty*. Washington, DC: World Bank.

Gough, Ian (2008): Welfare Regimes in Development Contexts: A Global and Regional Analysis. In: Gough, Ian/Wood, Geof (eds.): *Insecurity and Welfare Regimes in Asia, Africa and Latin America. Social Policy in Development Contexts*. Cambridge: Cambridge University Press, pp: 15–48.

Gough, Ian/Wood, Geof (eds.) (2008): *Insecurity and Welfare Regimes in Asia, Africa and Latin America. Social Policy in Development Contexts*. Cambridge: Cambridge University Press.

264 Katrin Fröhlich

Hanlon, Joseph/Barrientos, Armando/Hulme, David (2010): *Just Give Money to the Poor. The Development Revolution from the Global South.* Sterling: Kumarian Press.

Harris-Curtis, Emma/Marleyn, Oscar/Bakewell, Oliver (2005): *The Implications for Northern NGOs of Adopting Rights-Based Approaches.* Oxford: INTRAC.

HelpAge International (2011): *Pension Watch—Social Protection in Older Age. Social Pension Database.* http://www.pension-watch.net.

Holzmann, Robert/Jorgenson, Steen (1999): *Social Protection as Social Risk Management: Conceptual Underpinnings for the Social Protection Sector Strategy Paper.* Social Protection Discussion Paper Series, No. 9904. Washington, DC: World Bank.

Holzmann, Robert/Robalino, David A./Takayama, Noriyuki (2009): *Closing the Coverage Gap. Role of Social Pensions and Other Retirement Income Transfers.* Washington, DC: World Bank.

Hopf, Christel (2004): Research Ethics and Qualitative Research. In: Flick, Uwe/ Kardoff, Ernst von/ Steinke, Ines (eds.): *A Companion to Qualitative Research.* London: SAGE, pp. 334–339.

Hurrelmann, Achim/Schneider, Steffen/Steffek, Jens (2007): Introduction: Legitimacy in an Age of Global Politics. In: Hurrelmann, Achim/Schneider, Steffen/ Steffek, Jens (eds.): *Legitimacy in an Age of Global Politics.* Basingstoke: Palgrave Macmillan, pp. 1–18.

ILO (International Labour Organization) (2001): *Social Security. A New Consensus.* Geneva: ILO.

ILO (International Labour Organization) (2008): *Tanzania Mainland. Social Protection Expenditure and Performance Review and Social Budget: Executive Summary.* Genf: ILO.

ILO (International Labour Organization) (2011): *Social Protection Floors for Social Justice and a Fair Globalization.* Geneva: ILO.

ISSA (International Social Security Association) (2011): *Social Security Programs Throughout the World. Africa.* Washington, DC: International Social Security Association/Social Security Administration.

Javad, Susanne (2011): *Sozialgeldtransfers als Instrument der Entwicklungszusammenarbeit.* Berlin: Friedrich Ebert Stiftung (FES).

Krennerich, Michael (2013): *Soziale Menschenrechte. Zwischen Recht und Politik.* Schwalbach/Ts: Wochenschau Verlag.

Leisering, Lutz (2010): *Social Assistance in Developed and Developing Countries. A Case of Global Social Policy? No Place of Publication Given: Financial Assistance, Land Policy and Global Social Rights.* FLOOR, Working Paper No. 4.

Leisering, Lutz/Buhr, Petra/Traiser-Diop, Ute (2006): *Soziale Grundsicherung in der Weltgesellschaft. Monetäre Mindestsicherungssysteme in den Ländern des Südens und des Nordens; weltweiter Survey und theoretische Verortung.* Bielefeld: Transcript.

Lewis, David/Kanji, N. (2009): *Non-Governmental Organizations and Development.* London/New York: Routledge.

Loewe, Mark (2003): *Soziale Sicherung und informeller Sektor. Stand der theoretischen Diskussion und kritische Analyse der Situation in den arabischen Ländern unter besonderer Berücksichtigung des Kleinstversicherungsansatzes.* Inauguraldissertation. Heidelberg: Fakultät für Wirtschafts- und Sozialwissenschaften. Ruprecht-Karls-Universität Heidelberg.

Nabalamba, Alica/Chikoko, Mulle (2011): Aging Population Challenges Africa. In: *African Development Bank (AfDB),* 1, 1, pp. 1–19.

From Alms to Rights 265

Oxford Policy Management (OPM) (2010): *Evaluation of Retirement Systems of Countries Within the Southern Development Community. Country Profile: Tanzania*. Oxford: OPM.

Rosenau, James N. (1992): *Governance Without Government, Order and Change in World Politics*. Cambridge: Cambridge University Press.

Rossow, Judith (2012): Einführung: individuelle und kulturelle Altersbilder. In: Berner, Frank/ Rossow, Judith/Schwitzer, Klaus-Peter (eds.): *Individuelle und kulturelle Altersbilder*. Wiesbaden: VS-Verlag, pp. 9–26.

Samson, Michael/van Niekerk, Ingrid/Mac Quene, Kenneth. (2006): *Designing and Implementing Social Transfer Programmes*. Cape Town: EPRI Press.

Sandhu, Swaran (2012): *Public Relations und Legitimität. Der Beitrag des organisationalen Neo-Institutionalismus für die PR-Forschung*. Wiesbaden: VS-Verlag.

Schubert, Bernd (2005): *Social Cash Transfers—Reaching the Poorest. A Contribution to the International Debate Based on Experience in Zambia*. Eschborn: German Technical Cooperation (GTZ).

Seifer, Kerstin (2007): *Governance als Einfluss-System. Der politische Einfluss von NGOs in asymmetrisch strukturierten Interaktionsarrangements*. Wiesbaden: VS-Verlag.

Spitzer, H./Rwegoshora, H./Mabeyo, Z. M. (2009): *The (Missing) Social Protection for Older People in Tanzania. A Comparative Study in Rural and Urban Areas*. Final Report. Feldkirchen/Dar es Salaam: Carinthia University of Applied Sciences, Austria/Institute of Social Work, Tanzania.

Standing, Guy (2010): Social Protection. In: Cornwall, Andrea/Eade Deborah (eds.): *Deconstructing Development Discourse. Buzzwords and Fuzzwords*. Rugby, Warwickshire: Practical Action Pub, pp. 53–68.

Strauss, Anselm L./Corbin, Juliet M. (1996): *Grounded Theory. Grundlagen Qualitativer Sozialforschung*. Weinheim: Beltz.

Troyer, Lisa (2007): Legitimacy. In: Ritzer, George (ed.): *Blackwell Encyclopedia of Sociology*. Blackwell Publishing. http://www.sociologyencyclopedia.com.

UN (United Nations) (1966): *International Covenant on Economic, Social and Cultural Rights*. Adopted and opened for signature, ratification and accession by General Assembly resolution 2200A (XXI) of 16 December 1966, entry into force on 3 January 1976.

UN (United Nations) (2007): General Comment No. 191; *The right to social security* (art. 9). Adopted on 23 November 2007 by Economic and Social Council; Commitee on Economic, Social and Cultural Rights.

UN (United Nations) (2008): *Guide to the National Implementation of the Madrid International Plan of Action on Ageing*. New York: United Nations.

UN (United Nations) (2011a): *World Population Prospects. The 2010 Revision. Highlights and Advance Tables*. New York: United Nations, Department of Economic and Social Affairs, Population Division.

UN (United Nations) (2011b): *World Population Prospects. The 2010 Revision. Volume II: Demographic Profiles*. New York: United Nations, Department of Economic and Social Affairs, Population Division.

Van Ginneken, Wouter (2009): *Extending Social Security Coverage: Good Practices, Lessons Learnt and Ways Forward*. Working Paper No. 14. Geneva: International Social Security Association (ISSA).

Weible, Katharina/Leisering, Lutz (2012): South Africa's System of Social Cash Transfers. Assessing Its Social Quality. In: Burchardt, Hans-Jürgen/ Tittor, Anne/ Weinmann, Nico (eds.): *Sozialpolitik in globaler Perspektive. Asien, Afrika und Lateinamerika*. Frankfurt, New York: Campus-Verlag, pp. 247–270.

266   Katrin Fröhlich

Wietler, Katharina (2007): *The Impact of Social Cash Transfers on Informal Safety Nets in Kalomo District, Zambia. A Qualitative Study*. Berlin: Ministry of Community Development and Social Services (MCDSS)/Zambia and German Technical Cooperation (GTZ).

World Bank (2001): *Social Protection Sector Strategy. From Safety Net to Springboard*. Washington, DC: World Bank.

Zacher, Hans F. (1988): Traditional Solidarity and Modern Social Security Harmony or Conflict? In: Benda-Beckmann, Franz von/ Benda-Beckmann, Keebet von (eds.): *Between Kinship and the State. Social Security and Law in Developing Countries*. Dordrecht: Foris, pp. 21–38.

Contributors

Canan Balkir is Jean Monnet Professor and coordinator of the Jean Monnet Centre of Excellence at Dokuz Eylül University, Izmir, Turkey. Her fields of interest include international retirement migration, European studies, and the economy of northern Cyprus.

Désirée Bender, Dipl. Päd., Dipl. Soz., is a research associate and a PhD candidate at the Institute of Education, University of Mainz, Germany. Her fields of interest include qualitative research, sociology of knowledge, poststructural theories, transnationalism, discourse analysis, biography research, and social support.

Anita Böcker is an associate professor at the Faculty of Law, Radboud University Nijmegen, Netherlands. Her fields of interest include regulation of migration, international retirement migration, and antidiscrimination law.

Eralba Cela is a postdoctoral researcher in demography at the Department of Economics and Social Sciences, Università Politecnica delle Marche, Ancona, Italy. Her fields of interest include well-being, aging, loneliness, migration, integration, transnationalism, and return migration.

Tineke Fokkema, PhD, is a researcher at the Netherlands Interdisciplinary Demographic Institute (NIDI), The Hague. Her fields of interest include older adults, loneliness, solidarity, and return migration.

Katrin Fröhlich, PhD, is a consultant in development policy and career counseling. Her fields of interest include (local) development policy, social protection, social cash transfers, transnational non-governmental organizations, human rights, and images of old age in sub-Saharan Africa.

Carmen Grimm is a PhD candidate at the Netzwerk Alternsforschung (Research on Aging Network, NAR), University of Heidelberg, Germany. Her fields of interest include anthropology of aging, Peru, and Mexico.

268 Contributors

Ralf Himmelreicher, PhD, is affiliated with the Free University Berlin and founder of the Research Data Centre of the Federal German Pension Insurance (FDZ-RV) in Berlin, Germany. His fields of interest include social stratification in the life course and research on the influence of social policy on work, retirement, family, and health in Europe.

Tina Hollstein, Dipl. Päd., is a research associate and a PhD candidate at the Institute of Education, University of Mainz, Germany. Her fields of interest include migration and transnationalism, social support and coping strategies, illegality, and transnational aging and care.

Vincent Horn is a PhD candidate and research associate at the Institute of Education, University of Mainz, Germany. His fields of interest include transnational aging, care circulation, Peruvian migration, long-term care policies, and qualitative and quantitative research.

Wolfgang Keck, PhD, works with the Unit on Statistical Analyses at the German Pension Insurance, where he is responsible for social policy analyses. His fields of interest include intergenerational relations, comparative welfare state analyses, the reconciliation of long-term care, and pension policies.

Sarah Lamb is a professor of anthropology at the Anthropology Department, Brandeis University, US. Her fields of interest include social-cultural anthropology, aging, gender, personhood, families, India, and the US.

Susan McDaniel, PhD, FRSC Canada Research Chair in Global Population & Life Course, Prentice Research Chair & Professor of Sociology, University of Lethbridge, Canada. Her fields of interest include social policy, life course, demographic aging, health/well-being, health care, generational relations, family change in a global comparative perspective, and international migration and care work.

Jason Pribilsky is an associate professor at the Department of Anthropology, Whitman College, United States. Fields of interest: Ecuadorian and Peruvian Andes, applied anthropology, ethnographic methods, migration and transnationalism, indigenous identity and activism.

Cornelia Schweppe is a professor of social pedagogy at the Institute of Education, University of Mainz, Germany. His fields of interests include transnational aging, transnational social support, migration, poverty, social work theory, and professionalization

Elena Sommer is a research associate at the Institute of Gerontology, University of Vechta, Germany. Fields of interest: migration studies, intergenerational relationships, labor market integration, social network analysis.

Tatiana Tiayanen-Qadir is a postdoctoral researcher at the School of Social Sciences and Humanities, University of Tampere, Finland/Faculty of Social Sciences, University of Turku, Finland. Her fields of interest include transnational anthropology, ethnography of aging, everyday religion, family studies, and selfhood in self-help literature in Russia.

Eva Soom Ammann, PhD, is an associate researcher at the Institute of Social Anthropology, University of Bern, Switzerland. Her fields of interest include migration studies with specific focus on old age, gender, family and work, diversity and inequality, aging and care, institutional care, dying and death, public health, biographical and ethnographical methodology.

Seonggee Um is a postdoctoral researcher at the Prentice Institute for Global Population & Economy, University of Lethbridge, Canada. Her fields of interest include social and demographic changes in East Asian countries; care policy and practice for the elderly, migration of women and low-skilled labor, inequality, exclusion and marginalization, and qualitative research methods.

Karin van Holten, MA, is an academic Collaborator at Careum Research, Kalaidos University of Applied Sciences, Department of Health Sciences, Zurich, Switzerland. Her fields of interest include migration studies with specific interest on care migration, transnational care, gender, family care, family and work, work and care, and reconstructive research methods and methodology.

Claudia Vogel, PhD, is a researcher at the German Centre of Gerontology (Deutsches Zentrum für Altersfragen DZA), Berlin, Germany. Her fields of interest include intergenerational relationships, income and wealth in old age, participation and volunteering, migration.

Yvonne Witter, PhD, is an advisor at the Aedes-Actiz Kenniscentrum Wonen-Zorg (knowledge center of housing and care), Utrecht, the Netherlands. Her fields of interest include aging, welfare and care, client participation, and loneliness.